SOCIAL WORK PRACTICE
Problem Solving and Beyond

Third Edition

TUULA HEINONEN
University of Manitoba

LEN SPEARMAN
University of Manitoba

NELSON / EDUCATION

NELSON / EDUCATION

Social Work Practice: Problem Solving and Beyond, Third Edition

by Tuula Heinonen and Len Spearman

Vice President, Editorial Director:
Evelyn Veitch

Editor-in-Chief, Higher Education:
Anne Williams

Marketing Manager:
Ann Byford

Developmental Editor:
Liisa Kelly

Permissions Coordinator:
Beth Yarzab

Production Service:
Macmillan Publishing Solutions

Copy Editor:
Wendy Yano

Proofreader:
Barbara Storey

Indexer:
David Luljak

Production Coordinator:
Ferial Suleman

Design Director:
Ken Phipps

Managing Designer:
Franca Amore

Interior Design:
Sarah Battersby

Interior Design Modifications:
Katherine Strain

Cover Design:
Peter Papayanakis

Cover Images:
Inset: *Autumn Ground* by Tuula Heinonen, Background: FMNG/istockphoto

Compositor:
Macmillan Publishing Solutions

Library and Archives Canada Cataloguing in Publication

Heinonen, Tuula, 1952-
Social work practice : problem solving and beyond / Tuula Heinonen, Len Spearman. — 3rd ed.

Includes bibliographical references and index.
ISBN: 978-0-17-650038-2

1. Social service—Canada—Textbooks. 2. Social service—Vocational guidance—Canada. I. Spearman, Leonard B. II. Title.

HV40.H45 2009
361.3'20971   C2009-902414-4

ISBN-13: 978-0-17-650038-2
ISBN-10: 0-17-650038-3

A portion of Chapter 12, which appeared in the *Native Social Work Journal/Nishnaabe Kinoomaadwin Naadmaadwin* (Vol. 2, No. 1, 1999, pp. 91–1121) as "Seeking Mino-pimatasiwin: An Aboriginal Approach to Social Work Practice," by Michael Anthony Hart, is used with permission.

We also thank Wayne Antony at Fernwood Press for granting us permission to reuse content from his book, *Seeking Mino-pimatisiwin: An Aboriginal Approach to Helping* (2002), in Chapter 12.

Brief Contents

Preface   xv

About the Authors   xxi

Chapter 1

Introduction: About This Book   1

Chapter 2

The Emergence of Social Work in Canada   13

Chapter 3

Ideological Foundations and Values of Social Work   29

Chapter 4

Social Work Roles   47

Chapter 5

Practice and Policy in a Field of Social Work Practice: Child Protection Services as an Illustration   73

Chapter 6

The Client–Social Worker Relationship: Voluntary and Involuntary Relationships   97

Chapter 7

Cultural Diversity, Cultural Awareness, and Social Work Practice   125

Chapter 8

Problem Solving in Social Work Practice   143

Chapter 9

The Broad Knowledge Base of Social Work   167

Chapter 10

**Application of Focused Assessment within a Broad
Knowledge Base**   203

Chapter 11

Strengths-Based Practice as a Development Process   225

Chapter 12

An Aboriginal Approach to Social Work Practice   247

Chapter 13

A Feminist Approach to Social Work   275

Chapter 14

Structural Social Work and Social Change   297

Chapter 15

Putting It All Together: Problem Solving and Beyond   319

Glossary   335
References   343
Index   367

Contents

Preface   **xv**

Goals   xv

What's New?   xvi

    New Content   xvi

    New Supplementary Materials   xviii

Acknowledgments   xviii

About the Authors   **xxi**

Chapter 1

Introduction: About This Book   1

Introduction   2

What Is Social Work?   6

    Problem Solving and Beyond   6

    The Context of Social Policy   7

    Generalist and Specialist Social Work Practice 7

        What Is Generalist Practice?   7

        What Is Specialized Practice?   8

This Book Is about Generalist Social Work Practice   9

Looking Ahead   10

Chapter 2

The Emergence of Social Work in Canada   13

Introduction   14

Social Work and the Industrial Revolution   14

The Charity and Settlement House Movements, 1850–1930   15

    The Charity Workers   16

    The Settlement House Workers   17

        The Early Settlement House Worker 18

        The Reformers   18

        The Service Providers   19

The Social Gospel Movement and J. S. Woodsworth,

   Social Worker and Social Work Educator   20

The Development of Professional Social Work, 1925–2009   23

The Generalist Emerges in Canada   25

Chapter Summary   26

Notes   27

Chapter 3

Ideological Foundations and Values of Social Work   **29**

A New Ideology: Helping People   30

Ideology and Social Welfare (Macro) Policy   30

Ideology in Social Work Practice   31

What Are Values?   32

Ideological Lens of Social Work   32

The Core Values of Social Work   32

   IFSW   33

   CASW Core Social Work Values and Principles   34

   Some Explanations and Observations   36

      Similarities   36

      Provincial Differences   36

      The Values Are Inclusive   36

      The Values Are Abstract   36

Applying Social Work Values   37

   Expansion of the Principle of Self-Determination   37

      Conflict of Values   37

      Resources Must Be Available   37

      People Need Choices   38

      Self-Determination as a Value and Type of Intervention   38

      Some Want Decisions Made for Them   39

   Values and Culture   39

      Clashes in the Priority of Values   40

Ethics and Ethical Dilemmas   41

Chapter Summary   45

Notes   46

Chapter 4

Social Work Roles   **47**

What Is a Professional Role?   48

Types of Social Work Roles   48

   Social Work Roles Specific to Fields of Practice   48

   Generic and Generalist Roles   49

Common Generalist Social Work Roles   49

   The Story of Kim and Ann   50

   Micro and Mezzo Systems: Working with

      Individuals and Families   53

      Case Manager   53

      Counsellor   56

Micro, Mezzo, and Macro Systems: Roles for
    All Levels of Practice 57
        Advocate 57
        Enabler or Facilitator 59
        Group Worker 60
        Educator, Teacher, or Coach 62
        Mediator 64
        Outreach Worker 66
        Social Broker 67
        Evaluator 68
    Macro Systems: Generalist Roles in Community Development 68
        Community Practice or Organizing Roles 68
Chapter Summary 70

Chapter 5

Practice and Policy in a Field of Social Work Practice: Child Protection Services as an Illustration — **73**

Introduction 74
Child Protection Services in Canada 74
    Recent Changes 77
Social Work Practice in Child Protection 78
An Illustrated Connection between Policy and Social Work Practice 79
Generalist and Specialist Practice 94
Chapter Summary 94

Chapter 6

The Client–Social Worker Relationship: Voluntary and Involuntary Relationships — **97**

Defining the Social Work Client 98
Helping versus Social Control 98
Defining Social Work Relationships 100
Components of the Client–Social Worker Relationship 102
    Care and Concern 103
    Empathy and Honesty 104
    Acceptance 105
    Client Capacity for Change 106
    Self-Determination and Autonomy 108
    Confidentiality 109
        Limits to Confidentiality 110
    Power, Authority, and Control 111
    Purpose and Commitment 112

Context and Structure	113
Other Perspectives on Relationships	114
Relationships with Involuntary Clients	114
Assessing Involuntary Clients	115
Social Labelling	116
Reaching Out	119
Decision Making, Assessment, and Best Interest	120
Negotiation and Contracting	121
Ending Relationships	122
Involuntary Relationships and Social Supports	122
Chapter Summary	123

Chapter 7

Cultural Diversity, Cultural Awareness, and Social Work Practice	**125**
Introduction	126
Culture, Ethnicity, and Race	126
Awareness of Ethnoculture and Identity	126
Culture	127
Ethnicity	128
Race	129
Racism	129
Social Work across Cultures	130
An Etic Approach	130
An Emic Approach	131
Antiracist Practice	132
Discrimination and the Role of Social Work	133
Education Equity and Affirmative Action	134
Social Work with Newcomers	135
Intersection of Multiple Forms of Oppression: The Example of Lola	135
Group and Community Helping in Immigrant Communities: The Example of Lola	138
Anti-Oppressive Social Work	138
The Practice Relationship	139
Gaining Ethnic Competence	140
Chapter Summary	142

Chapter 8

Problem Solving in Social Work Practice	**143**
Introduction	144

The Problem-Solving Process in Social Work   145
    Problem Definition   146
    Assessment in the Problem-Solving Process: A Brief Introduction   148
        Assessment and Diagnosis   149
    Goal Setting   151
    The Contract in the Problem-Solving Process   152
        Power and Social Work Contracts   154
    Intervention   154
    Evaluation   156
        Evaluation of Progress in Everyday Practice   156
        Evaluation in Short-Term and Involuntary Relationships   159
    Endings   160
        Referral   160
        Termination (Planned Ending)   161
        Unplanned Endings   161
Implications of the Problem-Solving Approach   162
    Individual Orientation: A Limited Scope   162
    Restorative versus Promotional Approach   163
    Social Worker as Expert: An Issue of Power   164
    Involuntary Problem Solving, Social Control,
        and the Principle of Best Interest   164
Chapter Summary   165
Note   166

Chapter 9

The Broad Knowledge Base of Social Work   **167**
Theoretical Diversity   168
Broad Knowledge Base   169
Theory in Social Work   170
Links to Social Sciences   171
Ecosystems as a Framework   172
    Background   172
    Ecosystems   173
    Summary of Essential Principles   175
Theoretical Diversity and Assessment   176
Organization of Diverse Theory: The Micro to Macro Continuum   177
    Cognitive Theory   178
        Using Cognitive Theory in Assessment   179
    Ego Psychology   179
        Using Ego Psychology in Assessment   180

Crisis Theory and Intervention   181
    Using Crisis Theory in Assessment   182
Knowledge about Family Relationships and Processes   183
    Using Knowledge about Family Relationships and
    Processes in Assessment   184
Group Work Principles   185
    Using Theory about Groups in Assessment   186
Principles of Community Development   187
    Using Knowledge about Community
    Development in Assessment   188
Structural Social Work   189
    Using the Structural Approach in Assessment   189
Principles of Anti-Oppressive Practice   190
    Using Anti-Oppressive Practice in Assessment   191
Culture   192
    Using Culture in Assessment   192
Ecosystems   193
    Using Ecosystems in Assessment   193
Role Theory   194
    Using Role Theory in Assessment   195
Labelling Theory   196
    Using Labelling Theory in Assessment   196
Strengths Approach   197
    Using the Strengths Approach in Assessment   198
An Aboriginal Approach   199
    Using an Aboriginal Approach in Assessment   199
Feminist Theory and Practice   200
    Using a Feminist Perspective in Assessment   200
Chapter Summary   202

Chapter 10

Application of Focused Assessment within a Broad Knowledge Base   203

Introduction   204
The Road to Assessment   204
Inductive versus Deductive Assessment   204
Determinants of Assessment   205
    The Social Worker   206
        Professional Lens   206
    The Client   208

Risks 209

    Intervention as a Risk 209

    Risk of Client to Self or Others 210

The Workplace 211

Application of the Assessment Process 212

    Assessment Illustrated: A Case Example 214

Chapter Summary 223

Notes 224

Chapter 11

Strengths-Based Practice as a Development Process   **225**

Introduction 226

Strengths, Deficits, and Problem Solving 226

Promotion of Personal Growth and Quality of Life 227

Strengths Applied to Problem Solving 228

    Principles of Strengths-Based Practice Used to Problem Solve 230

Examples of Types of Strengths-Based Practice 230

    Recovery in Mental Health 231

    Solution Focused Brief Therapy 231

Key Elements of Strengths-Based Practice 232

    Empowerment 232

    Professional Relationships and the Strengths Approach 233

        A Consumer-Driven Approach 233

        Reciprocity 235

    Membership and Belonging 236

        Personal Niche 237

        A Social Niche and a Macro Connection 238

        Self-Help: An Enabling Niche 239

    Resilience 239

    Culturally Sensitive Social Work Practice and

        Strengths-Based Practice 241

        Reciprocal Relationships in Cross-Cultural Practice 241

        The Importance of the Client's Story 241

        Cultural Support 242

        Cultural Membership and Belonging 242

Chapter Summary 243

Chapter 12

An Aboriginal Approach to Social Work Practice   **247**

Making Connections 248

Understanding Aboriginal Peoples' Historical Context 248

The Present Context 250

Social Work's Participation in the Oppression Processes 252

An Aboriginal Approach 253

    Background of This Approach 254

    The Central Pillar and Frame of This Approach 254

Key Concepts 255

    Wholeness 255

    Balance 256

    Relationships 257

    Harmony 258

    Growth 258

    Healing 258

    Mino-pimátisiwin 259

Key Values 259

    Sharing 259

    Respect 259

Perceptions of Persons 260

    View of Human Nature and Activity Orientation 260

    View of Individuals, Time Orientation, and Relationships 260

Perceptions of Functioning 261

    Role of History 261

    Individual Development: The Cycle of Life 261

    Importance of Consciousness and Unconsciousness 261

    Nature of Change and the Role of Motivation 262

    Power 263

The Helping Process 263

    Focus of Helping 263

    The Helping Relationship and Specific Techniques 264

    Specific Knowledge and Skills of the Helper 265

    Goal Setting 266

Application 266

An Aboriginal Approach and Conventional Social Work 271

An Aboriginal Approach and Ecosystems 272

Chapter Summary 273

Notes 274

Chapter 13

A Feminist Approach to Social Work   **275**

Introduction 276

Women and Social Work 277

Feminism and Social Work: Background and Context 278

Feminist Research   280
Liberal, Radical, and Socialist Orientations   281
    Liberal Orientation   281
    Radical Orientation   282
    Socialist Orientation   283
    Illustration of Differences in Orientation   284
Divergent Meanings and Significance of Feminism   285
Applying Feminist Principles in Practice   288
    Validation   289
    Consciousness-Raising   290
    Transformative Action   291
    Affirmation   291
    Development of the Whole Person   291
    The Role of Power   293
    Working with Men   294
    Recognizing Diversity   295
Chapter Summary   295

Chapter 14

Structural Social Work and Social Change   **297**
Foundations of Structural Social Work   298
    Connection between Radical and Structural Social Work 298
    Anti-Oppressive Social Work   299
    Background of Structural Social Work   300
    A Conflict Perspective   301
    Framing   302
    The Place of Structural Social Work in Practice   302
    Structural Social Work and Direct Practice   303
    Reflection and Reflexivity in Social Work   304
Applying the Structural Approach in Practice   304
    Overview   304
    Problem-Solving Approach: Family Intervention   305
    Structural Approach: Collective Action   305
    Structural Social Work and the Environment   306
    Roles in Structural Social Work   309
Example of Structural Social Work and Direct Practice   311
    Direct Service or Social Change?   314
    Strategies of Action   314
        The Proposed Workfare Program 315
        The Ban-the-Boarding-Homes Movement 316
Chapter Summary   318

Chapter 15

Putting It All Together: Problem Solving and Beyond   **319**

Introduction   320

Extending Problem Solving   320

Context and Foundations of Social Work Practice   322

Use of a Range of Approaches and Knowledge   323

Comparative Summary of Five Approaches to Social Work Practice   325

Chapter Summary   334

Glossary   **335**

References   **343**

Index   **367**

Preface

This is the third edition of a Canadian social work practice textbook that both students and instructors have found helpful. This new edition of *Social Work Practice: Problem Solving and Beyond* attempts to bring the world of social work practice to students who can engage the material and imagine themselves as social workers in the case situations and examples.

Our students continue to tell us that this book, even after they have graduated, remains an important source book to be re-read, marked-up, and drawn from. It is also known and used in some European countries, the US, and elsewhere. We think that this new edition, written in a friendly and inviting style, offers much opportunity for students to learn about, reflect on, and apply social work theories and approaches. Instructors will also find the Instructor's Manual and PowerPoint® presentation slides useful.

Some years ago we had the challenging task of developing a print-based and teleconferenced distance education course in social work practice. In writing the course manual, we were constrained by the fact that generalist social work practice textbooks were invariably limited to traditional problem solving, often within a systems or ecological frame, and by lack of content based on the Canadian experience. The first edition of *Social Work Practice: Problem Solving and Beyond* was the result of our experience in writing the distance education manual.

GOALS

As teachers of social work practice, we believe that social workers need a broad understanding of the foundations of and approaches to practice.

Goal 1 To present the problem-solving process as a foundation of traditional practice. We then develop, in four chapters, approaches to practice that takes social work beyond problem solving. These approaches (strengths, Aboriginal, feminist, and structural), consistent with generalist social work practice in Canada, both critique and enrich the problem-solving process in generalist social work practice.

Goal 2 To write a social work practice textbook that is based on Canadian social work practice. We believe Canadian experience, often without fanfare, has greatly enriched the profession.

This book is intended for several groups of readers. Most directly, it is designed for social work students, mainly at the undergraduate level, who need to understand the principles, values, and knowledge behind generalist social work practice in Canada. All social workers should find the book useful as both a description of generalist practice and a reference source. Other professionals who need to know or are interested in social work practice that draws from the strengths, Aboriginal, feminist, and structural approaches and from cross-cultural social work should find the book useful.

WHAT'S NEW?

The decision to write the third edition was based on feedback from students and social work professors from across Canada. We and they continue to believe that the book captures social work practice in the Canadian context and also reflects good practice anywhere. While the key thrust (problem solving and beyond) and much of the organization and content of the second edition remains, we have made substantial additions and revisions.

Based on feedback, the theme that drives the changes in the third edition is increased application: application of conceptual and theoretical material to social work practice. While all chapters were revised with this theme in mind, application was emphasized in three ways: (1) two new chapters that focus on application; (2) considerable use of new case material; and (3) increased content about ***mandated practice***.

New Content

1. **Two new chapters:** This edition includes two new chapters.
   - One is an expanded chapter (Chapter 5) on child protection policy and practice that replaces a chapter on health and mental health policy and practice. One of the reasons for focusing on child welfare and protection is that this is a field where many social work graduates work. This chapter is intended to exemplify and describe policy and practice in the field of child protection and to apply the important connection between policy and practice. The chapter also recognizes and illustrates the often controversial social control function of social work (e.g., child protection) and how social control and the care or helping functions co-exist in mandated practice.
   - The second is an all new chapter (Chapter 10) on social work assessment. We regard assessment as a central part of social work practice and, hence, it is now emphasized in this text. For example, assessment in Canadian generalist social work depends upon a broad knowledge base and diversity of theory. However, assessment also needs to be focused. An important way that social workers do this is through what we call determinants of assessment, which are articulated in Chapter 10.

     Determinants define boundaries and focus an assessment and include much more than a theoretical understanding and analysis of a case situation. Every assessment is highly influenced by a wide variety of determinants that includes the knowledge, culture, and life experience of the worker; the client and the client's situation; risks associated with intervention; and the workplace in which the social worker is employed.
2. **Case Illustrations:** Much more than in the first and second editions, the text is built around cases. The intent of case illustrations is to show how practice principles can be applied.

   In the third edition, we use cases in two different ways. Often, as in the previous editions, we write a case to illustrate a conceptual point. However, in this edition we sometimes reverse this process. We first describe a case and then draw generalized principles from the case description; an inductive approach. Both new chapters as well as the revision of Chapter 1 are designed using this new inductive approach. This manner of presentation can nicely lead to fruitful class discussions and debates.

Examples of use of case material abound:

- The introductory chapter begins with a case example. This is intended to set the stage for learning about generalist social work practice. The case example helps explain the basic conception of the text and guide the reader as to what to expect in the coming chapters.

- Chapter 5 is constructed around a significant and controversial case example. Partly because of controversies in child protection, the case has two scenarios that lead to different outcomes. This should lead to good class discussion. As outlined above, the chapter weaves the connection between policy and practice around a case illustration from child welfare.

- The second half of Chapter 10, the new chapter on assessment, uses a case example to show how social workers engage in an analytical assessment of the "facts" of a case.

- New case material has been added in many other chapters. For instance, a new case in Chapter 12 helps illustrate and explain an Aboriginal approach to social work practice.

- In Chapter 6, we explain how social work relationships might begin by using the following excerpt from a potential child neglect case: "Kim [the social worker] was calm and warm even though Ann was angry with her and others. Ann soon began to feel that Kim understood how she felt because Kim's gestures and comments showed that she felt empathy for Ann. Kim also expressed honestly her view that Ann's emotional reaction was normal given her distress." Often such case material can be used to generate class discussion.

3. **Mandated practice:** In mandated practice social workers carry out the directives and functions of an employing agency that has the responsibility to implement legislation. Many, if not most, social workers are employed in mandated agencies. Unlike many social work practice textbooks, this textbook clearly recognizes that much of social work practice is mandated. In many chapters we illustrate and address important mandated functions of social work.

   For example, Chapter 5, which uses child protection to address the connection between policy and practice, is based on mandated practice. Chapter 6 suggests ways to build relationships with "clients" who do not want help. Most social work intervention with people who do not want help takes place in mandated agencies.

4. **Reflection:** In some chapters, we ask social work students to reflect on important issues of the day. For instance, in Chapter 5: "The dual sides of social work, social control, and care are evident in this kind of work. How does a social worker come to terms with these dual roles when she or he performs child protection work?"

5. **New content on ideology and values:** Much of Chapter 3 on ideological foundations and values of social work has been rewritten and reorganized. It now presents the ideological principles and values of social work as articulated by the Canadian Association of Social Workers and the International Federation of Social Workers. The discussion in Chapter 3 applies and analyzes these principles.

6. **Use of Internet:** We encourage students to make responsible use of the Internet. New to the third edition is use of many Internet resources. We particularly use the Internet to reference "official" sites such as sources from codes of ethics, agency policies, and government papers and policies. This use of the Internet permits easy access to much information necessary for students of social work. Although we have cited material from websites that we found useful and relevant, we cannot ensure that websites will be accessible in the future.

7. **References:** Sources have been updated in all chapters.

New Supplementary Materials

Supplementary materials available for instructors and students to draw from in this edition include the following:

- PowerPoint® slides that correspond with each chapter ✓**NEW**
- Revised and updated Instructor's Manual, including a Test Bank of questions, assignment ideas, and tips ✓**NEW**

This Instructor's Manual is designed to assist educators who use the book in their courses. It offers rich case material, exercises, reflection questions, and ideas for assignments. Instructors can select and copy from the manual what they will use in group or class discussions and for assignments. This manual centres around a "day in the life of a child welfare social worker," a number of vignettes, chapter highlights, teaching tips, reflection questions for small group and class discussion, and suggested exercises. We have updated this manual for the current edition so that it fits better with the third edition content of the book.

ACKNOWLEDGMENTS

Many people have contributed directly or indirectly to this book. Some have been our colleagues and students in the Faculty of Social Work, University of Manitoba, and those who read the book and sent emails from many parts of Canada and from around the world in Estonia, China, and other countries. Others are social work practitioners whose experience and insights have strengthened the book. We would particularly like to acknowledge Sandi Taylor, Jennifer Curtis, and Joyce Cabigting Fernandez for their contributions to the book. We thank our colleagues Esther Blum, Al Curtis, Sid Frankel, Kendra Nixon, and Juliana West from the Faculty of Social Work, University of Manitoba, for their reviews and helpful suggestions. We would also like to acknowledge the Faculty of Social Work's Endowment Fund for their support for the development of Chapter 5 on child protection policy and practice.

To Michael Hart, we give special thanks for again collaborating with us to enhance this book and for framing Aboriginal concepts on helping for our readers.

Thank you to Anne Williams, our acquisitions editor, and Liisa Kelly, our developmental editor at Nelson Education. For formatting and carefully reviewing the manuscript to correct grammar and enhancing its style, we thank Susan Calvert, our content production manager, and Wendy Yano, our copy editor.

It is important that any new book have good reviewers who can bring an instructor's perspective in reading each chapter. We were fortunate to have received constructive and useful suggestions from a number of reviewers, to whom we owe a debt of gratitude for the thoughtfulness and care evident in their reviews. We are very appreciative of the help and guidance that we received from our reviewers, who provided many helpful suggestions and ideas:

Dr. Margaret Wright	University of British Columbia
Philip Durrant	Niagara College
Bruce Northey	College of New Caledonia
Paul McKinnon	Sir Sandford Fleming College
Brent Angell	University of Windsor

We also thank the many students from our own and other social work classes who gave us comments on the book.

I would like to acknowledge Dr. David Woodsworth, friend and mentor, whose encouragement and generosity have meant so much to me. I am grateful to know him and Sheila Woodsworth and look forward to again sharing tea and ideas with both of them.

Thank you to the Yarmeys for use of their wireless network and to Aiti for the space to spread out materials and write. I am also grateful to good colleagues and friends who listened and reflected with me.

Tuula Heinonen

I would like to thank my wife, Marietta, for her support and patience while I worked on the book. I would also like to again apologize to our border collies, Heidi and Mickey, who could not understand why we missed so many outings and playtimes.

Len Spearman

About the Authors

Len Spearman and Tuula Heinonen have spent the majority of their academic careers at the Faculty of Social Work, University of Manitoba. Len Spearman is now retired but continues to be very active with the Faculty of Social Work as a Senior Scholar. Tuula Heinonen is Professor and teaches both undergraduate and graduate courses. Both have played a major part in developing the social work practice curriculum, and together they wrote a distance education course manual that became the framework for the first and subsequent editions of this book.

Dr. Heinonen's background is social work in health care and international social development. Her current interests are social work and rural women in China, experiences of newcomers to Canada, and health issues. She co-directs a large social work project in rural China and collaborates regularly with social work colleagues in Finland. She has been active in both undergraduate and graduate curriculum development and teaching.

Dr. Spearman has practised in the field of mental health in both Canada and the United States. At the University of Manitoba, he has played a major part in designing the Bachelor of Social Work (BSW) curriculum and the northern off-campus and distance education programs. He chaired the BSW Curriculum Committee for more than a decade.

Dr. Michael Hart, guest author of Chapter 12, "An Aboriginal Approach to Social Work Practice," and a colleague at the University of Manitoba, has had much experience teaching and working with Aboriginal and northern peoples in Manitoba. He has taught a variety of courses on Aboriginal peoples and social welfare policy, social work practice, and northern social work at the University of Manitoba's Faculty of Social Work in Thompson. He has also held positions in policy development, program management, and practice, primarily with organizations that provide services to Aboriginal peoples. Dr. Hart has conducted research and written articles and book chapters on sharing circles and Aboriginal approaches to social work.

Introduction:
About This Book

Chapter Goal ▼

To introduce key themes of the book and the context of what follows.

This Chapter ▼

- illustrates, by use of case example, principles necessary for competent generalist social work practice
- explains the meaning of the book's title, *Social Work Practice: Problem Solving and Beyond*
- explains the importance of the context of social policy in generalist practice
- distinguishes between and defines generalist and specialist social work practice
- outlines the scope of this book
- introduces each chapter in the book

INTRODUCTION

We begin this book with a case example. The case example illustrates the principles of social work that are addressed in this book. In Chapter 10, we return to the story of Alberto, to illustrate the process of assessment.

For those new to social work, some of the terminology used in this chapter will be unfamiliar. This is okay, because terms and concepts mentioned here will be defined and expanded upon throughout the textbook. We simply want to give readers an idea of what to expect in the book and set the stage for understanding social work.

Case Example

Alberto and His Family ▼

This is the story of a family's immigration to Canada and a summary of the difficulties that the family encounters. Like the story of many other newcomers, it describes the situation of a person and a family in which generalist social workers can provide help. Of course, each case and situation is different in many ways. But each case can be used to illustrate principles, often very different from each other, that are necessary for competent generalist social work practice. We will selectively highlight a few of the principles found in this book by referring to Alberto and his family.

City Immigrant and Refugee Services or CIRS (not a real organization) is funded by the United Way and provincial government grants. The mandate of the CIRS is to help newcomers from diverse regions of the world to adjust to Canadian life. CIRS has several programs, including employment services, a housing program, counselling services, English as a second language instruction, a crisis hotline, and easy referral access to specialty programs such as a women's networking group, anger management counselling, and parenting programs. The agency also has a large community hall that is used by a variety of newcomer and ethnocultural groups for educational and social activities.

Omar, aged 28, is a university-educated, generalist social worker who has worked for CIRS in counselling services as a case manager and counsellor for just over three years. He emigrated from a West African country 15 years ago and received a BSW five years ago. Omar's professional lens emphasizes a culturally competent strengths approach in the context of ecosystems. He is a strong advocate of a *consumer*-driven and anti-oppressive practice. Omar is now Alberto's case manager.

Discussion: Let us refer to some important concepts used in the description of Omar. In the above description, we used the following: concepts consumer-driven approach, case management, counsellor, professional lens, culturally competent strengths approach, anti-oppressive practice, and ecosystems. All are important in understanding social work practice. This book introduces, explains, and discusses these and many more concepts that are necessary to practise social work.

Case Example

Alberto and His Family ▼

Client Information: Alberto, aged 46, has a grade 12 equivalent education. He immigrated to Canada from Peru two years ago and his use of English is only fair. He is married to Maria, aged 38, and they have a 12-year-old boy, Carlos. The family is Catholic.

Request for Help: Alberto broke a leg by falling on ice in front of a grocery store and as a result lost his job as a construction worker. His Canadian Employment Insurance is about to expire although Alberto is still unemployed. This is so discouraging that Alberto has begun talking about returning to Peru. He tells Omar that he needs to have a source of income and he wants to "feel better."

Immigration: Alberto's brother-in-law, Paolo, and Paolo's family had immigrated to Canada five years earlier. He likes Canadian life and had encouraged Alberto to follow him here. The client's brother-in-law sponsored Alberto and his family. By Peruvian standards, Alberto and his family lived a reasonably comfortable life when they lived in Peru. Yet all members of the family were excited about the new opportunities that immigration afforded. Now Alberto is discouraged, even to the point of feeling somewhat depressed. However, Maria and Carlos, the couple's son, are happy in their new country.

In Peru, the family lived in a small city in a friendly neighbourhood. They were closely knit. After immigration, the family did not feel comfortable in Canadian churches and, even with support from Spanish-speaking friends, lost interest in church activities.

Current Family Situation: Maria has worked as a full-time sewing machine operator for two years. Her level of English is good. Maria learned English at work and by talking to neighbours and people at their church.

Alberto is frequently angry. He feels that his brother-in-law, who is a manager at a department store, looks down on him. Alberto has had serious arguments with his wife and sometimes slaps or pushes her. They had a huge argument

Continued

about how his education in Peru hadn't helped him. She has fewer years of education than he does but has a job. Alberto could not control his anger. He hit his wife and bruised her so badly she did not want to go out in public.

Maria packed her clothes and, with her son, moved in with a friend, but did not make a police report. Alberto begged her to return home. With some anxiety, three days later she complied. The family relationships remain tense and Maria continues to threaten to leave Alberto if he cannot control his anger.

Their marriage was stable and rewarding for both until Alberto lost his job. Maria thinks her husband has lost self-confidence because he speaks poor English, has job difficulties, and feels inferior to her.

Alberto is very proud of his son, Carlos, who does very well in school, speaks English well, and thinks the sun rises and sets on his father. Carlos is on a local soccer team and has asked his father to coach it. His father has not yet given an answer.

Work Skills and Work History: In Peru, Alberto worked as an electrician for five years before immigration. Provincial officials in Canada would not license him as an electrician because, he is told, he lacks suitable training and experience in Canada. Without a lot of enthusiasm, he managed to find night work as a custodian for Tower Insurance Company. He also has been able to find a part-time summer job in highway construction.

The man is unhappy and discouraged because he cannot find a job as an electrician, a trade he worked at in Peru. He is now unemployed. His employment insurance is about to expire and he is having difficulty finding new employment. Poor skills in English prevent him from entering training programs, and his attempts to speak English cause much frustration.

Education: Alberto received the equivalent of Canadian high school in Peru. He then completed an apprenticeship-type program for electricians. Maria has been encouraging Alberto to take an electrician training program that will permit provincial licensing. Alberto's brother-in-law has offered to help fund the training through a no interest loan. But Alberto is angry about the provincial policy that requires him to train in a trade he already knows well and he refuses to enroll. Maria thinks her husband is unreasonable.

Social Relationships: The family finds the Catholic church close to them to be very different from the church they attended in Peru. Maria attends but Alberto does not. In Peru, the church was the centre of their life. The family expected the same in Canada. The main pastime of the family is now watching television.

Alberto has made a few friends with fellow custodians at his previous workplace. Normally Alberto makes friends easily but has had difficulty in the past year.

Current Economic and Living Situation: The family can make ends meet. However, when EI benefits run out, an income crisis could result. The family rents a small home that badly needs repairs, but they cannot afford better housing. This is a source of embarrassment for Carlos. He does not want friends to see their house and its lack of furniture.

Summary of Strengths: Alberto has many strengths. They include a close relationship with Carlos. He is an affable person and has had a stable marriage up until a year ago. His problems are recent and seem to be situational. Importantly, he is a skilled worker, is motivated to work even though he is currently discouraged and wants to speak better English. Alberto completed the immigration process, which is not an easy task. His church and church life were very important to him in Peru.

Summary of Obstacles: Alberto's anger is sometimes out of control and his relationship with his wife is deteriorating. His use of English could be better, which is related to his feelings of low self-confidence and self-esteem. A major obstacle is unemployment, particularly obstacles faced due to provincial licensing requirements for those with training and work experience outside of Canada. In Canada, he does not find church satisfying and misses his experiences in Peru. He has very few friends and social supports.

Discussion: Do you wonder, after reviewing this case scenario that offers little analysis and no solution, "How does Omar, a social worker, help Alberto?" We hope so! A central focus of the textbook is to address this issue.

The story of Alberto raises many practice issues and questions. All of them are dealt with in the book. For instance, Omar needs to establish a working agreement (sometimes called a *contract*) with Alberto. Why? What will this accomplish? Omar also needs to develop a professional relationship with Alberto. Why? What is the nature of a professional relationship? How do social work values and ideology influence Omar's approach to Alberto? Why, in the case example, are the strengths of Alberto highlighted? Why do we use the term *obstacle*? How will Omar assess the situation of Alberto and his family? Assessment is a crucial process that generalist practitioners must learn. How should Omar intervene with Alberto? His family? How do social and agency policies affect Omar's practice? Is provincial policy regarding educational and work experience requirements for non-Canadian electricians oppressive? How do cultural differences affect the family and Omar's relationship with the family? How can principles of, for example, feminist practice be applied in this case? And the list of questions could go on, and on, and on! This textbook addresses principles raised by each of these questions as well as many, many more.

WHAT IS SOCIAL WORK?

Social work is a profession that has two very broad and overlapping dimensions. On the one hand, social work is a helping profession: it focuses on helping people solve or prevent the occurrence of personal or social problems. Social work practice, on the other hand, also aims at social change. The foundation of professional practice is built on humanitarian and egalitarian ideals, the right to *social justice,* and the elimination of oppression and exploitation in society.

The following is a definition of social work by the International Federation of Social Workers that is consistent with the content of this textbook:

> The social work profession promotes social change, problem solving in human relationships and the empowerment and liberation of people to enhance well-being. Utilising theories of human behaviour and social systems, social work intervenes at the points where people interact with their environments. Principles of human rights and social justice are fundamental to social work. (International Federation of Social Workers, 2000.)

The IFWS cautions that social work itself is always changing. Hence, as social work changes, the definition may also be updated.

Problem Solving and Beyond

During the past 60 years or so, social work has developed and honed a process called *problem solving.* In its simplest form, problem solving means identifying a client's problems, understanding them, and then engaging with the client in a process to solve the identified problems. In practice, problem solving is a sophisticated means of helping that is based on a purposeful set of values and assumptions and a broad set of knowledge about human and social behaviour, the social environment, the connections between people and the environment, and methods of helping. The first ten chapters of this book address principles that are common to most social work. Chapter 8 describes the problem-solving process itself.

In recent years, ideas have emerged that challenge, critique, inform, extend, and enrich traditional problem solving. No longer can social work practice be only understood as problem solving. Many of these new ideas have strong Canadian roots and connections. We develop four approaches in this book that have important practice implications and extend social work beyond problem solving: the strengths, Aboriginal, structural, and feminist approaches.

We accept problem solving as a basis of social work but argue that we must also move beyond it. To understand this and to place this book about generalist social work in the context of current Canadian practice, we need to distinguish between generalist and specialized practice.

The Context of Social Policy

Social work practice takes place in the context of social policies, often reflected through legislation. Most agencies, public and private alike, operate within the ***framework*** of social policies that refer to family, health, criminal justice, child welfare, mental health, and many more fields. Social workers need to understand and analyze (for some, policy analysis is a highly specialized form of practice) the social policies that are relevant to their practice. For example, a child welfare worker who is mandated to carry out child protection must be intimately aware of child and family social policy and legislation. The community health social worker can effectively counsel people with health problems only if the worker understands the social policies that drive the health care system and the implications of these policies for social work practice.

The other part of the social work–social policy equation involves knowing how to facilitate social change. Promoting social change almost always involves influencing policy. To illustrate, obviously a social worker who works directly with clients has an obligation to provide them with quality service. Inevitably, the worker will encounter a policy or regulation that she or he views as a problem. The worker not only must have the ability to understand the problem and the related policy but also must begin to enable and mobilize resources to address the policy.

Generalist and Specialist Social Work Practice

In Canada *generalist* practice is most often associated with undergraduate social work education, while *specialist* social work is the primary domain of graduate work. The *Standards of Accreditation* of the Canadian Association for Social Work Education, or CASWE (formerly the Canadian Association of Schools of Social Work), are clear that undergraduate social work must be general practice:

> Curriculum at the first university level will ensure that graduates will be broadly educated and prepared for general practice and have sufficient competence for an entry level social work position. Competence is evidenced by an ability to arrive at professional judgements and practice actions, based on integration of theory and practice within the context of professional values and the relevant social work code of ethics. (CASWE, *Standards for accreditation* (2007), Sec. SB 5.3)

The Canadian standard holds that "Curriculum at the second university level will prepare students to have sufficient competence for advanced, specialized or supervisory social work roles" (CASWE, *Standards for accreditation* (2007), Sec. SM 5.2). The "second university level" generally means the MSW level.

In this book, we focus on generalist practice.

What Is Generalist Practice?

Generalist practice underpins and is the foundation of social work and is part of all accredited Canadian entry-level social work programs. Yet the accreditation standards do not clearly define what constitutes generalist social work, but leave it up to each individual school of social work to determine the substance of practice within a set of guidelines: "The [individual] school shall have agreed upon core content with coherence, consistency and sequence within the curriculum" (CASWE, *Standards for accreditation* (2007), Sec. SB 5.6).

Theorists began to articulate generalist practice in the 1960s (e.g., Bartlett, 1970; Gordon, 1962). Early conceptions of a common base of practice were unclear and divergent. Nevertheless, North American universities began to offer degrees based on generalist practice. Like the current IFSW definition of social work, early and current generalist practice theories emphasize that social work should intervene "…at the points where *people interact with their environments*" (IFSW, 2000; emphasis added). As discussed later in this book, ecosystems theory helps focus practice on people's interaction with their environment.

Probably the most important characteristic of generalist social work is that while the concept refers to the ability to practise in a wide range of settings, it also refers to incorporating and understanding a particular set of principles, values, and knowledge.

What Is Specialized Practice?

Most specialized practice, as required by the accreditation standards of the CASWE (2008), is built upon a generalist base. Practice may be specialized according to the method of practice, the field of practice, the system size, the level of position held (usually distinguished by the degree of responsibility involved), or a combination of these features.

Specialization by method means that one's practice is essentially driven by the application of a set of specific helping techniques. During the first half of the 20th century there were three major methods, each of which involved a set of helping techniques (for example, see Perlman, 1957; Konopka, 1983). These were *casework* (one-to-one work with individuals and sometimes families), *group work,* and *community organization* (social work in communities and neighbourhoods). Nowadays, social workers generally do not identify themselves solely with these categories. New or different specializations by method have emerged, some of which include solution-focused ***therapy***, mediation and conflict negotiation, and community development.

Fields of practice are the settings of social work—the areas within which practice takes place. Examples are child welfare, family services, health, corrections, mental health, social assistance (welfare), and addictions. Many, if not most, social workers specialize within a field of practice.

Another way to think of specialization is by system size. For example, some types of practice involve working with individuals, while others involve working with families and groups, and still others with organizations, neighbourhoods, and communities. In recent years the term *micro* social work practice has been used to refer to small systems that include individuals and usually families. *Macro* systems refer to large units, such as organizations, communities, and neighbourhoods. *Mezzo* practice is in between: working with small groups.

Finally, specialization may be according to the level of position held. Social workers may work in direct practice as line workers or, in some instances, as private practitioners. Some social workers are supervisors, while others are coordinators and administrators. These positions generally involve greater responsibility over staff and for organizations.

Most social workers, as their careers develop, specialize in one or a combination of the above areas. For example, a social worker may become a family therapist in child welfare; another may devote his or her career to using methods of community development to work with young people in transitional or core areas of cities.

Specialization is the product of considerable social work education and experience. Often it is a lifelong endeavour. Many social workers begin their careers as generalists, and most undergraduate social work education programs are designed to train generalist practitioners for career entry.

THIS BOOK IS ABOUT GENERALIST SOCIAL WORK PRACTICE

This book is about the principles and theory of generalist social work practice. In fact, the core elements of generalist social work are imbedded in the questions that are listed below. Again, we recognize that some of the terminology will be new. This is to be expected. As we address the issues raised by the following posed questions in various chapters, we describe and analyze generalist social work practice.

Do you want to appreciate and understand:

- the foundations of Canadian social work practice?
- social work practice principles and theory that are generic and common to all of social work?
- the very wide range of *fields of social work practice* and how generalist practice fits into these diverse fields?
- connections between delivery of services in a field of practice and social and agency policy?
- the ideology, values, and ethics that guide social work practice?
- how and why the practice of social work is inseparable from social and agency policies?
- the importance of building helping relationships and what constitutes a helping relationship?
- the seeming contradiction that while social work is a helping profession, social workers are often called upon to act as agents of social control? (For example, in child protection work.)
- the practice roles that we assume as professionals?
- oppression as a serious, continuing, social problem and the importance and nature of anti-oppressive practice?
- the importance of culture? The principles of cultural diversity and engagement in culturally appropriate intervention?
- the very wide knowledge base and diversity of theories?
- fundamental elements of assessment of client situations including use of a wide knowledge base?
- use of assessment and intervention knowledge and skill that
  - ranges from micro to macro and
  - includes, but goes "beyond" problem solving, the subtitle of this book?

- how and why, unlike many other helping professions, the emphasis of social work practice includes
  - ° interaction between persons and the environment;
  - ° working with people's strengths, abilities, and capacities as opposed to deficits?
- newly developing theories of an Aboriginal approach to social work practice?
- the importance of gender?
- the important contributions of feminist social work?
- social work practice in which personal helping is engaged by addressing social structures?

Do you want these questions addressed? Then, read on! Understanding all the above is necessary in order to competently practise generalist social work.

LOOKING AHEAD

Previously we connected principles of generalist practice to the content of this book. Keeping in mind the connection to generalist practice, we now present a chapter-by-chapter overview of what is to come.

This book will first describe traditional social work, which is primarily reflected in the problem-solving model of practice and its current emphasis on person-in-the-environment systems, ecological perspectives, and the older—but only recently articulated—strengths approach. The book stresses that building reciprocal helping relationships is at the core of the social work process. However, good practice must go beyond these traditional ideas. Newer approaches, partly shaped by the Canadian experience, not only make major contributions to social work practice but also critique and inform more traditional ideas. The newer approaches that we argue enrich generalist social work practice are Aboriginal, structural, and feminist approaches, in addition to anti-oppressive and cross-culturally appropriate practice.

Much of this book addresses practice with individuals and small groups. However, working with communities is also very important. In numerous places in the book, we emphasize community development practice both through discussion and case examples. In the past decade or so, social workers have understood that oppression is often a huge factor in explaining why people have difficulties. Oppression is frequently a factor in all kinds of problems ranging from abuse to criminal behaviour to mental health problems. Sometimes oppression is a causative factor in explaining difficulties. For example, the residential school system forced upon Aboriginal children in the first half of the 20th century has oppressed not only the children but also their families. At other times people who have difficulties must deal with programs and systems that are oppressive: for example, a mental health system that demeans people. In a variety of chapters in this book we discuss anti-oppressive practice and show, through illustrations, how social workers can engage in anti-oppressive practice.

Social work practice did not just happen. Current practice cannot be fully comprehended unless it is understood in a historical context. A variety of events and social forces led to the development of modern social work. Chapter 2 summarizes many of these forces and describes the emergence of social work in Canada.

Chapters 3 through 9 present the basic principles and concepts in social work that are foundational to generalist practice. Chapters 11 to 14 extend practice beyond problem solving.

Chapter 3 sets out the ideology and values that are central to social work, influencing and giving perspective to practice. Social work is situated within the ideological context of helping that emerged primarily in the 20th century. Social work values, often expressed through codes of ethics, guide social workers; particularly important is the value of self-determination. The connection between values and culture in social work is also central, in that culture shapes our values and beliefs. Resolving ethical dilemmas in social work is of primary importance in today's environment.

The roles that social workers take on are discussed in Chapter 4. In everyday practice, social work integrates a wide range of practice roles from micro to macro—individual to organization or community.

Chapter 5 explains the connection in a field of practice between social welfare policy and social work practice by using the child protection services field as an illustration. Social work practice in this important field is diverse but similar to those in other fields of practice; today, social work in child protection is challenging and changing as social and agency policies change. These changes require those who work in this field to be flexible in performing a variety of roles.

Chapter 6 describes the nature of the social work relationship and the importance of building a partnership between worker and client based on trust, acceptance, respect, and the inherent right to self-determination. The professional relationship is seen as the core of the helping process. The difficulty of establishing helping relationships with people who do not want help is recognized, but the chapter argues that working with all people is an essential part of social work.

The importance of practice that is anti-oppressive has brought renewed attention to the need to critically reflect on our work, examine how oppression occurs at individual and societal levels, and ensure that we do not contribute to oppression but strive to counter it. Social workers, through their codes of ethics, aim to eliminate discrimination and inequality in society.

Culturally aware, appropriate and anti-oppressive practice is discussed in Chapter 7. Recognizing and responding to cultural diversity in ways that value and respect uniqueness is also a focus in Chapter 7. Culture offers social work a lens to look through, one that adds depth and breadth to practice.

The problem-solving process, detailed in Chapter 8, offers a rational, step-by-step way to help people solve problems. It is a person-in-the-environment approach—that is, it emphasizes the individual's relationship with the environment rather than, for example, concentrating on the inner psychological experiences of people or the social structure.

The theories and approaches that provide social work with its wide knowledge base are discussed in Chapter 9. The broad knowledge base focuses on diversity of theory but also holds that life experience, culture and tradition, observation, and testing are important contributors to social work knowledge. The chapter begins to link the wide knowledge base to assessment.

Chapter 10 is about social work assessment. Social work assessment is multidimensional and assumes theoretical diversity and a broad knowledge base. We introduce four determinants that guide and focus social work assessment. The heart of this chapter is the application of assessment. The chapter demonstrates this through a major illustration.

The strengths approach presented in Chapter 11 focuses on people's ***resilience*** and capacity for dealing with problems in everyday life by drawing on their strengths, abilities, and internal and external resources. This approach stresses empowerment of the client as an important goal.

Chapter 12 presents an Aboriginal perspective on healing, helping, and social work. Culturally specific ways of dealing with human situations and problems have only begun to make inroads into social work. Although there are similarities between some social work models and Aboriginal approaches, there are also many differences. Recognizing the importance of the relationship between an individual and the natural and spiritual worlds is one major Aboriginal contribution to social work.

Feminism has shed light on sexism in society, social policy, and the social work profession, offering alternative ways of understanding and practising that seek to eliminate the constraints of rigid social roles and expectations for both women and men. Chapter 13 explains how some of these ideas have been integrated by social work into various settings; however, feminist practice has been less well integrated into social work practice areas such as child welfare, income security, hospital-based health care, and so on. Although a core of common principles can be identified in feminist social work, there are numerous strands to feminism that reflect the realities of diverse groups of women, and not necessarily all in the same way.

Structural social work uses ideas from socialism and critical theory to focus on the structures and ***institutions*** in society that oppress people. Through the structural approach, described in Chapter 14, we appreciate that people are not solely responsible for the difficulties encountered in their lives, and that the broader social environment plays a significant role.

Chapter 15 is a summary of the major principles that form the foundations of generalist practice. The chapter concludes the book by systematically comparing problem solving, strengths, Aboriginal, feminist, and structural approaches.

chapter 2

The Emergence of Social Work in Canada

Chapter Goal ▼

To broadly understand and appreciate the heritage of social work in Canada and the vision of social work as shaped by more than a century of experience.

This Chapter ▼

- explains that social work is the product of the Industrial Revolution and urbanization
- shows that much of what is now social work emerged from two social movements: the charity and settlement house movements—1850–1930
- describes the influence on early Canadian social work of the social gospel movement and J. S. Woodsworth, a social worker and social work educator
- presents the professional development of Canadian social work in the years 1925–2005
- summarizes how generalist social work emerged in Canada

INTRODUCTION

Social work developed in Canada, the United States, and Britain at about the same time. It began to play a prominent role in society as life changed from an agrarian to a capitalistic and industrial system. In this chapter, we provide a broad view of social work's Canadian heritage[1] from the emergence of the fledging profession in the last half of the 19th century to the present day. While the path taken by Canadian social work is somewhat different than that in the United States and Britain, the history of the profession is interrelated between all three countries. (See Herrick and Stuart, 2005, for a comparative North American history of social welfare and social work.)[2]

SOCIAL WORK AND THE INDUSTRIAL REVOLUTION

For most of recorded history until the 18th century, people relied on human labour, draft animals, and, to a lesser extent, such forces as water and wind to drive machinery and transport goods. For most people in Europe and colonized North America, life revolved around agriculture. However, about 200 years ago, things began to change with the Industrial Revolution.

"The phrase 'industrial revolution' refers to the replacement of craftsmen by the factory, handicraft operations by power-driven machinery, the local market by one that was distant and impersonal" (Lieby, 1978, p. 71). Life changed drastically as people began to harness technology. The steam engine was invented. Factories making a wide variety of products sprang up. The rural family way of life was disrupted. People moved to cities as workers were needed for the factories. Workers made, used, and repaired the machines that were the engines of commerce and industrialism. Unlike in rural areas, where a large family meant more workers to grow crops, in cities children were an economic liability. To offset this, children were sometimes used as industrial labour, often at bargain-basement wages. The industrialists exploited the workers in order to make profits in their new and growing industries.

A way of life that took centuries to develop was, in fewer than 100 years, changed forever, first in Western Europe, particularly England, and then in the United States and Canada. The family was a different social unit, unable to cope using traditional ways. The church tried to fit in, but in the end it too was changed. The clergy in cities were more distant from their parishioners than they were in closer-knit rural areas. The church was no longer the centre of the community but merely part of a much larger system. Agrarian life gave way to industrial, urban centres.

In the cities, slums emerged and crime increased. The education of children changed: the one-room schoolhouse gave way to a much more impersonal and formal system. Children who were used as labourers were often not educated and almost always exploited. In North America, immigrants flooded to the cities, often living in slum conditions. The old, formerly stable institutions of family, church, education, and farming were disrupted and permanently changed. These *social institutions* could no longer meet their former social obligations.

It was these gaps left by social institutions that set the stage for the emergence of social work. Urban charities appeared to help the poor, child welfare agencies replaced some of the functions of family and church, **philanthropy** became common, and *settlement houses* were started that addressed life in the urban slums (Daly, 1995; Lieby, 1978, pp. 71–89; Pumphrey and Pumphrey, 1961). There is no doubt that social work is the product of industrialization and urbanization.

The predecessors of social work in Canada emerged at the end of the 19th century, later than in both Britain and the United States, mainly because urbanization and industrialization occurred later in Canada. For example, the population of Toronto in 1834 was about 9 250 and in the 1880s to 1890s was only about 100 000, when London's population was about 4 000 000 and New York's about 1 500 000 (Irving, Parsons, and Bellamy, 1995, pp. 4–8). "Canada's economy was largely agricultural rather than industrial, and urban problems were not pressing in the 1880s and 1890s as they had been for more than a hundred years in Great Britain and had quickly become in the United States" (Irving, Parsons, and Bellamy, 1995, p. 8).

THE CHARITY AND SETTLEMENT HOUSE MOVEMENTS, 1850–1930

Social work has its roots in many sources, including, for example, the development of child welfare, the social gospel movement in Western Canada, and the cooperative movement in Nova Scotia led by Moses Coady (Bellamy and Irving, 1986). However, early social work was probably influenced most by two social movements that originated in the last half of the 19th century: the *charity movement,* epitomized by the Charity Organization Society, and the *settlement house movement* (Brieland, 1995, p. 2249; Camilleri, 1996; Daly, 1995; Ramsey, 1984). The two movements occurred during approximately the same time period, initiating first in England and then spreading to the United States and Canada. Both social movements were responses to industrialization and urbanization. While the ultimate goals of the early charity workers and the settlement house workers were similar, their view of the world and their approaches to helping were radically different.

The charity movement, based on religion and religious thought (Daly, 1995; Jennissen and Lundy, 2008; Lieby, 1978, pp. 111–12; Wills, 1995), was the product of a belief that held that it is better to help (treat) people with problems than to banish, punish, or ostracize them. (See Chapter 3, which explains how social work ideology is bound to an ideology of helping.) The movement's supporters assumed that the new industrial system was fundamentally sound and that their task was to help disadvantaged people adjust to or cope with their surroundings. *Casework,* work with individuals, can trace its direct heritage to the charity movement.

Not unlike present-day structural (see Chapter 14) social workers, others viewed the industrial system as badly flawed. These were settlement workers and other reformers who saw such problems as poverty, poor working conditions, and unhealthy living environments in industrial parts of cities as products of the capitalistic industrial system. These reformers and social activists generated and promoted new ideas, such as workers' compensation, unions, social insurance, and public and universal health insurance. Some settlement workers also saw an immense need for a variety of social, health, and recreational services in slum areas of large cities. Many settlements organized or provided services to meet such needs. Much of group work, community development, and community organization can trace its beginnings to the settlements. As we will discuss later, the methods of casework, group work, and community organization subsequently became known as methods of social work.

The Charity Workers

The first Charity Organization Society (COS) was established in Britain in 1869. A leading spokesperson for the charity movement was Thomas Chalmers, a Scottish minister who is credited with leading the charity movement toward the goal of providing aid, based on strict religious principles, to people in distress. The first North American COS opened in Buffalo, New York, in 1877. The Toronto COS opened in 1888 (Kidneigh, 1965; Lieby, 1978, pp. 111–16; Wills, 1995). The society expanded rapidly, with 92 cities in North America reporting a COS by 1892. In the early 1900s, the numbers would have been in the hundreds. Through a process that unfolded during the first half of the 20th century, which included a name and function change, the COS evolved into the modern family service agencies that continue to thrive in Canada and the United States. In 1965, for example, there were more than 300 such agencies in North America (Kidneigh, 1965, p. 5), and many Canadian cities today have an agency.

At first the charity workers—almost always women, and from the middle and upper classes—were volunteers called "friendly visitors." Wills (1995) writes, "The COS was notorious for its rigid moralistic stand, which rested on a firm belief that poverty was the hallmark of a sinful life and its relief a matter of Christian uplift" (p. 14). Charity was provided on the basis of moral character. People in need were more likely to get friendly advice from the COS than any kind of tangible aid such as goods or cash. The COS organized or coordinated relief but generally did not provide direct relief services (Brieland, 1995, p. 2247; Carniol, 1995, p. 24).

Later, while still called friendly visitors, these volunteer workers became paid staff, albeit poorly paid. These workers were the first to suggest that the key to personal helping was the interpersonal relationship formed between helper (usually a friendly visitor) and person in need. The friendly visitors also firmly believed that sound assessment would lead to good advice. As a result, they began to articulate a process of helping (Lieby, 1978, pp. 116–23; Pumphrey and Pumphrey, 1961, pp. 341–43).

By 1910, many were calling the friendly visitors *caseworkers*. They were beginning to be viewed as professionals, and some were taking leadership roles in society. Probably the most notable from a social work point of view was Mary Richmond. A caseworker at the Baltimore COS, Richmond was the first person to attempt to formulate a theoretical base for social work. In 1917, she published her famous and highly influential book, *Social Diagnosis*.

In her book, Richmond outlined a process for social work practice that has had considerable influence on the profession. According to Richmond, the process of casework is study, diagnosis, and treatment, with the concept of helping—treatment—at its centre. But the process she outlined is the same as that used in medicine. Diagnosis implies that after examination (study), a person's problem can be diagnosed just like a disease, and the treatment that follows must be based on the diagnosis. Thus, Richmond's process was a medical model. This simply stated process set the ***theoretical framework*** for all casework for the next half-century. It finally evolved, another half-century later, to the social work problem-solving process that is still in widespread use today (see Chapter 8). Richmond's work also articulated and shaped two cornerstones of current social work practice: first, that intervention depends on an assessment process (which Richmond called diagnosis), and second, that the key to social work intervention (treatment) is the relationship between client and worker.

In 1928, J. H. T. Falk, then–General Secretary, Council of Social Agencies in Montreal, and in 1918 the first director of the McGill University social work program (Wills, 1995, p. 20), presented a paper at the First International Conference of Social Work held in Paris. In his paper, Falk clearly, but almost apologetically, connected Canadian social work with the charity movement and then distanced social work from the charity view that social ills are the responsibility of the individual. He wrote that social workers in Canada

> would be frank to admit that they have inherited from past generations ideas and practices which are part of the programme of charities established in the nineteenth century, and which at the best are well-meant attempts to relieve want and suffering prompted by the sympathy and conscience of the well-to-do. (quoted in Wills, 1995, p. 28)

He then defined social work as follows:

> Social work therefore concerns itself in the main with the prevention and cure of diseases physical and mental, the prevention and cure of poverty, and the prevention and cure of delinquency; for any of these conditions implies maladjustment to society for which social and economic factors are often responsible. (quoted in Wills, 1995, p. 28)

Falk's definition on the one hand is a clear reflection of Richmond's concept of social diagnosis and the medical model. He even seemed to view poverty and delinquency as things to be cured like a disease. But, importantly, he also saw social and economic factors as often responsible for the problems that people face; unlike the charity view that people's deficits are responsible for their problems, Falk saw as important—and even emphasized—social and environmental factors. He described a modern and current approach.

The impact of the charity movement on social work in Canada was enormous. While social work has undergone considerable change since the days of the COS, this organization established that when social institutions such as family and school are unable to provide needed services, personal helping should be the responsibility of professionals. People began to believe that poor people had the right to a minimum acceptable standard of living. While poverty continued to be viewed as a moral issue, it was felt that help in the form of relief and guidance could be offered based on an assessment of worthiness. If the poor person passed this kind of "morality means test," then relief would be given. More important to the emergence of social work, the advice and guidance provided by caseworkers of the time were early forms of counselling.

The Settlement House Workers

The second major social movement that led to the development of social work was the settlement house movement that began in the late 1800s. Much of this movement was very critical of the charity movement and the COS. Settlement house workers saw the charities as a form of social control. Giving people charity and advice only perpetuated poverty and the ghetto structure of industrial urban centres where most immigrants lived. They offered people no real way out of their plight. What was needed, it was argued, were reforms and services that would help poor people shake the bonds of poverty and industrialization so that they could enjoy a better quality of life. In Canada and the United States, the settlements focused much of their work on immigrant populations.

The Early Settlement House Worker

Some of the early settlement house workers were activists and service providers. Others tried to understand and study the nature of the slums, poverty, and the effects of industrialization. Often the latter were university students and professors, intellectuals, and union and political leaders, frequently socialists (Camilleri, 1996, p. 33). Some settlement houses, like University Settlement in Toronto and Chicago Commons in Chicago, became closely connected with leading universities and were influential in establishing major social policies (Irving, Parsons, and Bellamy, 1995). The settlement that probably had the most political and social policy influence was Toynbee Hall in London (Barnett, 1950; Camilleri, 1996, p. 33).

Many of the early workers were women, and some were the daughters and wives of industrialists. Historical literature clearly shows these women as idealists (Addams, 1910, 1930; Chambers, 1986). However, they were more than that. They were highly skilled, often well-educated, competent people in their own right who had limited avenues for using their talents. These women found an important niche in the settlements. They decided to do something about the plight of the poor; ironically, this poverty was often a result of the low wages paid by companies owned by some of the women's own families (Addams, 1910, 1930; Barnett, 1950; Chambers, 1963). Many found satisfaction in their work because it challenged their skills and because they observed real progress as the conditions experienced by immigrants did improve (Irving, Parsons, and Bellamy, 1995, pp. 211–12).[3]

The word "settlement" means to settle in, as in settling into a new home. The settlements were houses in the slums in which many of the workers lived. Imagine living 24 hours a day, 7 days a week in the inner-city social agency in which you work—that is exactly what the settlement workers did!

The settlements had two general functions. Some settlement houses had strong reform agendas and were heavily involved in social and political action. In Canada, this was less true than in Britain and the United States (Irving, Parsons, and Bellamy, 1995).[4] Their second function was to provide services to people who lived in the poor areas of cities. These services varied greatly according to such factors as demographics, community needs, and available resources.

The Reformers

Consider a teeming slum in the late 1800s and early 1900s. The streets were grimy. Pollution from industrial smokestacks darkened the sky at noon on otherwise bright, sunny days. Men, women, and children worked in the factories for wages that perpetuated their poverty. In Britain, the low-paid factory workers were members of the lower class. In North America, many, if not most, were immigrants, often of Irish or Eastern European background. Many immigrants had difficulty with the English language, and there were few schools where they could learn it. Few kindergartens existed to enable immigrant children who did not understand much English to begin to attend school.

There were few social services that these people could turn to for help. Adequate medical care was generally not available, let alone health insurance. If a person was injured on the job, it was unfortunate; workers' compensation programs were not yet in place. In most jurisdictions, if a child committed a crime he or she was treated by the justice system as an adult.

There were no unions to protect workers. In short, there was no *social safety net*. In North America, particularly the United States, the settlement house workers contributed greatly to reforms that led to the establishment of kindergartens, social insurance, public health insurance, workers' compensation, labour unions, juvenile courts, and more (Addams, 1910, 1930; Chambers, 1963; Daly, 1995; Lieby, 1978, pp. 127–35). In this role, the settlement workers were social reformers.

Probably the two most famous and most reform-minded settlement houses were Toynbee Hall (the first settlement, opened in 1884 by Samuel and Henrietta Barnett) in London, England, and Hull House (opened by Jane Addams in 1889) in Chicago. Most major Canadian cities had at least one settlement house (Valverade, 1991). The first in Canada was Evangelia in Toronto, which opened in 1902. However, the movement did not really become established in Canada until a series of events in Toronto between 1910 and 1912, including rapid growth and industrialization, led to the development of several settlements (Irving, Parsons, and Bellamy, 1995, pp. 26–33).

The early settlement workers recognized that the root of many of the problems facing people in urban areas was social conditions. The causes, in their view, were not due to personal defects, as the charity organizations assumed, but to the economic and social structure of the industrial and capitalist systems (Addams, 1910, 1930; Barnett, 1950; Chambers, 1963; Daly, 1995).

The truly activist characteristics of most of the settlements waned with the First World War.

The Service Providers

In both Canada and the United States, many settlement house workers provided services, mainly to immigrants. Some of the workers who performed these functions became known as *group workers,* while others were called *community organizers* and *community developers.*

Providing services accounted for most of the settlements' functions. According to Irving, Parsons, and Bellamy (1995), this was the primary role of Canadian settlements from the beginning, although many individual workers were socially and politically active. Often they acted as advisers or consultants to help people in the neighbourhood address a social injustice or some other issue. Settlement workers are credited with starting kindergartens in many urban centres.

Group workers would often use a task as the backdrop to accomplish an important goal. For instance, they might start a sewing group for a few immigrant women with the real goal of helping them learn English. Community organizers from Toronto settlements started, among other services, a well baby clinic in 1914, a library for local immigrants, ice rinks, and hundreds of other such community projects, all designed to improve the lives of disadvantaged people (Irving, Parsons, and Bellamy, 1995, p. 80).

Irving, Parsons, and Bellamy (1995) also report that during the Great Depression the settlements in Toronto, while still neighbourhood-oriented, tended to focus on providing relief in kind (food, clothing, and other goods) rather than in cash: "During the 1930s the Toronto settlements ... did not initiate or participate in much political action directed at changing the inadequate relief structure" (p. 126). During the Second World War, many services were directed to people who were affected by the war. By 1960, there was still another change, and the settlement as originally conceived was gone forever. Most of the remaining settlements in Canada became neighbourhood or community centres (some complete with swimming pools and gyms) where people in inner cities could meet their neighbours and spend leisure time with others.

THE SOCIAL GOSPEL MOVEMENT AND J. S. WOODSWORTH, SOCIAL WORKER AND SOCIAL WORK EDUCATOR

The Canadian settlements were different from those of the United States in other respects. First, they started later—largely because industrialization and urbanization also occurred later in Canada.

Unlike their U.S. counterparts, the Canadian settlements had strong ties to the Protestant churches. Irving, Parsons, and Bellamy (1995) go so far as to use the word "dominate" to describe the influence of the churches over the development of social services in Canada, and write that "the social gospel was behind much of the social reform of the time" (p. 36). For example, J. S. Woodsworth—a powerful social reformer and Methodist minister—in 1907 became superintendent of All Peoples Mission, a settlement in the north end of Winnipeg (Ziegler,[5] 1934, p. 37), and was a major leader in the social gospel movement (Irving, Parsons, and Bellamy, 1995, p. 36).

The social gospel movement—with strong roots in the Prairie provinces but a force throughout Canada—was a social reform movement built on Protestant religious thinking and a form of Christian socialism. The movement began in England in the mid- to late 19th century, and viewed the problems of society "as the result of flaws in the institutions of society" (Bellamy and Irving, 1986, p. 33; Wills, 1995).

Unlike the British experience, "The Canadian movement developed a radicalism through exposure to Western populism and industrial unionism" (Wills, 1995, p. 17). The social gospel movement influenced the settlement workers. For example, All Peoples Mission in Winnipeg, with J. S. Woodsworth as superintendent, supported the ideology of the social gospel movement (MacInnis, 1953; Ziegler, 1934). Woodsworth was also influenced by other settlements and received much of his education about the poor while visiting missions and settlements in London and the United States in 1899. "His appointment as superintendent of the All Peoples Mission in Winnipeg enabled him to develop institutes, settlements, clubs and hospital-visiting and relief programs" (Bellamy and Irving, 1986, p. 34).

Woodsworth, an important political leader in the social gospel movement, was a primary force behind the establishment of the Co-operative Commonwealth Federation (CCF) in 1933, the forerunner of the New Democratic Party (NDP) of Canada. First elected to Parliament in 1921, he held his seat for 21 years until his death. He is credited with many ideas that later formed the basic foundation of Canadian social policy, health care, and the social safety net. Woodsworth was instrumental in the "implementation of many reforms championed by the CCF and adopted by the Liberal government of Prime Minister Mackenzie King. These included old age pensions, health care benefits, unemployment measures, and a great many environmental programs that were intended to humanize modern society" (Bellamy and Irving, 1986, p. 34).

Before his political career began, Woodsworth was a social worker and social work educator. Mann (1968), in a short monograph, reports that in 1914—the same year that the University of Toronto initiated its Department of Social Services (Yelaja, 1985, p. 18)—one of the first training programs for social workers in Canada started in Winnipeg under the aegis of the Canadian Social Welfare League, a social research organization that Woodsworth founded and served in as secretary (Bellamy and Irving, 1986, p. 34; MacInnis, 1953, p. 90; Ziegler, 1934, p. 62). Woodsworth was the director of the training program as well as a committed social activist and a strong supporter of social welfare services (MacInnis, 1953, pp. 85–95; Ziegler, 1934, pp. 27–77).

The Winnipeg social work training program continued for two years. Woodsworth gave a number of the lectures. Interestingly, Falk, quoted earlier in this chapter, also gave several lectures. This was a very early training program and probably one of the first that used the term *social work* to describe social service, welfare, and charity work.

Often we ask the question, how did social work evolve? By carefully comparing the 1915 social work curriculum with the current curricula of generalist programs, one can see the changes as well as many of the similarities. Exhibit 2.1 shows the reproduction of a brochure that describes the curriculum of the training program,[6] almost certainly under the authority of the University of Manitoba,[7] that was given in 1915, the second year of the program. The brochure gives a sense of social work in at least one Canadian centre in 1915. The training program dates from before professional social work is generally considered to have been well established in Canada.

The social work training program is illuminating for a number of other reasons. Woodsworth, a major political figure in the establishment of Canadian social policy, clearly saw social work as important and was an early social work educator. His use of the term *social work* to describe the course of studies was unusual in that the term was really not widespread until the 1920s and 1930s. Also somewhat surprising for the time period, the description repeatedly uses *social work* to describe a professional activity.

The curriculum reflected a balance between charity work and reforms. While we have no solid information on the content of the courses, probably what is most important is that the curriculum covered the range of casework and work in charities, to social reform, to social and economic policy, to community organization. It is not a big leap to conclude that this range probably reflected Woodsworth's conception of social work, the views of the Social Welfare League, and social workers in the various community agencies that sponsored the program. Certainly it would have been influenced by the social gospel movement. Remarkably, many undergraduate generalist social workers in Canada today are educated in universities covering the same breadth of material as in this early training program.

Many of the issues and titles covered bear an uncanny resemblance to 21st-century issues (and modern curricula): unemployment, underemployment, immigrant issues, feminism, organized labour, health, volunteer work, and delinquency, to name a few. On the flip side, topics like unmarried mothers, the inefficient, and the backward child would raise many red flags in today's schools of social work. Some of early Canadian social work focused on immigrant populations and, based on the titles of some of the lectures, attempted to assimilate, contrary to current Canadian polity, immigrants into Canadian society. Most modern university-based social work programs also do not emphasize the role of the church in social work.

Exhibit 2.1 ▼ Winnipeg Training Class in Social Work

SECOND SUMMER SESSION, 1915

In view of the success of the Training Class last year the University authorities have authorized the holding of a session this summer.

The course is designed to help (a) those already professionally engaged in social work; (b) volunteer social workers, members of Boards of Charitable Institutions and Associations, and church workers; (c) University graduates or senior students looking to further study in special service.

Special attention will be given to the needs of out-of-town students.

The course is divided into three Institutes of two weeks each: (1) Community problems; (2) Modern Philanthropy; (3) Neighborhood workers.

Arrangements are made to visit the institutions described in the classes and others of special importance to social workers.

Instruction in Playground Supervision may be substituted for visits of inspection and group discussions.

DATE—July 5th to Aug. 13th.
HOURS—10 to 12 noon—Visits of inspection, and group discussion held in Board Room, Industrial Bureau.
 5 to 6 p.m.—Lectures held in University.
 8 to 9 p.m.—Lectures held in University.
FEES—$5.00 for course; $2.00 for one Institute.
LIBRARY—A specially selected library will be arranged for.
EXAMINATIONS—In lieu of, an essay will be expected on one subject in each Institute.
CERTIFICATE—At the conclusion of the course any student may obtain a certificate stating the work covered and an estimate of his fitness for Social Work.
REGISTRATION—Should be made at once to the office of the Secretary, Miss Elinor Mitchell, Room 10, Industrial Bureau, Winnipeg, Phone Main 6091.

I. Institute on Community Problems.

JULY 5–16

A Statement and Interpretation of Modern Social Developments—*J. S. Woodsworth*

July 5th 5 p.m.	—The New Era.
" 6th "	—Modern Industry.
" 7th "	—The Twentieth Century City.
" 8th "	—The Rural Problem.
" 9th "	—Social Reconstruction.

Special Problems—

July 12th 5 p.m.	—Municipal Ownership *A. W. Puttee.*
" 13th "	—Unemployment—*J. H. T. Falk.*
" 14th "	—Recreation—*H. R. Hadcock.*
" 15th "	—Town Planning—*Prof. Stoughton.*
" 16th "	—The School and the Community.
July 5th 8 p.m.	—Education—*Pres. Maclean.*
" 6th "	—Organized Labor—*Alderman Rigg.*
" 7th "	—Agriculture as a Solution of the Unemployment Problem *Mayor Waugh.*

" 8th "	—The Health of the Community *R. T. Riley.*
" 9th "	—The Relation of Economic Problems to Health and Disease *Dr. H. P. H. Galloway.*
" 12th "	—Recent Tendencies in City Government—*Theo. Hunt.*
" 13th "	—Municipal Finance—*Theo. Hunt.*
" 14th "	—Housing—*William Pearson.*
" 15th "	—Public Services *Controller Cockburn.*
" 16th "	—Charities Endorsement *N. T. McMillan.*

II. Institute on Modern Philanthropy.

JULY 19–30

Organized Charity—

July 19th 5 p.m.	—History of Organized Charity—*J. H. T. Falk*
" 20th "	—Technique of Family Investigation—*G. B. Clarke.*
" 21st "	—Special Cases—The Unemployed; The Underemployed; The Inefficient; The Delinquent *G. B. Clarke.*
" 22nd "	—Special Cases—The Sick; Widows; The Deserted; The Unmarried Mother *G. B. Clarke.*
" 23rd "	—The Volunteer in Social Work *Rev. G. H. Broughall.*
" 26th "	—The Homeless Transient *Roy Austin.*
" 27th "	—Social Resources—*J. H. T. Falk.*
" 28th "	—Hospital Social Service *Miss Inga Johnston.*
" 29th "	—Laws Affecting Social Workers *J. H. T. Falk.*
" 30th "	—Standards of Living and Labor *J. S. Woodsworth.*

The Promise of Politics

—*Prof. Harold Laski, McGill University.*

July 19th 8 p.m.	—Methods of Politics.
" 20th "	—Materials of Politics.
" 21st "	—Orthodox Sins and Heretic Dangers.
" 22nd "	—The Necessity of Transformation.
" 23rd "	—The Promise of Feminism.
" 26th "	—The Promise of Labor.
" 27th "	—The Meaning of Industry.
" 28th "	—The Reconstruction of Party.
" 29th "	—The Organization of Education.
" 30th "	—The Will to Succeed.

III. Institute for Neighborhood Workers.

AUGUST 2–13

Special Problems—

Aug. 2nd 5 p.m. —Problems in Connection with Boys' Club Work—*W. Finnegan.*
" 3rd " —How to Help Working Girls
Miss M. Tweedie.
" 4th " —Instruction in Sex Hygiene
Dr. J. Halpenny.
" 5th " —Causes of Juvenile Delinquency
Rev. H. Atkinson.
" 6th " —The Backward Child
Miss M. H. Kelly.

The Church and the Community—

Aug. 9th 5 p.m. —The Church and Changing Conditions— *J. S. Woodsworth.*
" 10th " —The Development of a Community Conscience
Dr. A. G. Sinclair.
" 11th " —A Constructive Programme for the Local Church
Dr. A. G. Sinclair.

" 12th " —Organization and Training of Christian Forces
J. S. Woodsworth.
" 13th " —The Rural Church
J. S. Woodsworth.

Immigration Problems—*J. S. Woodsworth.*

Aug. 2nd 8 p.m. —The Immigrant.
" 3rd " —Maintaining Canadian Standards.
" 4th " —Conserving Immigrant Resources.
" 5th " —Forces Canadianizing the Immigrant.
" 6th " —Elements of a Constructive Policy.

Immigrant Groups—

Aug. 9th 8 p.m. —The Slavic Peoples
Rev. A. O. Rose.
" 10th " —The Poles—*Louis Kon.*
" 11th " —The Hebrews—*E. A. Cohen.*
" 12th " —The Ruthenians
P. H. Wojcenko.
" 13th " —The Russians
Joseph A. Cherniack.

(Archives of Manitoba. Welfare Supervision Board Papers. File # GR 1557.)

This type of information is important to us as social workers almost a century later: our past helps us to understand and appreciate our current knowledge and practices, and shows us how "everything that changes remains the same."

THE DEVELOPMENT OF PROFESSIONAL SOCIAL WORK, 1925–2009

It is clear that early social work was strongly influenced by religious values and theology. This was true of the charity, settlement, and social gospel movements. There is no doubt that current values in social work are influenced by these pioneer movements (Wills, 1995). As well, the Great Depression and the two world wars influenced the development of social work.

By 1920, many methods of practice existed. There were group workers and community organizers, who tended to come from the settlement movement, and caseworkers, who came from the COS. And each of these methods was even further specialized. For example, there were, among others, medical caseworkers, public welfare workers, psychiatric caseworkers, corrections workers, and child welfare workers. Each branch tended to be an entity in and of itself, and there was no professional body for people who called themselves social workers. Many of these specialists had their own professional associations and were not yet organized as a social work profession. Falk (1928) adds another dimension to this fragmentation, suggesting that in 1928 the practice of social work in Canada varied greatly from province to province: "As to the methods [of social work] in vogue, they differ so greatly in different Provinces that any attempt to generalize is impossible" (quoted in Wills, 1995, p. 28).

By the mid-1920s, however, some began to argue that there were common threads between the various specialties, using such phrases as "a common base" or "generic social work."

In 1926, the Canadian Association of Social Workers (CASW), a federation of provincial associations, was established (Graham, Swift, and Delaney, 2000). The CASW, through its provincial branches, remains the primary professional social work organization in Canada. Through the national and provincial branches, standards of practice are established. Today the CASW is an important organization and helps unify social work across Canada.

From the 1930s to the mid-1960s, Canadian social work was strongly influenced by its American counterpart, the National Association of Social Workers (NASW). The first Canadian university-based social work program began in 1914 at the University of Toronto, 11 years after the first American programs (Chandler, 1986, p. 335; Graham, Swift, and Delaney, 2000, p. 29). In 1918, McGill University in Montreal followed suit. But it was not until 1947 that the University of Toronto graduated the first master's level student in Canada (Yelaja, 1985, p. 18). In comparison, the United States had developed many graduate programs in the 1920s (Brieland, 1995, p. 2249), and in 1939 the accrediting body of the time decided to accredit only university-based, master's level programs (Frumkin and Lloyd, 1995, p. 2239).

Until the late 1940s and early 1950s, although social work training programs were offered in Canada, students often had to attend an American university for professional education and certainly for advanced training. In fact, the lack of training in Canada was so acute that in 1960 the CASW requested that the federal government grant special funding to universities so that more students could enroll in social work programs (Akman, 1972, quoted in Yelaja, 1985, p. 18).

As social work began to mature, the fledging profession became closely connected with the social sciences (Lieby, 1978; Pumphrey and Pumphrey, 1961). Canadian social work was influenced by several, sometimes divergent, disciplines. One of the most important was theory from psychology and psychiatry, most notably **Freudian** and **neo-Freudian theory**. For nearly half a century, beginning in the 1920s, Freudian and neo-Freudian theory greatly influenced much of social work practice and education (Johnson, McClelland, and Austin, 2000; Leighninger, 1987). Even today much of social work practice heavily borrows theory from psychology.

Social work also began to adopt interactional theories that focused on the connection between people and their environments. In Chapter 9 we discuss three of these: ecosystems, role theory, and labelling theory. However, Canadian social work, unlike mainstream American practice, was also influenced by British socialism, which developed the intellectual foundations of the welfare state (Wills, 1995, pp. 19–20). The roots of this influence can be traced to the London School of Economics and Toynbee Hall (Barnett, 1950; Wills, 1995). To this day socialist ideals have an important place in Canadian social work services. Chapter 14, on structural social work, is based on critical theory and socialist ideology.

By the 1950s, the emphasis of practice on the inner person was waning. In 1957, Helen Perlman published her seminal book *Social Casework: A Problem Solving Process*, which tied case-work practice to role theory and, although within the context of ego psychology, shifted practice emphasis toward the environment. In the late 1950s, the NASW established a commission to re-examine a common base of practice. They began to lay the framework for a theoretical, common foundation in social work based on the interaction of a person with the environment. In the 1980s, others, including Meyer (1983, 1988), Germain and Gitterman (1980, 1995), and Gitterman and Germain (2008), articulated an ecosystems view of social work that some even today argue should be the common base of all social work (see Chapter 9).

This movement toward finding a common base for social work coupled with practice theory that connected people with the environment were important steps in the development of generalist social work practice.

THE GENERALIST EMERGES IN CANADA

In Chapter 1, we emphasized that this book is about generalist social work. This section summarizes how the Canadian schools of social work developed this new generalist form of social work practice, a made-in-Canada mode of practice.

By 1960, master's level social work education was common in Canada. However, most of the Canadian schools were accredited by the American-based Council on Social Work Education (CSWE). Canadian social work education mirrored its American counterpart.

Several events of the 1960s and 1970s dramatically changed Canadian professional social work. During the 1960s, both the profession of social work and Canadian universities were in a period of rapid expansion. Also during this time period, some began to look seriously at the longstanding contradiction of how a professional graduate program (Master of Social Work) could be offered as a beginning degree. Further, many in the 1960s viewed the content of some MSW programs to actually be of an undergraduate calibre. For instance, sometimes an MSW program was part of another faculty, such as Faculty of Arts, and not the Graduate faculty.

Most MSW degree programs specialized in one or any combination of casework, group work, and community organization methods. Many believed that this distinction did not reflect the reality of social work practice. Educators and practitioners agreed that many workers actually practised in all three areas and hence required generalist skills. Also, there was a shortage of university-educated social workers in Canada. Canadian social workers and educators viewed all of these problems seriously enough to change the conception of practice and chart a course that led to a different kind of social worker: a "made-in-Canada," university-educated, professional generalist social worker at the BSW level.

A first step was to create a new educational structure. By the early 1970s, many Canadian universities with social work programs had established a three- or four-year Bachelor of Social Work (BSW) degree as the first professional degree. Some of these universities then established a graduate level MSW degree based on the undergraduate BSW. (A few, including the University of Toronto and Wilfrid Laurier University in Waterloo, Ontario, retained the MSW as a graduate degree without offering a BSW.)

In order to make these changes, the practice of social work needed to be re-defined. The front-line worker was expected to have an undergraduate degree and work in a variety of settings using multiple types of intervention, not to specialize in casework, group work, or community organization as was common at that time. This meant that university curriculum needed changing because the old division of methods did not fit. The answer was to create this new type of social worker: a generalist social worker.

This was a marked departure from the American educational system. At the time, many Canadian schools belonged to the American-based Council on Social Work Education (CSWE). These Canadian schools were accredited by the American CSWE. The Council's accrediting process did not accommodate a professional BSW and a one-year MSW. The Canadian schools needed not only a new curriculum but a Canadian accreditation body. As a result, the Canadian Association of Schools of Social Work (CASSW) was established in 1967, with the goal of setting curriculum standards and accreditation processes for the new BSW and MSW programs. (In 2008, the name was changed to Canadian Association for Social Work Education or CASWE.) The accreditation process, under the aegis of the CASSW, was in place by the early 1970s (Yelaja, 1985, p. 19), with several schools admitting BSW students as early as the mid- and late 1960s. At the university level, the pattern of a generalist BSW education followed by graduate level MSW education is now the norm in Canada and has grown since the late 1960s.

Alongside university-based social work degree programs are many college programs across Canada that also educate students for jobs in social services. Their students may find employment in the social services upon graduation or elect to continue social work studies to obtain undergraduate university degrees, through negotiated agreements with university social work programs. Some of these colleges teach courses in generalist social work practice. We encourage you to seek out websites of social work programs in different Canadian provinces to learn more about how these programs "ladder" with or connect to social work education programs in Canadian universities.

CHAPTER SUMMARY

The emergence of social work as a profession has been the product of many forces, probably the most important of which were industrialization and urbanization. Social work grew as the institutions of agrarian societies dramatically changed and could not adequately cope with many of the industrial and urban problems of the day. Early social work filled gaps left by failed social institutions.

As a response to urbanization and industrialization, the charity and settlement house movements were born. They were both highly influential in the development of social work. Casework can trace its genesis to the charity movement, particularly the Charity Organization Society. Group work and community organization/community development were highly influenced by the settlements.

Social work developed later in Canada than in Britain or the United States, an important reason being that industrialization and urbanization occurred much later in Canada. Social work did develop somewhat differently in the three countries. It seems, for instance, that in Canada (particularly Toronto) the settlements emphasized providing services and focused less on reforms, whereas in both Britain and the United States the settlements had a strong social reform goal.

The 1915 social work education program developed by J. S. Woodsworth and influenced by the social gospel movement is an important example of the breadth of social work in Canada in the early part of the 20th century.

During the middle part of the 20th century, Canadian social work borrowed heavily from American practice. Many Canadian social workers were trained in the United States. It was not until the 1950s that advanced training was generally available in Canada, and it was the late 1960s before Canadian social work education began to chart a course that was different from its American counterpart.

NOTES

1 While social work in Quebec and English Canada developed in parallel, the roots of social work in Quebec are somewhat different. For instance, the Catholic religious orders in Quebec were instrumental in the development of early social work in the province (see Bellamy and Irving, 1986). This chapter mainly discusses the roots of social work in English Canada.

2 The book by Herrick and Stuart, *Encyclopedia of Social Welfare History in North America,* is a useful source book that compares the history of social welfare and the profession of social work between Canada, Mexico, and the United States. It is available both in hard copy and online. John Graham, University of Calgary, is associate editor and a Canadian contributor.

3 The role of women in early social work, including those who worked in the settlements, is controversial. There is little dispute that women made huge contributions to the development of early social work and took leadership roles in the reforms of the late 19th and early 20th century. Some, such as Chambers (1986) and Walton (1975), as suggested by Camilleri (1996), go further and argue that social work "was a movement and an occupation, from 1890 to the 1920s, created for and with women" (p. 36). This view holds that women occupied positions of some power and professional responsibility and were able to create important careers for themselves in a patriarchal world.

Feminist and radical thinkers present an alternate view and suggest that many of the early women social workers were exploited. Carniol (1995) holds that the women who were charity volunteer workers (friendly visitors) and early caseworkers were low-paid staff who served to mask the problems of poverty from men in power and "confirmed [the men's] views about being superior mortals and gave them a clear conscience about their relationship to the poor" (p. 25). In 1929, J. H. T. Falk, like many settlement house workers and social reformers of the time, took a similar position that charity was a way to ease the conscience of the industrialists.

Some also suggest that settlements and charity agencies were usually run by men but staffed by women. This meant that the role of women was undervalued and that "women in social work would play an important but secondary role in the professional hierarchy" (Daly, 1995, p. 11).

4 Historical information on American settlements is considerably more abundant than that on Canadian settlements. One of the best Canadian sources is Irving, Parsons, and Bellamy (1995), who generally describe the settlement movement in Canada but focus on examining in detail three settlements in Toronto. Of the three, only one had a clear social reform agenda. The other two were service-oriented.

5 Olive Ziegler was an influential settlement house worker and social activist in Toronto.

6 This document was obtained from two sources. Professor Len Kaminski of the Faculty of Social Work, University of Manitoba, discovered the brochure in the Welfare Supervision Board papers, File # GR 1557, Provincial Archives of Manitoba. We also received a copy from Professor John Cossom, School of Social Work, University of Victoria.

7 The reference sources refer to the "University," which in 1915 would have meant the University of Manitoba. Wesley College and Manitoba College also existed in Winnipeg at that time (later they merged to become United College and still later the University of Winnipeg), but neither were considered universities.

chapter

3

Ideological Foundations and Values of Social Work

Chapter Goal ▼

To explore and establish the ideology and values of social work that both shape and filter practice.

This Chapter ▼

- connects social work practice with the ideological foundations of professional helping that have emerged mostly in the 20th century
- distinguishes between knowledge and values
- suggests that social work is strongly influenced by an ideological lens that filters and shapes social work practice
- presents the core values of social work as articulated by the Canadian Association of Social Workers (CASW) and the International Federation of Social Workers (IFSW)
- shows how values are applied in practice by
  - illustrating the usage of the important but complex value of self-determination
  - connecting social work values with culture
  - addressing the issue of clashes between values
  - exploring ethical dilemmas

A NEW IDEOLOGY: HELPING PEOPLE

In Western societies, the ideology of helping and the concepts of treatment and rehabilitation are barely 150 years old. Up until the latter half of the 19th century, public policies dealing with vagrancy, deviance, and morality were punitive. People who could not fend for themselves or who were defined as deviant were generally punished, ignored, or forgotten in institutions. Often people who committed crimes were given corporal punishment. Vagrants, orphans, paupers, and elderly people were placed in institutions, sometimes called almshouses or poorhouses, that provided minimal levels of care and no attempts to rehabilitate. Similarly, asylums were built to care for people referred to as insane, usually without any real hope that those admitted would ever leave. Frequently, conditions in these institutions bordered on squalor, circumstances that certainly would not be tolerated today.

During the last half of the 1800s, major social reforms in North America and Western Europe changed all of this. Mental hospitals replaced insane asylums. This was much more than just a name change—it reflected a commitment to treatment. Penitentiaries were built as prisons with a rehabilitation focus. In many places, corporal punishment was abolished. Orphans were placed in foster homes or adopted. Today orphanages have largely disappeared. Programs were provided for disabled and elderly people that gradually focused on building a better quality of life. Slowly but surely over the next century, society began to accept the ideology of helping in the form of treatment, rehabilitation, and therapy for people with personal and social problems.

Out of this change in society's view emerged the helping professions. These professions included social work, psychology, and psychiatry, all well established in 21st-century Canada. In the early 1900s, however, the ideology of professional helping was new. Professions were being established to provide the treatment and helping services that flowed from the emerging acceptance of a helping or rehabilitation ideology. Freud was just beginning to publish. Psychologists, social workers, parole officers, probation officers, psychiatrists, personal counsellors, marriage counsellors, and other *human service* workers either did not exist or their respective fields were just in the formative stages. The use of professionals to help others with personal and social problems is a practice that is barely a century old.

IDEOLOGY AND SOCIAL WELFARE (MACRO) POLICY

Social policies greatly influence the practice of social work. Chapter 5 discusses in some detail the connection between policy and practice. Here we describe three political ideologies that help shape social policies and in turn social work practice.

A belief in individual interest and responsibility, personal freedom, and acceptance of unequal power and resources in society characterize conservative ideology. This lens tends to shape approaches to social welfare that see individuals as responsible for their own problems and solutions. For example, if Nina, a mother with two children subsisting on an inadequate social assistance income, finds it difficult to pay her rent each month, she may be seen as a poor planner who needs to be more resourceful and work harder to budget the money she receives. Policies related to workfare (requirement to work in exchange for social assistance benefits) and courses in household budgeting and parenting might be used to solve Nina's problems. Rather than examining why social assistance benefits are kept low and why caring for children is not worth more, it is assumed that there is nothing wrong with the system, only with people like Nina who can't manage well.

Adopting some features of the conservative position, a liberal lens includes a more humanistic view that people need to have a social safety net in case they become unemployed or face health or other crises. As Steve Hick (2004) explains, liberals "believe in a mix of targeted programs for those in need as well as universal programs, such as Medicare, that are available to all Canadians" (p. 61). Liberal social welfare, in the case of Nina and her children, adopts some conservative principles such as social assistance and food banks. A liberal position also advocates that community programs and self-help groups targeted to those in need, and particularly universal supports such as child benefits, government-funded income security programs, and basic health care, also comprise part of their available social safety net. Drawing from this mix of programs and services, a liberal approach strives toward greater social equality, but without much tampering with the system.

Moving away from individualism and minimal social service provisioning is the Fabian socialist (or social democratic) position, which Fiona Williams (1989) sees as including "equality, collectivism and social harmony" (p. 21). Society, it is viewed, needs to be organized so that human social connection and community are strengthened and the state plays a key role in creating social justice and equality, often by reducing large differences in wealth and poverty (Parrott, 2002). This social welfare ideology holds that universal programs and a just distribution of social goods are necessary in society to ensure equality. Important values in this social welfare ideology include equality, cooperation, and justice in society. In this type of social welfare environment, Nina would find herself in a better situation where her income would be sufficient to allow her to meet her family's needs for shelter, food, clothing, and other basic requirements of life, and other public programs (e.g., family holiday programs) would allow for a better quality of life. Many social workers might view this alternative as their preferred ideal scenario. Ideology influences social welfare policy, which in turn influences social services delivery and the practice of social work (see Chapter 5).

IDEOLOGY IN SOCIAL WORK PRACTICE

The social work profession has developed its own ideology, one that shapes, in varying degrees, the practice of social workers. As the use of professionals, often social workers, to provide personal and social helping services gained acceptance in society (and in the social welfare system), they began to provide more and more services. An ideology of social work emerged. This ideology consists of a set of ideas, knowledge, values, and principles that help structure the thinking and characteristics of social work. The ideology of social work has matured and has been influenced by social change over time, by movements such as the women's movement. In social work, a major part of the ideology is expressed as values. Over the years social work has spent considerable effort—perhaps more than any other profession—articulating a set of values, much of it embedded in the ideology of helping, to guide practice.

WHAT ARE VALUES?

Values cannot be proven. Gordon (1962, pp. 8–9) distinguishes between values and knowledge statements. Both values and knowledge statements are assertions of truth—assertions that something is so. Values, however, are based on a belief system. As the word "value" implies, we make an assertion because we like (value) it; it is desirable and important. We *believe* the statement to be true.

A statement of knowledge may also be valued. We may also believe it to be true. However, we have also either tested or intend to test its validity. We do not intend to test the validity of a statement of a value.

For example, "We believe in egalitarian ideals" is a statement of a value. For whatever reason, we hold this ideal to be important. It is so because we think it is so. It is a belief and we do not intend to rigorously test it. Now assume that we believe that a new intervention will benefit clients. We may like the new intervention and think it is a good idea, but it is not a statement of value if we intend to test (or have tested) whether it works. It is an assertion of a knowledge statement.

Many assertions of truth contain elements of both knowledge and values. In fact, the two can be conceptualized on a continuum ranging from "pure" knowledge on one end to "pure" values on the other. Making this distinction between knowledge and values can help us understand practice. We illustrate this later in this chapter under the section "Self-Determination as a Value and Type of Intervention."

IDEOLOGICAL LENS OF SOCIAL WORK

Throughout this book we show how social work practice is filtered and interpreted by each social worker. This is analogous to a camera lens with filters that shape colours and hues of the image that the camera receives.

Similarly, helping professionals use filters that shape their practice and define their understanding of people to whom they provide services. The ideological lenses of both the worker and the worker's profession, in part, filter the worker's image of the world.

This ideology shapes the image that that workers have of clients as well as the nature of practice, including assessment and intervention. Different helping professions may have a different image of clients because the ideological underpinnings of the professions are different. The concept of an image has further importance because often clients and social workers view things differently, based on their own ideological lens through which they view the world.

THE CORE VALUES OF SOCIAL WORK[1]

The International Federation of Social Workers (IFSW) articulates a clear statement of core values that is consistent with the positions taken in this textbook. The IFSW definition of social work (see full statement in Chapter 1) asserts, "Principles of human rights and social justice are fundamental to social work" (IFSW, 2004, Section 2, Definition of Social Work). The following is an unedited statement of the IFSW document that articulates these principles.

IFSW

4. PRINCIPLES

4.1. Human Rights and Human Dignity

Social work is based on respect for the inherent worth and dignity of all people, and the rights that follow from this. Social workers should uphold and defend each person's physical, psychological, emotional and spiritual integrity and well-being. This means:

1. Respecting the right to self-determination – Social workers should respect and promote people's right to make their own choices and decisions, irrespective of their values and life choices, provided this does not threaten the rights and legitimate interests of others.
2. Promoting the right to participation – Social workers should promote the full involvement and participation of people using their services in ways that enable them to be empowered in all aspects of decisions and actions affecting their lives.
3. Treating each person as a whole – Social workers should be concerned with the whole person, within the family, community, societal and natural environments, and should seek to recognise all aspects of a person's life.
4. Identifying and developing strengths – Social workers should focus on the strengths of all individuals, groups and communities and thus promote their empowerment.

4.2. Social Justice

Social workers have a responsibility to promote social justice, in relation to society generally, and in relation to the people with whom they work. This means:

1. Challenging negative discrimination* – Social workers have a responsibility to challenge negative discrimination on the basis of characteristics such as ability, age, culture, gender or sex, marital status, socio-economic status, political opinions, skin colour, racial or other physical characteristics, sexual orientation, or spiritual beliefs.
2. Recognising diversity – Social workers should recognise and respect the ethnic and cultural diversity of the societies in which they practise, taking account of individual, family, group and community differences.
3. Distributing resources equitably – Social workers should ensure that resources at their disposal are distributed fairly, according to need.
4. Challenging unjust policies and practices – Social workers have a duty to bring to the attention of their employers, policy makers, politicians and the general public situations where resources are inadequate or where distribution of resources, policies and practices are oppressive, unfair or harmful.
5. Working in solidarity – Social workers have an obligation to challenge social conditions that contribute to social exclusion, stigmatisation or subjugation, and to work towards an inclusive society. (International Federation of Social Workers (IFSW), *Ethics in Social Work, Statement of Principles* (2004). Available online at www.ifsw.org.en/)

---

* In some countries the term "discrimination" would be used instead of "negative discrimination." The word negative is used here because in some countries the term "positive discrimination" is also used. Positive discrimination is also known as "affirmative action." Positive discrimination or affirmative action means positive steps taken to redress the effects of historical discrimination against the groups named in clause 4.2.1 above.

Each of the principles is a value. It is an assertion of what IFSW, as a federation, believes in.

The Canadian Association of Social Workers (CASW) *Code of Ethics* is similar but organized differently. The preamble of the CASW *Code* includes the following:

> This *Code of Ethics* [of the CASW] is consistent with the International Federation of Social Workers (IFSW) *International Declaration of Ethical Principles of Social Work* (1994, 2004), which requires members of the CASW to uphold the values and principles established by both the CASW and the IFSW statement of values. (CASW, 2005a, p. 3)

The CASW statement on values is lengthy. The following section identifies each core value and related principles of the CASW *Code*. The full CASW *Code of Ethics* explains each core value in some detail. (*The Social Work Code of Ethics*, adopted by the Board of Directors of the Canadian Association of Social Workers (CASW) is effective March, 2005 and replaces the CASW *Code of Ethics* (1994). The *Code* is reprinted here with the permission of CASW. The copyright in the document has been registered with Canadian Intellectual Property Office, registration No. 1030330. pp. 3–8. Available online at www.casw-acts.ca.)

CASW Core Social Work Values and Principles

VALUE 1: RESPECT FOR INHERENT DIGNITY AND WORTH OF PERSONS
Principles:
- Social workers respect the unique worth and inherent dignity of all people and uphold human rights.
- Social workers uphold each person's right to self-determination, consistent with that person's capacity and with the rights of others.
- Social workers respect the diversity among individuals in Canadian society and the right of individuals to their unique beliefs consistent with the rights of others.
- Social workers respect the client's right to make choices based on voluntary, informed consent.
- Social workers who have children as clients determine the child's ability to consent and where appropriate, explain to the child and to the child's parents/guardians, the nature of the social worker's relationship to the child.
- Social workers uphold the right of society to impose limitations on the self-determination of individuals, when such limitations protect individuals from self-harm and from harming others.
- Social workers uphold the right of every person to be free from violence and threat of violence.

VALUE 2: PURSUIT OF SOCIAL JUSTICE
Principles:
- Social workers uphold the right of people to have access to resources to meet basic human needs.
- Social workers advocate for fair and equitable access to public services and benefits.
- Social workers advocate for equal treatment and protection under the law and challenge injustices, especially injustices that affect the vulnerable and disadvantaged.
- Social workers promote social development and environmental management in the interests of all people.

VALUE 3: SERVICE TO HUMANITY
Principles:
- Social workers place the needs of others above self-interest when acting in a professional capacity.
- Social workers strive to use the power and authority vested in them as professionals in responsible ways that serve the needs of clients and the promotion of social justice.
- Social workers promote individual development and pursuit of individual goals, as well as the development of a just society.
- Social workers use their knowledge and skills in bringing about fair resolutions to conflict and in assisting those affected by conflict.

VALUE 4: INTEGRITY OF PROFESSIONAL PRACTICE
Principles:
- Social workers demonstrate and promote the qualities of honesty, reliability, impartiality and diligence in their professional practice.
- Social workers demonstrate adherence to the values and ethical principles of the profession and promote respect for the profession's values and principles in organizations where they work or with which they have a professional affiliation.
- Social workers establish appropriate boundaries in relationships with clients and ensure that the relationship serves the needs of clients.
- Social workers value openness and transparency in professional practice and avoid relationships where their integrity or impartiality may be compromised, ensuring that should a conflict of interest be unavoidable, the nature of the conflict is fully disclosed.

VALUE 5: CONFIDENTIALITY IN PROFESSIONAL PRACTICE
Principles:
- Social workers respect the importance of the trust and confidence placed in the professional relationship by clients and members of the public.
- Social workers respect the client's right to confidentiality of information shared in a professional context.
- Social workers only disclose confidential information with the informed consent of the client or permission of client's legal representative.
- Social workers may break confidentiality and communicate client information without permission when required or permitted by relevant laws, court order or this *Code*.
- Social workers demonstrate transparency with respect to limits to confidentiality that apply to their professional practice by clearly communicating these limitations to clients early in their relationship.

VALUE 6: COMPETENCE IN PROFESSIONAL PRACTICE
Principles:
- Social workers uphold the right of clients to be offered the highest quality service possible.
- Social workers strive to maintain and increase their professional knowledge and skill.
- Social workers demonstrate due care for clients' interests and safety by limiting professional practice to areas of demonstrated competence.

- Social workers contribute to the ongoing development of the profession and its ability to serve humanity, where possible, by participating in the development of current and future social workers and the development of new professional knowledge.
- Social workers who engage in research minimize risks to participants, ensure informed consent, maintain confidentiality and accurately report the results of their studies. (CASW, 2005a, pp. 4–8)

History shows that values are subject to change. So are codes of ethics. We urge you to check the CASW and IFSW websites for updates at www.casw-acts.ca and www.ifsw.org respectively.

Some Explanations and Observations

Similarities

The core principles and values of the IFSW and CASW may appear to be rather different. However, this is more due to organization than substance. Careful reading of each will show that, in the end, very similar values are captured. (Also see CASW, 2005b.)

Provincial Differences

In Canada, each province is responsible for the regulation of social work (CASW, 2005a, p. 2). This means that each province's social work association may choose to adapt the CASW *Code,* develop its own code, or expand the CASW *Code* for the unique situation of its province. Since codes of ethics are subject to change, we recommend that you visit the website of individual provincial associations to learn about provincial codes in different provinces and territories of Canada. You can access the provincial associations (except Quebec) through the CASW website (CASW, 2009).

The Values Are Inclusive

A basic theme of both the IFSW and CASW statements is inclusiveness. This is evidenced throughout by use of such concepts as diversity, equitable distribution of resources, worth and inherent dignity of *all* people, upholding human rights, challenging discrimination, working for social justice, and more.

The Values Are Abstract

The values in the codes are intended to guide practice. However, they are general and most are quite abstract. Many do not prescribe specific behaviours for social workers. For instance, the CASW *Code* holds that "social workers uphold each person's right to self-determination, consistent with that person's capacity and with the rights of others." (CASW, 2005a, p. 4). The statement identifies two limits to self-determination: a person's capacity and the rights of others. The code, however, does not address what constitutes "capacity" and "rights of others."

The *Guidelines for Ethical Practice* (CASW, 2005b) help. For example, see Section 1.3 of the Guidelines, "Promote Client Self-Determination and Informed Consent" (pp. 4–5).

Section 1.3 offers rather specific guidelines on application of the principle of self-determination. Social workers in Canada should use the *Code of Ethics* and the *Guidelines for Ethical Practice* in concert with one another.

APPLYING SOCIAL WORK VALUES

The values articulated by the IFSW and CASW are held by many people, perhaps the majority in our society, and are not characteristic solely of social work. There is some disagreement between social workers about which principles are most important in our practice. Further, these principles are applied differently by social workers in different practice situations.

Expansion of the Principle of Self-Determination

Self-determination is one of the most important principles and yet it is difficult both to articulate and apply. In this section, we elaborate on the principle.

Conflict of Values

Dilemmas between different practice principles in real-life situations are well known and require careful thought and considered action. For example, the right to self-determination of an angry man under the influence of crack cocaine who aims a gun at his family conflicts with the right of his family to a safe environment. The rights of others are violated. It is clear to most of us that in this case the family's right to safety is the uppermost priority. This means that we must override the man's right to self-determination in this instance in order to help his family. If he is later requested by the court to seek the services of a social worker for assessment and treatment, the social worker would treat him with dignity, respecting his right to self-determination as much as possible given the circumstances. Unfortunately, in many situations, action is not as clear as in our example. Thus, professional judgement is important.

Resources Must Be Available

The principles and values outlined in the above sections speak to values that are related to people's rights and responsibilities. Mullaly (2007, pp. 39–41) presents a different ***paradigm*** that agrees with these principles but adds a set of values that outlines the responsibilities of social institutions. His paradigm offers a challenge to current practice. It is not possible to have equality or equal rights in a society that is characterized by vast differences in access to the resources that provide people with a good quality of life. In an earlier work, Mullaly (1997) explains that social equality means "every person is of equal intrinsic worth and should therefore be entitled to equal civil, political, social, and economic rights, responsibilities, and treatment" (p. 28), but it does not rest on a uniform division of resources among all. Instead, his view takes into consideration individual differences and potentials. This, according to Mullaly, is necessary so that people can voice their ideas and wishes and participate in making decisions about a wide variety of issues and concerns in which they have a stake. For social equality to be realized, it is necessary to address the responsibility of social institutions to promote justice for citizens. In practice, this requires a serious re-examination of social, economic, labour, and other policies. To illustrate, the right to self-determination of a poor, lone mother with two young children is meaningless unless she has available to her the resources that allow her to be self-determining—adequate shelter, food, clothing, and childcare. Only then will she realistically be able to express her views publicly and participate in the decisions that affect her, her children, and her community.

People Need Choices

The following expands on Mullaly's ideas. For example, to what extent can the woman and her two children who live on a meagre social assistance income (described above) be self-determining about their lives? The low income very likely limits many of their choices and chances in life. How can a community where plant closures have created mass unemployment be self-determining about its future? The community is limited by the problems caused by the closure. Can a man who is confused and hospitalized for a serious brain injury determine for himself that he will be able to care for his young children? Is a 12-year-old child who has become a ward of the court able to determine with whom she will live? All of these examples suggest how self-determination may be constrained. The areas in which choices can be made are limited by circumstance.

Self-Determination as a Value and Type of Intervention

Suppose you are working with a homeless client who has few social skills and whose decision-making capacity is limited. Your goal is to help the client find suitable housing within her means. You are considering two strategies. One is that your client's need for housing is the highest priority and you will scour the area until you find suitable housing for her. The advantage of this plan is that you will likely be able to find the housing, your client will not have to experience the stress of the search, and you reduce the risk that her limited social skills will result in the failure of her own search, which for her could be traumatic. However, this approach would eliminate some of the client's choices and her own ability to make decisions. Her right to self-determination would be thwarted. Yet, these may be acceptable costs if the search successfully ends with finding suitable housing. If you choose this option for the client, you will have decided that the limit to client self-determination is justifiable. The primary goal is to find suitable housing, and you do not want to risk failure.

Your other option is to support the client in her own search. While you believe this option has a higher risk of failure, you think a more important goal is to help the client to make decisions for herself. The goal of finding suitable housing is secondary to the primary goal of enhancing her decision-making capacity. In this instance, your strategy is to maximize her self-determination.

In much of the social work literature, self-determination is seen as an expression of a value. But often social workers use self-determination as a strategy of intervention based on knowledge and ***theory***. In the second option, self-determination is both a desired end (a value) and a strategy of intervention (based on knowledge). In part, it is a value because the worker holds that all have the right to self-determination. However, it is also an assertion of knowledge because the worker will test the efficacy of self-determination by finding out whether the strategy of assisting with self-determination is successful if suitable housing is found and the decision-making abilities of the client improve. In this sense, self-determination is not a value but an outcome—a specific, testable strategy of intervention, and therefore a form of knowledge.

Some Want Decisions Made for Them

Social workers may also face situations where clients do not want to be self-determining. Clients sometimes want social workers to make decisions for them. For example, a refugee family fleeing persecution in another country may not yet understand how to get things done in Canada, or may not be accustomed to open communication with people in authority. In other circumstances, persons who feel overwhelmed by circumstances in life, such as major crises or trauma, may be unable to make decisions or take action on their own behalf. They may want the social worker to make decisions for them about how and what help is to be secured.

Rarely can any kind of choice in life be made without some constraints to free and independent selection. People can make choices only when they perceive that they have a range of options to select from and when the rights of others are not diminished by their decisions.

Values and Culture

Sometimes the core and other values held by social workers can conflict with the values of various cultural groups. For example, some of the important values of Aboriginal groups conflict with some European values, causing misunderstanding and frustration in practice situations when social workers who do not understand Aboriginal cultural values work with Aboriginal people whose values are drawn from their culture (see, for example, Elliott et al., 2005). In social work, we learn from our clients before we know how we can be of help. We need to begin our work with an awareness that there are different ways of seeing one's world, the people in it, and appropriate courses of action. In the urban, white environment, some important values include independence, skills in verbal communication, acting quickly ("taking the bull by the horns"), and being assertive. In the practice of social work in Western cultures, we are trained to view client independence and, in some cases, assertiveness (but not aggressiveness) as strengths that are to be encouraged. Our profession is highly dependent on verbal communication, provision of expert help, efficiency in decision making, and even confrontation when it is deemed helpful or necessary. Furthermore, we encourage clients to show their emotions, verbalize their feelings, and assert their needs when appropriate, often during time-limited interactions.

Particularly when working with clients of cultural backgrounds different from our own, social workers must clearly understand the clients' values and how they conflict with the social workers' professional and ethnocultural values. To illustrate, many of the values and behaviours mentioned above conflict with those of some Aboriginal peoples (recognizing that there are differences among different Aboriginal peoples as well). For example, in many Canadian Aboriginal communities assertiveness and independence are not revered; instead, cooperation and collective experiences are valued. Mores that dictate acceptable means of communication may differ; ways of showing emotions also differ.

Another example relates to the concept of *noninterference* (see Chapter 12 for a discussion of noninterference). People in some traditional Aboriginal communities do not interfere with another's decisions or behaviour and consider it inappropriate to confront others by criticizing their behaviour or giving advice. In Aboriginal cultures, as in many others, it is good practice not to embarrass people by showing in front of others that they are wrong. Ross (1992) notes the need to forget grief and sorrow as quickly as possible, even destroying evidence that could bring back such feelings (e.g., a picture of a loved one who died). Talking about such things is seen as burdening others; thus, communication about these events is often indirect. This principle is different from that of most European-based cultures.

Another common Aboriginal principle that shapes behaviour is the need to carefully weigh all the facts available before doing anything. This may involve periods of physical immobility and silence, not the intense dialogue that is often a strategy of the non-Aboriginal person.

One's culture contributes to what is seen as right, true, or desirable. There may be similarities across cultures and individuals with different cultural backgrounds, but these can never be assumed. In situations where the client's ethnocultural background and identity differ from the social worker's, values that guide thinking and behaviour may not be similar. For example, in some South Asian cultures, traditional values and practices define the status of men, women, children, and extended family members. Sometimes the eldest male determines what will be done by others in the family. Young females may be protected by the family until they marry. Dominant North American (and social work) values that stress an individual's right to self-determination can fly in the face of values that clearly limit what less influential family members can say or do. In cases where a daughter is seeking increased freedom to date or travel like her peers, value conflicts can create dilemmas for families adhering to another set of values. Social workers must recognize these differences and try to find a way to work across worldviews and cultural practices or to negotiate between them in a given situation. To illustrate, the social worker providing services to a South Asian family facing such a value conflict can help by understanding the place of such values within the family's and each individual's cultural context. Then the social worker can work with family members to discuss the source and meaning of the conflict, ease tension, and help them to find an acceptable solution. Chapter 7 discusses the role of culture in social work practice in detail.

Clashes in the Priority of Values

People differ in how they prioritize values. As social workers, we come across situations in which our personal and professional values clash with those of clients, other professions, or the ***agency*** that employs us. Our work in a particular agency may pose problems for us if our values cause us to disagree with some aspect of service provision or agency functioning (e.g., when client benefits are cut in order to save money).

Frequently, the personal values of social workers clash with those of clients. A social worker may personally disagree with the plans of a woman who is fully capable of making decisions for herself to return to an abusive partner. The worker may have as her highest priority the safety of the abused client. While the client may be fearful, she may value the maintenance of the family unit above all else. If the client chooses to carry out her plan with full knowledge of its implications, most would agree that the worker should respect her right to make her own choice. Of course, the social worker would assess the safety risks, offer ongoing help, and help the woman plan what to do if she or her children are in danger.

In general, the social worker must respect the values of the client, and when there is a clash in values or a difference in priority of values, the client's values must take precedence over those of the worker. This is particularly important when the client and worker are from different cultures. However, there are exceptions to the precedence of the client's values over those of the social worker. The primary limiting factors are the safety of the client and others, and beliefs that advocate breaking the law. One example is seeking a physician's services for the purpose of circumcising a female child. Female circumcision has continued for centuries in a number of cultures, but in Canada it is illegal and is seen as a form of child abuse.

Sometimes there are conflicts of values between employing agencies and professional standards. There are some guides that can help resolve conflicts. Obvious ones are the professional codes of ethics. The CASW *Code of Ethics* does not clearly prioritize but outlines a process to be applied in situations of conflict (*The Social Work Code of Ethics*, adopted by the Board of Directors of the Canadian Association of Social Workers (CASW) is effective March, 2005 and replaces the CASW *Code of Ethics* (1994). The *Code* is reprinted here with the permission of CASW. The copyright in the document has been registered with Canadian Intellectual Property Office, registration No. 1030330. P. 2. Available online at www.casw-acts.ca):

> Social work is a multifaceted profession. As professionals, social workers are educated to exercise judgement in the face of complex and competing interests and claims. Ethical decision-making in a given situation will involve the informed judgement of the individual social worker. Instances may arise when social workers' ethical obligations conflict with agency policies, or relevant laws or regulations. When such conflicts occur, social workers shall make a responsible effort to resolve the conflicts in a manner that is consistent with the values and principles expressed in this *Code of Ethics*. If a reasonable resolution of the conflict does not appear possible, social workers shall seek appropriate consultation before making a decision. This may involve consultation with an ethics committee, a regulatory body, a knowledgeable colleague, supervisor or legal counsel. (CASW, 2005a, p. 2)

ETHICS AND ETHICAL DILEMMAS

Ethics has to do with what is right and wrong in human actions, one's duty to others, and striving to understand what underlies ethical behaviour. Morals refer to what is good or right or bad or wrong behaviour of people (Antle, 2002). According to Antle (2002), ethics in social work are based on humanitarian values and the belief that "all people are intrinsically worthy and should share in the benefits and burdens of society" (p. 5). Abstract principles about what is good are applied to specific situations by social workers in order to determine a course of action. The study of ethics is concerned with identifying standards that can be applied in practice (see, for example, Reamer, 2006). There are numerous ideas that are important in ethics and in ethical decision making. These are helpful to social workers, who daily face many situations that involve ethics and the need to employ ethical practice principles.

Another issue related to values and ethics that sometimes faces social workers is that of ethical dilemmas. An ethical dilemma occurs when a social worker is caught between two courses of action, both of which involve certain beneficial and/or adverse consequences. For example, a social worker is given a beautiful and expensive emerald bracelet by a wealthy female client, who insists that in her culture such gifts are expected and represent mutual respect and a good way to end any effective partnership. What should the worker do? Accept the gift? Return it and risk offending the client and perhaps hurting her feelings? Discuss the incident with and seek advice from her peers or supervisor? What consequences could the social worker's quietly slipping the bracelet into her desk drawer have on the social worker, the client, and the organization? There are gentle ways to explain to clients that it is thoughtful to offer such a gift, but a "no, thank you" along with a polite, gentle explanation is sufficient and most appropriate.

Ethical dilemmas are experienced by clients in many situations. Often we don't hear of them until after they have been dealt with, for better or worse. At other times, a client's ethical dilemma may be the reason for seeking help from a social worker. Consider the situation of Julia, a young woman who wants to marry her boyfriend in the near future. She has just found out that she is HIV positive. She is fearful that her boyfriend will break up with her when he learns of the diagnosis, but she is also concerned about already having passed the infection to him. What should she do? Pretend she doesn't know, but start taking precautions? Put off any talk of a wedding until she can tell him? The social worker can begin by helping the client to explore the options available to her and the potential consequences of each.

Basic survival needs to take precedence when there is a conflict between ensuring life and maintaining confidentiality. Consider again Julia. When the social worker meets with Julia, she hears from Julia that she is very concerned about keeping her HIV positive status private and does not want her friends, family, or workplace colleagues to know about it. She has agreed to visit the clinic regularly as part of her health care, but has declined to participate in post-diagnosis counselling. She is very concerned about maintaining her privacy. She does not want to tell her boyfriend about her diagnosis, as she is afraid that he may leave her. Julia says that she does not want anyone from the clinic calling her home or revealing her medical situation.

As discussed earlier, an important principle in social work is self-determination. A person has the right to self-determination. In this case, we can understand the need for self-determination and why Julia wants to decide for herself whether she will seek health care or other treatment. Self-determination assumes that people have choices in the actions they pursue and can make their own decisions. Young children or people who are cognitively impaired (e.g., debilitated by Alzheimer's disease) usually cannot make important decisions for themselves, limiting their self-determination.

We are also aware that the principle, protection of life, takes precedence over the principle of autonomy and freedom (Reamer, 2006). One person's activities should not jeopardize another's life and well-being. Social workers would not want to see someone risk harming another person if it could be prevented. In this case situation, the social worker does not want Julia's partner's health to be jeopardized by Julia's refusal to tell him about her diagnosis. We believe that he should be tested and counselled on how to take care of his own health. Not telling him may be harmful to him and may also damage the couple's relationship. We also see that, given the controversy about the spread of HIV/AIDS to partners who are unaware of possible transmission, Julia is worried that her privacy would not be maintained. She is clearly vulnerable and may experience social stigma if others learn that she is living with an HIV diagnosis. The social worker would want to ensure that the principle of self-determination be applied whenever possible and appropriate. (Although policies may still be developing, provincial health departments stipulate the obligation of people diagnosed with HIV/AIDS to contact past and current intimate partners to inform them of possible transmission.)

Of course, other ethical dilemmas take place within the social worker–client relationship. Often these have to do with issues of confidentiality and preserving autonomy. As mentioned earlier, an ethical dilemma occurs in situations where a social worker is caught between several courses of action and is unable to choose between them because of possible adverse consequences. Often, social workers can avoid these situations by clearly stating the limits to confidentiality and the helping process. (Of course, respecting client confidentiality as a general rule is fundamental to social work practice.) For example, not giving a client information about situations in which confidentiality cannot be guaranteed can pose serious problems in cases where a report must be made to authorities (e.g., if the client confides that her child is being abused by her partner).

Ethical dilemmas are often best approached using some systematic way of sorting out the characteristics of the dilemma. One could use the code of ethics as a guide to what principles are important in each potential course of action, and then attempt to weigh the positive and negative consequences of each. The code can be a good resource for resolving a dilemma for a number of reasons. First, it is written by and for social work practitioners. Second, it is accountable to social work and is recognized by our professional associations and most agencies as a guide for practice. Third, it has been revised over time to respond to the current practice environment. The difficulty in applying the code of ethics to an ethical dilemma is that it does not help determine which value or principle is uppermost in a given situation. It guides the social worker in identifying the relative importance of certain ethical principles, and, as shown in the previous section, the CASW *Code* does suggest a process for resolution.

Some have attempted to prioritize a list of principles or values that can be used as a guide for practice and as a way to help handle social work dilemmas (e.g., Loewenberg, Dolgoff, and Harrington, 2000; Reamer, 2006). The Ethical Principles Screen (Loewenberg, Dolgoff, and Harrington, 2000, p. 69) is organized in a pyramid, similar to the hierarchy of needs put forward by Maslow (1970).[2] From the top of the pyramid, the order of screening items to consider in ethical decision-making are as follows:

- the protection of life
- equality and inequality
- autonomy and freedom
- least harm; quality of life
- privacy and confidentiality
- truthfulness and full disclosure

For social workers, these principles require that basic survival requirements such as shelter, food, air, water, and the sustaining of life be the first concern. Next, we can be guided by the four principles drawn from the International Federation of Social Workers document (IFSW, 2004, Section 2, Definition of Social Work) and defined above: self-determination; people's participation in decision making; treating the whole person in her or his own social and natural environment; and working in ways that identify and develop people's strengths.

Other ethical principles are also important in social work practice. Respect for privacy and confidentiality is particularly important in a profession that works with problems that are personal and private. Disclosing information truthfully (and appropriately) is also necessary in social work practice. This refers not only to information provided to a client regarding social work services, but also to supervisors and authorities such as the courts, and in research activities (CASW, 2005a, 2005b; Loewenberg, Dolgoff, and Harrington, 2000).

Most of us can understand the primacy of the right to basic needs (life itself, food, shelter, and safety). Social workers support this principle by delivering, for example, programs and services that help people when they lose a job or become ill or disabled. Addressing social inequality and injustice that adversely affect people who are most vulnerable—those who are old, homeless, young, or ill—is a duty of social workers. Social workers have an obligation to ensure that vulnerable people are given the aid they need through public policy so that people are treated fairly and not subjected to discrimination. It is possible to use the CASW *Code of Ethics* principles above to provide a guide for practice in situations that pose ethical dilemmas. Another guide that can help in solving ethical dilemmas is the Ethical Principles Screen (Loewenberg, Dolgoff, and Harrington, 2000, p. 69).

When we accept the code of ethics as social workers, we agree to abide by certain rules and laws that we are usually not free to break (Reamer, 2006), even when we may have some personal conflicts with them. For example, a law that requires social workers in a social assistance (welfare) agency to refer clients to a job placement program that forces them to work as street cleaners, tree planters, or in other public works jobs may seem demeaning and punitive to a social worker, but the worker cannot simply refuse to participate. Instead, he or she can seek ways to act that don't break laws, such as requesting and evaluating the program's results or seeking alternatives. A final option for the social worker would be to seek other employment if no other solution can be found.

To understand an ethical dilemma adequately, questions need to be asked about the factors that have created it. Robison and Reeser (2000, p. 9) suggest that in each case, social workers ask themselves who are the participants or actors and who else is affected, what it is that these people do or do not do that might cause harm, and why the participants act or don't act in these ways. Making a decision about which course of action to take involves weighing the possible consequences to the participants to select the option that minimizes harm for those involved.

To resolve the ethical dilemma, a social worker can assess the situation from various perspectives, determine the key values and principles involved, examine possible courses of action and their consequences (seeking consultation when needed from peers or supervisors), select and implement a course of action, monitor and review the process, and follow up and conclude. It may be useful to step back and consider the situation from a distance to ensure that an ethical dilemma, rather than a disagreement or emotional response, actually exists (Robison and Reeser, 2000). For further information about resolving ethical dilemmas, it may be helpful to read an analysis of an ethical dilemma involving the mother of a 9-year-old child who is using intravenous street drugs online at http://www.socialworker.com/home/ Feature_Articles/Ethics/Analysis_of_an_Ethical_Dilemma.

CHAPTER SUMMARY

Social work practice emerged as the idea of professional helping took hold during the 20th century. Practice is based on a complex ideological foundation that includes a set of values that guides the nature of practice and helps set the goals for intervention.

Values are assertions that we believe to be true. Knowledge consists of assertions that we may believe but that we either have tested or intend to test to determine whether the assertions are true. Understanding the difference between knowledge and values can help us understand our practice.

Social work's view of the world is filtered through an ideological lens that most members of the profession share. This ideology shapes the way that clients are viewed and social policies are conceptualized, developed, and implemented. This, in turn, shapes the nature of practice, including assessment and intervention.

The IFSW holds that there are two fundamental principles: (1) Human rights and dignity; and (2) social justice. It then organizes a number of more instrumental and less abstract principles according to the two fundamental values that guide practice. They are important and most are reflected in the CASW *Code of Ethics*.

The CASW *Code* identifies six core values and then lists a number of principles related to each core value. The core values are as follows:

1. Respect for inherent dignity and worth of persons
2. Pursuit of social justice
3. Service to humanity
4. Integrity of professional practice
5. Confidentiality in professional practice
6. Competence in professional practice

"This *Code of Ethics* [of the CASW] is consistent with the International Federation of Social Workers (IFSW) *International Declaration of Ethical Principles of Social Work* (1994, 2004), which requires members of the CASW to uphold the values and principles established by both the CASW and the IFSW statement of values" (CASW, 2005a, p. 3).

The chapter explains that the two codes are similar, that there are some provincial differences in codes of ethics, the principles and values are inclusive, and they tend to be abstract. The chapter continues by illustrating how values are applied in practice, partly by illustrating usage of the important but complex value of self-determination. While we assert its importance, the right to practise self-determination is limited by many factors.

The chapter ends by connecting social work values with culture, showing clashes between values, and highlighting the problem of ethical dilemmas.

NOTES

1 The values of social work are embedded in the codes of ***social work ethics*** of many countries. Links to these codes can be found at the website of the International Federation of Social Workers, www.ifsw.org. There is some variation of values between nations.

2 Maslow's well-known model hierarchy of needs is usually pictured as a triangle divided into five levels. Beginning from the widest, bottom level are (1) the basic survival needs (food, water, and sleep); (2) the need for security (a safe environment); (3) the needs for belonging and love (caring relationships); (4) feelings of self-esteem and individual worth (through accomplishments and competency); and (5) self-actualization needs (optimizing potential and experiencing personal growth).

chapter 4

Social Work Roles

Chapter Goal ▼

To explore a variety of professional roles that are generic (common) to generalist social work practice.

This Chapter ▼

- defines professional roles
- distinguishes between social work roles that are specific to fields of practice and generalist roles that are generic to most fields of practice
- explores a wide range of generalist social work roles organized according to micro, mezzo, and macro levels of practice

WHAT IS A PROFESSIONAL ROLE?

Simply stated, people in all professions are expected to do certain things. These expectations define the roles of a profession. Often those in a society share and set the expectations. Clients of professionals also have expectations of what professionals should do. Likewise, members of the profession have expectations for themselves. Some roles are identified in codes of ethics and *licensing* regulations. The point is that professional expectations come from a variety of sources. Consider a family lawyer. The public, clients, and fellow lawyers may expect the lawyer to counsel, advocate, consult, and so on. In this example, some expectations, such as advocating in a court of law, may even be defined by legislation. It is also possible that the public, clients, and fellow lawyers may have differing expectations.

Similar roles are often shared between several professions. For example, many professionals such as psychologists, physicians, pastors or priests, and social workers provide personal counselling. On the other hand, some professions have unique roles, roles that only members of that profession can perform. For example, only physicians can prescribe medications.

The roles that social workers perform are not unique to social work, nor are they unique to any other profession. For example, nurses and psychologists frequently act as case managers and counsellors, and a variety of professionals may be mediators. However, what each professional brings to his or her role helps to determine how he or she performs it. For example, a nurse brings a different orientation to the role of case manager in the mental health field than does a social worker or psychologist. The personal and professional values, culture, life experience, and knowledge base of social workers helps shape the manner in which they perform their roles.

TYPES OF SOCIAL WORK ROLES

Social Work Roles Specific to Fields of Practice

One way to view social work roles is according to *fields of practice*. A field of practice is a broad area in which social workers are employed. Sometimes a field of practice is referred to as a setting. Each field provides services to a select group of clients. (See Turner and Turner, 2009, pp. 270–352, who group services according to select groups of clients.) Child protection and family services, health, mental health, school social work, criminal justice, and international social work are but a few examples of fields of practice. The field in which a worker practises partly determines the roles of the social worker.

Roles often differ between fields of practice. For example, the expectations of a social worker in mental health centres are very different from those in child protection. A hospital mental health worker might work with people who have long-term illnesses and require considerable help with *discharge planning*, family relationships, and/or community living. A child protection worker would most likely, in part, define her or his role as ensuring child safety, helping with family connections, risk assessment, and the like.

Roles such as discharge planning and risk assessment are not generic to social work practice. They are specific to the field and often require specialized skill.

Generic and Generalist Roles

Necessary and prerequisite to the development of many roles specific to settings are roles common to all of social work and that are applied in a variety of, if not most, fields of practice. Some call this "cutting across fields of practice." These are generic roles; they are common to and underpin social work practice. Generic roles flow out of the purpose, values, ideology, and theories adopted by the profession. Generalist social workers are expected to attain competency in a wide range of diverse generic roles.

Let us illustrate the connection between specialist roles defined by a field of practice and generic roles. Two roles discussed later in this chapter are advocacy and counselling. Again, assume a hospital mental health worker is helping a person with a serious and long-term mental health problem plan his discharge. One of the worker's hospital roles is discharge planning. In order to perform this field of practice-defined role, the worker needs skills in advocacy and counselling. Most likely the worker will counsel the client on decision making on topics such as housing and family connections. Depending upon circumstances, the social worker may need to advocate for the client in order to find affordable and adequate housing. Thus, the social worker needs skills in generic practice roles, such as counselling and advocacy, in order to perform specialized functions that are required in specific fields of practice.

Generic roles are diverse. A useful way to conceptualize the diversity of generic roles is to cast them into the context of ecosystems theory. (See Chapter 9 for discussion of ecosystems theory.) Drawing from ecosystems, we organize generic roles by ***micro, mezzo***, and ***macro systems*** (see Kirst-Ashman and Hull, 2009).

Think of micro to macro systems as a diverse continuum that ranges from small to large. The boundaries between micro, mezzo, and macro are blurred. Micro social work practice generally focuses upon individuals and sometimes families. Mezzo practice is aimed at small groups and sometimes families. Macro practice centres upon helping communities, neighbourhoods, or organizations. (See Chapter 9 for further discussion of micro, mezzo, and macro practice.)

Earlier we argued that generalist social workers must be able to function in a wide range of diverse generic roles. However, the roles that social workers perform in generalist practice are too many and too diverse to expect that any one person can become competent in all. In practice, social workers develop different roles and related sets of skills and competencies. The roles to learn and hone depend on the interests of the individual, the fields in which the social worker will practice, the requirements of unique client situations, relevant social and agency policies, and factors such as the social, cultural, economic, and political contexts of practice. Generalist social work practice is too fluid and broad to definitively circumscribe or define its functions. In fact, it is likely that, as new opportunities and challenges arise over time, new social work roles will emerge. For example, in some countries and contexts, disaster intervention is a new role for social work.

COMMON GENERALIST SOCIAL WORK ROLES

The social work roles that we describe in this book do not constitute an exhaustive list, but rather a range of roles on the micro to macro continuum. These roles are selected because they are ones that we perceive are commonly required by agencies, range from micro to macro, and are all generic to practice and social work in general. Further, they are not performed in isolation. At any given time, a social worker may be performing two or more roles.

Micro and mezzo systems: Roles for working with individuals, families, and groups

- case manager
- counsellor

Micro, mezzo, and macro systems: Roles for all levels of practice

- advocate
- enabler or facilitator
- group worker
- educator, teacher, or coach
- mediator
- outreach worker
- social broker
- evaluator

Macro systems: Roles in community development and social policy

- community practice or organizing
- community developer
- social activist

The Story of Kim and Ann

The story of Kim and Ann begins in this chapter and continues through later chapters, spun into scenarios used to illustrate various roles, theories, and approaches to social work practice.

Case Example

Kim and Ann ▼

Kim is a family social worker in the Child Protection Agency (CPA). She is an experienced worker with a generalist BSW degree who has taken many refresher and training courses in child welfare. Kim has earned the respect of her colleagues, family court judges, and numerous clients. For the most part, Kim really likes her front-line social work job and realizes she can provide a valuable service with a great deal of confidence and competence.

Ann is a 27-year-old lone mother of three children (Jim, aged 9; John, aged 4; and Amy, aged 18 months) with a grade 10 education. A child of Dutch immigrants, Ann was raised with her two older brothers and one sister in a working-class section of the city. The family is Protestant but rarely attended church.

Jack and Ann were married when he was 18 and she was 17. Ann was pregnant with Jim at the time of their marriage. Jack left the family just after Amy was born. He pays very little child support even though the family court has ordered him to increase his contribution.

Brief History of Events

Recently the CPA nightshift worker placed Ann's three children in a temporary, overnight shelter. The worker had received a call at 1:30 a.m. from a neighbour that the children were home alone, unattended by an adult. He discovered that Ann was at a party and indeed had not arranged for adult care of her children.

The nightshift worker found the three children alone. Amy was crying and needed her diaper changed. Jim did not want to do it. All three had colds and runny noses, and looked like they had been wearing the same old, torn clothes for days. Food was scattered all over the house, and the sink and kitchen were cluttered with dirty dishes. Amy had a bottle, but when Jim filled it he had spilled much of the milk and it had run under the refrigerator. Jim was still awake watching TV, but John was asleep. Ann is a smoker, and there were several packs of matches scattered around the house. Three or four used matches were on the floor. The nightshift worker wondered whether Jim or John had been playing with them.

The family is known to the agency, and neglect has been suspected, but there has been no evidence of direct physical abuse. The next day Kim was assigned to work with the family. CPA decided that temporary custody of the children needed to be extended to at least several weeks. The final decision on custody was made after Kim's assessment. Ann was initially an involuntary client (required to accept CPA's services), but over time Kim and Ann have formed an amiable relationship.

Circumstances ▼

Ann has been on social assistance (from Public Social Services) for almost two years. She is very frustrated that she cannot find a job that pays enough to feed, clothe, and house her family. Her stress level is very high, and she is unable to cope with both a job and parenting. Her problems are compounded by the fact that she has only a grade 10 education and no vocational training.

Ann and her family live in the core of the city in an area that, during the past five years, has deteriorated badly. There are many vacant houses, and

Continued

neighbourhood kids have set fire to several of them. Youth gangs have grown rapidly in the last two years, and the neighbourhood is covered with graffiti. Banks and grocery stores have moved out. Many people are afraid to venture outside at night, and some worry about safety even during the day.

Ann lives on the upper floor of an old house, next to a vacant one that has been burned. The house is divided into three apartments. Some of the windows have no screens. The toilet is not working, and the family has been unable to use it for more than a day. The house is badly run-down, and Ann has a lot of difficulty getting her landlord to make even basic repairs. One of the main reasons that he does not want to make the repairs is that he has not been willing to pay the high cost of fire insurance on the house.

As a youth, Ann had hoped to continue schooling so she could have a career but found herself pregnant. Her parents insisted that she marry, and she did not give abortion any real consideration. Jack was an exciting and fun-loving young man and she liked to be with him, but neither of them really wanted to be a parent. At first Jack took his parenting responsibilities seriously. He held a fairly good job as a highway maintenance worker for the provincial government. His wages met the family's basic needs with some left over for a few extras. Then, three years ago, Jack began to drink and to resent the responsibilities of being a parent. He became abusive. While Ann was never afraid of him, she was often glad when he was not around.

Despite these problems, Jack would often take over parenting tasks that reduced some of Ann's stress. While the relationship between them was not really close, they often complemented each other. About two months before Amy's birth, Ann discovered that Jack had a new woman friend. Marriage breakup followed very quickly. Jack is now living in a common-law relationship with his new partner.

While Ann often feels relieved that she does not have to contend with her ex-husband's drinking and abuse, the marriage breakup has caused other very serious strains. Now she is on social assistance and cannot make ends meet. Jack does not make the support payments that he is supposed to. Before the breakup, the family lived in reasonable accommodations. Now, because of the lack of income, Ann and her children live in inadequate housing. Her stress has mounted over the years.

Ann is close to her older sister and often confides in her. On occasion she has been able to get her sister to take care of the children in order to give her a break. Ann sees little of her parents, who are elderly; her mother is in poor health. Ann still has a couple of high-school friends that she sees occasionally but has no really close friends.

In the past year, Ann had more trouble with parenting, and Public Social Services had referred her to Family Counselling and Assistance Services, a sister agency of CPA, for help in developing parenting skills. The family counselling worker thought that Ann was under considerable stress. Some of it was caused by her environment, some because she felt trapped by her children, and some because she believed she would never be able to achieve any of the goals of her youth. Her workers at Family Counselling were concerned that Ann sometimes neglected her children, yet they were also convinced that she was capable of providing a loving and quality home life for her children. Over the past nine years, Ann has grown to love her children and deeply wishes she could be a good parent, but she feels overwhelmed by the stress of her living conditions and the frustration of not being able to attain a better quality of life.

Several times in the past three months CPA had reports that Ann had left her children alone. However, each time the agency investigated, her children were with an adult and Ann denied ever leaving her children unattended. Nevertheless, it was clear that sometimes Jim would prepare meals for himself and his two younger siblings, and the children were often dirty and unkempt.

Kim's Initial Assessment ▼

Ann is very upset that her children have been taken away from her and badly wants them returned. Kim, aware of the assessment of Family Counselling and Assistance Services, quickly recognized the stress that Ann feels. She concurred with the family counselling workers that Ann, with coordinated help, does have the potential to provide a good home life for herself and her children. It seems likely that the neglect of her children is not due to an uncaring attitude but to the mountain of stress Ann faces, which has been constantly rising. While long-term foster care will not be necessary, Kim decided that she will ask the court to extend temporary custody for three months. She is unmoved in her decision that Ann must prepare to have her children returned to her. Kim's essential task will be to help Ann get her life in order before she resumes her parenting functions.

Micro and Mezzo Systems: Working with Individuals and Families

Case Manager

The role of case manager is very common in general social work practice and is often referred to in the social work literature. This role arose almost overnight in the 1970s as the result of psychiatric hospital depopulation. As people were discharged from hospitals, community professionals were needed to help them access scarce and fragmented resources. These professionals, not necessarily social workers, became known as case managers in programs developed by the influential National Institute for Mental Health in the United States (Gerhart, 1990, p. 206).

The fundamental purpose of case management is to provide supports and resources to clients so that they can maximize the use of these services and, to the extent possible, mobilize their own resources, skills, and capabilities.

Case management involves the following:

1. It attempts to ensure that clients are able to access and benefit from appropriate resources and services. Case managers help clients receive the maximum benefit from each resource and use only those that are beneficial. This is sometimes called case coordination.
2. It requires that the worker monitor effectiveness and efficiency of services and hence involves an important evaluation component.
3. Good case management is the application of multiple direct service and other generalist roles. To mobilize and coordinate resources, case managers must be advocates, brokers, sometimes mentors, counsellors, facilitators, mediators, evaluators, and more. The mark of good case management is to combine the use of multiple roles that include case coordination.

For the most part, case managers work with clients who are very vulnerable and have to overcome significant challenges. They often require coordinated services that meet several areas of need, such as physical care, counselling, financial assistance, and home-based support. Examples of such clients are frail elderly people, people with serious mental illnesses or physical disabilities, and children requiring foster care. To manage all of the complex needs and ensure that the services required are provided in a satisfactory manner and at the appropriate time, someone must take responsibility.

To illustrate, assume a case manager is working with an elderly man who has recently had a stroke, has trouble walking, and has slurred speech. He is on the road to rehabilitation and is seeing, among others, a speech therapist and a physiotherapist. He is also receiving homemaker services. The case manager ensures that the man receives these services effectively and efficiently and that his recovery proceeds smoothly. However, suppose a few days into his recovery the man's home is invaded and, while he is not hurt, he is badly traumatized. A good case manager, educated as a social worker, can provide immediate, on-the-spot crisis counselling and help to mobilize the man's social support network (family members, friends, and neighbours). Further, the case manager is able to assess the need for longer-term counselling and decide whether referral to other services is best or whether the case manager should undertake the counselling.

The role of case manager is not unique to social work and is often performed by a variety of professionals. In the above example, a registered nurse might be the case manager. If so, she or he would likely bring a different set of skills and another orientation. For instance, a nurse might immediately refer the man to a crisis counsellor. But suppose that on a home visit the nurse finds that the man has cut himself and needs medical attention. The nurse might provide the required treatment without any referral, while a social worker would most likely seek medical help.

Case management can be misused. Governments, particularly in times of cutbacks to services, seem to use case management as a way to classify what social workers do. This opens the door for many poorly trained and less expensive personnel to qualify for positions that formerly required higher levels of expertise. In turn, this can—and does—reduce helping to simply coordinating resources and services required by clients. Some continue to see "case management as a convenient device to save money by emptying out large and expensive physical facilities and dumping clients on the streets without ample service back-up. According to this view, case management is used by canny politicians to protect the public coffers while giving the illusion of meeting the needs of the people" (Rothman, 1994, p. 277).

Case Example

Kim and Ann ▼

Kim's primary role is that of case manager. As she attempts to determine the course of action to take regarding the temporary custody of Ann's children, she needs to work with many agencies and the court system. After consulting with agencies that previously provided services to Ann (including Family Counselling and Assistance Services, Public Social Services, and Local Child Guidance) and assessing the circumstances of the events that led up to Ann leaving her children unattended, Kim made the decision that she will ask the court to keep the children in temporary custody for three months and leave the door open for an extension of time. During this period she will help Ann develop a plan to achieve more independence and a better quality of life for her family. Kim needs to prepare documents for court presentation and also coordinate services among various agencies. The case management function of coordination is and will be a major role for Kim.

Kim recognizes, contrary to common belief, that case coordination is difficult and has pitfalls that are often not considered. It will not be enough for her to assume that each service is being carried out. If, for instance, an important part of the plan is for Ann to receive some form of adult education, it will be necessary for Kim to ensure that this education meets its intended goals and even to ensure that Ann is regularly attending classes and receiving passing grades. If Ann is not, then this might make it very difficult to help her achieve her goals of independence and a reasonable quality of life for her children and herself.

However, there is more to Kim's case management role. Above we argue that good case management is not just case coordination. Probably Kim's most important function is to help Ann plan how to get her family back together, which is a counselling role. Kim is convinced that Ann's desire to have her children returned is genuine.

Continued

As mentioned in the initial summary of the case, Kim's assessment is that, with coordinated help, Ann is capable of providing a loving and quality home life for her children. Kim will spend the next few months helping Ann get her life in order first so that she can resume her parenting functions. Fortunately, Ann has already developed working relationships with two important resources: Tamar at Family Counselling and Assistance Services and the counselling services at Local Child Guidance.

▲

Counsellor

Generally the purpose of counsellors is to help individuals and families change, maintain, or stabilize their social and psychological well-being. Counselling is a common direct practice role. **Direct practice,** sometimes called *clinical practice,* is work that usually involves micro intervention with clients in a process of counselling (see Jaco, 2002, p. 257). Generalist social work counselling is usually supportive. Examples include enabling clients to more effectively cope, supporting them in meeting their own goals, helping them establish meaningful relationships, assisting them to make constructive decisions, helping them better understand their feelings and behaviour so that they can gain more control over their lives, and establishing an environment in which people can empower themselves. Counselling in generalist social work should have a clear focus on growth and development. It is a voluntary arrangement that depends heavily on the relationship between social worker and client. Supportive counselling requires that the social worker must be able to apply basic, generic skills such as interviewing, communication, and relationship skills.

The above description of the counselling role is basic and generic to all of social work. However, many social workers develop advanced and specialized counselling skills through advanced education. Examples include a variety of cognitive therapies, **solution-focused therapy**, feminist therapy, and an array of **family therapies**. Even so, generic social work counselling principles remain the base of advanced work.

Note that assessment is an important part of all counselling, and we address the assessment process in social work in some detail in Chapters 8, 9, and 10. These chapters are particularly relevant to social workers as counsellors.

Case Example

Tamar and Ann ▼

Kim, in her role of case manager in a child protection agency, may not provide ongoing counselling with Ann. Instead, she would use an appropriate resource.

Tamar, a social worker with Family Counselling and Assistance Services, had been providing direct counselling services to Ann with the primary goals of helping her learn better parenting and decision-making skills and how to manage stress. Tamar helped Ann with stress management and how to deal with the specific problems she was having as a parent. The clear focus of the counselling was to promote Ann's growth and development. However, three months ago, Ann abruptly stopped coming for counselling. Tamar had attempted to reach Ann but was unsuccessful.

A few months ago, during one of the counselling sessions, Ann had talked about the noticeable change in behaviour in Jim, her 9-year-old son. All Jim seemed to want to do was watch TV and play video games on an used machine they have. He used to play with friends almost every day, but since his father left he no longer asked them over. His schoolwork had also deteriorated badly. Tamar was concerned enough to refer Jim and Ann to Local Child Guidance. There they would assess Jim for psychological and possible learning problems. If they found that Jim was suffering from major psychological problems, one course of action might be to engage him in play therapy with the goal of helping him deal with his negative feelings and psychological difficulties. However, along with this restorative goal, the agency would focus on activities to help Jim grow and develop in school and with his friends. While part of the treatment provided by the agency is usually restorative (treats the problem), it is also oriented toward growth and development.

Note that the counselling provided by Local Child Guidance requires specialized assessments and interventions to address possible learning or psychological problems. A team of helping professionals, including social workers, may accomplish this work. While the workers should have a generic background, they also would need to have developed specialized skills.

Micro, Mezzo, and Macro Systems: Roles for All Levels of Practice

Advocate

As advocates, social workers act on behalf of others primarily to improve social conditions and promote social justice.

Case advocacy refers to action undertaken on behalf of individual clients. It is micro practice in that the client is usually an individual or family. However, intervention often requires macro skills because the worker's target is a large social institution or organization. Very often the advocacy is directed toward a bureaucracy that the client needs to access. Often the client is perceived as being treated unfairly. Sometimes the social worker's action is directed at the worker's own agency.

Ordinarily, *empowerment*—helping people to help themselves to take control of their own lives—should be a primary goal of intervention. But advocating on a client's behalf probably does not directly aid empowerment, even if it significantly improves a client's situation. Advocacy is frequently justified on the basis that many of the clients for whom social workers advocate are vulnerable or in difficult circumstances and may be unable to take action themselves. These include frail elderly people, people who are seriously mentally ill or disabled, people affected by natural disasters or crimes, and children. As a general rule, case advocacy should be used in situations in which the client cannot advocate for herself or himself or the social worker and client agree that the skills and access of the worker to resources will more likely achieve the desired results.

It is important to carefully consider whether the needs of the client are better served by encouraging or supporting clients to advocate for themselves, or by the worker directly acting for the client. For example, a woman who has been battered by her spouse and has experienced increasing feelings of powerlessness in her marriage may feel that only another person who has more power can change her situation. Some advocacy on her behalf may be required, say, for legal protection. But it would also be necessary to support and encourage her to begin to draw on and use her own resources and strengths to effect change in her life. The social worker would then be helping the client to increase her own agency (capacity and initiative), which can lead to greater feelings of personal empowerment.

As in all social work, the worker and the client (except small children and others who are unable to make decisions for themselves) must agree on the need for and goals of advocacy and who should carry it out. One of the goals can be to use advocacy to help create better conditions for the client to take further action by himself or herself. In this limited sense, advocacy has an empowering function.

Class advocacy is direct action taken by a social worker on behalf of a group of people. Usually class advocacy is aimed at the policies of social institutions or legislation. More than case advocacy, class advocacy is a political process that takes place in the public arena.

Case Example

Kim and Ann ▼

Kim has presented the family court with the position that Ann's children should be kept in foster care custody for three months or more until Kim and Ann can develop a workable parenting plan. Kim is acting as an advocate for the three children and sees the children as her clients. Often social workers advocate on children's behalf without the children or parent(s) agreeing to this action. However, almost always if the client is an adult, the social worker and client must agree that case advocacy on behalf of the client is an appropriate intervention.

The court has agreed to place the children in custody for three months. While Ann is very upset with this decision, Kim and Ann have learned to respect each other and Ann is beginning to trust Kim. A week after the court grants temporary custody of the children to foster care, Ann learns that her social assistance payments will stop. While she expected a decrease in the payments, she did not expect complete denial. Both Kim and Ann believe this is very unfair, is probably against the policy and related rules of Public Social Services, and will make it very difficult for Kim and Ann to develop a workable plan that will help Ann's family. Kim and Ann agree that Kim should advocate with Public Social Services to get the organization to reverse its decision. (In this role, Ann is now the client.) They decide that Kim should do the work because she is most familiar with the bureaucracy, she knows the staff at Public Social Services, and she is skilled in advocacy. The risk of failure is too high if Ann acts on her own behalf. Kim knows that Ann's basic survival needs are threatened without the support income.

Note that an alternative to Kim's intervention is discussed in the next section, "Enabler or Facilitator."

Enabler or Facilitator

The fundamental principle that underpins enabling is empowerment. In social work vernacular, enabling is doing "with" a client rather than "for" the client. The focus of enabling is to help clients empower themselves. To this end, enabling usually has two different purposes. One is to achieve goals agreed upon by the worker and client. These goals are often concrete and task oriented. The second purpose, frequently more important and empowering, is to use the process of meeting these goals to promote a client's growth and development.

The enabler role is used in micro, mezzo, and macro practice. Consider the following example from micro practice. (Note: enabling is also discussed as used in mezzo practice in this chapter under the topic, "Group Worker.") Suppose a mental health worker, Julian, is helping a client find suitable housing. Amos has a serious and persistent mental illness and was recently discharged from a psychiatric hospital. Both Julian and Amos agreed that attainment of affordable and suitable housing was the immediate goal. The worker felt that he had two intervention options. One was for Julian, with permission from Amos, to locate housing *for* the client with no or limited input from Amos. The worker might choose this intervention option if, for example, Amos has sufficiently limited skills that he is unable to do the apartment search by himself even with the worker's support and help.

The second option for Julian is to act as a catalytic helper (who encourages and coaches). Amos would engage the process of apartment searching by himself, but with Julian's support, guidance, coaching, and counselling. The purpose of this option not only includes the attainment of the concrete goal but also the promotion of Amos' growth and development.

This example illustrates two underlying principles of enabling.

1. The focus on growth and development means that clients will use their capacities to achieve their own goals. If so,
   a. Successful goal achievement should help clients with such factors as self-confidence, self-esteem, and decision-making capacity.
   b. The enabling process should enhance empowerment.
   c. The learning that takes place should assist clients in meeting future life challenges and future goal achievement.
   d. Growth and development would not likely occur if the worker "did *for* the client."
2. Enabling almost always requires the use of other roles such as coaching, teaching, and modelling.

We recognize that enabling is not always possible. Enabling requires that the social worker must make the judgment call that the client has the capacity to achieve agreed-upon goals. Second, enabling requires that the client wants help from the worker. When the client is not voluntary (does not want the worker's help), enabling is usually not possible.

Case Example

Kim and Ann ▼

In the previous example, Kim agreed to advocate, on Ann's behalf, with Public Social Services. However, Kim has an alternative intervention strategy. It is enabling.

Kim and Ann have agreed that Ann's social assistance needs to be reinstated, albeit at a rate lower than if her children were living with her. In this scenario, Kim and Ann agree that there is a goal of higher priority. While the social assistance is very important, Ann has considerable difficulty in doing things for herself. This causes her to rely too much on others and leads to some of her parenting problems. Both women recognize this as a problem. Instead of agreeing to advocate on Ann's behalf, Kim encourages Ann to do the work herself. Kim stays behind the scenes, helping, encouraging, and sharing her expertise (coaching) with Ann. Kim's role is no longer advocacy but involves enabling Ann to do the work for herself. The advantage of Kim taking this role is that if Ann is successful, she may develop improved self-esteem and confidence as well as meeting the goals of the immediate task. It may also help Ann to develop her decision-making skills and ability to address future challenges of life.

Group Worker

Group work has a long, established history in social work and is used by nearly all social workers at one time or another. The social worker can lead or facilitate groups in many different social work settings and for different purposes (see Mesbur, 2002).

Sometimes the purpose of the group is to help individuals within the group. The individual group members are the clients. Group therapy, support groups, and self-help groups are often used in direct practice as a process to counsel, provide emotional support, and/or educate. Often, the sharing of experience and ideas in the company of others dealing with similar life problems can be very powerful and helpful. A good group worker can play a key role in creating a safe space to talk and encouraging a positive experience for members. As Johnson and Johnson (2003) hold,

> [S]trengths and positive interpersonal behaviour will be revealed in a setting in which they can be enhanced. In creating a microcosm of the outside world, groups provide an arena for participants to interact freely with others, help them identify and understand what goes wrong and right in their interactions, and ultimately enable them to change maladaptive patterns and use their strengths more effectively. (p. 525)

At other times the group itself is the target of the social worker's intervention. Group work is important when working with interdisciplinary professional teams, task committees, boards of directors in organizations, workplace peers, and many more. The group worker's skill in balancing the dual roles of keeping to task and attending to group process is critical (see Johnson and Johnson, 2003). While most group work is practised in micro or mezzo arenas, community organizing can offer a good site for group work where a worker can use skills in facilitating meetings, building capacity for leadership in others, mediating in conflicts, brainstorming ideas for action, and many other activities (see Sullivan et al., 2003).

The enabler role is often used in group work. The role of the worker may be to use group process in order to strengthen and develop client skills. Goals of groups are wide-ranging and may include goals that vary from anger management to improved parenting to group discussion skills, to learning English as a second language, and so on. In the following example, both the group and individuals within the group are clients.

Suppose some teenaged girls from the inner city have formed a group at a local community centre. Their stated goal is to initiate and implement organized weekend activities at the centre. They are a diverse group from a variety of cultural backgrounds. While enthusiasm is high, the group does not have a good bond, and they do not know how to organize themselves to accomplish their goals, which remain vague. The role of the social worker is to enable the group so that they can first clearly define the goals of the group and then meet them. This group might be called a task group.

To accomplish the goals of the task group, the social worker needs to ensure that all members are involved in the group. They must all feel important and that they are contributing. This may improve the self-confidence of group members. The process will likely enhance members' discussion skills and group bonds. The social worker may also help develop leadership within the group not only to strengthen group structure and performance but to enhance the decision-making capacity of each member. The group process then is not only used to accomplish a group task but to develop a variety of skills in group members. The group provides the girls with an educational experience that is enabling.

The enabling group worker does not do the work for the girls. That is, he or she does not organize the weekend activities. In the end, the girls will do the work and make the effort to meet their own goals. The worker only helps them to make this happen. These same principles can be applied to work with individuals, families, and, particularly, communities and neighbourhoods.

Case Example

Kim and Ann ▼

Recall that Ann wants to have her children returned to her. Kim will help Ann make reasonable decisions that will help show that she is a competent and caring parent. Ann is a single mother and needs to deal with considerable stress. She has a good understanding of herself and believes that she needs help with parenting. Kim agrees.

Earlier Ann was receiving some help with parenting from Tamar at Family Counselling and Assistance Services. Kim wonders if Ann would rather use a group experience to help her with parenting. For an unknown reason, Ann stopped coming to her counselling sessions. However, Ann did like to work with Tamar.

Kim, Ann's case manager, knows that a program at Family Counselling and Assistance Services has had considerable success in using groups of single moms in order to help members cope with stress and at the same time learn tips, mostly from each other, on how to become better parents. The group is led by a generalist social worker who has developed advanced skills in group process. The worker recognizes that by group members sharing experiences, including both problems and solutions to problems, people with difficulties can move forward; the experience should be enabling. Members also can understand that others have had experiences similar to theirs. Ann might not only be able to validate her experiences but learn how to handle some of her parenting problems through the group experience. Ann, who has a rather outgoing personality, welcomes the referral. She also states that while she felt okay when working with Tamar, she now believes that she needs a different kind of help with parenting.

Educator, Teacher, or Coach

The social work role of educator or teacher is an empowering and enabling role that has a number of functions. Frequently clients need information or need to learn a skill before they can take action themselves. For instance, in the enabling example of the teen group, the worker needed to teach the girls how to structure a group so that they themselves could make effective decisions toward goal attainment.

Teaching involves a number of functions that range from micro to macro practice. Some of these are modelling, public education, teaching daily living skills, coaching, and role-playing. Note that all of these examples assume empowerment—that the teaching is provided so clients can take effective action by themselves.

Modelling, a common intervention technique, is teaching by example. It may be a natural spinoff of the helping relationship. For instance, if a client is shown acceptance and understanding, the client may, in turn, show tolerance to others in her or his own life, thereby improving the client's relationships with others. At the other end of a continuum, modelling may also be a complicated and specialized technique, such as what might be used in child therapy to help a child learn a new behaviour or develop different attitudes.

Public education is a role often practised by social workers. For example, social workers might arrange to speak to children in schools about the effects of bullying. Or in the health care field, they might sometimes join with other health professionals in public presentations about healthy lifestyles or dealing with medical conditions. In this type of work, social workers can be especially helpful in illustrating the roots of poor health when they are related to poverty, unemployment, discrimination, or lack of security in inner-city neighbourhoods.

Many clients, particularly those who are highly vulnerable, lack necessary social and other daily living skills. For example, lone parents on welfare do not always know how to cope with the limited amount of money they receive. They may not know about programs or additional help to which they might be entitled. When they run out of funds, they may not know what to do. Lack of skill in determining other available help and not knowing how to use local resources such as community kitchens, low-cost programs for children, and self-help groups can add to their difficulties. These limitations in skills and knowledge may even contribute to the fact that these clients see social assistance as their only option for survival. Perhaps they do not know about job training or childcare subsidies. When the money runs out, frustration levels can run high and self-esteem can be low. Social workers for such clients may teach them how to extend their resources, negotiate additional help, and seek other support to enhance their quality of life.

Basic coaching skills are necessary in generalist practice. Like most roles, the teacher/ coach role can be complex and can require specialized skill inherent in a field of practice. For example, many parents who are clients of the child welfare system may lack fundamental parenting skills. They may not have had good parenting themselves as children, or they may have experienced abuse that hindered their development. Social workers in child welfare agencies sometimes convene and lead parenting skills classes by coaching and guiding parents. Both basic coaching skills are needed as well as knowledge of effective parenting practices and child development.

Coaching is usually undertaken when a client needs to approach something new or is apprehensive or unsure about how to do something. Often coaching is aimed at developing or honing a skill. The social worker might suggest or give advice on how to approach the task. For example, a worker could help a client with an upcoming employment interview by instructing the client on how to highlight the strengths he or she would bring to the job.

The situations in which role-playing is used are similar to those of coaching. In role-playing, the client enacts, with the social worker or others, how to undertake a task. For example, an 18-year-old who has been convicted of some crimes needs to find a job but is fearful that his criminal record will be held against him. A worker may coach him on how to approach an employer and how to react if the employer begins to ask questions about his criminal past. Alternatively, the social worker may role-play a job-seeking interview with the client.

Case Example

Kim and Ann ▽

The previous example using enabling (Ann's attempt to reinstate social assistance) is also an example of *coaching*. The following illustrates a number of possibilities that entail additional educational functions. Kim and Ann would need to agree on which, if any, options that they would take.

The only jobs that Ann has had are low-paying minimum wage positions. Both Kim and Ann know that maintaining a home will be very difficult without a higher income. Kim could *teach* Ann how to work out a budget that demonstrates how much income Ann will need in order to maintain a household of four persons. Kim might also help identify realistic options for Ann. These include vocational training or finding a better paying job without further education. Kim might *coach* Ann on how to determine if vocational training is practical for her. Or she could *role-play* with her client how to search for a job and how to highlight her strengths and existing skills to prospective employers.

When the night worker was in Ann's home and apprehended the children, the children were living in an apparent unhealthy environment. Implied is that Ann does not have a good understanding of the health care needs of her children. Kim might choose to help Ann better understand good hygiene or, more likely, refer Ann to a public health care agency that *teaches* about good practices for children's health.

Note that the above possible actions that Kim might take involve multiple roles. For instance, all of the educational roles, in varying degrees, enable. Referral to a health care agency assumes a broker role.

Mediator

The mediator is a direct practice role that is used to help people solve disputes and negotiate conflicts. Usually the intent is to resolve conflicts by having parties to the dispute address the blocks to settlement.

The social work role in mediation has many similarities with education and enabling. In each instance, the work of the professional is to find ways for people to arrive at solutions themselves. In mediation, all parties must do the work. The social worker is the catalyst; the parties who have the dispute must arrive at their own solutions. Note that mediation differs from arbitration. In arbitration, the professional is in a position of authority and may impose a solution for the dispute.

Let's return again to the example of the group of teenaged girls. They had proceeded nicely toward developing a set of activities for Saturday afternoons until they discovered that another group also wanted to book the community centre at approximately the same time. Neither group would change its preferred time, and the executive of the centre would not permit either to book times until the dispute was resolved. In this example, the social worker might mediate the dispute between the two groups. Both groups have their self-interests at stake, and they probably have difficulty communicating. The likely task of the social worker is to seek a compromise solution that meets the needs of both. Generalist social workers should have the skill to mediate such a dispute.

However, other situations require more specialized mediation skills. For example, Miguel is a 15-year-old who has run away from home three times. While away, he spent most of his time on the streets. Miguel and his father do not get along. They fight over trivial things. Miguel's father has threatened to kick him out of the house many times. His mother, while caring, does not want to get into the arguments between the other two.

The relationship problem has become severe. A child welfare agency has considered placing Miguel in a foster home. However, his mother begs for one last chance for him to live at home. Sara, an experienced generalist-educated social worker and an employee of the child welfare agency, has been assigned to help mediate the dispute between Miguel and his parents. The goal is to arrive at an agreement and contract among the three family members (and probably Sara's agency) that will permit Miguel to remain in his home.

Generalist social workers, as pointed out earlier in this chapter, need to develop specialized skills required by employing agencies in different fields of practice. Family mediation is a common skill required of social workers in child welfare practice. Sara has learned special mediation skills through a number of workshops and continuing education programs.

Case Example

Kim and Ann ▼

The following illustrates a type of mediation that is common in generalist practice.

Ann finds out that her landlord is going to raise her rent by $33 per month. Ann will have a very hard time making this extra payment. Her landlord has told her it is necessary because he has decided to increase fire insurance on the property despite its high cost.

Kim and Ann agree on two courses of action. First, Kim will try to help Ann and her landlord arrive at a more modest increase. She will attempt to mediate this dispute, which may seem minor but is a very important one to Ann. Note: Alternatively, Kim might act as Ann's advocate or coach. Kim's role would depend upon her judgment regarding how best to help Ann.

Outreach Worker

Usually an outreach worker attempts to extend services to people in the community by defining who is in need and then offering services or referrals. The attempt is often to provide a service to people who are not clients. Part of the work may be defining who is a client. Sometimes the client is an individual. For example, some agencies assign staff to work with a general population of young people on the street in a downtown core. The service may be as straightforward as helping a youth to locate a friend who has disappeared or the complicated task of counselling a young person who has an addiction. Other times, the client may be the entire population. For example, a social worker may disseminate information, such as how to reduce the risk of illness from sharing needles, to all youth.

A common function of community outreach workers is educating community members. For example, a remote Aboriginal community may be concerned about the extent of communicable diseases such as tuberculosis or AIDS in the community. The government may have a health education program designed to disseminate information, but the leaders of the community do not think this is enough. They need someone who is either Aboriginal or who has a good understanding of Aboriginal culture and traditions to work directly with the people. The work might start with finding out the needs and concerns of the community and who might be at risk. After identifying those at risk, the goal may be to offer information, services, and referral. In community outreach, the social worker would likely need community development skills. Community development and outreach often overlap.

Social workers who work as case managers also are often required to perform outreach. The next case example illustrates outreach work with individuals.

Case Example

Kim and Ann ▼

Sometimes, outreach services are provided by community and neighbourhood social workers. However, workers in most fields need to reach out to people who are perceived as needing help. Thus, while most child welfare workers would not be community outreach workers, they often are expected to "reach out" to clients or potential clients. In our ongoing case example, Ann lacks many life skills but is loving toward her children and seems willing to take the difficult steps necessary to restore order and quality to her family life. Kim did not have to "reach out" to her.

Often, however, parents who neglect or abuse their children do not want the help of social workers. Suppose Ann did not want help from anyone and showed considerable anger with the social agencies and courts. If so, Kim's initial responsibility would change. Instead of beginning to develop with Ann a plan for the return of her children, Kim would need to spend much more time outlining alternatives and consequences—negative and positive—of both the agency's and Ann's decisions and explaining services that her agency could offer to Ann. Kim would need to work to reach out to Ann and search for ways that she (or others) could be of help.

Social Broker

A major function of case managers is to act as a social broker. The main goal of the social broker is to connect clients with needed resources. It includes referral but encompasses more than that. Linking a client with services or programs usually requires assessing both client needs and available resources. To conduct an assessment, social workers need a thorough understanding of both client and local resources.

As in all of social work practice, linkage requires that a relationship be established between worker and client. This includes developing a partnership with the client in which referral options are mutually explored. A basic task of the social worker is to ensure that the client has a good understanding of the resources that are available and, to the best of the worker's ability, an understanding of the quality of these services. In most instances, the goal of the social worker is to enable the client to access the resources herself or himself and for the client to make the best possible decisions.

The broker role can sometimes be used to begin to establish a relationship with an involuntary client. Clients who resist the services of a social worker frequently want to gain access to resources that they think they need. Offering to help the client obtain these resources may open the door to further communication and relationship building between the worker and the client. Of course, the social worker's intention is genuine help, not just getting the client in the door.

Case Example

Kim and Ann ▼

Ann has been referred to a group parenting program at Family Counselling and Assistance Services. Previously Ann had terminated a counselling service at the same agency by simply missing appointments. At first the agency is not sure that they want to accept Ann for a new program, given their perception that she is unreliable.

Both Kim and Ann think this group program is important. However, because of the reservations of the agency, Kim needs to broker the referral. In this instance, Kim approached Family Counselling and Assistance Services and argued that the situation with Ann has changed. Ann is now motivated because Ann wants to have her children returned to her. To help satisfy the concerns of the family agency, Kim agrees to help monitor progress and encourage Ann to attend. As a result of Kim's intervention as a broker, the counselling service agrees to permit Ann to enroll in the group program.

Evaluator

The evaluator role is not often referred to explicitly as a social work role. Yet it is a necessary part of the repertoire of social work practice. Social workers should be required to evaluate their practice, not only in their day-to-day reflection on their work with clients, but also as a way of showing what they have achieved through their actions and how effective these actions have been. The evaluator should use basic ***research methods*** to understand and describe practice, programs, or other change efforts and to make sense of the related processes (what happened, who participated, what was learned, and other information). (See Bloom, Fischer, and Orme, 2003.)

Sometimes this is called ***clinical evaluation***. Clinical evaluation is done at many levels. For instance, some types of clinical designs require considerable background in research methods and clearly require specialist education.

However, evaluating practice should be seen as necessary to all practice, including front-line generalist practice. Minimally a social worker and client need to monitor and evaluate the progress of intervention. The case example below introduces how a generalist worker can and should begin this evaluation process.

Case Example

Kim and Ann ▼

Kim and Ann have set a clear goal, that is, to regain custody of Ann's children. There are at least two other important goals upon which Kim and Ann have agreed. In good practice, this agreement should become part of a contract (agreement) between worker and client (see Chapter 8).

One goal was to gain better parenting skills, which is a subgoal that Ann must achieve before she can have her children returned. To this end, Ann was referred to a parenting group. Second, also a subgoal, Ann needs to develop achievable short- and long-term plans for a source of income sufficient to maintain a family of four. This may require vocational training.

As case manager, Kim needs to monitor Ann's progress. If she does not, how will anyone determine if Ann should have her children returned to her? In Chapter 8 we articulate a straightforward way for front-line social workers to monitor progress. The process begins, as we have done in this example, by client and worker agreeing upon goals to be achieved.

▲

Macro Systems: Generalist Roles in Community Development

Community Practice or Organizing Roles

Regardless of the economic times, social work is a political enterprise. Oppression and poverty continue to exist, and conditions will not improve without social change. Community (macro) practice is an important way to address social change, particularly in local neighbourhoods. Social work practice needs to incorporate community and social change. This is a position emphasized throughout this book, but particularly in Chapter 14, concerning structural social work. The roles of community developer and social activist are important vehicles necessary for carrying out social change (see Fisher and Karger, 1997).

Community organization may be seen as having several subsets. Two of these are community development and social action. Both are roles that generalist social workers perform. (See Banks, 2002, for an interesting discussion of regional community practice in Canada.)

Community Developer   A community developer (sometimes called a *locality developer*) acts as a catalyst to assist members of a community or neighbourhood to help themselves. The emphasis is on a democratic process in order to build community. The developer acts as an advisor, resource person, and catalyst to promote and mobilize self-help, indigenous leadership, and action. Many community developers work in core areas of cities, rural areas in Canada, and in other parts of the world (Campfens, 1997). Community development is a common role of generalist social workers employed in remote communities and in the North. Even child welfare and mental health workers perform community development functions by helping small communities address their own problems.

Social Activist   History brims with old-style activists. They were at the foundations of the profession in the early part of the 20th century and included such notable people as Jane Addams, a major leader in the settlement house movement in the United States, and J. S. Woodsworth, active in government and social policy in Canada. Their aim was to directly implement social change through a variety of tactics, usually aimed at policies of governments and powerful social institutions such as industrial firms. Often the goal was to redistribute power or resources. Unlike community developers, social activists often devise and directly implement strategies for change. Activists are champions of causes and work on behalf of those whose lives are adversely affected by unjust or exploitative practices and policies. Participation in social action is a common role for all social workers.

To illustrate social activism, Moses Coady—not a social worker by profession, but an activist priest—was instrumental in initiating the cooperative movement in Nova Scotia. He targeted the large companies that controlled the lives of fishers and miners, introducing cooperatives to change the exploitative practices that shaped the workers' lives. By using cooperatives in single-industry communities, workers not only were able to buy products at reasonable prices, but also were able to shake the authoritarian bonds of the large companies. Modern cooperatives today can be traced to Coady's pioneering work (Trecartin, Tasker, and Martin, 1991).

Today, many social activists work through self-help groups and grassroots community organizations with limited funding and uncertain futures. Individuals do not seem to have the high visibility in social change they once did. Instead, their work, like that of the community developers, is more behind the scenes and involves mobilizing action groups. This does not mean that community development and social action are unimportant—on the contrary, they are more essential than ever, given the current environment of global economic problems and their domino effects that lead to industry closures, job losses, and government cost-cutting.

These, in turn, create gaps in *social welfare* provision. The quality of life for many people is and will be diminished by regressive economic and social policies. Although most health care and child welfare workers in front-line practice (common social work jobs in Canada) engage infrequently in community development or social activist roles, opportunities often arise in which skills in these roles are important and necessary.

Case Example

Kim and Ann ▼

Kim has helped Ann become involved in an organization that is lobbying for lower property insurance rates for Ann's inner-city neighbourhood, which is deteriorating. Kim has recognized this neighbourhood deterioration as a growing problem. She often works in this area and believes that incidents of child abuse and neglect reflect the condition of the neighbourhood. She believes that action must be taken and that she needs to get involved in a way that uses her skills effectively but does not draw her away from her primary job as a child protection worker.

Recently, a nongovernmental organization that provides funds for voluntary and community services has funded a new agency in the area called Neighbourhood Action Services. The new agency has a mandate to help the community organize in order to combat the problem of decay. One of the agency's first steps was to establish a board of directors, made up mostly of local residents but also including some experts in problems associated with poverty and urban deterioration. The board is to set policy and oversee the operations of Neighbourhood Action Services. Kim was quick to agree to be on the board, even though this will involve one evening of her time per week for at least the next six months, or until the agency establishes itself. She has considerable knowledge of the area and can use her social work skills to help set effective policies and help the organization plan programs to meet local needs.

CHAPTER SUMMARY

Some social work roles are generic while others are specialized according to fields of practice. Necessary and prerequisite to the development of many roles specific to settings are roles common to social work and applied in a variety of, if not most, fields of practice. These are generic roles; they underpin all of social work practice. Generic roles flow out of the purpose, values, ideology, and theories adopted by the profession. Generalist social workers are expected to attain competency in a wide range of diverse generic roles.

Generic roles are diverse. A useful way to conceptualize the diversity of generic roles is to cast them into the context of ecosystems theory. Drawing from ecosystems, generic roles are organized by micro, mezzo, and macro systems. The following generic roles, each discussed in the body of this chapter, are all front-line generalist roles.

Generalist Social Work Roles

Micro and mezzo systems: Roles for working with individuals, families, and groups

- case manager
- counsellor

Micro, mezzo, and macro systems: Roles for all levels of practice

- advocate
- enabler or facilitator
- group worker
- educator, teacher, or coach
- mediator
- outreach worker
- social broker
- evaluator

Macro systems: Roles in community development and social policy

- community practice or organizing
- community developer
- social activist

Practice and Policy in a Field of Social Work Practice: Child Protection Services as an Illustration

Chapter Goal ▼

To show, using the example of child protection services, the connection between social work practice and social welfare and agency policy.

To draw students into the practice of child protection and to help them see how practice is shaped by policies, which are in turn determined by an ideological lens.

This Chapter ▼

- describes policy, practice, and social work roles and functions in child protection
- shows that social welfare policy is filtered through the professional lens of social work
- describes the historical development of child protection services in Canadian society
- identifies common social work roles found in child protection services delivered by social workers
- reviews the development of selected **social welfare policies** and legislation in child protection services and how they have shaped practice
- illustrates the impact of large-scale (macro level) and small-scale (micro level) social welfare policies on social work practice through examples

INTRODUCTION

Child protection is a major part of the field of ***child welfare***. Other areas include adoption; family services including family supports; placement of children in foster homes, group homes, and the like; and development of foster homes (Hick, 2006, p. 112). Children may be taken into care on an involuntary basis in cases of neglect or abuse (as defined in provincial acts). At other times, placement may be voluntary. In such instances there may be no abuse or neglect, but the parent is unable through factors such as illness, infirmity, or economic reasons to care for the child.

We have chosen to use child protection services to illustrate the connection between social policy and social work practice. We could have used health, corrections, income security, or any other field of practice to write this chapter. Also, our decision takes into account that a large number of social workers, including those with a BSW degree, become child protection workers whose major role is child protection. Many provinces require social work education for employment as child welfare workers (Albert and Herbert, 2008).

The ideological lens discussed in Chapter 3 can help us understand how social welfare policy can be interpreted through a filter or lens. Social workers develop an understanding of social policy as seen through an ideological lens. This occurs as a result of professional education and socialization (see Chapter 3). The values and ethics of social work (based on the 2005 CASW *Code of Ethics*) are an important feature of this lens, framing how social welfare policy is viewed. For example, the trend toward privatization of public services and cuts to social programs is generally seen negatively by social workers because those who are poorest will likely suffer additional hardship and an inequitable and unfair outcome. However, additional provisioning for women or families on social assistance is viewed positively because it can be seen as promoting social work values such as dignity and respect of persons, social equality, and justice. Other groups in society hold different sets of values that in turn influence how they see social policy through their ideological lens.

The next section sets out the context in which child protection services developed over time. Although not a detailed history, it shows how social work practice has been linked to micro and macro policies. After child protection history is reviewed, a case situation with two scenarios in the child protection field is described, including decisions related to social work practice in the field. The two scenarios illustrate different outcomes that result due to a turn of events. Throughout the case description, we emphasize key ideas that connect social work practice to agency and social welfare policy. These are found in a number of text boxes in different sections of the case description. This chapter will also draw from the discussion of generalist and specialist roles in Chapter 4. In addition to this, other boxes provide websites and various reference sources that provide further information for readers.

CHILD PROTECTION SERVICES IN CANADA

Throughout Canadian history, society has viewed and treated children in many different ways. These views are often a reflection of the political, social, and economic climates of the time.

The protection of children in need can be traced back to medieval and Renaissance (proper noun) times and was considered pre-industrialization social welfare. During this time, women were considered the caregivers and nurturers and men were the economic providers. There was little understanding of childhood as a time of need and therefore children were considered mini-adults by the age of seven years (Bala, 2004). Gradually provisions to care for orphaned children were made by communities of people, such as churches, hospitals, court systems, and extended families. Factors such as poverty, war, and death of parents were common issues. For children who were deserted or orphaned, apprenticeship was sometimes used. This meant a child would work in exchange for being cared for by a family or organization (Child Welfare League of Canada [CWLC], 2007, p. 2; Hick, 1998). Like most arenas of helping, such as the Charity Organization Societies (COS) and the settlements, early child protection centred on issues of morality. The focus was on ensuring the moral development of a child.

Industrialization meant there was a shift from agriculture and raw production of natural resources to manufacturing and a shift from rural and cottage industries to urban centres where production took place under a factory system (Daly, 1995; Lieby, 1978, pp. 71–89; Marr, 2008). Along with these shifts came difficult experiences involving transitions from rural to urban living, which meant a decrease in familial supports, harsher working conditions, and increased economic divisions between social classes. This period was considered the transition to a welfare state and saw an increased awareness of the child, including their physical and educational needs. "With the need for systematized care for disadvantaged children and the absence of legislation specifically directed at neglected and abandoned children, the inauguration of the *British North America Act* and the establishment of Confederation in Canada allowed for a fundamental template for child welfare service philosophy and delivery" (CWLC, 2007, p. 2).

With the initiation of the *BNA Act* in 1867, the state claimed responsibility for the best interests of children. It also provided a "legal context" for caring for neglected and abandoned children (CWLC, 2007, p. 9). In Canada, this was the first step toward modern child protection legislation. Between 1874 and 1915, a number of organizations and legislations were created to promote caring for children. While state responsibilities for caring for children occurred across Canada during this time period, we illustrate these developments by mostly using the Ontario experience. (Excerpts from "History of Child Welfare in Canada" from the Child Welfare League of Canada (CWLC) publication *The Welfare of Canadian Children: It's Our Business, A Collection of Resource Papers*. Available online at http://www.cwlc.ca/files/file/policy/Welfare%20of%20Canadian%20Children%202007.pdf.)

- In 1874, Ontario legislation permitted charitable institutions to intervene to prevent the maltreatment of apprenticed children.
- In 1888, the *Act for the Protection and Reformation of Neglected Children* or the *Children's Protection Act* was created in Ontario. This gave the province authority along with parents, effectively eliminating children as the exclusive property of their parent(s).
- In 1891, the Children's Aid Society of Toronto was established to deliver government authority as outlined in the 1888 act. The Toronto CAS was founded by the influential Henry Kelso, a leader in early child welfare. Kelso was a strong advocate for passage of the 1893 act.
- In 1893, the *Act for the Prevention of Cruelty to and Better Protection of Children* passes in Ontario. "With this legislation, children's aid societies became semi-public agencies with the legal power to remove children from their homes, supervise and manage children in

municipal shelters and collect monies from municipalities to cover the maintenance costs for wards." (Excerpt from Ontario Association of Children's Aid Societies (2008), *History of Child Welfare*. Available online at: http://www.oacas.org/childwelfare/history.htm.)

- By 1912, 60 Children's Aid Societies had been established across Ontario (Ontario Association of Children's Aid Societies, 2008; also see CWLC, 2007; and Hick, 2006, pp. 116–19).

As these formal services and documents were put in place, caring for children shifted to a practical, "scientific" service that focused on efficacy and outcomes. For example, a shift was made to helping children who lacked education and skills so that they could obtain life and work skills that would carry on into adulthood (CWLC, 2007, p. 3). Standards of practice were created, and formal training programs for working with children at risk and their families were established. This shift not only shaped the work of caring for children, but also established the groundwork for the professional social worker designated to deliver social services to children (CWLC, 2007, p. 3).

Yet many child protection "workers" remained volunteers. Use of volunteers to deliver social services, including the COS and most settlements, was common during the late 19th and early 20th century. The change to professionalization and the widespread use of professional social workers to provide child welfare services emerged as governments took more responsibility for child protection services, and placement of children changed from institutional arrangements (e.g., orphanages) to community-based arrangements, for example, foster homes (Hick, 2006, p. 120; Ontario Association of Children's Aid Societies, 2008, p. 1).

As these and other social service programs were developing, professional schools of social work also began to emerge. These schools began to educate service providers. As shown in Chapter 2, the first school of social work was opened in 1914 at the University of Toronto, followed four years later by a new school opening at McGill University. The University of Manitoba's summer curriculi in 1915 was an early effort to educate professional social workers, many of whom worked in child and family service agencies.

Other shifts in the philosophy of child welfare occurred beginning in the mid-1950s. The previous thinking on child protection principles moved toward the more pathological philosophy of "maltreatment of children as 'child abuse'" (CWLC, 2007, p. 3). This era also saw the amalgamation of federal and provincial funding in many different areas that overlapped the social services boundaries.

In the 1950s, orphanages were still common, but use was fading as the number of foster homes was increasing. Policy makers began to make this change based on the still-current belief that home-like environments are far superior to institutional life. In the 1960s and 1970s, the following events took place:

- In 1966, federal government created The Canada Assistance Plan (CAP), which provided funding for a wide range of social assistance programs and services.
- The mid-1960s saw a change in terminologies from child protection to "child abuse" and child "rescue."
- The mid-1960s and into the later part of the 1970s saw a significant increase in the number of children in the care of child welfare agencies or placed in substitute care.
- By mid-1960s, child abuse registers were established in many provinces to help keep track of abusers and abused children, and help facilitate research.

- "Child rescuing" was targeted at First Nations populations. Placing Aboriginal children in non-Aboriginal homes as a method of child protection was widely practised. Such practice has been widely discredited.
- The late 1970s and early 1980s were marked by a "discovery" of child sexual abuse as researchers found children were often too intimidated, felt ashamed, or were too ill-informed to report it (Bala, 2004; CWLC, 2007, pp. 3–4).

Recent Changes

Over the past 30 years many changes have occurred within the child welfare field. An increased awareness and understanding of sexual, physical, and emotional abuse and child neglect have led to changes in the focus of services available to children and families, as well as legislation changes that require professionals and the public to report suspected cases of child abuse. Child abuse registries have been established. Professionals have the legal duty to report suspected abuse. During the 1980s, women's shelters that also protected children increased in importance.

The declaration of the *Canadian Charter of Rights and Freedoms* in 1982 created a sociopolitical backdrop for the changes to policy and practice. The idea of "child protection or child rescue" (best interest of the child) changed to familial support for a period of time. Although this was well intended, funding for field workers was lacking and the mandate soon returned to a "child rescue" philosophy again (CWLC, 2007).

Currently, changes have been implemented as follows:

- Provincial governments mandate agencies to deliver child protection services. Different provinces use different names for their mandated agencies.
- In all provinces professionals deliver child protection services. Child welfare agencies employ many professional social workers.
- Institutional services such as orphanages have been replaced by services such as foster homes.
- While actual provincial legislation varies from province to province, the principles of the legislation are similar. All provinces hold that child safety and acting in the best interest of the child are priorities.
- Some provinces have adopted legislation and policies that include increased family involvement. For example, in Ontario,

  in 2006, Bill 210 introduced a number of improvements for children and families. These included greater emphasis on placing children with kith and kin in an effort to prevent them from entering care. As well, the Act allowed for a greater role for permanency options for children in care, including customary care, adoption and kinship care. During the same period, the Child Welfare Transformation Agenda was introduced, which included a new focus on Differential Response, allowing for alternative, clinically-based options for children and families, at the referral stage. (Ontario Association of Children's Aid Societies, 2008, p. 1)

- In many provinces, children's exposure to violence in the home is seen as a form of child maltreatment and potentially warrants child protection services intervention (Nixon, 2009).
- Provinces, including British Columbia, Alberta, Saskatchewan, Manitoba, Ontario, and Nova Scotia, have negotiated agreements (or are in the process of negotiation) with Aboriginal organizations that have established Aboriginal child welfare agencies to provide

services to Aboriginal children and families (see CWLC, 2007; Hick, 2006, p. 120; and Ontario Association of Children's Aid Societies, 2008). For documentation on Aboriginal child welfare, see Bennett, Blackstock, and De La Ronde (2005).

At the present time, child welfare services are the responsibility of provinces and every province has enacted child protection legislation. This legislation, augmented by provincial regulations and standards, mandates specific agencies in each province to protect children and ensure their well-being. Services to First Nations are either administered by the provincial agencies or through a negotiated agreement that mandates direct administration by Aboriginal agencies (Hick, 2006, p. 113).

Child welfare legislation changes quite often. New agencies, particularly those that are Aboriginal agency–administered, are emerging. The specifics of child protection differ from province to province. To keep up to date, refer to online sources. By searching for a simple phrase such as "child protection in Nova Scotia," "child protection act in Nova Scotia," or "child welfare in Canada," a rich variety of resources can be located. Many are agency and government documents that explain and detail provincial child protection legislation, policies, and practices.

SOCIAL WORK PRACTICE IN CHILD PROTECTION

As the values and beliefs of society changed, so too has provision of child protection services. In earlier times, parents were presumed to be capable of acting in their child's best interest. As shown above, the state has taken increasing responsibility since the passage of the *BNA Act*. As implied above, in the last 30 years or so researchers and professionals in the field have shown that abuse and neglect is common. This has resulted in major changes. Child protection has evolved and adopted the prevailing view that the state must be prepared to act in "the best interest" of the child when child abuse, neglect, or other child safety issues emerge. In one way or another, all provinces, in their legislation or policy, direct child welfare social workers to always act in the child's best interest.

An emphasis on best interest means that the social worker must assess risk to a child and be prepared to apprehend (or rescue) the child if necessary. The role is mandated by legislation. This role of the worker is not a traditional "helping" role of social work. It is, in part, one of social control; the worker has the legal authority to take away the rights of others, usually parents, and require improvement of conditions for care of a child or placement of a child in an environment approved by practising social workers. The rights of parents are clearly secondary to the well-being of the child. As Hick (2006, p. 121) points out, the best interest principle has been emphasized partly because of high-profile negative press concerning decisions of child welfare workers.

Importantly, legislation in many provinces also reflects another principle. Hick (2006) calls this a "least restrictive" approach. In this approach, the worker strives to keep the child in his or her own family and environment. Family support is seen as important. For example, the 2006 Ontario Bill 210 referenced above allows for more emphasis upon kinship relationships and customary care. Long-term effects on the child, as well as the family, may be emphasized.

Nixon (2009) points out, "The best interests of the child implies that children's interests do and should trump their mothers' interests. This representation mistakenly assumes that children's interests are not interconnected with their mothers' interests" (p. 215). She further argues that children's well-being is inextricably connected to their mothers' well-being (Nixon, 2009, p. 215; Radford and Hester, 2006). Child protection workers, in order to help children, should also address the needs of their mothers.

While best interest of the child remains paramount, the door is opened wider for the enactment of a helping role by social workers.

Questions for Discussion

What might child protection services look like if they were based on prevention of child maltreatment and support to families (and communities) in caring for their children? What would social workers do if these were their primary roles? What can social workers do now to prevent maltreatment of children? What can they do now to enhance their practice with families and communities (without forgetting their current child protection mandate)?

AN ILLUSTRATED CONNECTION BETWEEN POLICY AND SOCIAL WORK PRACTICE

Of all the fields of social work practice, none carries more responsibility than child protection. There is no doubt that child protection is a challenging task. The following case illustrates this challenge, how social welfare policy and legislation mandate child welfare practice, the social control function of social work, and the opportunities within mandated practice for a supportive, helping role of the social worker. Following the discussion of the case situation, we will return to exploring the role of social work in mandated child protection practice.

The case examples illustrate the connections between social policy and social work practice in a child welfare agency. These connections are discussed following the text boxes. The case scenarios draw from policies and practices in a number of provinces and have been developed according to actual policy, practices, and procedures that vary across Canada. Child protection policies, practices, and procedures change over time. We have strived to make the case descriptions as realistic as possible, but there are a variety of ways that the scenarios could be approached.

The scenarios below involve a family where child abuse is reported. Social workers become involved in a number of ways in order to investigate, plan, make decisions, and implement them. We describe the background of the family, what is learned, the actions that social workers take, and how these are related to laws and social and agency policies that shape practice. The case situations involve Raisa, a young child living with her mother, Valentina, and her mother's new boyfriend, Barry.

Case Example

First Scenario: Raisa ▼

Gina is a child protection worker (sometimes referred to as an intake worker) in the Child Protection Agency (CPA). She is an experienced worker with a

Continued

generalist BSW degree who has taken many refresher and training courses in child welfare. Gina likes her front-line social work job and realizes she can provide a valuable service to children and families, and this is important to her. Her role is to respond to reports by conducting investigations of new child protection cases, which involves risk assessment, planning, and goal-setting.

Kim (featured throughout the book) also works at the CPA. She has a social work degree and her main responsibility is case management. Some might call this role a treatment role. (See Chapter 4 for a general discussion of case management.) Kim will provide direct supportive services to Valentina and arrange and follow up with any other services required for Raisa and Valentina. Both Gina and Kim have a good understanding of the provincial policy and legislation that mandates their practice.

Gina and Kim are guided by the overriding principle that a child protection worker must always act in the best interest of the child (see CASW, 2005c). Their employer also abides by this principle and is mandated to protect children from child abuse and neglect.

Gina's role of child protection sometimes involves apprehension of a child, which often means a court appearance. Kim's role is directed at family intervention and support yet, like Gina, her main concern remains safety of the child.

Ideally, as illustrated in the current case, different workers perform the child protection and case management functions (although provinces may vary). This separation of roles is important and can be therapeutically effective. However, particularly in rural areas, the same worker sometimes performs both roles.

The social welfare policy pertaining to child protection is translated at the delivery level of agencies into programs and services. It is at this level that agency policies, responding to broader policies of governments, are implemented. The work that Gina and Kim do at CPA is shaped and determined by legislation, detailed policies, and written procedures at provincial and agency levels. Their agency's guidelines and procedures guide them in making decisions.

It is necessary to keep in mind that each province or territory may differ in its policies and practices. Manitoba currently differs from Ontario, for example, in roles for child protection workers (i.e., apprehending worker and current worker). Case management may also be shaped and practised differently across provinces.

Case Example

First Scenario: Raisa ▼

Valentina is a single mom who has been working at a local restaurant for the past three years. She is well-known and liked by everyone in the community. Her daughter Raisa is just over 2 ½ years of age and has been attending the daycare centre since she was 15 months old. She is considered a very outgoing, happy child who has a positive bond with her mom.

> The owners of the restaurant decided to close and Valentina was laid off from her job. Because she had been at the restaurant for a number of years, she applied for and is receiving Employment Insurance (EI) benefits. As well, EI has agreed to retrain Valentina and she is now attending classes three days per week. As a result, Raisa continues to go to daycare on these days.

▲

Valentina has experienced some challenges in her life that have no doubt resulted in added stress and worry. However, she shows strength and resilience despite having lost her job. She is receiving Employment Insurance (EI) cheques that help her to support her child, Raisa, and herself. Raisa is attending a daycare centre while Valentina is in training classes. In the meantime, she is actively improving her knowledge and skills. She hopes to get a better job soon. There is no child protection issue and no need for social work services as Raisa's needs are being met both at home and in the community. The fact that Valentina is doing well despite her job loss is a positive factor that would be considered by any CPA worker asked to assess the family's situation.

Case Example

First Scenario: Raisa ▼

Four weeks later: The daycare has recently noticed that Raisa has become more withdrawn over the past week and is not playing as actively with her friends. She has not been interested at all in toilet training. In fact, she has begun to squat in the corner after having soiled or wet her pants. This appears to be out of character for Raisa. Today, when Raisa was dropped off by her mother, there were some new bruises on Raisa's legs and back. Based on what she has observed, the daycare worker phones the intake line for the Child Protection Agency.

During this phone call, the daycare worker describes Raisa's behaviour over the past week and mentions the bruises she has observed on Raisa's body. The daycare worker states that there have been a number of times in the last month that Raisa has not attended daycare and Valentina has not called to let the centre know that Raisa would be absent. This seems unusual to the daycare worker because all of the time that Raisa has attended daycare prior to this she has not missed any days without a call from Valentina. The day care worker reports that she thinks that Raisa is also showing regressive behaviour.

▲

The childcare worker has experience and knowledge about normal child development. She also knows that she has an obligation by law, as do other professionals, to report suspected child abuse or neglect. This is required by law in her province. (In most, if not all, provinces community members are also obliged to report child abuse to the authorities.) Since the daycare worker notices behaviour that is unusual for a young child and bruises on Raisa's body, she makes a call to CPA. Even though she is not sure that abuse or neglect of Raisa is occurring, the daycare worker does what she is required to do: she contacts the appropriate authority so they can assess the situation.

Case Example

First Scenario: Raisa ▼

Due to the report given by the daycare worker, a file is opened. Gina, the child protection social worker, is given this file so she can begin an investigation of risk to Raisa. She will make a home visit the next morning.

Before she could leave for the home investigation, a second phone call is received. This time it is from a neighbour who asks to remain anonymous, indicating that there had been several domestic disturbances over the past few months and the neighbour has concerns about the young child who has been seen crying outside with her mother after being locked out of the house. He adds that a man whom he had never seen until last month seems to be living in the apartment with them. The two reports raises numerous red flags and confirms to Gina that the investigation must begin immediately.

Gina's first checks with the child abuse registry and finds that Valentina has no past history of child abuse. Next she conducts a home visit. Due to the report about possible domestic conflict at home, Gina requests that another worker accompany her. Gustav is asked to join her in the home visit to conduct the investigation.

As soon as a call about suspected abuse or neglect of a child is received, a case file is opened and a social worker is assigned to the case. The second phone call raises additional concerns. It supports the report given by the daycare worker that the child is being harmed. The policy is clear: the response must be immediate. These procedures are part of provincial and agency policy and procedures regarding responses to reports received by the CPA and must be followed.

Steps in the family-based investigation usually (depending on the province) include: checking the child abuse registry and child protection case history; medical check-up of the child; age-appropriate interview of the child; interview of alleged perpetrator of child abuse (with help from police if needed); home-based observation of the child about whom a report was made and any other children being cared for; assessment of the child's living situation and conditions at home; interviews of others who live in the home to identify anyone else at risk; obtaining of information from medical, school, and other professionals about the child's situation (See, for example, Ministry of Children and Youth Services – Ontario, 2007a, p. 33; and Hick, 2006, pp. 130–33). A priority would be to check whether there is bruising and have the child examined by a doctor, seek explanations from the parents, and, if possible, the child.

In cases where there is some risk to the worker or others, child protection workers may travel in teams so that an investigation can be carried out. Child protection work can be challenging, as few parents or caregivers want to have authority figures come to investigate or question their parenting or behaviour. This is why child protection workers often conduct home visits in teams to carry out investigations or are sometimes accompanied by a police officer if there is personal risk when they apprehend children. Agency policies stipulate how social workers can take precautions to protect themselves on the job, although many social workers essentially work on their own.

Case Example

First Scenario: Raisa ▽

Gina and Gustav arrive unannounced at the home around 9:45 a.m. Valentina greets them at the door and appears surprised and even shocked after they identify themselves. She recovers rather quickly when the workers explain why they have come. Valentina appears tired.

Surprisingly, she is gracious in welcoming them into her home. Raisa is in her room having a nap. Valentina's home appears pleasant and clean. Toys are stored on a corner shelf in the front room. The dishes are all washed and put away, and as Valentina reaches into her cupboard for a teabag, Gina notes that there is food in it. Accustomed to being a good observer in child protection investigations that require detailed assessment of children's home situations, Gina makes notes for her report. The fact that the home appears to be comfortable and clean indicates to Gina that Valentina is able to provide for her child's basic needs, cares about her environment, and knows how to maintain it. These are strengths that Gina wants to include in risk assessment report.

Gina informs Valentina that there is concern about abuse in the home, and therefore the safety of Raisa (and also of Valentina, the child's primary care provider). The workers explain the purpose of their visit, noticing that Valentina has a cut on her left wrist. She also seems to be cautious when using her arm. When Raisa wakes, the workers note that Valentina hesitates in picking her up, but eventually manages to collect her and carries her to the living room. She is not very affectionate with Raisa and seems exhausted. Raisa begins playing with her toys and scatters them throughout an area of the living room. Valentina tells her daughter that she can only have one toy out at a time as Valentina picks up the toys and puts them back in their places. The social workers ask

Continued

Valentina about her arm and ask to see the cut. The cut is rather deep. Although it is healing, it probably should have been seen by a doctor, who could have stitched it. Valentina says, "I was rearranging my bedroom on the weekend and the headboard accidently fell on my left side. I got my arm caught under it as I tried to keep it from hitting the floor." As she explains this to Gina and Gustav, she looks away from them. The workers looks at one another and Gina decides to speak. She asks, "Valentina, has someone hurt you?" Valentina gets up and moves to the window. She looks away again. Reviewing the intake reports, the social workers ask Valentina if she is being abused and if she and/or her daughter are in any danger.

▲

The social workers want to know if there is a risk of violence in the home and if Raisa (and Valentina) are at risk of being harmed. They do not suspect that Raisa is at risk of abuse from her mother. However, due to the reports received, they think that someone else may be abusing Raisa. They will want to assess whether Valentina and Raisa are at risk and, if necessary, carry out safety planning with Valentina (e.g., information about women's shelters, telephone crisis help, and laws that are meant to protect women [and children] from violence in the home). If Gina and Gustav determine that Valentina's and Raisa's safety are at risk, they will work with Valentina to review her options. In effect, there are two investigations occurring: 1) to determine whether the child is being abused by someone, and 2) to examine if the mother is able to successfully protect the child from being abused.

Depending on provincial laws, it would be up to the woman who has experienced the violence to report it to the police when it occurs. The police may or may not lay a charge at that time, and a restraining order against the partner whom they deem has enacted violence may be obtained. Although laws and policies in child protection are different and changing across the country, if social workers determine that there is reason to be concerned about violence in the home affecting a child, action will be taken to protect the child (for example, in this case, Valentina might go to a shelter with Raisa).

In this case scenario, it is presumed that the mother is capable of protecting the child because the workers determined that the mother has the capacity to protect her child. This is a part of the assessment. A factor that helps them in making this determination is the mother's reaction to the violence in the home and her willingness to work with CPA.

Case Example

First Scenario: Raisa ▼

After some silence, Valentina turns to Gustav and Gina, and tells them that Barry, her boyfriend, has been living with her for the past few months. She then admits that they have had some arguments, but these were nothing serious and arose because she did not have meals ready when Barry came home. Valentina says that Barry is having a hard time getting on his feet after being released from prison recently and she wants to help him. They met at the EI office where she helped Barry fill out forms while she was waiting for her training class to begin. Barry asked to see Valentina again and she agreed. Soon they became closer and began dating; then Barry moved in with her.

Valentina explains that she had been relying on Barry to take care of Raisa when she has had to go out, but Barry did not really enjoy small children. At this moment, Gina points to the bruising on Raisa's body and asks how it had happened. For now, Valentina avoids the question.

Valentina explains that she and Barry plan on marrying within the next year. She does not disclose why he was in prison. Gina will follow this up, as it may be important to address. Barry is not at home at the time of the interview with Valentina, but an interview will be set up immediately with Barry alone to investigate his role in the family and to question him about Raisa's injuries. A computer check will be also be conducted to see if he has any history with the agency.

To protect the safety of Valentina and Raisa, it is important to interview the suspected abuser separately from those who might be his victims. If the situation cannot be resolved (for example, by Valentina and Raisa going to stay at a women's shelter or other safe place), social workers will assess the risk of emotional and/or other injury that might warrant apprehension of Raisa. The options available depend upon provincial child protection laws and policies.

It would be useful to think about whether Valentina and Raisa should have to move from their home to escape from someone who has moved in with them and who has been violent toward one or both of them. Shouldn't they have the right to stay in their own home? Valentina might have sought for a long time to obtain the housing they have now. What other actions could help to protect them and disrupt their lives less than moving to a women's shelter?

Case Example

First Scenario: Raisa ▼

Gustav asks Valentina to tell him about the two incidents when Raisa was seen crying as she and her mother stood outside, apparently unable to enter their own apartment. Valentina explains, "It was only a misunderstanding when I got locked out those times. I forgot my key and Raisa wanted her toy. That's why she was crying. There is really nothing to worry about." Gina and Gustav note that Valentina is trying hard to convince them that everything is fine in the

Continued

home; however, it seems to them that she was afraid of Barry as she spoke about these incidents.

Valentina hesitates when answering questions and tends to avoid eye contact, often looking off to one side. She tries on a number of occasions to change the subject when a direct question is asked and asks for confirmation that the answers she gives are "right" for the workers. Valentina does not volunteer information and answers questions with the least amount of information possible. The workers know that often women in abusive relationships are controlled by the partners or boyfriends who have abused them and may have good reason to be afraid of disclosing the abuse. Often many supplementary questions are needed to gain additional information. Gina then explains to Valentina that abuse in intimate relations is not uncommon and that women are often afraid to speak out about it because of possible repercussions. Gina then asks her directly if Barry cut her on the arm and locked Valentina and Raisa out of the apartment. Valentina does not answer them directly and appears fearful.

Valentina reports to the workers that she is saddened about losing her job at the restaurant, but she is being retrained and so hopefully she will be able to get work again. She says when EI benefits run out, she is not sure what she is going to do if she can't find work. She explains that she doesn't want to go on social assistance because that is what she lived on as a child and she did not want that for her child. Gustav asks Valentina if she depends on Barry to help her with living costs. Valentina tells him that she has asked him to buy groceries sometimes and also to babysit Raisa. Valentina describes that when she was a child her mother was an addict who was unable to care for her and, as a result, she was placed into foster care at the age of 6, along with her two younger siblings. She says that she does not ever want that to happen to Raisa.

Gina, the child protection worker, returns to her question about bruising. Raisa has a number of visible bruises, consistent with the report from the daycare centre, with some that appear to be healing and a few fresh ones. When Valentina is asked about this, she indicates that Raisa tends to fall a lot because she is clumsy. She adds that Barry had been taking care of Raisa on one occasion and she got bruised due to a fall from the sofa. But Gustav and Gina are worried about possible abuse of Raisa by Barry. This could also explain her withdrawn behaviour at the daycare. Gina and Gustav determined that they would learn more about Barry's history and take action to protect Raisa.

Gina and Gustav conclude the interview by telling Valentina that they are concerned about both Raisa's and Valentina's safety and particularly the bruising on the child. Because of the risk from Barry, the workers believe that action is urgent and must take place quickly. **Safety planning** is carried out with

Valentina and Raisa so they can prepare in case they need to leave the home quickly for their own protection. The safety planning is carried out to protect the child; the mother may not have requested any protection. Valentina is Raisa's primary caregiver and the CPA wants to support and enhance her ability to care for her child. It is also decided that Raisa will need to be examined by a doctor to assess the bruises. Valentina will take Raisa to the doctor that day, and the doctor will send her report back to the CPA office.

Gina asks questions of Raisa in an age-appropriate manner to learn more about her. She uses basic language skills; however, they seem less developed than they should be at 2½ years. Although a doctor is to examine Raisa later that day, Gina notes that Raisa displays some behaviour that concerns her.

After returning to the office, Gina does a background check on Barry and discovers that he had been in prison several years ago for domestic violence involving a previous partner. This was a concern for Gina, since there might be some risk to both Raisa and Valentina with Barry in the home.

The doctor's report is also faxed to Gina at the CPA office. Her report said that sexual abuse was not evident, but that there was bruising that indicated physical abuse. Gina then initiates a face-to-face meeting with Valentina to ask about her knowledge about Barry's history and whether she has any concerns. Valentina states that Barry was not in prison for any assault, but rather had been jailed for pushing his ex-fiancée slightly when she tripped and fell down the outside stairs. She had become angry with him because he wanted to break up with her; she then called the police and they laid a charge against him. Valentina said it was all a misunderstanding and that he suffered for nothing, was really sorry for what happened, and would never do anything to harm another person. When Gina informs Valentina that the charge of assault against a former partner was real, and asks Valentina if she is concerned about this, Valentina dismisses it, saying, "That's not true. Barry told me what happened; he was the victim, not that woman."

During the meeting, Gina also tells Valentina about the findings from the doctor's report. Upon hearing the news, Valentina is shocked and angry. At first, she asserts that she was sure that Raisa had fallen downstairs and Barry had tried to stop her but could not. "That's what he told me. Kids move so fast. You can't keep them from falling all the time." Valentina then begins to cry and admits that it could have been that Barry lost his temper and hit Raisa. She then says that Barry had beat her up on a few occasions, but she hoped that he would change now that he was in a family situation. Gina questions Valentina about why she had changed her story about the bruising. Valentina explains that she had believed what Barry said, but now sees that he could be violent

Continued

when he loses his temper. Sometimes she was frightened by his need to be in charge. Valentina had no idea that he was also hurting Raisa. After a period of crying and more revelations of Barry's violent behaviour toward her, Valentina says to Gina that she would ask Barry to leave her home right away and stay away from Raisa and her. Valentina also says that she is angry with Barry for hurting Raisa and with herself for trusting him.

Later in the meeting, Gina, with her supervisor's agreement, explains that there is enough evidence present—unexplained bruising on Raisa and the child's regressive behaviour—to take action against Barry. Gina also talks to Valentina again regarding safety for herself and Raisa. Gina knows that it was important for safety planning to occur so that both mother and child will be protected while action is taken against Barry. In the meantime, CPA provides the police with information based on reports from the community, the social workers, and doctor. It is likely that Barry will be charged.

In provinces with a zero-tolerance policy on domestic violence, a report about abuse can be made to the police by the person who experiencing the violence. The police may lay a charge once they investigate the situation. This policy aims to protect women, who are most often the victims of violence in the home. It may also protect children who live in the home. Many provinces in Canada have additional legislation to protect victims of violence and others may be implementing them.

According to provincial and agency policies, a social worker has the right to inquire about past charges against someone when there is a concern about the safety of a child living with him or her. The need to investigate child, abuse or neglect cases overrides the right to privacy of such individuals. Social workers may receive privileged information about those who may be abusing or neglecting a child, as they are mandated to protect children (see Ministry of Children and Youth Services – Ontario, 2007). Of course, it is good practice to ask the person's permission before conducting such record checks.

Case Example

First Scenario: Raisa ▼

Based on the information gathered from the risk assessment report conducted during the home visit, the home visit itself, the criminal record check of Barry, and the doctor's report, the decision is made that there is sufficient evidence of short- and long-term risk of harm to Raisa and that intervention is required.

The preferred choice of action may be to help Valentina develop a safety plan that leaves Raisa in the home with her. This could include a restraining order placed against Barry if Valentina consents. If there is danger to Valentina and Raisa in returning home right away, they might be able to reside in a women's shelter until it is safe for them to return home. Kim, as case manager, would help in these and other referrals for services.

The next scenario uses the same basic facts as the first but depicts what might happen if Valentina decides to stay with Barry. Such a decision leads to a very different sequence of events that would be especially difficult for Raisa.

<blockquote>

Case Example

Second Scenario: Raisa ▽

If Valentina refuses to leave Barry or ask him to leave her home, CPA would be left with the option of apprehending Raisa and placing her into care. Both Gina and her supervisor realize that this move will be difficult for both Raisa and Valentina, as the bond between them is important to maintain. It has been established that there has been abuse against Raisa and Barry is the perpetrator. With Barry in the home, it is not a safe place for Raisa. It should be noted that foster homes in many areas are in short supply, and even when one is available the children placed there need to adjust to new surroundings and people, creating a significant amount of stress for them. It may also be necessary to move children from one temporary placement to another, making them even more susceptible to trauma and stress.

</blockquote>

Removing a child from her or his home environment and parents is always disruptive for both child and parent(s); a decision to apprehend and place the child into alternative care cannot ever be made lightly. Removing a child from parents or care providers, even if the relationship is not very nurturing or healthy in our judgment, is stressful on children and may be accompanied by emotional effects and behavioural difficulties. If a family was once functioning well, a social worker needs to assess whether it might not be best to support the strengths in the family and find ways to help restore healthy functioning. However, when there is evidence that a child is at risk of abuse and is experiencing distress and maybe crisis (and medical reasons are not a factor), that there is a clear risk to a child's well-being at home, and no other options are available, apprehension of the child may be necessary for his or her own protection.

Social workers in the child protection field follow provincial legislation and policies in acting in the best interest of the child. They need to complete a standardized risk assessment form so that risk can be measured in each case. This helps to quantify what the level of risk is in a particular case situation and indicates whether the social worker needs to take action. The completion of the agency's risk assessment form shows the degree of risk to the child. Social workers document their assessment so that there is a record that justifies why they intervened in the way they did (e.g., placement of a child in temporary foster care). Social workers may also ask for expert opinions or assessments from psychologists or physicians to obtain further evidence to help them make decisions.

Weighing evidence and making judgments to protect a child are not easy. If Valentina was unwilling or unable to remove Barry from her home, what would you do if you were the responsible CPA social worker? State the reasons for your actions. How could the family have been left intact? Could the disruption that taking Raisa into care caused have been avoided or reduced? How?

Difficult decisions like the one that would have been made by Gina and her supervisor (in the above situation) are made every day by child protection social workers. Social workers need to concern themselves with the best interest of the child. Yet, by doing so, they are acting in a social control capacity. The dual sides of social work, social control and care, are evident in this kind of work. How does a social worker come to terms with these dual roles when she or he performs child protection work?

Case Example

Second Scenario: Raisa ▼

In this scenario, where Valentina stays with Barry, a temporary guardianship order would be sought by CPA. The order requests from the courts a short (3–6 months) length of time to keep the child in care to continue their investigation and to plan for services and supports that can help the family move toward reunification. The short time would help focus the agency's actions on reuniting mother and daughter.

The needs of the family are apparent in child protection work. Good social work requires that workers support families and enhance their capacities and strengths to care for their children. In fact, the apprehension of children from their homes and parents is seen as a last resort. This is what would also occur in the case of Valentina and Raisa.

Reunification would take place only if Raisa's safety was ensured. It would be necessary for Barry to have no contact with Raisa. Notwithstanding the mother's situation, safety planning is for the child's protection. The mother has not clearly stated yet that she requires protection. Her safety is not directly being assessed; rather, her capacity to protect her child. Of course, because she is the primary caregiver, the goal of the agency would be to support and/or enhance her ability to care for her child.

Second Scenario: Raisa ▼

The risk assessment, the daycare worker's information, facts about Barry's history, observations of the home situation and conditions, evidence from medical or other experts, and interviews with other family members provide information to help the social workers conclude that Raisa is in need of protection. Valentina might deny that Barry has been abusive, as she is afraid of him. If she insisted that Barry was blameless and wanted him to remain living with her in her home, it might have been necessary to take Raisa into care for the child's own protection. Leaving her at home with Barry could possibly result in physical and emotional harm to Raisa. Raisa's regressive behaviour and the bruising on her body strongly suggest abuse (See Government of Ontario, 2007, for tools and topics in risk assessment).

Agency policy stipulates that when the situation is determined to be unsafe and apprehension is possible, a child protection worker and her or his supervisor go to the child's home and explain at the time of apprehension why the child is being taken into care and what will occur next. When a child is to be apprehended and placed into foster care, the child protection social worker or her or his supervisor and often a police officer meet with the parent(s) to explain the rationale for their actions. Apprehension of a child from the child's home usually involves emotion and tension, and in some cases there may be concern about angry reaction from parents or caregiver. This can be a very dangerous time for women who are living in violent home situations. It may be that the parent who is responsible for abuse or neglect is taken into custody by the police at that time. Measures are taken to ensure the safety of the child. The social worker wants to be sure that the apprehension process is safe. Usually another meeting is arranged to discuss the range of options and conditions for return of the child.

Second Scenario: Raisa ▼

In this scenario, Valentina would be informed that probably the quickest and best way to have Raisa returned is for Valentina to end her relationship with Barry. If Valentina is able to remove Barry from her home and agree not to associate with him, then it might be possible for Raisa to stay in the home. Follow-up would be needed to assess whether these conditions were met. A support worker (to support the family to establish stability in the home) could be provided by CPA to ensure that Raisa's needs were met and that Valentina was given support in making

Continued

childcare decisions. It is important to consider what would be the risk to Valentina if Raisa was placed into foster care. Would Barry retaliate against Valentina? Why or why not? Discussing safety plans with Valentina would be a good idea.

If Barry remains in the home, the process will likely be much longer and more difficult.

If you were in Gina's shoes and were considering the options available to you, how would you make a decision? What evidence would you want to obtain to help you make the best decision? If the Ontario policies on protecting children from harm (see the Children's Aid Society of Toronto website, http://www.torontocas.ca) were your guidelines, which of these could you draw on to justify the action you would take?

Child protection—with a legislated mandate—is a field of social work where there is a dual purpose, that is, to care and to control. Social workers must protect children from harm and take action when necessary to do so. The language of control may be used when writing reports about cases. This language consists of short-cut terms that social workers might find oppressive (e.g., non-compliant, resistant, cooperative, etc.). However, the controlling function in this case serves to protect children from harm and neglect. Social workers may find it appropriate to include a strengths or anti-oppressive approach in some of their child protection work. Respect, empathy, and concern for clients fit well with social work principles of practice. We know that many people who become social work clients are affected by structural inequalities in our society that often pose barriers in access to good housing, educational and employment opportunities, secure incomes, and high quality childcare services. Working as partners with and advocating for families (described in Chapters 13 and 14) can often be very helpful even in mandated social work, such as child protection.

Case Example

Second Scenario: Raisa ▼

In this scenario, Kim, the case manager, would contact Valentina after a few days. She would recognize that Valentina's life is in disarray and she is an involuntary client. (See Chapter 6 for discussion of involuntary clients.) Kim must first gain Valentina's trust and respect before she can be of real help. As part of this process, Kim would need to find out what Valentina wants. For example, what does Valentina want in planning for the return of Raisa? Does she need help in finding a job? Does she need help in finding an immediate source of income? And so on. However, this may be difficult because Valentina is an involuntary client and may not want help from CPA. The social worker is concerned for Valentina's safety as well as Raisa's, and would need to work with Valentina to assist her with her needs.

Assuming Valentina does begin to trust Kim and wants her child returned to her, Kim's primary role as case manager would be to help her plan for this eventuality, to help her access resources, and coordinate and monitor them as necessary. If Valentina does not want or is unwilling to accept help from Kim, then the case manager would still have the responsibility to help her if and when help is requested. From time to time, Kim will report about progress to her supervisor.

In addition to helping Valentina plan and make decisions, Kim's role as case manager involves monitoring the process and progress of the case. She remains involved with the members of the family to facilitate the ongoing work of the programs and services required. Kim receives and documents information from each professional involved and continues to add information to the case file to consult when further decisions are made.

The emphasis and priority in child protection is upon the safety of the child. However, in almost all child protection situations, parents or other caregivers are vulnerable. We consider services provided to parents or caregivers as very important. Often plans are made to eventually return children to their own homes. Prevention of further maltreatment can be aided by providing help to those to whom the child returns. This is in the best interests of the child, and such services should be made available to families. In this case, we attempt to show how this help can be an important part of child protection work through Kim's role as case manager and the help of the support worker.

Case managers work with vulnerable clients who need to overcome significant challenges. Such clients often require direct support and assistance as well as coordinated services that meet several areas of need, such as physical care, counselling, financial assistance, and home-based support. Children requiring foster care often require supportive services. Ensuring that appropriate services are effectively provided to meet these multiple needs of clients is also a responsibility of a case manager (see Chapter 4).

Agency policy and procedures manuals guide social workers about their duties and responsibilities. Case managers in child protection follow child protection manuals that tell them about their function in open cases. (See, for example, Ministry of Children and Youth Services – Ontario, 2007b.)

Case Example

Second Scenario: Raisa ▽

As Kim, the case manager, continues to provide support and to monitor the progress of the family once Raisa is returned to Valentina, she notes that Raisa's behaviour appears to be improving and she seems to be growing and developing normally. Raisa has been able to express herself, has adjusted relatively well, and has progressed behaviourally to an age-appropriate level. Gina continues to visit with the family to ensure that things are working well. Eventually the file is closed.

GENERALIST AND SPECIALIST PRACTICE

In the second scenario of the case example, the functions of two social workers are highlighted: Gina and Kim. Gina is portrayed as the decision maker and is primarily responsible for the safety of Raisa. Her role is defined by legislation. She must be intimately familiar with policies and laws that protect children. Valentina does not want Raisa apprehended. Yet, in the interest of safety, Gina, with the support of her supervisor and following legislated and agency policy, apprehends the child. Gina has considerable power, and her actions regarding both Valentina and Raisa suspend their rights to self-determination. This is an important social work role of social control and Valentina is an involuntary client (see Chapter 6).

Kim's role, cast as case manager, is different. Her main goal is to help Valentina plan and prepare for the return of Raisa. She reports progress to the supervisor. Her supervisor and Gina then make decisions regarding placement and return of Raisa. Kim's role is much more of a helping and enabling role. She helps Valentina reach her goals. Kim's role is not really one of social control and Valentina is a voluntary client to the extent that she wants and/or accepts Kim's help.

Both roles as described above are specialized according to the field of protection and the particular province and agency. Policy and legislation define these roles. However, both require generalist skills; both are roles of social workers. The professional lens of social work filters the practice of child welfare.

Gina needs to approach her work with sensitivity. Even though Valentina is probably angry and upset with Gina, the worker must use her social work relationship skills. Gina must understand that Valentina is very vulnerable and that she must be treated with dignity and respect. She needs to abide by the CASW *Code of Ethics*. All of these are important generalist functions.

Within the context of social control, Gina must use acceptable social work skills and principles. In the end, her goals are "helping" Raisa have a quality childhood, including aiding Valentina in providing the environment in which this can happen.

The case manger role adopted by Kim is a generalist role that Kim must adapt to child welfare. She is an enabler and counsellor, for example, in helping Valentina make informed decisions. A primary role for her is brokerage. She helped Valentina gain access to resources and monitored them.

In this example, the roles of case social worker and case manager have been separated. In another case situation described in this book (see Chapter 8), Kim is cast as assuming both case manager and case social worker role. One can argue which of these is preferable.

The first case scenario describes a more straightforward child protection situation than the second, which involves involuntary clients and a more prescriptive process requiring careful planning and monitoring. In both scenarios, the social worker is guided by provincial child protection mandates, laws, and policies.

CHAPTER SUMMARY

The main purpose of this chapter was to connect and show how social work practice is directly connected to social policy. The chapter also shows how social workers carry out their work and provide services in the context of a mandated practice field. We chose to use child protection to illustrate this important part of social work, using the Child Protection Agency as a backdrop. We described key features and roles of social work practice in the field of child protection services. These were discussed in relation to historical developments and shifts in social welfare and agency policy.

The majority of this chapter describes the case of Raisa and Valentina. The two scenarios were written to draw students into the work of child protection, including assessment of risk, review of social work responsibilities, determination of client options, planning and setting goals, and implementation of actions to realize goals. This chapter aids students in understanding social work practice in child protection and helps them see how practice is shaped by laws and policies, which are, in turn, partly determined by an ideological lens.

The decision-making process and actions taken by Gina, the case worker, and Kim, the case manager, are illustrated throughout the description of the case situation. We showed that the dual function of social care and social control are characteristic in social work in the child protection field.

The Client–Social Worker Relationship: Voluntary and Involuntary Relationships

Chapter Goal ▼

To describe the nature of the professional social work relationship, both voluntary and involuntary.

This Chapter ▼

- defines the social work client and distinguishes between voluntary and involuntary clients
- defines the nature of the professional helping relationship and describes key components of this relationship
- describes social work relationships with involuntary clients and suggests ways that social workers might form relationships and work with clients who do not want to engage with them

DEFINING THE SOCIAL WORK CLIENT

Fundamental to social work practice is the professional relationship that social workers develop with clients in order to provide a helping service to them and to effect change. Much of the remainder of the book elaborates on this relationship, particularly Chapter 8 on problem solving, Chapter 11 on the strengths approach to social work, Chapter 12 on an Aboriginal approach, Chapter 13 on a feminist approach, and Chapter 14 on structural social work. No matter what approach is used by the social worker, the need to establish and develop a relationship for the work together is essential.

The client is not necessarily the person with whom the social worker is working. What may seem obvious at first is, in fact, rather complicated. Suppose you are a child welfare worker working with a 1-year-old child who has been abused. Is the child the client? One or both of the parents? Or is it the society or state, represented by the child welfare agency that is responsible for protecting children? What if the community in which the child lives with his family has been involved and wants to voice some ideas about the situation? Is the community also a client?

The Canadian Association of Social Workers (CASW) *Code of Ethics* defines a client as "a person, family, group of persons, incorporated body, association or community on whose behalf a social worker provides or agrees to provide a service" (CASW, 2005a, p. 13). The service may be provided on request or in agreement with the client, or as the result of a legal mandate received from legislation or from a judge of a court of competent jurisdiction who orders that the social worker give to the Court an assessment (CASW, 2005a, p. 10). In cases where there is "a valid court order, the judge/court is the client and the person(s) who is ordered by the court to participate in assessment is recognized as an involuntary client" (CASW, 2005a, p. 10). In this conception, the client is presumed to be voluntary if the service provided is sought by the client and is the result of agreement with the client concerning the nature of the problem and the action required to address it. In the case of an involuntary client, the relationship is voluntary if the client and worker agree to work on a problem (establish a contract) beyond what was originally mandated. (Some provincial social work associations have adapted wording that slightly alters that of the national association.) (*The Social Work Code of Ethics*, adopted by the Board of Directors of the Canadian Association of Social Workers (CASW) is effective March, 2005 and replaces the CASW *Code of Ethics* (1994). The *Code* is reprinted here with the permission of CASW. The copyright in the document has been registered with Canadian Intellectual Property Office, registration No. 1030330.)

The word *client* implies a power differential between the social worker and the client, particularly if the client is involuntary. Those who advocate a strengths approach (see Chapter 11) often prefer the word *consumer*. Other alternatives might be *partner* or *helpee*. However, *client* is the most common and generally accepted word used by social workers, and is the term used in this textbook.

HELPING VERSUS SOCIAL CONTROL

The function of **social control** and its impact on involuntary clients are important issues in social work. Social control is an action of a professional worker, agency, representative of a court, or other legally ***mandated organization*** that is intended to regulate, govern, or restrict the activities and behaviour of a client. Often the action is taken to protect a third party, such as children in abuse cases or the public when the client has been convicted of a crime. At other times, as in the case of mental illness, social workers (and other professionals) may make treatment decisions in the best interest of a client even if the client objects. Importantly, in all situations, the purpose of social work intervention remains to help, and the social worker must always act in the best interest of those with whom she or he works.

Many social workers are employed in fields in which strong mandates for social control are attached to their work. Probably the three fields at the top of this list are corrections, child protection, and mental health. It is likely that many social work clients are involuntary, but keeping accurate and complete statistics on the number of involuntary clients social workers have worked with has been difficult.

There are two types of involuntary clients, but they are often difficult to separate. Some are involuntary because the justice, mental health, or child welfare system or other social institution takes some form of action toward the client. This group includes clients who are or have been convicted of a crime, those who have neglected children, and those who are mentally ill and are forced to seek treatment. Such clients might be called *mandated involuntary clients*. Valentina, a single parent and mother of a child who was apprehended, is the centre of a case illustration in Chapter 5. She is an example of mandated involuntary client.

Probably most mandated involuntary clients, like Valentina, are also unwilling. However, an unwilling client can also be one who seeks help because of pressure from family, social agencies, the police, or other outside sources. A client in a hospital or long-term care setting may be provided social work services if requested by the institution, even if they are not wanted by the client. Another common example in which a client may be unwilling occurs when a partner in a troubled marriage reluctantly sees a counsellor at the insistence of the spouse. A person who displays eccentric behaviour that is not harmful to anyone but that some consider a sign of mental illness may resist treatment even though others think it is important. He or she is also viewed as an unwilling client.

The second group of involuntary clients, then, are unwilling clients. They are involuntary because they do not want a service when others think the service would benefit them. Unwilling clients are reluctant to accept social work services and frequently resist seeing a social worker or participating in treatment.

Often social workers work with openly resistant clients. An example is a parolee who wants no part of the treatment program developed by her or his parole officer at the order of a parole board. Or, it could be the parents of an abused child who aggressively reject help, perhaps because they do not agree that their child should have been apprehended. Social workers in the mental health field often treat people who are forced by the legal system to undergo treatment or are coerced by others, such as family or police, to seek help. They may lack many social skills but refuse to recognize this as a problem. The fact is that much of social work involves working with people who do not want help. Yet textbooks on intervention in generalist social work practice with these people has been limited. (In Chapter 8, we address the ethical principle of best interest and the involuntary client.)

> ### Case Example
>
> ## Kim and Ann ▼
>
> Our ongoing story about Kim and Ann can be used to illustrate how social work conceptualizes clients.
>
> Since Kim is a child protection worker and Ann's children are under the legal care of the Child Protection Agency (CPA), the children are Kim's clients. Ann is, on the one hand, a mandated involuntary client because the agency removed her children from her without her permission. However, since Kim and Ann agree that Kim will provide a useful service to Ann and they agree on the problems and a plan for solving them, Kim has been able to form a voluntary relationship with Ann even though Ann did not ask for service in the first place.
>
> Now suppose that Ann views herself as a victim of the agency and the courts and, as often happens, actively rejects help from Kim or any other child welfare worker. Using the concept of client as presented above, if Kim still provides a service to Ann (for example, to help Ann understand the legal processes and alternatives available to her), Ann is a mandated and unwilling involuntary client. The children would still be clients because Kim is working on their behalf.
>
> Suppose that the judge requires that Kim file an assessment report with the court after 60 days of custody. In this instance, the court or judge, representing society, is also Kim's client.

DEFINING SOCIAL WORK RELATIONSHIPS

Throughout our lives, human interaction and the quality of the relationships that develop from them provide meaningful experiences for us. We learn from childhood how to get along with people, how to meet our own needs, and how to give in to the needs of others in relationships. Through social and cultural experiences we become aware of how conflict and reciprocity feel and what methods and skills we can draw on to make relationships work—or leave them altogether. In social work, this learning forms a foundation on which we build professional relationships that exist for a specific purpose and in a particular organizational context. There are differences among relationships between friends and family members and those between clients and social workers. Deliberate effort and considerable skill are needed to initiate, develop, maintain, and end client–social worker relationships.

A relationship in social work practice can be thought of as an exchange at the emotional level and a dynamic interaction between people in a professional meeting. It also connects people in a mutual process (Biestek, 1957) that includes a purpose and expectations (Compton, Galaway, and Cournoyer, 2005). Relationships involve process (the quality and flow of interchange) and content (what is being discussed), both of which are necessary to attend to. Above all, relationships are connections between individuals based on some expectations of shared rules of conduct. These rules may be contested in practice, where the different parties in the relationship may negotiate for more flexibility in them and for other changes.

The duration of a relationship depends on the level of commitment, will, and purpose in keeping it going. In social work, some relationships can be long term, continuing over years with the same clients, whereas others are limited to the short term. Relationships are built and shaped over time by the shared rules, purpose, roles, expectations, and needs of those involved. In any client–social worker relationship, you can identify certain points where changes take place in the relationship. This is natural in a process that unfolds as work proceeds, and as Locke, Garrison, and Winship (1998) state, "it is necessary to attend to the ebbs and flows of the process" (p. 113). For example, when clients have achieved some identified goal that has been a focus of work, the purpose of the relationship will shift to different issues and interests. To illustrate, a social worker's relationship with a family whose crisis situation is being resolved changes in intensity and focus, perhaps from the immediate crisis to longer-term issues or new problems. Both parties may then renegotiate the purpose, roles, and expectations of their work together.

Social workers have clear responsibilities in helping relationships with clients. As Perlman (1957) explained over 50 years ago, using oneself in a purposive or disciplined way is a feature of this relationship. The need to respect (not necessarily to like), to be concerned about, and to care for clients in ways that acknowledge that they have the capacity to decide their own actions is central to the relationship. Social workers also strive to communicate integrity and honesty while maintaining client confidentiality and privacy, for example, by not seeking information from the client that is not essential or relevant to the problem or situation being addressed.

We cannot overestimate the importance of the relationship in social work—and we may not even realize its importance in the client's life. The client may not either, at least while in the process of working with the social worker. Here's an example: A social work researcher is conducting interviews with women who are former social work clients and who have experienced addictions, abuse, and other issues. After having introduced herself as a social work researcher, she is told by the former client that the person who really cared about her when no one else did was a social worker. The client added that although she did not realize or acknowledge it at the time, the social worker listened to her, didn't judge, and carefully guided and encouraged her to decide for herself about a course of action. The few sessions she had with the social worker helped her to take the first steps to change her life for the better. The research participant told the researcher that it was only several years later that she was able to reflect on the changes in her life and how they came about. The social worker she had met with then never knew what an important role she played at that very difficult time in the woman's life. The social worker's compassion and belief in the client and the client's capacity to respond to these helped build a strong, caring relationship between them. To the interview respondent, this relationship was more important than any information given, referrals made, or *practice approaches* used by the social worker. Probably there are many stories of effective and compassionate relationships between social workers and clients that remain unheard. Research studies (e.g., Apollo et al., 2006; Hubble, Duncan, and Miller, 1999) have pointed to the importance of the relationship between a client and service provider. Apollo et al. (2006) found that caring for the whole person, listening to the client, and mutuality between the client and professional providing services were very important to clients in a health care setting. The work of Hubble, Duncan, and Miller (1999) highlights the importance of relationship with service providers as perceived by clients. They concluded that positive outcomes in therapy were less dependent on professional theories and methods of a therapist but had much more to do with the existence of a good relationship with the therapist, one that helped the client to feel better about herself or himself. However, without social work skills and knowledge, a good relationship will not be sufficient for effective practice.

Communication is a key feature of any helping activity. Communication can involve speech or sign language and gestures or it can take a written form, including memos, letters, reports, records, position papers, or articles. The form of communication depends on what is needed in the situation. For example, in community work, a social worker may communicate the community members' need for a children's daycare centre through facilitating a petition and letter to city hall.

There must be a purpose for both the social worker and the client in maintaining a relationship. The benefit for the client is, for example, the hope or expectation that something favourable will ensue. Social workers gain satisfaction from seeing that their efforts at building relationships with clients are successful. For clients, the purpose in establishing a relationship with a social worker is to gain access to certain resources or to seek help in making changes in their lives. Clients must view the relationship as an important part of the helping process.

For both the social worker and the client, the relationship is a means to an end. If the worker is able to establish a caring and empathic relationship, then the helping process will more likely be successful. Citing Perlman (1957, pp. 64–83) again, we note that in her writing on the problem-solving process, she clearly recognized this and saw the growth of clients, particularly in their ability to solve their own problems, as a major purpose of helping. She wrote, "[T]hroughout his life each person seeks (and feels secure only when he has found) a relationship with one or more other human beings from which he can draw nourishment, love or sustainment and the stimulus of interaction" (pp. 64–65). She goes on to argue that the purpose of the professional relationship is to engage the helping process, which "like every other process intended to promote growth, must use relationship as its basic means" (p. 65). The fact that social workers agree, through an employment mandate and a professional ethical code, to work with people to achieve certain ends provides them with a purpose for and a direction to the relationship. This relationship is structured according to its purpose, which may take the form of a written contract, an informal agreement, or some understanding of what will follow (Boyle et al., 2009).

COMPONENTS OF THE CLIENT–SOCIAL WORKER RELATIONSHIP

The relationship between a client and a social worker is a partnership. The partnership conception of the relationship is strengthened in feminist social work, where clients and workers share power and create a nurturing environment (see Chapter 13). The importance of sharing the responsibility of helping clients solve their own problems is emphasized in feminist social work.

Social work texts identify the components that are most common in social work relationships with clients. They include care and concern; empathy and honesty; acceptance of people; acknowledgment of the client's capacity for change; self-determination and autonomy; confidentiality; power, authority, and control; purpose and commitment; and context and structure (Biestek, 1957; Compton, Galaway, and Cournoyer, 2005; Johnson, McLelland, and Austin, 2000; Kirst-Ashman and Hull, 2009; Sheafor and Horejsi, 2008).

Care and Concern

Showing care and concern toward others is basic to social work values and practice, and refers generally to caring for people and what troubles them. Although we may not approve of a client's behaviour (for example, in the case of a parent who abuses a child), we need to respect and value each person's humanity and affirm his or her right to be heard, understood, and helped. The Canadian Association of Social Workers *Code of Ethics* also stresses this requirement (CASW, 2005a). The well-being of others is necessarily one of the most fundamental concerns of client–social worker relationships. This means ensuring the safety and security of clients, not only in their own social and physical environments, but also in the social work process. It also means expressing interest in and concern about their well-being by, for example, helping them to feel comfortable in our first meeting with them.

The tendency to want to be helpful and the human need for professional success or esteem can sometimes be obstacles that hamper a helping relationship. As Sheafor and Horejsi (2008) state,

> Some type of relationship will develop whenever a social worker and client interact. This relationship may be either positive or negative, depending on the client's interpretation of the worker's words and actions. Thus the social worker cannot *make* a positive relationship happen. At most a social worker can strive to be the type of person and type of professional that most clients find to be helpful. (p. 136)

Social workers must consider the goal and purpose of their actions to ensure that they focus on the client's needs and balance those with building a good working relationship.

Case Example

Kim and Ann ▼

Returning to the story of Kim and Ann can help us to illustrate how caring and concern are applied. Suppose that Ann was angry that she needed to meet with Kim, the child protection worker. Ann did not agree with the decision to apprehend her children and wants to let Kim know it.

Kim understands that most parents would feel powerless and angry when an authority intrudes and makes a decision in which they had little input. Kim genuinely cares about what Ann feels and believes in and is concerned for her. Kim knows that her demonstration of care and concern will help establish an initial relationship even if the beginning will likely be rocky. Kim waits while

Continued

Ann shouts at her and insists that the decision to apprehend her children was wrong and unfair. Kim knows that Ann is feeling vulnerable and stressed and wants her children back. Kim understands that Ann needs to be heard. She also knows that Ann needs to hear that Kim cares about her and is concerned about Ann's needs and interests. Ann is now more open to working with Kim, not just because the court has mandated it, but because she sees that Kim cares about her and her situation.

Empathy and Honesty

Empathy refers to the ability to understand clients in their situations and from their perspectives, and it is integral to social work. It also means that each individual client's uniqueness is appreciated. In explaining empathic skills, Shulman (2006) writes: "The acceptance and understanding of emotions and the worker's willingness to share them by experiencing them frees a client to drop some defenses and to allow the worker and the client more access to the real person. The worker also serves as a model of an adult with empathic ability" (p. 133). (See Shulman, 2006; and Hepworth, Rooney, and Larsen, 2002, for a more detailed discussion of empathy.)

We demonstrate empathy by listening actively and communicating understanding of the client's story. Although the concept of empathy might seem simple, it draws on the skill and experience of the social worker. Without a good grounding in knowledge about human behaviour across the lifespan, stress, crisis, resilience, responses to problems in living, and other elements that affect a range of people in diverse situations, a social worker is less able to empathize with clients. Empathy occurs at the feeling level but also requires cognitive understanding of people's problems and their reactions to them.

Social workers can learn from each client they meet, and this knowledge will help them to become more aware of their own emotions in specific situations. As Shulman (2006) explains, "The worker will more readily allow a client to share more difficult emotions as the worker becomes more comfortable with their effects, particularly those of negative feelings, both worker's and client's, which form a natural part of any helping relationship" (p. 135).

In a helping relationship, it is also important not to lose perspective on the client's situation and to react only emotionally. Empathy means being honest with yourself and the client. Consider, for example, what might happen if you became completely focused on the emotions and obstacles faced by a young disabled man who has come to you seeking help with life choices. You might feel unable to help him in dealing with his problems, but might instead try to solve them for him to relieve some of his distress. There is no sense in telling the man, for instance, that you can help him resolve his problems and that "everything will be okay" if it might not be. Expressing honestly, without destroying any hope, what seems realistic in a situation promotes better practice relationships. For the beginning social worker, it is often difficult to keep oneself sufficiently separate from the client's situation, yet it is necessary to find a balance between empathy and separateness. This takes practice and is usually helped by additional experience in drawing on skills and knowledge to avoid getting "stuck on" or overwhelmed by problems presented by clients.

Demonstrating empathy can involve appropriate and timely verbal or nonverbal affirmations. Showing that you empathize with clients, however, does not mean constantly nodding or saying "Mm-hmm," since such behaviour can seem mechanical. With practice, it is possible to change most distracting behaviours that impede empathy and good communication in social work. Most importantly, being genuine helps in communicating empathy and honesty.

Case Example

Kim and Ann ▽

Kim had listened actively and Ann saw that Kim genuinely wanted to be helpful to Ann. She could also see that Kim empathized with her situation. The way Kim did this was to encourage Ann to talk about her feelings, and as she did so, Kim nodded while making eye contact with Ann and commented that she knew that Ann would likely feel upset because if Kim was in Ann's shoes, she might feel the same way too. Kim was calm and warm even though Ann was angry with her and others. Ann soon began to feel that Kim understood how she felt because Kim's gestures and comments showed that she felt empathy for Ann. Kim also expressed honestly her view that Ann's emotional reaction was normal given her distress. Kim's honesty helped Ann to see the possibility of working with Kim.

Acceptance

Acceptance of people, even when their behaviour is difficult to understand or is repulsive to the social worker, is necessary in effective social work practice. Acceptance is related to concern and empathy. It means not judging, idealizing, or assuming what people are, were, or should be. Sometimes assumptions about a person or group of people have harmful effects in social work practice. This can certainly occur in cases where the worker and the client come from different cultures. For example, a non-Aboriginal social worker who has little knowledge about Aboriginal helping methods might not see an Elder as a useful resource for a traditional Aboriginal client (see Chapter 12).

Not being able to accept and work with certain clients poses problems in a practice situation and can create serious barriers in developing a relationship. Recognizing and appreciating the rich diversity in people and the uniqueness of each individual can help social workers approach and work better with clients. It can also prevent them from judging another's actions hastily when they do not really know what it is like to be in the client's shoes. Social workers do not need to approve of behaviours that they do not accept or that others likely wouldn't accept–for example, beating someone up for money. However, social workers do need to view the client holistically and understand the client's behaviour based on his or her own perspective.

Consider how people's *constructions* of their own realities guide their decisions and actions. Striving for a holistic appreciation of people in their situations discourages stereotyping and labels like "the welfare mother," "the schizophrenic," "the juvenile delinquent," and so on. Listening to the experiences of people from their own viewpoints can be useful in highlighting the lives of those whose voices have not been heard very much, for example, refugees and immigrants, street-living youth, those with serious mental health challenges, poor people, and others. The ways in which people construct meaning from their life situations can reveal commonalities and differences in what they and their social workers interpret as problems. In social work, there is more than one kind of knowledge; there is the body of knowledge that is derived from theories and research that informs social work practice, and there is knowledge that is local, subjective, and rooted in people's daily lives.

Saleebey (2006b) stresses that when clients and social workers work together, social workers become mutually engaged partners with clients, which "requires us to be open to negotiation and to appreciate the authenticity of the views and aspirations of those with whom we collaborate. Our voices have to be quieted so that we can give voice to our clients" (pp. 14–15). People's knowledge about their experiences and lives becomes an important resource rather than a series of problems.

In fact, our ideas about a person and his or her situation may prove quite different from those who actually live the experience. For example, a boy of 14 who is receiving cancer treatment tells a social worker that his biggest concern is how his classmates will react to his changed appearance. He explains that his hair was what he liked best about his looks. Due to chemotherapy, he has lost it all. The social worker is surprised to hear about this being so important to him; she expected him to identify other problems, which she perceived as more significant. However, she accepts his version and works with him to resolve the situation.

Case Example

Kim and Ann ▼

Kim knows that acceptance of people by others is basic to self-esteem and actualization. Kim accepts Ann, even when she does not approve of Ann's behaviour. Along with empathy and honesty, Kim's unconditional acceptance of Ann helps Ann to feel that she is valued as a human being. Kim shows acceptance by listening to Ann and treating her with respect and fairness. Ann feels that her feelings and ideas matter to Kim.

Client Capacity for Change

Acknowledging client capacity for change and client resilience is a key feature of client–social worker relationships. The strengths perspective outlined by Saleebey (1992, 1997c, 2006b) stresses the importance of actively seeking with clients the range of strengths and resources open to them in the external environment and within themselves. When people's difficulties obscure the fact that they have strengths on which to draw, their capacity for change is also hampered. Recognizing one's strengths can increase self-esteem, hope, and motivation for change. A strengths perspective in social work thus takes the position that people have natural internal resources that can be harnessed for healing and growth and can be expressed by all people. Articulation and expression of care, concern, hope, and the value of clients' strengths, gifts, and capacities is done through the client–social work relationship.

Consider the situation of an unemployed, despondent woman who has fled Sierra Leone as a refugee, having had her schooling interrupted. In her new country, she has had trouble finding a job due to her limited education and poor English-language skills. It is apparent to the social worker that the client faces many barriers and feels unable to deal with them. At the same time, the woman has survived war and found the courage and resources to leave her home and extended family for the hope of a more safe and secure life in a foreign land. The social worker identifies and explores with the client some of the many strengths that her experiences suggest. The social worker's knowledge helps him understand that capacity for change is inherent in all humans. They move toward growth and development. He takes the time to get to know her and her experiences, fears, and hopes as he begins to build a relationship with her. The social worker also works with the client to draw out and find specific strength areas that can be used to improve her current situation. Thus, believing in clients' capacity for change can encourage them to see at least some of their obstacles as surmountable.

A person's capacity for change, according to the strengths perspective, comes from within. We cannot, however, ignore the fact that client situations are often complex and require more than tapping inner resources and capacities. People face many constraints that often call for examination and identification of the structural features in society that contribute to or create difficulties, such as discrimination based on class, ethnocultural background, ability, sexual orientation, age, gender, and so on, and that call for interventions that reach beyond the client. To illustrate, imagine the situation of a homeless young man with a heroin addiction. Although a search for his internal strengths may be helpful, many other external resources will likely be needed to help him. He may be able to use his own resources to some extent to secure his own safety and security, since he has survived considerable difficulties until now, but these will likely not be enough to deal with his current situation. There are many issues to deal with, such as how he can be safe, find shelter and food, and begin to regain his self-esteem (see Buchanan, 2005). Acknowledging the client's capacity for change is important and can be an impetus for building a relationship and sustaining the client's life changes.

Case Example

Kim and Ann ▼

In beginning a relationship with Ann, Kim knows that Ann has a number of strengths, some of which she has yet to learn. Kim will take the time to learn about these soon. Kim also thinks that Ann has the capacity to make positive changes in her life and makes sure that Ann heard that Kim was confident that

Continued

Ann could make the needed changes for the return of her children. Kim knows that people can change, grow, and thrive even when their circumstances may appear hopeless. This is an important belief that would generate hope and meaning in Kim's relationship with Ann.

Self-Determination and Autonomy

As explained in Chapter 3, self-determination refers to clients' rights to make life choices for themselves. Social work codes of ethics highlight the value of self-determination. It presupposes that decisions can be made between a range of options and that being able to make choices for oneself is both empowering and helpful to people (Miley, 2002, p. 239). In establishing professional relationships, a key element in work with clients is ensuring that, within the limits of agency and societal mandates and client capabilities, they have the opportunity to make free choices. Social workers may generate and explore options, opportunities, and constraints and their potential consequences with clients, but they cannot select a course of action for clients or take responsibility for it.

Often one of the goals of intervention is to help clients make choices for themselves. A free exchange between client and social worker on courses of action, their potential consequences, and how to select among them can be of great benefit because the client may realize new options and strategies that he or she had not considered before. This can be both empowering and motivating.

However, self-determination in any organized society has many constraints. For example, there are considerable limits on the rights of children to make free choices. People who are incarcerated or in mental hospitals have many of life's "normal" decisions made for them by people in authority, including social workers. Frequently, social workers in child welfare settings often severely limit the choices of parents who neglect or abuse their children. (See Chapter 5 for examples.)

People can make choices only when they perceive that they have a range of options to select from. When clients and social workers meet, there is often an exchange of ideas and information that may influence the client's decision making. As a result of this process, client autonomy may be reduced, especially when the social worker is seen as an authority. The client may have very little interest in establishing or maintaining a relationship with the social worker, yet it may be in the client's best interest to do so.

The concept of self-determination reflects *individual agency,* where a person makes autonomous decisions and takes action according to personal wishes and motivations. For some people, collective needs and wishes are more important than an individual's. This may be the case in many ethnocultural communities, where family aspirations or collective goals are considered more important than those of an individual. For example, in some cultures, families rely on the earnings of older daughters or sons to pay for the school fees of younger children or the purchase of a new home for the whole family. In such cases, individual autonomy of the son or daughter is sacrificed for the common good. Self-determination might be viewed primarily as a Western notion, one that may not be relevant for some people or in some situations. We need to understand whether it is an important value of a client and, if not, be open to different perspectives. Thus, personal and cultural values can affect self-determination.

Case Example

Kim and Ann ▼

Ann felt strongly that she had a right to determine her own course of actions and that no one should interfere with decisions that she makes in her life. Thus, the decision to apprehend Ann's children made Ann angry. She was unable to be self-determining. However, Ann can work with Kim so she can determine for herself how she will plan for the return of her children. Likely there are some choices that Ann can make in the services she will make use of, when she will use them, and what other resources she requests from Kim. Although Ann is unable to be completely self-determining in this situation, there is some leeway for her to make decisions for herself. Kim knows this is important to Ann, and points out choices that Ann has, explaining that she will help facilitate Ann's own decision making as much as is possible given her child protection mandate.

Confidentiality

Confidentiality in social work relationships is a central concern due to the often sensitive personal information clients provide. The client's right to confidentiality and privacy is very important and social workers, like all helping professionals, must make every effort to protect it. The Canadian Association of Social Workers *Code of Ethics* holds that all information provided by the client or others during the helping process must be, within limits, kept confidential (see discussion later in this chapter). Provincial laws (e.g., the Manitoba *Freedom of Information and Protection of Privacy Act*) also regulate access to personal information and the protection of private information by public bodies (Government of Manitoba, 2003). These generally affect all social work agencies.

Some of these provincial laws set stringent requirements in health and human service organizations that govern to whom professionals can release information about clients. They tend to be more specific—and sometimes in the fields of health and mental health, even more rigorous—than those in the CASW *Code of Ethics*. All social workers need to be acutely aware of the provincial legislation that governs their practice. Also, in some jurisdictions and some fields, such as health care, clients have a legal right to see all or a portion of their files.

Social work deals with intimate details and private difficulties that people do not want revealed to others: social workers hold this information in trust. However, information can be shared if the client gives permission to do so in writing or if statute or a court so authorizes (CASW, 2005a, p. 7). For example, if a referral for mental health services is to be made, or if advocacy on behalf of a client is needed for housing or residential care, it is important to discuss with clients and receive their permission as to what will be shared and why. When the client is unable to act on her or his own behalf, social workers can talk to designated trustees or guardians. Most often, clients agree to information being shared with others who need it or when this is in their best interest. In some organizations and in some cases, signed consent forms are used to permit social workers to discuss clients' situations with others. It is also possible that consent to share client information need only be verbal in some circumstances. ***Organizational policy*** and legislation will determine the practice in most social work settings.

Limits to Confidentiality

There are important limits to clients' rights to confidentiality. In a number of circumstances, courts can and do subpoena records of workers even if the social worker has promised the client that all information will be kept confidential. If abuse of a child or other vulnerable person is reported, most jurisdictions have legislation that requires professional helpers to share the information with proper authorities. In such situations and in a client–social worker relationship, client self-determination and confidentiality are superseded.

Importantly, social workers need to discuss the limits to confidentiality with their clients when they begin their relationship and agree to work together. (This is also the case in social work research.) For example, a worker in a family service agency may help partners in a marriage resolve relationship difficulties. Even if there is no history or indication of child abuse, the worker is obligated to set the limits of confidentiality. Many agencies have protocols that specify how to do this. It should include informing the couple that if they make mention that abuse of a child is occurring, then the worker is required to take certain steps that usually involve reporting to proper authorities. The worker should describe limits to confidentiality honestly, as a matter of fact, in a manner that is clearly understood by clients, and as part of the relationship-building process. Such discussion helps define the relationship between worker and client and helps establishes its boundaries. This discussion seldom harms the helping relationship, and often enhances it because it promotes honesty and transparency.

In general, when the social worker has cause for concern about a client's or another person's safety, the worker has a moral, ethical, and often legal duty to act. For example, if a client tells a social worker about an active suicide plan, requesting that this be kept confidential, the worker is obligated to try to prevent the suicide by mobilizing emergency, and, within the boundaries of the client's legal right to privacy, supportive assistance and other resources, and following up during and after the crisis (Golightley, 2006; Parker and Bradley, 2007; Sheafor and Horejsi, 2008). Client confidentiality in this case is not the primary concern.

There is another exception to confidentiality that must be shared with clients. Most social workers are employed in agencies and have colleagues and supervisors. Often other professionals are also part of the organization, such as in hospitals. All agencies should have policies regarding who has access to confidential information. Usually this right is extended at least to colleagues and members of the professional team. At the beginning of the relationship, the social worker needs to tell clients who within the agency or organization has access to client information. It is also a good idea to know and communicate to clients whether and how they can view material about them in the records kept by the agency or organization.

Case Example

Kim and Ann ▼

In any child protection case, there are standards of confidentiality and rules that govern when confidentiality can be breached for the protection of children or others. Kim was careful about speaking to others about Ann's situation, but she knew that she was mandated by the court to provide an assessment that would include privileged information about, for example, Ann's economic situation, behaviour, and psychological functioning. To protect Ann, she would not reveal any of this information to her colleagues or other persons unless she had permission from Ann and it was necessary for service provision.

▲

Power, Authority, and Control

Social work is not a profession associated with the same degree of power or authority as, for example, medicine or law. Nevertheless, social workers do exercise authority in direct practice situations. In fact, sometimes they find themselves dealing with "grey areas" in which they need to make judgments and determine actions autonomously (e.g., in child protection). This authority may be seen as a threat by clients in cases where the actions taken by a social worker determine access to their children or the return of a probationer to prison. The control function (covered in more detail later in this chapter) of social work should, however, be carried out in an appropriate and respectful manner. Although we may have strong feelings about the best way to resolve a problem, we need to refrain from controlling a client's situation ourselves. "The special trust they [our clients] often feel for us, along with our access to agency and community resources and our professional knowledge and expertise, leave us in a potentially controlling position" (Compton, Galaway, and Cournoyer, 2005, p. 329). One could say that social work is a profession with some inherent contradictions.

Fields of practice in which social workers are sanctioned to provide services—for example, to people who have abused their children—call for the appropriate use of power and authority. The state gives social workers the right to use their mandate to protect children at risk and to prevent potential or continued abuse (see Chapter 5). It is critical to acknowledge to ourselves and to our clients what kind of authority we have and how it is to be used. As Compton, Galaway, and Cournoyer (2005) point out, "Our own feelings about authority, may complicate matters. However, social workers must be able to deal comfortably with both our own and others' exercise of authority" (p. 153). This is not easy, since social workers often experience conflicts that inhibit their use of authority, as they may feel that using their authority will adversely affect the social worker–client relationship. We understand the importance of empathy, respect, and concern for clients, recognizing that often people's issues or problems are not completely of their own making but reflect structural inequalities in society based on class, gender, ethnoculture, age, sexual orientation, or disability (Carniol, 2005; Mullaly, 2007). At the same time, our mandates in many fields of practice (e.g., probation services or the criminal justice system, child protection, and sometimes health care) guide us to use the authority and sanction of the state in our work with clients (Bala, 2004; Fusco, 1999, p. 53). The control aspect of social work is especially evident in relationships with involuntary clients, creating a source of conflict for both parties when clients don't want to receive services from the social worker, for reasons that may make sense from their perspective. Most people feel intruded upon in circumstances where they are required to tolerate the scrutiny of the state or its agents.

The issues of authority and power between an involuntary client and a social worker need particular attention and thus must be addressed honestly and openly. Although building a relationship with clients in such situations may be difficult, it is best to be frank and clear about the purpose of social work involvement and communicate in a way that is respectful and understanding of the client's reluctance to engage with the social worker. In all social work relationships, whether or not the client wants the services of the social worker and whether or not the social worker likes the client, the Canadian Association of Social Workers *Code of Ethics* must guide the practice relationship.

Case Example

Kim and Ann ▼

Kim knows that her role is mandated and she has the potential for considerable control in Ann's life. Ann, of course, is worried about this and upset that the Child Protection Agency, represented by Kim, has taken her children into its care and that the court will determine what will happen. Kim has carefully explained to her the rationale for the CPA's action, the role of the court, and of Kim herself. Kim has also told her that she must complete the assessment for the court, but would also work with Ann to develop a plan to re-gain control over her life and family situation. Although Kim knows what she would do if she was in Ann's shoes, she cannot direct Ann's decisions. However, she can give Ann information, offer resources that might be helpful, and discuss the consequences of any actions being considered. Ann appreciates Kim helping her to look at different options and consequences, but leaving decisions for Ann to make.

Purpose and Commitment

A relationship between a client and a social worker requires purpose and commitment from both to sustain it. However, the social worker must take the lead because it is his or her mandate to provide help. Thus, there is a purpose or intention for initiating the social worker–client relationship. Commitment in a relationship occurs when there is agreement that working together for a specific purpose and goal is possible and desirable. Often the initial contact, whether on the phone or in person, begins a tentative relationship. A longer-term relationship can then be explored. At this early stage, there is no agreement to continue working together. This is so even when clients have been ordered by a judge to accept social work services. A decision by an involuntary client to reject social work services may invoke intrusions into the client's life (e.g., court proceedings, criminal charges, or other actions). Although difficult, it is possible to build commitment in such a relationship, but much depends on the success of discussion, conflict management, and negotiation.

The assessment stage of the client–social worker relationship includes the early, exploratory work that precedes any agreement to work together. It is at this point that a client decides whether she or he will accept the help of the social worker or agency. The client may choose not to pursue the relationship if, for example, she perceives that the kinds of services available are inappropriate for her; the waiting period for help is too long; the organization's mandate, principles, or service delivery is unacceptable; the distance is too far; or some other reason. Likewise, a social worker and agency might determine that they cannot offer services for some reason (e.g., they have no one with the required knowledge).

If, however, the client and social worker establish that they will work together, a relationship can be developed. The social worker commits to helping the client, bringing to the relationship concern, commitment and obligation, acceptance, empathy, and any power and authority that is accorded to her or him by this position (Compton, Galaway, and Cournoyer, 2005, pp. 147–53). Commitment involves concern for and acceptance of the client's uniqueness and humanness within a process of helping. Social workers need to tell clients of their obligations to them as required by the profession and agency. Their actions must reflect these obligations and responsibilities.

Case Example

Kim and Ann ▼

The purpose of Kim's work with Ann was to prepare and produce an assessment for the court so that a decision could be made about what would happen to Ann's children, who had been apprehended by the CPA. Kim had a commitment to the court and to the CPA for completing this work so that Ann's children could be safe and protected. At the same time, Kim made a commitment to Ann to work with her to determine what she wanted to do and what she needed to carry out the plan. In this case, Ann wanted to have her children returned to her so that their family could be together. Purpose and commitment shape Kim's relationship with Ann. Should Ann refuse to participate in a relationship and refuse to meet with Kim, the purpose of Kim's work with Ann may be different.

▲

Context and Structure

Social work practice occurs within a context, usually a social agency, characterized by organizational policies, values, regulations, and practices. An agency context gives structure to some aspects of the relationship, such as how, where, and when meetings occur, what resources are available for use, and which other professionals work with the social worker and the client. The context also limits what social workers can do and the kinds of help clients can receive from the social worker and agency.

Sometimes the structure of such a relationship becomes clearer to clients after an initial meeting with a social worker. Such information is important, as it can reduce anxiety in clients. Expectations as well as limitations due to the agency context and structure and that shape the social worker–client relationship should be discussed with the client. This might include topics such as the rights of clients, the mandate, approaches, and practices in the agency, who has which responsibilities, and how the client and social worker will work together.

Case Example

Kim and Ann ▽

The context and structure of the CPA shaped Kim's mandate and purpose. The agency's policies, practices, and procedures, as well as the roles of its workers, formed a backdrop to Kim's work with Ann and the limits of their social worker–client relationship. Kim needed to let Ann know how the context and structure of the CPA would determine aspects of their work together.

Other Perspectives on Relationships

The qualities that a social worker needs to bring to client relationships are the same in Aboriginal, feminist, and structural approaches (see Chapters 12 to 14). However, the nature of the relationship may differ from more conventional approaches, since acknowledging that subordination, oppression, and exploitation shape human experience gives rise to other dynamics in relationship building (Bishop, 2002). Acknowledging and using one's authority and power in the social work relationship, as discussed by Compton, Galaway, and Cournoyer (2005), may conflict with some of the values and principles in Aboriginal, structural, and feminist approaches. This is so, for example, in approaches that aim to reduce power differences between clients and social workers. Such a situation may occur when a feminist social worker discloses to a client that she has had similar experiences as her client. She shares this information with her client in a conscious effort to find common ground and better understanding. The social worker strives to become an ally or partner of the client in order to foster a collective consciousness with those who experience oppression. In feminist social work, sharing and validating a woman's experiences, in which sexism and gender inequality may have shaped those experiences and access to resources, are important. Although power differences between female clients and their social workers exist, feminist social workers attempt to reduce them (see Chapter 13).

RELATIONSHIPS WITH INVOLUNTARY CLIENTS

Relationships with involuntary clients merit specific attention. Earlier in this chapter we defined involuntary clients, and we talked about the use of authority and power as a control function of social work. Chapter 8 will describe how the principle of best interest, widely accepted by social workers, provides a rationale for working with involuntary clients.

People sometimes become involuntary clients through court mandates in fields such as corrections and child protection, and are required to accept social services. Some are involuntary clients because they are hospitalized, often in mental hospitals or in residential facilities, and targeted for social work intervention. Some involuntary clients shun any effort to develop a relationship with the social worker. Probably most, as well as being fearful and angry, are reticent, want to avoid contact, and may be resistant. Yet they still leave room for the worker to attempt to negotiate a helping relationship. In other words, there are varying degrees to which clients are involuntary.

Particularly in fields like forensic psychiatry and corrections, a major responsibility of the social worker is to the public. The public, as represented by the judicial system, is really the primary client in a sense. The service that the social worker provides is usually to both protect the public at large and to help rehabilitate persons charged with criminal offences. Nevertheless, social workers have the responsibility to provide services to offenders and to consider them clients, albeit usually involuntary ones.

Helping in social work is presumed to depend on a working relationship between the worker and the client. The first sections of this chapter have shown that all of the essential helping tools that social workers have at their disposal require meaningful communication between worker and client. The nature and quality of the relationship and the communication contained within it will determine the success or failure of the helping attempt. Social work helping depends on the nature of communication with clients.

We have also shown that, to develop this helping relationship, social work practitioners must form partnerships with clients who seek help. All of the approaches used in this book tend to make the assumption that the client is seeking or willing to accept help. This includes the problem-solving, strengths, Aboriginal, and feminist approaches.

Still, developing helping relationships with unwilling clients who do not want our help is not an easy task.

Assessing Involuntary Clients

While assessment frameworks such as those presented in Chapter 9 and other chapters in this book are applicable, there are other approaches to assessing involuntary clients. The social worker needs to see the involuntary client through a different set of lenses, to understand that he or she has probably experienced many difficult, stressful, and possibly even traumatic problems in life. There are important reasons for the client having these problems. The client has probably been a victim in the past, even though others may currently see him or her as deviant. The client may have committed serious crimes or may be a danger to others. While using the lens of assessment to understand the client, one does not make excuses for behaviour but seeks to set the stage for a helping process. It may be very challenging, for example, when a social worker experiences strong feelings of dislike for a client who has seriously injured a young child or killed someone. In such situations, it can help to consult a colleague or supervisor for help. It may also be useful to regard the client as someone who, rather than being a victim, has survived adversity in life.

Assessment *must* include both how others see the client and how the client sees herself or himself. For example, a criminal justice worker who is assigned to work with a man who has a long record of violent crime must understand how others view him. These others include a wide range of people, including those close to the man, those responsible for the legal system, and perhaps even his victims. But the worker must also attempt to understand the man's point of view and his story. The same principle applies to working with a young woman who has recently had an episode of schizophrenia, threatened close family members, and been forced into hospital. The worker needs to understand the implications of the views of the mental health staff (including diagnosis and prognosis), the woman's family, and other relevant systems. But, primarily, the worker needs to understand the client from her own viewpoint.

Why are people who experience personal and social problems often unwilling to seek help? There are many possible answers. Some people may feel that their problems are surmountable given time or luck. Most pride themselves on their independence. They like to be able to handle their own emotional, social, and financial affairs and to meet their own basic needs. If they are unable to do so, they often view this as a failure, as may their friends and family. To ask for help is not only an embarrassment but also an acknowledgment of failure, and may open the door for stigma. There may also be anger or resentment with authority figures who attempt to control the person's behaviour or limit his or her choices in life.

Many clients of social workers in the justice and child welfare systems particularly have had numerous previous encounters with those referred to as "helpers." Often these encounters have had negative consequences. Think of the impact of the abuse that many Aboriginal people experienced in residential schools. Few teachers and religious leaders served as role models and earned the trust of the students, and some of them abused their students (Milloy, 1999). Certainly, this experience would lead to mistrust of those people who purport to help.

Think of the fear that a small Aboriginal community would have of child welfare workers when it was common (as it was in the 1950s and 1960s) for them to apprehend children and place them in non-Aboriginal foster homes in Canada or the United States. Often members of the community did not understand the reasons for the children being sent away, let alone the need for placement in a different cultural environment. The deep grief, pain, and anger felt by parents and communities can only be imagined.

Or think of the embarrassment that some people feel when they wait in line to receive groceries from a food bank. They may also worry about running out of food before they are eligible for more and how to manage until then (Bidgood et al., 2005). Their circumstances may have little to do with any failing of their own, but could be the result of unemployment, racism, or other structural issues in society.

There are many more possible examples. However, most of them have at least two common threads. First, people have often had negative experiences with a system that was supposed to provide them with a service and earn their trust. Second, all of these people have been defined as deviant.

Social Labelling

Understanding the labelling process is important in working with involuntary clients. The concept of labelling helps us understand how the perceptions of others and their actions toward a client affect him or her. It also helps us understand why some people have been defined as deviant, and ultimately why some clients are unwilling to accept help from social workers.

Most clients who are involuntary may also be viewed as deviant. Likely they have broken a social rule, and possibly the law. Many social rules or norms are not codified in law. Often rules set by families and other primary social groups are more important than cultural or legislated rules. Deviance is a category of behaviour that does not conform to normative expectations and toward which others take negative sanctions. These negative sanctions often take the form of stigma, ostracism, punishment, and other means of social control.

Deviance covers a wide range of behaviours. Probably all who enter the criminal justice system are seen as deviant by society, even if they are only charged with or merely suspected of a crime. Parents who have a child removed from them may be seen as deviant. The behaviour of a person who is psychotic and threatens others or seems "mad" will be seen by others as a rule breaker and hence deviant, even if the psychosis has clearly been defined as an illness. It is not necessary for this person to break the law—she or he has broken a commonly held social code that prescribes "normal" behaviours (Becker, 1963; Kitsuse, 1962; Lemert, 1951; Schur, 1971; Suchar, 1978, pp. 165–242). Golightley (2006) describes models of mental illness that define different ways of treating persons with such illnesses.

Labelling theory holds that the label or tag by itself is of relatively little consequence. Such a tag, a name for a deviant activity, is sometimes called the *primary deviance.* Critically important is how others react to the tag and how this reaction affects the person who is labelled. Social labelling is the process of defining someone as deviant and condemning that person for a behaviour or trait that she or he has or expresses.

A gay man who has just found the courage to "come out" to his coworkers after five years of working with them may be seen as deviant by some at his workplace. They avoid him because they are unsure how to relate to him now. They may be homophobic and fear that they too might be seen as gay by association, so they do not join him for coffee or lunch any longer. (Others, however, might be encouraged by his openness, sharing their own identity issues or providing him with the validation and support he needs at this time.) This example illustrates differences between primary deviance and subsequent labelling. The primary deviance, according to labelling theory, is the man's homosexuality. Labelling theory holds that there would be no consequences in being defined as homosexual if others did not label his behaviour as deviant.

However, the man's family may be embarrassed and possibly ashamed of him. Former friends might not want to continue to associate with him. Fellow employees may shun him. He may be passed over for promotions at work, or his job may even be in jeopardy. If such reactions occur, then the man has been labelled. According to labelling theory, these are the factors that are important. The labelling process has defined the man as deviant, and he must now contend with this as part of his life.

The labelling process can have devastating effects, causing severe stress, guilt, defensiveness, fear, anxiety, and a host of other emotional and social problems. If the response to the labelling is further deviance, this response is called *secondary deviance* (Golightley, 2006; Lemert, 1951; Rooney, 1992, pp. 121–24; Schur, 1971; Suchar, 1978, pp. 165–242).

Labelling theory can help us work with involuntary clients. Most involuntary clients (and many voluntary clients) have experienced labelling. If the labelling was perpetrated by professional helpers, as frequently happens, this often helps to explain some of the problematic behaviours of clients and why clients do not want help. Assessment must include a clear understanding of the social labelling process (not just the tag) and a clear understanding of how it affects clients. This understanding may provide clues on how to engage involuntary clients in a helping relationship. An acknowledgement from the social worker that she or he understands how the labelling happened and its effects may be a starting point, helping to validate the client's past experiences. A social worker trying to develop a relationship with a client who has been labelled needs to acknowledge the effects of such labelling for the person, including the impact on his or her current situation.

Case Example

Tom ▼

Tom is an 18-year-old Aboriginal boy who moved to the city from a reserve at age 7. When he first enrolled in school he was behind the other students in his grade. Teachers quickly labelled him "slow." Other students taunted him because he was different, and he was often the butt of teasing that had racial overtones. Tom's teachers and fellow students defined him as deviant. At that young age, he began to believe that he was not as good as or equal to the other children.

By age 9, Tom had begun his delinquent career. At first it was petty shoplifting. Then he began to sniff solvents. His parents, who were both unemployed, were having difficulty controlling him. At age 10, Tom was placed by the courts in the first of four foster homes. The first home was very strict. The people there had no understanding or appreciation of Tom's Aboriginal heritage. Like his teachers, they considered Tom incapable of keeping up with others in school. His social worker visited only when there was a crisis and, in Tom's eyes, was cold and uncaring. The school considered him a troublemaker, and he was expelled twice. After nine months, Tom ran away and was placed in yet another foster home. Four years later, the police arrested him after he was caught shoplifting. They took him to a group home for delinquent boys.

The negative experiences in foster homes were repeated three times. Tom's teachers and social workers continued to believe that he had little potential. As the years passed, the severity of his delinquency increased. Tom, now 18, has been convicted of armed robbery and trafficking in heroin.

You have been assigned by the courts to complete a pre-sentence report. As you interview Tom, you discover that he has little use for professionals, particularly teachers and social workers. You find that he is not only a mandated involuntary client but a resistant one as well.

In the case example, Tom has been labelled almost all of his life—at least since he moved to the city. The psychological and social consequences of labelling are huge. This may be particularly so because those who were supposed to help him—teachers, foster parents, and social workers—either actively dehumanized him or displayed an uncaring attitude. The system had failed him. Understanding the dynamics of this process of labelling often helps explain the difficulties in working with involuntary clients. Tom has learned not to trust others. There is good reason for him not to want to seek help. Why should Tom seek help from professionals who dehumanize him?

This process is not uncommon. Aboriginal people often experience labelling because they are Aboriginal. When they encounter the social service system, like Tom, why should they trust it? Their experience may tell them not to do so. Likewise, people living in poverty who have been dehumanized by their plight may have difficulty trusting those who wish to help. Labelling can occur as the result of many social processes, including intolerance, racism, and prejudice.

It is best to avoid communication or action that labels. While avoiding labelling completely is probably impossible, its effects can be mitigated. For instance, it is possible to separate condemning certain behaviour from condemning the person. If the goal is to establish a helping relationship, it is all right to appropriately condemn a behaviour, but it is not all right to condemn a person. Think of how such condemnation has affected Tom throughout the course of his young life. How can we begin to establish a relationship with him that is built on respect and trust?

To further illustrate, assume a young woman has been given a diagnosis of schizophrenia. When her illness is active, she is paranoid and sometimes threatening and potentially abusive. Also, assume that your goal is to begin to engage her, an unwilling client, in a helping relationship. There is a subtle but big difference between defining her as a schizophrenic and seeing her as a person who has schizophrenia. The former implies that schizophrenia is the person and the person is deviant because of the paranoid and threatening behaviour. The second limits schizophrenia to a disease and implies that it is only part of the person. This attitude accepts that the person has dignity but suffers from a significant disease. If the disease leads to irrational behaviour, such as threatening actions, you can show that the behaviour is unacceptable and will certainly affect how others relate to the woman.

It is important to help clients deal with labels. For example, a social worker might offer to speak for a client who is fearful of seeking employment because she has been convicted of a crime. A social worker might also intervene directly with those who label—for example, by helping a teacher understand that a student is not unintelligent but has a learning disability that gives him trouble in school. He needs specialized help to adapt, and his family has not been able to afford this. Offering to help clients who have been labelled can open the door to a stronger helping relationship.

Reaching Out

Most social workers recognize that attempts to help a hostile client will not succeed unless the worker and client agree that a problem needs to be solved. On occasion, a client needs to be convinced that there is a problem. While the client may reject help, often the worker needs to continue trying to establish a helping relationship. This process is sometimes called *reaching out* and is often a major part of work with involuntary clients. Reaching out requires an effort by the social worker to connect or engage with the client. This might involve expressing that you understand that it is difficult to be in his or her situation and that you want to listen to what he or she has to say (See Shulman, 2006, for illustrations of contracting with clients who resist the social services. Also see Chapter 4 and 5 in this textbook.)

Decision Making, Assessment, and Best Interest

Most social workers who work with involuntary clients make decisions that affect clients' lives. However, unlike working with voluntary clients, these decisions are generally made *for* the client rather than *with* the client (see, for example, Golightley, 2006). Consider the decision of a social worker to support a family's attempt to force a member who suffers from bipolar disorder to be hospitalized. Think about the approach of a child welfare worker working with a mother who has apparently abandoned her child, requiring that the worker seek temporary custody of the child. Another example is a parole officer who reports that his client has broken the rules of parole.

In one sense, the assessment process for involuntary clients (see Chapters 8 and 9) is the same as for voluntary clients. However, assessment with an involuntary client is often not a dialogue between social worker and client. Instead, it is usually more like detective work, in which the worker tries to deal with conflict, establish what is wrong, determine the client's problems, and develop a treatment plan. Assessments of involuntary clients can involve completing official assessment forms for agencies or individuals with authority, such as court officials, the medical staff of a hospital, a child welfare agency, or a parole board. Often these documents not only assess the client but also include recommendations for action. The purpose of such assessments is to help the proper authorities, often courts, to make treatment or other judicial decisions, such as sentence length. In providing the information, the social worker is acting in the best interest of the clients, who are often both an individual and the public.

Case ¦ Example

Ravi and Maria ▼

Maria had left her children at home alone while she visited friends, and the local child protection service agency apprehended her children. Maria is very hostile to Ravi, the child protection worker assigned to her case. Ravi realizes that, despite Maria's hostility and rejection of his help, he may need to make decisions that could have a profound effect on her family's life. Ravi also understands that he is acting in the best interests of both Maria and the children, but that his highest priority is ensuring the safety and well-being of the children.

Ultimately, Ravi believes Maria will get her children back, so it is very important that he think in the long term. Ravi hopes that eventually he can establish a helping relationship with Maria. His current challenge is to begin to reach out to Maria.

As suggested above, working with clients who do not want services often requires the social worker to make decisions that affect the client's life but without the client's consent. Of course, these decisions must be made within the boundaries of the worker's and agency's mandate. The worker should be clear about the decisions and not withhold information from the client. Further, the worker needs to carefully explain the reasons for the decisions, the exact nature and content of the decisions, and the likely effects of the decisions on all those involved. The social worker must make a considerable effort to keep the decision making transparent and open, with no hint of deception or dishonesty. By keeping everything above board, showing how the social worker is acting in the best interest of a variety of stakeholders, the worker sets the stage for the later formation of a helping relationship with the client. The social worker must make known that she or he is available to the client if the client so wishes. This fact needs to be outlined clearly and regularly in order to open the door to future contact.

Negotiation and Contracting

Suppose, in our case example, that Ravi has clearly told Maria that he is going to petition the court for temporary custody of her children. Ravi has discovered that Maria has a history of abandoning her children. He is honest with her and lets her know that custody will be reviewed in 90 days, but that it is unlikely that the children could be returned to her then. Ravi emphasizes, however, that he is available to help Maria. After the end of the first month, he receives a phone call from Maria, asking to meet with him. Ravi sees this meeting as a possible opening for forming a helping relationship. His ideal goal is to form a contract (see Chapter 8) that outlines a plan and method to help Maria decide the best course of action, which probably, but not necessarily, includes return of the children.

Ravi may use this opening to begin negotiations with Maria. Unlike most voluntary relationships, engaging with involuntary clients usually requires substantial negotiation. Since Maria suggested the meeting, a good place for Ravi to begin might be to invoke the old social work adage "Start where the client is."

Case Example

Ravi and Maria ▼

Ravi meets Maria at her home. This is Maria's own environment, where she likely feels most comfortable and in control. Ravi lets Maria explain what she

Continued

wants and tries to clearly understand her point of view before reacting. As Maria talks, it becomes clear that she wants her children back immediately. She also says she is willing to attend a parenting group and accept counselling for herself. Once clear about Maria's position, Ravi makes explicit the non-negotiable items. For instance, Maria has to show progress before a decision to return her children can be made, and there is no chance of their return before the review date. However, within these confines Ravi is willing to help Maria enroll in the parenting group and seek counselling in addition to helping her develop a plan to get her children back. Maria still does not trust Ravi, the person who in her mind has taken her children from her. But she does ask him to help her get started with the parenting group and counselling.

In the case example of Ravi and Maria, the two negotiate a starting point—a limited contract. Neither Ravi nor Maria get what they want. Ravi is unable to develop a plan, and Maria does not get the immediate return of her children. But they do have agreement on a starting point. Most helping relationships formed with involuntary clients involve considerable negotiation, and most are much more complicated than our example. (See Shulman, 2006, pp. 329–34, for a description of working with an involuntary group as client for further discussion of negotiation and contracting in involuntary relationships.)

Ending Relationships

Endings in professional relationships between social workers and clients must also be considered. A professional relationship ends for many reasons. However, the ending process should be discussed during the process of helping and should not occur suddenly without planning. Of course, the client may end the relationship unexpectedly for some reason. In some cases the end of the relationship (sometimes referred to as *termination*) occurs because the goals set out for work together have been realized, for example, in the case of children being returned to a family in which they had experienced past neglect. Perhaps the parents participated in agreed-upon treatment groups or prepared themselves to care for their children better. In a study of voluntary clients by Roe et al. (2006), it was found clients terminated treatment because they had accomplished their goals, individual circumstances made it difficult to continue, or they were dissatisfied with the therapy. They also found that if clients became involved in new relationships and had other purposeful goals, they terminated therapy.

Involuntary Relationships and Social Supports

In mandated practice, clients often feel a lack of power and autonomy because they are not in charge of important parts of their lives. The social worker is usually in a clear position of power and control over the client. Instead of the relationship being a supportive one, it is controlling. However,

> All too often, individuals in the mental health, child protective and criminal justice services became involuntary clients, in part, because they did not have enough sources of social support. In other instances, these individuals had used up these supports by asking for too much help too many times, or by disappointing these sources of support. Without these supports, they were not able to hold things together and committed actions that brought them into one of these systems as involuntary clients. (Ivanoff, Blythe, and Tripodi, 1994, p. 92)

Often involuntary clients can benefit from engagement with enhanced formal and informal social supports. These may have been severed due to difficult circumstances or problems in the clients' lives. Networks of support might include self-help groups, community projects, volunteer work involvement, friends, and professionals.

Several studies about the contribution of case management (*Harvard Mental Health Letter*, 2006; Hangan, 2006; Shera, 2002) in recovery from mental illness found that community and effective case management support were important factors in clients' capacity to be more independent and to experience improved well-being. While medication is necessary for many clients of mental health services, providing professional support is very important in initiating recovery.

Social workers need to be innovative in building supports, even if clients are resistant. While they may reject efforts at support, resistant clients often appreciate them. In addition, support building may depend upon the ingenuity and resourcefulness of the worker. Support of client strengths and goals by social workers can have important benefits for involuntary clients.

We have attempted to outline some principles designed to engage mandated and unwilling involuntary clients. This is in reality a very complicated and, to some extent, controversial process. Further, exact processes are different depending on the field of practice. For example, forming relationships with someone who has a psychosis and displays paranoid thinking is very different from engaging with an angry man who has abused his spouse. A major part of our thesis is that good social work practice must account for work with both voluntary and involuntary clients. The strategies and methods discussed above can help in the development of a social worker–client relationship, but the skill, compassion, and commitment of a social worker in beginning, establishing, and maintaining a relationship with a client, even when doing so is very difficult, is of critical importance in any field of practice.

CHAPTER SUMMARY

Social workers must work with both voluntary and involuntary clients. Involuntary clients may be mandated, unwilling, or both. While all client–social worker relationships are important, the nature of professional relationships with voluntary and involuntary clients is different.

The features that are most important in forming relationships with clients are care and concern; empathy and honesty; acceptance of people; acknowledging client capacity for change; self-determination and autonomy; confidentiality; power, authority, and control;

purpose and commitment; and context and structure. Considering the situation of the client by hearing his or her own story from his or her own perspective is useful in understanding better the client's situation and in building a relationship for working together.

There are challenges in working with different kinds of people in diverse problem situations; social workers need to understand how social labelling can create feelings of shame, reduced self-esteem, and anger in people. Social workers' professional experience, knowledge, and commitment will help them in using the problem-solving process and other social work *practice approaches* for work with voluntary and involuntary clients.

chapter

7

Cultural Diversity, Cultural Awareness, and Social Work Practice

Chapter Goal ▼

To understand how culture provides a lens for social work practice and to learn how culturally aware and anti-oppressive practice enriches social work.

This Chapter ▼

- examines the meaning of culture, ethnicity, race, and racism
- describes anti-oppressive and antiracist social work in relation to immigrants, refugees, and visible minorities
- discusses etic and emic stances and ethnocultural competence in social work
- applies the above concepts to case situations and explores the implications for social work practice at micro, mezzo, and macro levels

INTRODUCTION

This chapter uses the lens of culture in relation to values, assumptions, orientation, and actions of social workers in their work at various levels. It also examines the meaning of concepts that are used in social work; those that often are not clear until applied to practice situations. For this reason, we introduce a number of case situations to illustrate their application. This chapter does not describe ethnocultural (pertaining to an ethnic group) demographics in Canada or laws and policies regarding immigration, multiculturalism, or settlement, as these are covered in other works (Driedger, 1996, 2003, 2008; Fleras and Elliott, 2006; Guo and Andersson, 2006; Halli and Driedger, 1999; James and Shadd, 2001; Li, 1999, 2003a, 2003b).

In the first part of this chapter, we define and discuss concepts such as culture, ethnicity, race, racism, and antiracist and anti-oppressive social work, among others, in order to explore how they influence people's lives. We also discuss their significance in social work practice with individuals, families, groups, and communities, primarily but not solely in relation to immigrants, refugees, visible minorities, and people from diverse cultural backgrounds. We acknowledge that many others in these groups also experience oppression due to disability, age, sexual orientation, or poverty.

CULTURE, ETHNICITY, AND RACE

North Americans are either Aboriginal peoples, immigrants, or descendants of immigrants. In the early 1900s, settlement house workers at St. Christopher's House and other settlements in Toronto headed by clergy and academics had a dual purpose—to Christianize and to assimilate newcomers (Irving, Parsons, and Bellamy, 1995; O'Connor, 1986, p. 6). Their work aimed not only to educate the poor but also to help them in accepting the dominant morality and culture. These activities reflected the social policy of the era. Settlement house workers later noted, however, that most newcomers maintained an affiliation with and followed the cultural practices of their countries of origin. We now recognize that original culture and cultural practices are important to many immigrants and often provide a source of strength and grounding in families and communities. Some cultural practices can be harmful and may conflict with laws or practices in Canada. One example is the practice of female circumcision, which can have serious health consequences for girls and women.

AWARENESS OF ETHNOCULTURE AND IDENTITY

Clearly understanding your own cultural background, whether or not you are a first-generation immigrant, can help you to empathize with and recognize the considerable and different challenges faced by newcomers, whether they are people who have come here through planned immigration or for refuge from a situation of persecution, war, or conflict.

For all social workers, self-awareness about identity and background is important, as this is part of who we are and shapes our relations with others. It may be that you view your own background or identity as significant in your life experience or of limited significance for you, perhaps because it is taken for granted. As helpers, we often work with members of cultures that differ from our own. In order to fully understand people from another culture, we need clarity about our own backgrounds. This is necessary so that we can appreciate and understand similarities and differences between ourselves and clients and how we mutually react to each other's cultures.

Consider some of the ways in which cultural heritage has been significant—or not—in your life and what importance it has for you now. It may even have some relevance in your decision to study social work. It might be useful to draw a family tree or diagram that shows your own family and your family of origin and notes the ethnocultural roots of your parents (and/or foster parents), your grandparents, and yourself and other details that highlight the places, cultural contexts, and events that are a part of your ancestry and social history. For example, if one grandparent immigrated to Canada from France and married a person of Cree background, what events and circumstances do you think brought them together in life? What obstacles do you think they had to face and overcome? What legacy are you left with? Has this cultural background been a factor in shaping your values, identity, life goals, and personal relationships? If so, how? Even if you do not identify with any particular culture, you may have developed a "culture" within your family where rituals and traditions are unique and important to how you live. Over the course of your life, you may have had many experiences with people from cultural backgrounds different from yours. Think of one or two examples that are particularly memorable. What effects did these encounters have on you? What did you learn from them? What learning can be applied in your work with people or groups whose cultural background differs from yours?

Throughout this chapter, we will look at the benefits of social work that respects and responds to the diversity in clients and in all people.

CULTURE

Culture for a group of people includes a shared but not necessarily identical home country, region, customs, language, beliefs, traditions, and worldview, which are expressed in everyday life. Culture has an influence on people's values and behaviour. For example, think about how the culture of traditional Inuit hunters in Nunavut differs from that of a middle-class urban family in Vancouver or the subculture of homeless people living in Toronto's streets. (A *subculture* represents a distinct group that varies in certain ways from the broader cultural environment in which it is located.) Culture can be shared by people living in a particular region or by a specific community of people who are not necessarily living in the same geographic area, such as Filipino or Somali communities whose members have scattered in various countries and cities. It can also refer to a common bond or interest between people who may have no other ties (e.g., alternative film culture, gay culture, dog breeders' culture, etc.).

Culture is dynamic, changing over time and place. For example, if you think of the culture of early French-Canadian settlers who lived mainly as farmers in rural Quebec and compare it with the primarily urban French-Canadian cultural context of Quebec today, you can appreciate the degree of change over time. Moreover, the culture and cultural practices of the same French-Canadians, when they relocate to a city in British Columbia, are differently adapted and perhaps differently expressed. Of course, some aspects of cultural life are retained as people adapt to a new environment. A useful idea drawn from Morrissey (1997) is that "'Culture' is not an item of baggage but a continuous process of renegotiation grounded in specific times and places and affected by other social processes" (p. 102). The idea that one's culture is fluid and changing is supported by Dorothy Herberg, who wrote in 1993 about the transitions and benchmarks of immigrants who come to Canada, explaining that they are affected by the culture they left, the culture they enter, and the changes they go through as they settle and make a life in Canada (Herberg, 1993).

Culture partly consists of a social structure that includes values, beliefs, and expectations. It sets guidelines for what is acceptable behaviour and what is not. People tend to abide by these guidelines if they belong to and identify with a particular ethnocultural group. Culture can also offer a map for understanding what goes on around us and for interacting with others. Some years ago, Barnlund (1988) referred to culture as a "symbolic universe governed by codes that are unconsciously acquired and automatically employed. [We] rarely notice that the ways [we] interpret and talk about events are distinctly different from the ways people conduct their affairs in other cultures."

Culture is also about how people view their world. It is difficult to ever fully understand the culturally embedded beliefs and behaviours of others, at least not from the group's own standpoint. Each person views the world and experiences events from the perspective of her or his uniquely created individual lenses (McIntosh, 1989).

The word *culture* can also be used in reference to harmful aspects in our society. Evidence of this is seen in a shared culture of violence among organized crime groups, a culture of sexual exploitation on Internet pornography sites, or when members of one cultural group seek to harm those of another due to notions of superiority (e.g., ethnic cleansing). We need to be cautious about portraying culture only as a neutral or positive feature in a society.

To some, culture refers to those who are non–English speaking, perhaps immigrants or members of particular ethnocultural or racial groups. This is especially likely if you are of Western European descent and are at least second-generation Canadian. Importantly, the Canadians who have descended from European settlers do have their own cultures. So do North America's Aboriginal peoples—Inuit, Indian, and Métis—whose identity has been subjected to classification by state legislation and policy. Sometimes, you hear people say that they don't have any special culture; they're just Canadian. It is difficult to experience our culture as unique when it is so much a part of our everyday thinking and living. It is not easily seen because it surrounds us.

Some features in Canadian society might contribute to a broader national culture. We are exposed to the same national laws, attend schools that impart certain common ideas and values, and are integrated through events and processes in which we all share. James (2003) describes how in Canada, people from various racial and ethnic groups learn through a process of ***acculturation*** to participate in and adopt the dominant culture in which they live. Despite the shared form of culture in which all people living in a society participate—at least to some degree—there is considerable diversity in how culture is expressed in other areas of life.

ETHNICITY

The word *ethnic* is derived from a Greek word that can be translated as "people." It is often used to refer to immigrants, refugees, and foreigners in general, but everyone belongs to an ethnic group. An ethnic group shares a common heritage. It tends to be assumed that ethnic groups also share a common identity, experience, and origin, including aspects such as beliefs, language, and traditions, an assumption that often leads to stereotyping. A useful definition and discussion of ethnicity is given on the Statistics Canada website (Statistics Canada, 2008a). Notable in the discussion are the elements that make up ethnicity; "Ethnicity is somewhat multidimensional as it includes aspects such as race, origin or ancestry, identity, language and religion. It may also include more subtle dimensions such as culture, the arts, customs and beliefs and even practices such as dress and food preparation (Statistics Canada, 2008a). Ethnic identity is a way for people in one ethnocultural group to see themselves as having a common feature that ties them together and establishes their uniqueness in society. The word *ethnicity* can be viewed as "essentially relative (historically and geographically) and social [in] nature," (Morrissey, 1997, p. 98), making it difficult to define in concrete terms. Individuals may identify themselves as members of a particular ethnic group, but there are variations in the strength of their affiliation. In addition, people's ethnicity may not be the most significant distinguishing social category for them. Perhaps class, gender, sexual orientation, or age is more important to them.

RACE

Race is also seen as a feature of ethnicity where a particular racial group might have some common physical features, such as colour of skin. However, race is difficult to conceptualize because it has been defined in relation to ethnic groups, biological traits, personalities, nationalities, and particular geographic regions. For more information on the difficulties in defining the term *race,* see Statistics Canada (2008b) and Ontario Human Rights Commission (2009). This book uses the words *ethnoculture* and *ethnicity* rather than *race*. We do, however, make use of the terms *racism* and *antiracist social work practice* as defined below.

RACISM

Attempting to define racism has been described as similar to "pasting Jell-O to the wall" (Fleras and Elliott, 1999, p. 67), because its meaning, much like the meaning of race, is difficult to pin down. It is easier to point to actions that are racist than to define racism. Some definitions of racism, for example, do not refer to colour of skin, seeing racism as any act against a group of people. Although we acknowledge these difficulties in definition, we have decided to define racism as a form of discrimination based on ethnicity, which may also include skin colour.

Oppression based on ethnicity and/or skin colour—racism—occurs due to an assumption of superiority by one group over another, whether or not this is conscious. When we hear the term *racism,* we often think of it as discrimination or negative views held by a person from one ethnocultural group against another. These kinds of attitudes can be seen when someone insults or is violent toward a person because of his or her culture. Legal processes offer individuals courses of action to take should they feel discriminated against. A considerable amount of attention has been given to the impact of individual acts of racism, often in the form of books and articles written by the victims or those who speak for them (see, for example, *In Search of April Raintree* [Culleton, 1992], the moving story of two Aboriginal sisters who coped with foster home placement and discrimination).

Institutional racism refers to the structural or systemic factors that support unfair treatment of people based on race or ethnic group. Institutional racism is often subtle and involves practices that have been developed over time and that support one another. Sometimes policies and practices in educational institutions, for example, are connected and supported by those in employment or some other area, creating a linked net that excludes some groups of people. Through these institutional arrangements, people can experience racism, for example, when a job requiring Canadian experience rejects a foreign-trained and experienced worker who also faces barriers in applying for post-secondary education due to her or his foreign education. Access to some kinds of housing may also result from racism, which can make the links in the net of exclusion even stronger. Another example we can draw from is university admission requirements that have tended to work against Aboriginal people and other cultural groups whose first language is not English or French or who may have had fewer supports to succeed in high school (e.g., language or other assistance). Some students may drop out of high school due to their feelings of exclusion and isolation.

Racism is not confined to the attitudes and behaviour of white people. Discrimination occurs across many groups of people (Dei, 1996)—for example, when members of one minority group discriminate against members of the same group (or another) according to class or religion. In social work, we recognize cultural racism (and discrimination) as issues that need to be discussed and dealt with in our society, and as concerns in social work practice.

SOCIAL WORK ACROSS CULTURES

The terms *etic* and *emic,* borrowed from anthropology, are useful in thinking about intervention when a client and social worker's ethnocultural backgrounds differ.

An Etic Approach

The etic approach involves a perspective from an outsider's position, allowing general comparison from one cultural standpoint to another. For example, when a social worker (an outsider) carries out research to compare community-organizing strategies practised by women in a number of cultural groups in Canada, she or he needs to first think broadly about the general features of community organizing by women. She or he might study the issues that each group of women organizers address, how activities are planned, who the group leaders are, and how community work is balanced with other responsibilities. These general topics might be explored so that a range of cultural groups can be included in the research and some generalizations about how women in non-dominant cultural groups in Canada do community organizing. From such a study, the researcher would obtain general findings that tell her or him about the general strategies and practices used, but the social work researcher would know little information about the unique cultural context and experiences of each of the women's community organizations. The etic approach filters everything through the lens of the outsider (in this case the social worker), who is an observer.

In social work practice, an etic approach suggests applying general principles that can be used for good practice with people from all ethnocultural backgrounds. Using such an approach would mean being open to different ideas and practices, learning from a range of clients whose cultures differ from our own, and appreciating different cultures and their enrichment to Canadian society. However, it does not focus on knowing about any one particular culture.

An Emic Approach

The emic approach refers to an insider's view—one that is local and specific to a cultural group. In the study of women's community organizing, an emic perspective would be one that deals with specific community organizing experiences and their relevance to women from one ethnocultural group in Canada, according to the women themselves. It may be that the social work researcher is also a member of the same ethnocultural group or that she or he learns a great deal about the group by spending time with them. This approach offers to the researcher the group members' or insiders' account of their community organizing work. The aim would be to focus on this particular ethnoculturally specific group of women to understand community organizing in their cultural context. It might be found that the women use unique forms of management, or include certain cultural practices in their activities. The information would include many details specific to this ethnocultural community organization and the people in it.

In social work practice, an emic approach means really getting to know persons we work with from their perspective. For example, we might want to learn more about child-rearing practices and ideas in a particular area of the world so that we are better prepared to provide services to families and children from that area.

In social work, we strive for an emic approach. We want to know about a client's perception of what has occurred, how he or she understands the situation, what factors in his or her life have played a part, and what the client thinks might help. While we may draw on general knowledge from our reading and from encounters we have had in similar circumstances, we cannot assume that the current client's situation is the same as in our past experiences.

For example, consider an Asian family with an elderly member. He is in hospital recovering from a severe stroke. You are the hospital social worker responsible for discharge planning. Likely, the man will not be able to manage at home alone and will need constant care. The family has stated that they are all working at several jobs and cannot afford to stay home to provide care. Past experience and your general knowledge tell you that grandparents in many Asian families (and in other ethnocultural groups) are highly respected and valued; families are usually willing to take care of sick extended-family members in their own homes. In assessing the family situation, you must take into account your past experience but also hold open the possibility that the family will not take their elderly family member home with them. They may feel seriously conflicted by having to make a decision about placement in a long-term care facility. While guided by your generalizations (which would be an etic approach), you must let the family members tell their own story so you understand how they perceive the situation. It will also be important for all members to express their feelings and talk about the significance of this decision for them. This will determine your course of action.

The reason that social workers strive to use an emic approach is because we need to learn from clients about their unique situations and understand their views and explanations. This means focusing closely and sensitively on our clients, not drawing only on general principles and views. This means recognizing that clients and their circumstances are unique, requiring us to maintain openness and flexibility as we intervene in each client situation.

ANTIRACIST PRACTICE

Actively and honestly exploring who you are, what you stand for, where you are situated in terms of *social location*, what has advantaged and disadvantaged you in relation to others, and how you have found strength to overcome challenges in your life are important questions for social workers. This exploration is not an easy undertaking and might reveal assumptions about race or culture that need to be unlearned over time. As Butler, Elliott, and Stopard (2003) state, "We must be comfortable with ambiguity, uncertainty, and remain open to challenges" (p. 279) They also point out that working in an antiracist way means being open to learning, reflecting on how we practise, appreciating difference in people, and building on their strengths.

Moving beyond a model that stresses cultural sensitivity is the antiracist approach to social work practice, in which social workers deal directly with attitudes and practices that promote prejudice and discrimination against ethnocultural groups. Writing from the field of education, Dei and Calliste (2000) refer to antiracist practice as "an action-oriented, educational and political strategy for institutional and systemic change that addresses the issues of racism and the interlocking systems of social oppression (sexism, classism, heterosexism, ableism)" (p. 13). This broad definition includes the examination of diverse forms of oppression along with racism. Thompson (1993) agrees, adding that oppression and discrimination are "aspects of the divisive nature of social structure—reflections of the social divisions of class, race, gender, age, disability and sexual orientation. These are dimensions of our social location [where we see ourselves fitting in relation to others in society] and so we need to understand them as a whole..." (p. 11).

Considering our social location means understanding ourselves in terms of our ethnoculture, gender, age, socioeconomic class, ability, and other characteristics and critically examining how these have advantaged or disadvantaged us in meeting our needs and life chances. Recognizing our own social location in relation to that of our clients and others is important for all social workers.

Antiracist practice is inherent in an Aboriginal approach to social work (see Chapter 12). The history of Aboriginal peoples and the policies of assimilation resulted in cultural loss to such an extent that efforts to reclaim traditional teachings and to promote culturally specific practices and languages must now be made (see Chapter 12; McKenzie and Morrissette, 2003; and Morrissette, McKenzie, and Morrissette, 1993). Bringing antiracist practice to one's social work practice can help to promote these aims.

How people feel about themselves has much to do with how others behave toward them. In Chapter 6, we described how Tom's experiences as an Aboriginal student in a school dominated by white students and teachers were characterized by discrimination and labelling that worked to oppress him. His treatment by students and teachers played a role in how he saw himself and subsequently behaved toward himself and others. The example shows clearly how important it is that the development of positive regard for oneself and others begins early in life, and how it can be seriously hindered through the negative actions of peers and authority figures and tolerance of these in our society. Internalized oppression, where a person who has experienced numerous acts of discrimination in our society comes to believe that he or she is inferior and unworthy, can lead to self-hatred. How an individual senses she or he is perceived by others in society, "whether in the media or in history books or among professionals such as teachers, doctors, and lawyers, has an impact on her [or his] perceptions of self-worth and ability" (Lundy, 2004, p. 132).

What we can learn from Tom's experience is that it is necessary to understand how racism diminishes people, not only those who perpetrate it knowingly or unknowingly, but rather all human beings. It is worthwhile for social workers to help people like Tom make connections between their past experiences and current reality so that they can begin to examine their strengths, build their self-worth, and develop hope that their lives can be better. We also learn from Tom's situation that investing time to help children develop self-worth and compassion for others is critical to their continued growth and well-being.

DISCRIMINATION AND THE ROLE OF SOCIAL WORK

According to the Canadian Association of Social Workers *Code of Ethics* (2005a), we are expected (*The Social Work Code of Ethics*, adopted by the Board of Directors of the Canadian Association of Social Workers (CASW) is effective March, 2005 and replaces the CASW *Code of Ethics* (1994). The *Code* is reprinted here with the permission of CASW. The copyright in the document has been registered with Canadian Intellectual Property Office, registration No. 1030330. P. 2. Available online at www.casw-acts.ca):

> to provide resources, services and opportunities for the overall benefit of humanity and to afford them protection from harm.
>
> Social workers promote social fairness and the equitable distribution of resources, and act to reduce barriers and expand choice for all persons, with special regard for those who are marginalized, disadvantaged, vulnerable, and/or have exceptional needs. Social workers oppose prejudice and discrimination against any person or group of persons, on any grounds, and specifically challenge views and actions that stereotype particular persons or groups. (p. 5)

The quotation above tells social workers that we not only take action on an individual or group basis to identify and confront discrimination and marginalization, but that we also act collectively. This may mean working with communities to oppose policies and practices that are discriminatory or harmful to some groups, conducting research to learn about incidents and experiences of oppression, and writing and teaching critically to expose injustice.

Mullaly (2002, p. 100), for example, criticizes multiculturalism when it is equated mainly with ethnocultural festivals but pays little attention to the obstacles and difficulties many immigrants face in finding good jobs and gaining access to the resources that enhance the lives of those who are in the Canadian mainstream. Adasme (in Fleras and Elliott, 1999, pp. 278–83) provides an account of her immigration experiences in Canada, noting that for immigrants an occupation is a critical link to who they are in relation to society. She notes that immigrants are found in occupations that tend to be the least valued and most poorly paid in contrast to those in which most mainstream Canadians are employed. She states, however, that, "There is nothing wrong with it if one is allowed to move away from that setting (through educational programs, etc.), if one feels the need to do so. But there is something very wrong if one has to remain a janitor, sewing machine operator, etc., for life … feeling enslaved." For many immigrants, upgrading and opportunities for training and education in Canada are the means to acquire better jobs, but access to education and training may be difficult because of high cost, lack of affordable childcare, no English-language assistance, and other reasons. Educational equity programs are one way that has been used to level the playing field and allow more access to education for people who may otherwise not be able to participate.

EDUCATION EQUITY AND AFFIRMATIVE ACTION

There is an ongoing debate as to whether affirmative action and equity programs are working. On the one hand, such initiatives open doors for people who have previously had less access to higher education or good jobs, and aim to better reflect the composition of society in education (Blum and Heinonen, 2001) and the workplace. On the other hand, some people believe that affirmative action threatens standards of excellence and quality in the university or workplace. Referring to the field of education, Dei (1996) counters, "The issues of diversity, excellence, quality and equity in education are inseparable" (p. 38), implying that equity programs promote better and richer educational and workplace environments by including all members of society. Removing barriers, offering supportive programs (such as mentorship), and building an inclusive learning environment can help increase the enrollment of students who previously felt shut out of post-secondary education.

Efforts to increase access to education and the labour market (equity or affirmative action) have become common strategies to deal with these problems, but obstacles to recognizing foreign credentials, for example, continue to pose serious barriers. Licensed occupations, including medicine and dentistry, continue to impose restrictions and deny accreditation, which results in blocking the entry into these professions of immigrants with foreign degrees or credentials outside Canada (Fleras and Elliott, 1999, p. 276). Social work is not immune to these practices, although they may vary across provinces. As licensing and standards for practice shape who can practise as social workers in Canada, it seems that Canadian experience and education will be more prominent than foreign experience and education, even when skills and knowledge requirements are similar. This is partly so because employers hire those whose experience and education they know about and to which they can relate. This is unfortunate, because immigrants who bring experience from their own countries enrich social work and add new perspectives and knowledge to the profession, not only about social work practice but also about their cultures and languages. Many will be cultural brokers and service providers for members of their own cultural communities, who often don't use mainstream social services because they are incongruent with what they have known or prefer. Immigrant social workers can also demonstrate alternative methods and unique skills that all in the profession can learn about. We lose their skills and talents if we do not examine practices and policies that exclude social workers from non-dominant cultures from making their services available.

SOCIAL WORK WITH NEWCOMERS

Social workers may encounter both new and more established immigrants and refugees as clients in large social service agencies or in organizations that specifically work with these groups. Such work may be carried out, for example, in social service delivery to new immigrants dealing with settlement issues and related needs, such as practical help or emotional support. These needs can arise from the circumstances in their home country (and/or refugee camps), departure and separation from family members and homes, and settlement in Canada. Sometimes these are related to problems in gaining access to English language learning, housing, and jobs. Social service programs reflect current immigration policy and may include a variety of public and voluntary social provisioning (e.g., financial help for settlement, access to legal resources, language and job training programs, housing assistance, and mental health services). Of course, this is not meant to imply that all immigrants will require these social services; many will not.

In social work practice, we need to work to support the successful settlement and integration of immigrants in Canada and identify the obstacles that stand in the way of full access and promote exclusion of newcomers (and others) from education, occupations, and other entitlements in our society. Doing so is part of our professional responsibility and is referred to as such in our code of ethics.

INTERSECTION OF MULTIPLE FORMS OF OPPRESSION: THE EXAMPLE OF LOLA

It is necessary to acknowledge and understand the intersections of all forms of social oppression. Mullaly (2002) mentions that there is a need to analyze multiple forms of oppression since one single form of oppression, such as sexism, often occurs in combination with another, such as ageism. He asserts that analysis of a "single strand" model of oppression needs to be replaced by an "intersectional model of oppression" that accounts for "intersecting, interlocking, and/or interacting oppressions" (p. 151). For example, class, race, and gender may work to oppress a Somali refugee woman who is living on social assistance income in Toronto. She may experience the effects of racism or other kinds of oppression when she tries to find a job. We need to understand how these forms of oppression work against and with the others in their effect on the woman, her family, and her community. McIntosh (1989) asserts that "Since race and sex are not the only advantaging systems at work, we need to examine the daily experience of having age advantage, or ethnic advantage, or physical ability, or advantage related to nationality, religion, or sexual orientation" (p. 12). The myth of equal opportunity and democratic choice in our society hides the fact that Canadian social structures do not offer an even playing field for all.

To illustrate how racism combined with other types of oppression constitutes intersections of oppression, we draw on the story of Lola. (This example is inspired by research findings reported by Migliardi, Blum, and Heinonen, 2004.)

Lola ▼

Lola Mendez, a 34-year-old immigrant woman from a South American city, lives in Calgary with her husband, Ricardo, 37, and their two daughters, Nita and Donna. The girls are 8 and 11 and attend school near the family's apartment in an older area of the city. The family has been in Canada for five years. Ricardo works as an apprentice mechanic in a gas station, and Lola works in a garment factory sewing jacket sleeves together.

Recently, the situation at home became difficult. Beginning a year ago, Ricardo started to abuse Lola. At first he yelled at her and pushed her when he was not happy with her cooking or the way she spent money. Lola at first tried to talk to her husband and say she would try to do better and that it was best not to fight in front of the children. She did not say anything to anyone for fear that the whole community would look down on her and that someone might even report her and have her deported. Lola is fearful of what will happen to her and the children. Already she could see that Nita, the youngest, was slapping her sister and demanding more of her mother's attention. The girls hid in Donna's closet when they heard the arguing start, because they were frightened of what would happen.

After the girls had gone to sleep one night, Lola began to prepare the children's school lunches for the morning. Ricardo came in after drinking and began to yell at her, pulling her hair, punching her, and throwing her against the door. Lola fell to the floor. Upstairs, Donna called 911; she had learned about it at school. When the police came, Ricardo was still yelling at Lola and trying to get her to stand up. He did not open the door for the police, so they entered by force. The girls were awake and crying at the top of the stairs.

Ricardo was taken to the police station to be charged with assault, and an ambulance was called for Lola. An after-hours social worker was called to help place the children temporarily. Both feared that their mother would not recover and had to be consoled for some time.

When Lola was discharged home from the hospital, a friend came to help her, and the children were returned to her a few days later. Lola decided that she would never accept this kind of treatment from Ricardo or anyone again. She had been visited by a hospital social worker, who asked if she could introduce her to another immigrant woman who was a volunteer counsellor for immigrants. The volunteer, Sari, had herself experienced physical abuse from her father-in-law and now knew a lot about the rights of women and laws against violence in Canada. The two women spent a number of hours talking as Lola began to recover from her injuries. Sari could see Lola's many strengths and asked if she wanted to work against violence against immigrant women herself someday. Lola agreed, saying, "Yes, because it is one thing I can contribute to my community so other immigrant women don't have to live like me."

After Lola moved to another location, separated from Ricardo, and started a better job in a unionized factory, she decided to call Sari. Sari told her that a special training course would be beginning in a month's time, where women from different ethnocultural communities were invited to learn how to help other women who were facing the effects of violence in their homes. Lola agreed to participate for one evening per week when she learned that childcare and transportation costs would be taken care of. Donna and Nita would enjoy the many activities in the playroom and the company of other children.

The training course lasted three months. In the course, Lola learned about laws against violence, women's rights, different kinds of abuse, how violence arises and is maintained, myths about woman abuse, effects of violence on children, how some cultural beliefs and practices sometimes work to support violence, how to be supportive of women facing abuse in their lives, and when to call for help. In the training course were many other immigrant women from a range of cultural backgrounds. Lola was surprised that, despite so many differences among them, there was so much they shared, too, as immigrants in Canada and as women. The guest speakers and immigrant women leaders who guided the training used visual aids and spoke clearly and explained things when some did not understand. The best part of the course for Lola was sharing experiences and views with the other women participants. Many of the women in the group said things like: "I would never have been afraid of my in-laws if I had known that I could not be deported for getting a job of my own"; "I feel so free now. I have rights and I can use this information, not just for myself, but to help others too. I feel strong"; and "Immigrant women really can understand what it is like. I would like to have another immigrant woman help me if I was being abused, I would be too ashamed to tell most people about it."

The training group helped Lola, a poor, immigrant, visible-minority woman, to use the help she got in the hospital and the knowledge she gained from the training to form a self-help group for women in her ethnocultural community to counter violence in their lives. One of the women's husbands heard about the group and thought something along the same lines would be good for men, too, so they could learn about nonviolent ways to deal with anger, frustration, and relationships with women and children. The men's group was advertised not as a support group for men who used violence, but as a group to support peaceful and healthy ways of being a father. (It was decided that this kind of group would be more attractive to men than a group with some other stated purpose.) Appropriately, the men's group began on Father's Day.

Just as in Lola's situation, the life experiences of some people bring them face-to-face with racism, poverty, and other challenges, often in very difficult ways. Lola's poor job, her lack of access to education, limited knowledge of human rights, and fear in her family situation were related to her being poor, an immigrant, and a woman. These featured as sources of oppression that intersected in her life, affecting her experiences in the home, the workplace, and the community. Her self-esteem, confidence, life chances, economic situation, and social position were adversely affected.

GROUP AND COMMUNITY HELPING IN IMMIGRANT COMMUNITIES: THE EXAMPLE OF LOLA

Community organizing and mutual help can often be useful where mainstream social services are not available or do not fit with immigrants' needs or ways of helping. In our case situation, the hospital social worker was aware of this and referred an immigrant helper to speak to Lola. If the hospital social worker had not done so, Lola might not have found the power in herself to heal and grow to the point that she could be a resource to others. A community of women, all with the common experience of immigration to Canada, offered her this opportunity.

Lola and her peers felt that it was important for immigrant men to examine violence and its meaning in their lives, since working with women alone was not enough. Men could not be excluded. They found a way to do this by finding a male ally who discussed with them the immigrant men's interests and what they wanted to learn from the group. This was an important means of offering a service that built on men's interests and promoted the prevention of violence in their homes and communities. Methods that fit with Western social work in professional practice may not fit for immigrant clients. It is important to explore what ways of helping are appropriate and most useful in a particular ethnocultural community and, if possible, how these might be adapted in the Canadian urban context. Immigrant social workers could be very helpful in developing such alternative models and methods and enriching existing ones in many social work agencies and organizations that are poorly utilized by immigrant clients.

ANTI-OPPRESSIVE SOCIAL WORK

Anti-oppressive social work involves intervention that is not confined to individuals but that spans the social structural level of society (Mullaly, 2002). It involves critical reflection about oppression and its harmful effects on clients and action based on learning from such reflection. As we have seen, social workers mainly provide services to individuals who face issues such as poverty, illness, addictions, and mental health conditions. Anti-oppressive practice avoids adding to existing oppression experienced by clients, viewing the cause of problems as lying outside individual control. Anti-oppressive social workers critically ask questions in their work with clients: "Why does this 88-year-old woman need to live in substandard housing? Who gains from this situation?"; "How is it that this 62-year-old, skilled worker was laid off a few years before his retirement and replaced by a younger, inexperienced employee? Who gains and why?"; "What brought this immigrant woman to the brink of suicide after she was beaten by her husband? How has Canadian society failed?"; "Why does this gay man need to fear for his safety when walking alone at night? In what ways is society to blame?"; and "What caused this young woman to turn to crack cocaine and steal from her family? How are social structures to blame?" They strive to understand the "oppressive conditions, processes and practices [that] exist at the personal, cultural and structural levels" (Mullaly, 2002, p. 171) and how these influence or shape an individual's situation. In doing so, anti-oppressive social workers can help clients to search for the roots of their difficulties outside themselves. In relation to the clients of social work, Mullaly (2002) explains,

> As awareness of injustice and oppression grows, oppressed people are less likely to blame themselves for their oppression and are more able to identify the social causes of their negative emotions and experiences. These insights, in turn, help them to develop their analyses of their oppression as well as to build confidence and the capacity for seeking social changes. (p. 173)

Anti-oppressive practice and culturally sensitive social work are appropriate for working with all clients, no matter what their background. They also offer an alternative perspective that draws on strengths, assets, and capacities first, rather than a primary focus on problems and limitations. This alternative way of practising is attractive to most social work students because it fits well with the values and principles in social work codes of ethics. (See Chapter 11 on the strengths approach.)

THE PRACTICE RELATIONSHIP

You may see your cultural background, offering some distinct ways of viewing the world, as different from that of your clients or coworkers. On the other hand, you may find yourself in a workplace in which there is a shared cultural heritage between most workers and clients—for example, an organization in which Aboriginal social workers are employed to help Aboriginal teenagers who are experiencing problems in school. Whatever the cultural environment in your workplace, social workers need to use empathy and effective communication to enhance understanding between themselves and their clients.

There may be other differences that, in addition to culture, are significant to the practice relationship. How, for example, does the age or gender of the social worker affect the development of a relationship with the client? Such issues may raise challenges for you in practice. Will you be able to understand the ways in which clients view their situation, identify what strengths and assets they have, and determine what help they will accept and how they would like to go about dealing with their situation? Is it possible for a middle-aged female social worker who is third-generation Scottish to develop a working relationship with a teenaged Eritrean male client? Can a young social worker of Polish ancestry understand why a Chinese family views their son's failing grades in school as a major problem for his grandparents? Can a new social worker from Nigeria appreciate the significance of an Aboriginal community's healing practices? In considering these questions, we need to see that social workers, like most people, are generally resilient and can learn to respond effectively in unfamiliar situations.

We gain knowledge from our experiences in social work and search for continuing social work learning opportunities. We can also be *reflexive* in our practice by critically and self-consciously evaluating the process of our work and its impact on clients.

Social workers may find themselves in situations where clients or other people make offensive comments about their (or someone else's) cultural background or traditions. For example, ethnic jokes can be insensitive and harmful. Social workers, through our codes of ethics, support the elimination of discrimination and racism, so doing nothing conflicts with our professional ethics. Finding a way to challenge such comments skillfully and appropriately is not easy, but it is necessary. It might be that the offending person lacks awareness about the impact of such comments or believes that her or his views are justified. Letting such comments go without speaking up could reinforce the view that it is okay to put people down. Of course, a social worker needs to be cautious in such a situation to prevent it from escalating and becoming threatening. Focusing on what is said and its effect rather than on the individual who makes the offending comment is useful. Remaining calm and clear, but at the same time empathic and respectful of the other person, can help.

If you know that some or all of your clients will be of another culture—say Latin American or Aboriginal—it is wise to learn something about their beliefs and traditions. Often these contain unique strengths and may offer keys for dealing with obstacles and problems in life. Such learning by a social worker may also provide some ideas (which cannot be generalized to all members of a cultural group) about spiritual practices, family relations, roles of men and women, accepted ways of raising children, importance of extended family and community networks, and other areas. People differ in the strength and form of their cultural identification, their expression of cultural traditions and practices, and in the significance of cultural values and ideals in their lives. Some people may even see themselves as belonging to a number of cultures, such as French, Japanese, and Aboriginal. As a guiding principle, people are viewed as unique individuals first before they are grouped together as Somalis, Chinese, Métis, Inuit, or members of another ethnocultural group.

GAINING ETHNIC COMPETENCE

Green (1995) refers to the concept of ethnic competence as helpful in social work practice across cultures. Ethnic competence involves a number of factors.

As a step toward attaining ethnic competence, it is necessary to be aware of your own cultural limitations in your work with clients, particularly as you form relationships with them and intervene in their private troubles. Although our profession trains us to encourage clients to express their feelings freely, some cultural groups see such expression to strangers, especially those in authority, as inappropriate. This may deter some from seeking any help from social service agencies.

Social workers need to be cautious about seeing persons who belong to a particular ethnocultural group as the same. As mentioned above, culture is not static nor is people's expression or adherence to a cultural identity. Seeing one ethnocultural group as unchanging and the same can lead to stereotypes, which we have likely become familiar with already. Such stereotypes about cultures and people from specific cultural groups are usually inaccurate, often outdated, and inappropriate.

Although it is not always necessary or even appropriate to ask clients what cultural group they belong to, it is helpful for social workers to consider that differing perspectives—for example, attitudes toward parenting or preventive health care—might be attributed to cultural factors. It is sometimes necessary for social workers to review with clients, for instance, parental responsibilities and obligations, including acceptable ways to discipline children. This information, rather than closing discussion, could be offered in such a way that clients feel able to ask questions, discuss options open to them in various situations, and inquire about any supportive programs or available help. The difficulties newcomers may face because of language barriers and fear of authority figures (e.g., school principals, guidance counsellors, and social workers) may be considerable, so the strengths and resources of parents trying to raise their children in a new environment should also be highlighted. In some cases, there may be distinct differences, some of which may conflict with Canadian laws. These will need to be discussed to prevent misunderstanding at a later time. Clients may be in a position to inform social workers about the best ways to help them with their specific issues or problems. Being empathic and open is necessary, but it is not sufficient.

The strength of a person's cultural beliefs and practices will give you some idea about which resources could be useful. Invoking a client's internal strengths, such as spirituality or previous persistence in the face of hardship, may help. External resources, such as cultural associations or culture-specific health and social services, may also be useful. Clients are the best people to decide whether these are appropriate, and they may have strong feelings about wanting or not wanting to use them.

Clients can help us understand what is most appropriate for them given their cultural traditions and practices. The social worker could learn whether a trusted midwife, godmother, community leader, or other resource person might be preferred for help rather than a formal agency. Helping resources that are most desirable to clients need to be explored so that misunderstanding and frustration can be prevented. Thus, the helping process can become a mutual learning context.

The resources to which a person has access (internal and external) vary across cultural groups and according to circumstances. For example, a man who has fled a conflicted and war-ravaged area with his young son to settle in Canada as refugees will almost certainly lack many of the resources others take for granted. (He most likely has many that we don't know about.) Supportive help from family members, friends, and trusted spiritual guides are not available. The man may be dealing with the loss of his spouse, his extended family, and his home. He may also have experienced imprisonment, torture and/or discrimination in his home country or in refugee camps. The man and his son have many needs as they adapt to life in a new country, and social service agencies and workers will likely become involved.

Expectations of how social services are delivered vary across cultures. For example, in seeking counselling for a depressed young mother, members of some cultures may expect that family members and extended kin will accompany her into the counsellor's office to support her. Most counselling agencies would find this unusual and likely inappropriate given their agency's practice.

The modes of social work practice for specific client situations may call for family, individual, group, or community intervention. The use of group work among women newcomers to encourage sharing and learning from others can build connections, support, and hope for a better future in their new homeland. For many, connecting with their ethnocultural group members to share information about resources, build friendships, and maintain cultural practices is important for successful survival in their new environment.

Encouraging and enabling access to informal networks can be a key role for social workers helping newly arrived immigrants, as shown in the case situation of Lola. Social work with families and communities may be most effective for new immigrants' success; however, social workers can also use their skills in policy analysis to improve the current situation for immigrants, advocating for inclusion of foreign credentials of immigrants, including social workers, and better, more comprehensive social services that respond to immigrants' needs in culturally appropriate ways.

In using an emic approach, we strive to understand how a situation looks from a client's perspective. This involves meanings: those attached to words spoken, gestures, and silences in communication. We need to feel comfortable about asking questions when we do not understand what is behind the client's words or gestures. It may be necessary to work with an interpreter when the client and social worker have no common language. This raises issues such as building the helping relationship through an intermediary, handling confidential material, and ensuring accuracy. In many cases, social workers will need to clearly explain their roles and the kinds of help they can offer, since newcomers may not understand what social workers are or what they do. Clients may fear, for example, that social workers have the capacity to deport immigrants. Or perhaps they may view social workers as having the power to provide all of the material help they require.

CHAPTER SUMMARY

In this chapter, social workers are encouraged to explore their own cultural background and what it means to them. By doing so, one can experience culture as a lens for looking at the world. This is important in order to practise effectively across cultures and within cultures.

The chapter presents a view of antiracist, anti-oppressive, culturally sensitive, and culturally appropriate practice that emphasizes an emic approach and cultural competence. The significance of culture in social work practice is highlighted in a multicultural society like Canada's. Social work practice has incorporated ways to understand the significance of culture for clients and ourselves by developing cross-cultural practice principles, culturally sensitive and culturally appropriate practice, and cultural competence. These enrich social work practice whether or not social workers and clients share similar cultural backgrounds.

Racism and other related forms of oppression work to keep some groups of people disadvantaged and others privileged. The social work codes of ethics guide the profession and encourage social workers to work at eliminating discrimination and all forms of oppression in society. It is, however, difficult to address the institutional racism that pervades organizations and institutions like an invisible mist. For example, the institutional racism and rigid requirements for Canadian experience work to marginalize immigrants with foreign professional credentials. Much can be learned from immigrant colleagues about alternative methods and viewpoints on helping and being helped. Applying such knowledge can enrich and broaden social work perspectives and lead to better, culturally appropriate services. Through mutual exchange and collective effort we can promote respect for and appreciation of human diversity in society.

Problem Solving in Social Work Practice

Chapter Goal ▼

To describe and analyze the problem-solving process in social work and to identify its contributions and implications.

This Chapter ▼

- outlines and describes the elements of the problem-solving process
- establishes the importance of contracting with clients
- describes a simple evaluation framework that can be used in almost any direct social work practice with individuals
- addresses some of the important implications of the problem-solving process

INTRODUCTION

The traditional model of social work practice is problem solving. This has been true since at least 1917, when Mary Richmond outlined a framework for casework practice in her book *Social Diagnosis.* The heart of her book described a problem-solving process. Although social work's conception of problem solving has changed, the process remains central to practice.

The business of social workers is to help people or communities solve serious, often complex personal and social problems. Social workers would not be asked to help if solving problems were easy. Part of solving difficult and complex problems is understanding the process itself.

The elements of problem solving are quite simple (see Exhibit 8.1):

1. Identify the problem.
2. Attempt to analyze or understand the problem.
3. Use the analysis to set goals.
4. Evaluate the appropriateness of the analysis.
5. Take action to solve the problem.
6. Evaluate, through ***feedback loops,*** whether the action accomplished the intended goals.

If successful, or if the decision is made that the problem cannot be solved, then the process ends. If not, the process begins again. This process is generally the same whether it is used in solving everyday problems of life or in professional practice.

Let's illustrate with an everyday example. Suppose, early one cold winter morning, a harried student discovers that his car will not start. He has an exam at 9:00 a.m. He has identified the problem and begins to analyze it. Quickly he decides that he must get to his exam at all costs. Within seconds he realizes that he has five choices: he could attempt to fix the car himself, call a tow truck, call a friend, take the bus, or take a taxi to the university. He is not very good at fixing the car, so he rules out that option. Calling a tow truck may take a long time on a cold morning. The frustrated student thinks his friend has already left for work. He has only $2 in his pocket—not enough money for a taxi. So, he decides that his best bet is to take the bus. However, he does not know the bus schedule.

By now the student has established a clear goal. He must write the exam! The analysis has narrowed down his options for action. To his chagrin, he finds that the bus will get him there too late. Quickly he evaluates his remaining options and calls his friend. Fortunately, she is still at home and can get him to the exam on time. The friend brings the process to a successful end.

Exhibit 8.1 ▼ The Problem-Solving Process

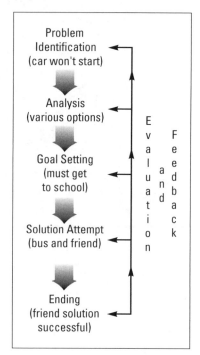

This example could have taken a different twist. Suppose the student chose to fix the car himself. He could have used the same analytical method to understand the process for fixing the car. Most likely he would have attempted to clearly understand the problem with the car, diagnosed it, and then taken the appropriate action to fix it. The problem-solving process can apply to almost any situation that requires a solution.

THE PROBLEM-SOLVING PROCESS IN SOCIAL WORK

Notice that the process outlined above and in Exhibit 8.1 proceeds in a generally linear fashion with feedback loops. Each evaluation establishes a ***feedback mechanism***. If in any of the evaluations an error, mistake, or omission is discovered in any of the steps, then the process will likely revert to a previous step for correction or revision. This was what happened when the student found that the bus was not an option. Evaluating the information related to the bus schedule led him to revisit the action step and devise a new plan—basically, to revert to plan B. Like the steps in the example, in social work each stage of the process is often revisited and reviewed, leading to changes in problem definition, assessment, goal setting, and intervention.

Understanding the historical context of problem solving in social work is important. As shown in Chapter 2, at the beginning of the 20th century social work was a fledging profession. Agencies were beginning to pay social caseworkers a salary rather than use friendly visitor volunteers. There were no social work textbooks. In fact, there was no literature that even conceptualized the helping process in social work.

This changed in 1917 when Mary Richmond published a seminal book: *Social Diagnosis*. Richmond outlined a process of social casework that has had enormous influence on today's social work practice. This was (1) study, (2) diagnosis, and (3) treatment. Richmond established the idea that assessment (diagnosis) and helping (treatment) were at the centre of practice. The process that she outlined was almost the same as that used in medicine (the medical model). Diagnosis implies that a person's problem can be diagnosed like a disease. Emphasis is often on pathology. Further, the diagnosis determines the prescribed treatment. This simply stated process set the theoretical framework for all of casework for the next half-century. Richmond's work also formalized two cornerstones of current social work views of problem solving: first, that intervention depends on assessment; and second, that the key to social work intervention is the relationship between the client and the worker. (See Boyle et al., 2009, p. 155; and Dewees, 2006, pp. 116–17.)

Over the years the conception of problem solving has evolved. Perlman (1957) articulated the basic problem-solving framework that remains in use today.

Today the social work problem-solving process involves the following elements (see Exhibit 8.2):

- Define the problem(s).
- Conduct an assessment.
- Set goals and objectives.
- Establish a contract.

- Intervene.
- Evaluate the process.
- End the process.

Exhibit 8.2 shows the flow from problem definition to endings, with evaluation occurring during and after each step. When feedback from the evaluation warrants, one or more of the earlier steps may be revisited. Review is frequent and important. Later in this chapter we suggest a simple scheme to evaluate everyday practice. Exhibit 8.2 shows that contracting, like evaluation, is a part of each stage of the problem-solving process. It is very fluid and involves frequent changes.

Chapter 6 discussed in some detail the social work relationship. The problem-solving process depends upon the relationship between worker and client. As emphasized in Chapter 6, the social work relationship is at the heart of all social work practice. Helping almost always is engaged through the relationship.

The helping relationship is important in all stages of problem solving. It is necessary in order to help clients define and articulate their problems. Effective goal setting and intervention also depend upon the worker–client relationship. There is not a single stage of problem solving that does not depend upon the social work relationship.

The exhibit suggests that the process is smooth and essentially linear with feedback mechanisms built in. In practice this is usually not the case. In real life, the problem-solving process is very fluid, and hits many bumps along the way.

Exhibit 8.2 ▼ The Social Work Problem-Solving Process

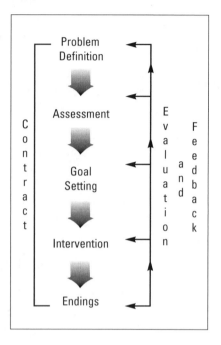

Problem Definition

A problem may be that of an individual, group, organization, or community. Often the person or persons who are experiencing a problem first identify it. The starting point may be their story. Other times, someone else reports the problem. A woman who suspects that her neighbour abuses his child is an example. Sometimes an authority such as the police first reports a problem.

The goal of problem definition is to begin to articulate the problem in a way that both the social worker and the client can understand. They need to agree on this definition before the worker can take action to help solve the problem.

This first step of the problem-solving process has several crucial elements. The place to begin is "where the client is." This means beginning with the client's story, and his or her understanding of the problem. It is essential to encourage clients to tell their stories in their own words. Only after the story begins to emerge should the social worker formulate his or her opinion of the nature of the problem.

Case Example

Kim and Ann ▼

Recall that Kim is a family social worker in the Child Protection Agency (CPA). The nightshift worker placed Ann's three children in temporary custody. The worker had received a call from a neighbour stating that Ann's three children were at home alone, unattended by an adult. He discovered that Ann was at a party and indeed had not arranged for adult care of her children. The family is known to the agency, but there has been no evidence of direct physical abuse—only neglect.

Kim's first concern was for the safety of the three children, but helping Ann was also a high priority. Agency workers in the past have felt that, with help, Ann could manage the role of lone parent.

Upon meeting Ann for the first time, Kim explained the reasons for apprehending her children, emphasizing that the children needed adult supervision. Ann was angry with Kim but particularly upset at the Child Protection Agency worker and the neighbour who reported the neglect. Kim let Ann express her anger, and, when Ann began to cool down a little, in a calm and encouraging voice she asked Ann to tell her story. Kim wanted to shift the attention to Ann's needs and problems, to let Ann know that her needs were important, and to let Ann know that she was there to help. As Ann told her story, Kim was better able to understand the stress that Ann felt.

Ann saw her problems as being related to her lack of income and blamed the intrusive nature of the Child Protection Agency for compounding them. Kim gently steered Ann toward telling about other parts of her life, including her relationships with her children and their daily activities. As Ann talked, Kim realized that Ann thought very poorly of herself. She was recently fired from a job in a store when her boss learned that she could not read the labels on products. Ann's lack of work and her family responsibilities were getting her down. When there was enough money, Ann could take care of her children. When there was no money, Ann seemed to drown her sorrows by drinking heavily. Kim, through Ann's story, began to get a different picture of the problem.

Often, the social worker defines the problem differently than the client. In the case example, Kim saw more dimensions to the problem than Ann did. Kim agreed that Ann's lack of income was important, but her limited parenting skills, lack of education, and problem drinking were also factors. To successfully conclude the identification of the problem, the client and the social worker need to agree on the main problems and which ones they will attempt to solve. This is part of contracting, which will be discussed later in this chapter.

Kim successfully merged the function of social control (apprehension of Ann's children) and helping. Often such an approach works when it is perceived by clients to be in their best interest. However, if Ann had refused to discuss her situation with Kim, clarifying the problem would have been much more difficult. Kim would have had to work hard to convince Ann that while her primary intent was the children's safety, she could also help Ann address her own problems that precipitated the apprehension. Helping Ann address her own problems is probably not possible unless Ann decides that she needs and wants such help from Kim.

The establishment of a helping relationship between Kim and Ann is necessary for them to engage in problem solving. Kim took several steps to do this. Of these, probably her encouragement of Ann to tell her own story was most important.

The success of all later steps depends heavily on the establishment of a professional relationship, as discussed in Chapter 6.

This example illustrates another important principle. Kim at first concentrated on Ann's telling of her own story. She listened and did not make quick judgments. Only after Ann and Kim began to be more comfortable together did Kim begin to draw her own conclusions. Again, this principle of social work is often called "starting where the client is."

Assessment in the Problem-Solving Process: A Brief Introduction

This section introduces assessment in the context of the problem-solving process. Chapter 10 discusses assessment in much more detail.

The purpose of assessment in problem solving is to set goals and devise a means (intervention) to reach these goals. Clarifying and articulating the problem generally leads to a better understanding of its nature. In a formal sense, assessment is a consequence of problem definition. However, in practice, assessment usually starts as soon as the social worker begins to understand the problem and take in information about the client. Problem definition and assessment are best viewed as roughly sequential, with many feedback loops and constant revisions beginning from the initial client–social worker contact (Specht and Specht, 1986).

Assessment has two key elements. First, the social worker and client must have a clear understanding of the nature of the problem; and second, they must translate it into a need. For example, suppose the parents of a 10-year-old boy, Tranh, agree with the social worker that the main problem is Tranh's aggressive behaviour. They are also worried about his poor performance in school. To solve the problem, the worker and clients must determine what Tranh needs. This translation of a problem into a need is necessary to begin to take steps toward a solution. Suppose the worker and clients then determine that Tranh, among other things, needs clear rules. They think this not only will help him recognize and set **boundaries** but also will provide him with a feeling of security (another need) that he lacks. To meet these needs, the social worker and parents agree on a plan to set clear rules at home.

Information for an assessment may come from many sources, including relatives, reports from authorities such as the police, referring agencies, and the like. However, probably the chief source of assessment data is the client's own story. Cowger (1997, pp. 63–64) and Cowger and Snively (2002, p. 112) argue that clients are, most of the time, the best source of information. Clients are not only the most reliable source of information but also, their story tells the social worker how they perceive their problems.

Assessment addresses such questions as the following: Why did the problem occur? What are the likely short-term and long-term effects? Does the problem affect other areas? If so, how? What is the context of the problem? What are the perspectives of the problem according to the client, the social worker, and possibly others with an interest in the situation? What goals are realistic? What strategies of intervention might enable the client to reach these goals and solve the problem?

Assessment and Diagnosis

In 1957, Helen Perlman published a landmark book, *Social Casework: A Problem Solving Process,* that carefully articulated problem solving in social work. Until then the social work process was generally seen as a social work version of the medical model (exam, diagnosis, and treatment). While Perlman used the word *diagnosis,* her articulation was more similar to current use of assessment than the earlier meaning of diagnosis. Perlman "… saw diagnosis as dynamic, as 'a cross-sectional view of the forces interacting in the client's problem situation.' Diagnosis was seen as an ongoing process that gives 'boundary, relevance and direction' to work. It was seen as the thinking in problem solving" (Johnson, McClelland, and Austin, 2000, p. 27). For the most part, the concept of assessment has replaced use of the term *diagnosis.* Generally current use in social work of the term *diagnosis* is limited and usually makes reference to a mental illness or disorder, not to the assessment process. Over time social work assessment has become very different than the concept of diagnosis. However, even today social workers sometimes use the concepts of diagnosis and assessment interchangeably.

Diagnosis is a very different concept than assessment. It may be easier to understand some of the principles of social work assessment by comparing them with the diagnostic process in medicine. As you read the comparisons in Exhibit 8.3, note that the process is parallel but the emphasis is very different. Also note that these descriptions represent a standard or ideal. As explained later in Chapter 11, on the strengths approach, it is still sometimes easy to slip into assessments guided by principles of disease and client deficits.

Exhibit 8.3 ▼ Medical Diagnosis Compared with Social Work Assessment

	MEDICAL DIAGNOSIS	SOCIAL WORK ASSESSMENT IN PROBLEM SOLVING
Categorization	• Uses categories of disease/ injury based on pathology	• Does not place people in categories
Purpose	• To provide a basis on which a disease can be prevented or cured	• To help people solve problems by providing a basis for selecting appropriate goals and intervention
Emphasis	• Pathology and disease	• Personal and social functioning, particularly personal strengths and connection with the environment
Problem	• Seen as a disease	• Seen as having psychological and environmental dimensions; may be seen as a weakness or deficit
Process	• Based on examination by an expert, who makes the diagnosis with little or no discussion with the patient	• Usually based on a contract between client and social worker; worker viewed as an expert skilled in helping
Final result	• Diagnostic category and label	• No attempt to condense assessment to a single category • End product is an analytical statement that usually describes the person in the situation
Goals	• To prevent or cure illness • Are clear and easy to measure • If cure or prevention is not possible, then goal is to reduce the effect of symptoms	• Fluid, with emphasis on improving quality of life • Depends on the assessment and varies considerably depending on needs of individual clients, agency setting, and orientation of helper
Treatment	• Diagnosis prescribes treatment; a fundamental characteristic of the medical model	• Prescriptive only in a most general sense; strategy of intervention depends on assessment and goals that derive from assessment • Goals and treatment methods frequently negotiated with clients
Bases of knowledge	• Based on science and scientific inquiry; knowledge is not acceptable if it cannot be empirically verified • Reliability of diagnosis is very important	• Partly based on the social sciences but also on life experiences and culture • Theoretical knowledge often used even though it has not been empirically verified • Research is often experience based, without empirical verification
Types of science	• Life sciences, with emphasis on biology, biochemistry, biomedicine, and psychology	• Emphasis on social and behavioural sciences, including psychology, sociology, economics, and anthropology
Place of	• Generally assumes illness occurs across cultures, so culture is a secondary factor	• Culture shapes personal problems and solutions in very important ways

	MEDICAL DIAGNOSIS	SOCIAL WORK ASSESSMENT IN PROBLEM SOLVING
Causation	• Presumes that illness is caused by biological or psychosocial factors, possibly triggered by environmental stress	• Biological and psychosocial factors play an important part in personal functioning, but so do social factors, values, culture, and economic conditions, as well as many other possible factors

Goal Setting

The next step in the problem-solving process is goal setting, though some see this step as part of or an extension of assessment. Goal setting determines the focus of intervention. Goals identify the problems that the client and social worker have chosen to solve. They must be measurable, communicable, and observable. We do not mean by measureable that goals need to be quantified—far from it. Most goals are complex and it is either difficult or counterproductive to attempt to quantify them. We mean by measurement that the worker and client must each have the same understanding of goals and that they can successfully communicate with each other progress to goal attainment. Often the goals are expressed in narrative, descriptive terms.

In our case example, suppose Ann tells Kim that she wants a better life. Probably Kim's first question would be, "What do you mean by a better life?" Unless Kim understands what Ann means, they cannot properly communicate. They need to be clear about what Ann means by "a better life." If Ann tells Kim that she would like a new job and to get her children back, and that if she can accomplish these two goals then she believes that her life would be better, Kim will better understand Ann because Ann has stated the goals in terms that can easily be communicated.

Change is important but it is not easy to measure all kinds of change—for example, shifts in thinking, attitude, or beliefs. But such changes may be significant in the course of work with clients. The critical point is that both client and worker must be able to arrive at the same definition and conception of the goals and both must be able to determine progress.

The values of the client and social worker help determine goals. As explained in Chapter 3, a value is an assertion of truth or belief. A goal is really no more than a valued end. A goal in social work, in simple terms, is the desired end result of the intervention process. A key function of social work values is to guide the worker in establishing goals with the client.

Often, goals must be prioritized. For example, Ann's primary stated goal is to get her children back.

Case Example

Kim and Ann ▼

Kim and her agency are firm. While their goal is also family reconciliation, they will not return Ann's children to her until other problems are solved. Most important to them is Ann's ability to handle her role as parent along with other key life roles.

Continued

Kim decides to engage Ann in a process that could lead to the return of her children. They must prioritize their goals. Number one is family reconciliation. When Ann resorts to social assistance benefits, her self-esteem suffers. The two of them decide that she must find a suitable job and appropriate childcare arrangements before her children can be returned to her.

Kim believes there is another, prior step. She convinces Ann that before she gets a job, they must find ways for Ann to cope practically and emotionally with the competing expectations of employment and parenting. They both also realize that her son Jim's learning disabilities and hyperactivity may pose a long-term threat to his well-being. Focusing on this problem is a high priority. To summarize, they agree that for Ann to get her children back she must first find a good job and show that she can handle her different roles. Kim agrees to help Ann arrange childcare, which is necessary if Ann is to accomplish her goals. They must also find help for Jim. The goals, as in most life situations, are complex, multiple, and dependent on one another.

Finally, goals must be achievable. The ability to judge the difference between goals that are achievable and those that are hopeless or involve extreme risk is key to professional practice. Proper assessment will help ensure that the goals selected are realistic.

The Contract in the Problem-Solving Process

In social work there are a variety of different kinds of contracts. The nature of contracts can be quite complex. There are at least three kinds that are important and that we highlight in this book. A social work *business contract* sets out the administrative details of intervention, including length of meetings, payment, responsibilities, and roles of client and worker, among others. This sort of contract is particularly important in **private practice** or when there are important administrative arrangements that need to be made between worker and client.

Another kind of contract is a *no harm contract*. Sometimes social workers need to have the client agree to a certain condition. Usually, such contracts are established when risk is involved. A common example is a *no harm to self contract*. This sort of contract is very common in crisis work where suicide is a possibility.

The worker may make the contract conditional. For example, if a client threatens suicide and hence violates the contract, the worker may notify the police. Another example of a conditional contract involves work with families in which violence has taken place. The worker may make "no violence" a condition of treatment.

Probably the type of contract that gets the most attention in the literature is the practice contract. Exhibit 8.2 shows contracting as an important part of all stages of problem solving. Contracting is the process of client and social worker negotiating and agreeing on the outcome of four of the steps in the problem-solving process. This means that to provide effective help, the social worker and client must agree on the problems to be solved, the understanding of these problems (the broad assessment), the goals and objectives that the worker is to help the client meet, and the means (type of intervention) to be used in meeting these goals. (See Boyle et al., 2009, pp. 190–201; Kirst-Ashman and Hull, 2009, pp. 203–7; and Tutty, 2002.)

Case Example

Kim and Ann ▼

A central part of the relationship between Kim and Ann were the contracts—sometimes partnerships—that they reached. For example, both agreed that Ann had several problems that needed resolution. These were limited formal education, loss of job and income, and role strain. Ann agreed with Kim's assessment that she had the capacity to hold a good job and was capable of pursuing formal education, but that strain in a variety of her roles hindered her job performance and the possibility of pursuing education. They also concurred that ultimately (primary goal) Ann should regain custody of her children. To reach this goal, Ann first had to upgrade her education, find a job, and work on her parenting skills. Ann reluctantly accepted this process, though she knew it would take at least a year. Kim had reached a contract with Ann.

Establishing a contract usually does not happen easily. Often a client and social worker begin from different positions and must make an effort to narrow the gaps or differences to move toward a contract. Again, the problem-solving process suggests a clear principle that helps this happen: start where the client is. For the social worker, this means using careful listening and other communication skills. She or he also needs a clear and informed understanding of the client's perception of the problems. Kim's task is to understand Ann's problems from Ann's point of view, make her own judgments about the problems, and attempt mutual definition of them. Throughout the problem-solving process, Kim intentionally attempted to arrive at mutual understanding.

The stronger the agreement between the worker and the client at each step of the problem-solving process, the more likely the worker will be able to effectively help the client solve the problems.

Although not always done, the contract should be put in writing. There are some important reasons for doing so. First, a written contract helps clarify possible misunderstandings. Second, it can be a good reference point for evaluations. Third, it provides documentation if required by the courts. Finally, it is a tool of intervention. Occasionally referring to the contract and updating it from time to time can help keep the intervention process on track.

Power and Social Work Contracts

Power is a central issue in establishing business, conditional, and practice contracts. This is so both in situations in which clients are voluntary and not voluntary. Particularly in no harm and conditional contracts, the worker attempts to directly exercise control over clients in order to reduce risk.

Kim, throughout, had both implied and real power over Ann. Ann, for example, was aware that Kim had the power to greatly influence whether her children were to be returned to her. This is power granted to Kim through the mandate of her agency, and it gave her a limited right to control Ann's behaviour. It was a form of social control. Kim has the legal (mandated) power to control regardless of whether Ann wants it.

Now, consider another kind of power that is also important between Kim and Ann. When a client seeks or accepts the services of the social worker (Ann wants Kim to help her have her children returned to her), there is the expectation that worker will have the expertise and skill to help the client. This expertise gives the worker a form of power over clients. If a client accepts and utilizes this expertise and skill, then the client grants the worker the right to influence the client. This is a particularly important type of power, because if the client accepts the influence attempted by the worker, then it increases the likelihood of positive change. The result is an implied contract; the client grants the worker the right to use her or his expertise to help (influence) the client.

Intervention

Intervention is the action that the social worker or client takes toward solving problems. Generally, intervention flows from the assessment and the established goals.

Intervention includes both treatment (action to alleviate a problem) and prevention of a problem's possible reoccurrence. There are two kinds of prevention: primary prevention is an attempt to keep a problem from occurring in the first place, while secondary prevention attempts to stop the development of new problems while working on an existing one. For instance, if one is attempting to help a person with a chemical addiction recover, one might also attempt to prevent the loss of his or her job.

Social work intervention consists of many parts. Social work roles have been discussed in Chapter 3. Chapter 9 addresses theory that is commonly used in assessment and intervention, while Chapters 11 to 14 discuss strengths, Aboriginal, feminist, and structural practices.

The following case example describing Kim's work with Ann highlights how a single case manager can perform a number of roles.

Case Example

Kim and Ann ▼

Kim begins her intervention by helping Ann contact the employment centre. She ensures that Ann has appropriate clothing for approaching employers and is clear about the type of job she wants. The two spend some time discussing how Ann will approach potential employers, and during this discussion they role-play some job interviews. Kim also arranges to have a report sent to her from the employment counsellor.

The next time Ann sees Kim, Kim has the employment report and Ann is somewhat dejected. Her employment counsellor told her that without better reading and writing skills, Ann will not be able to get a job that pays enough to support her family. So Ann and Kim are back at the beginning and must devise plan B.

Kim is there to give Ann support and encourage her to consider alternatives. She helps Ann lay them out, ranging from doing nothing to upgrading her education. The "do nothing" option would mean that Ann's children would remain in foster care. Going back to school would be a long-term effort and would require certain sacrifices. However, by this time, Kim is convinced that Ann has the strength to select this option and senses that Ann is leaning toward making this decision.

Returning to school would mean that Ann would have to go on welfare under a provincial program that encourages training of welfare recipients. However, applicants must first prove that their employment depends on further education. Kim helps and encourages Ann to check out the specifics of the local adult education program. Ann agrees to do this herself.

However, the welfare application poses a bigger challenge. Kim agrees to broker Ann's application with the department of welfare and, if necessary, advocate for her.

Kim also agrees to contact the school for a report on Ann's son Jim. Ann does not think that Jim has had a good medical and psychological assessment. Kim will find out what resources are available for him and lay out the alternatives for Ann and the temporary foster parents.

Note that in the case example, as intervention proceeds, the goals change. Returning to school was at first ruled out. However, when Ann found out that good employment depended on it, she reconsidered. This meant that there would be a delay in working out how to solve the important role strains and associated problems until her schooling had begun. However, help for Ann's son could not wait.

Let us summarize the interventions from the example. The overall role of the social worker, Kim, is case management. She also acts as a broker and advocate with the welfare department. By showing support and encouragement, she enables Ann. By helping her prepare for and go to the employment centre by herself, Kim attempts to help Ann do things for herself. We could call this empowerment. Kim also helps Ann with decision making by listing alternatives for her consideration. All interventions are in the context of building a strong helping relationship and problem solving.

Note how Kim uses multiple roles and interventions. If we were to present the contacts between Kim and Ann in greater detail, we would be able to see even more interventions. Social workers need to be able to use multiple interventions that vary depending on the case situation and relevant circumstances.

Evaluation

Social workers often seem to emphasize assessment and intervention and pay less attention to evaluation of the process. However, evaluation should be viewed as an important step in the problem-solving process, and it should occur at all stages of the process because it is the mechanism for feedback. For instance, as intervention progresses, the social worker and the client should regularly review and update the problems to be worked on.

Evaluation helps social workers decide whether to push on as planned or revisit earlier stages. Often evaluation results in reassessment and new strategies of intervention. It helps in making judgments about the progress and effectiveness of intervention. Another primary use of evaluation is to decide when and how to end intervention.

Direct practice evaluation helps the social worker and the client understand the progress that they have made, the effectiveness of the specific helping process, the need for further interventions, and, possibly, the decision to end the relationship. Evaluating client–social worker contact should take place during each intervention.

Often evaluation is informal. Informal evaluations are usually based on a specific type of formal evaluation but do not have a structured schedule or protocol. Many social work situations do not allow the time for formal evaluations.

It is the responsibility of the worker, with the client, to evaluate the process and effectiveness of intervention. While a formal process is probably best to evaluate practice, we argue that all problem-solving processes with clients should engage in at least an informal evaluation.

Evaluation in day-to-day social work practice is mostly qualitative rather than quantitative. **Qualitative evaluation** is generally a description of outcomes and process. A framework, usually one that is easy to construct, guides such evaluations. It may consist of merely a listing of reference points and goals with agreed-upon ways to chart progress. Quantitative evaluation often flows from qualitative efforts. Quantitative evaluations are methods that allow observations to be measured in numeric terms. For example, a couple that is experiencing nightly arguments might record the number of incidents on a chart over a 12-week course of therapy.

Evaluation of Progress in Everyday Practice

The method presented in this section assumes general adherence to a problem-solving approach and that all parts of the approach are flexible. This means that as social worker–client contact continues, all steps can be revisited and altered. For instance, during intervention an assessment may change and, as a result, goals may be reformulated and new interventions engaged. The evaluation of practice involves at least two factors: outcome and goal attainment, and process.

An outcome is simply the result of any intervention. Goal attainment is the extent to which goals have been met. Sometimes, outcome and goal attainment are the same thing. At other times, intervention can have an outcome that was not an intended goal. For instance, a couple in family therapy may have as a goal the reduction of hostile arguments. The achievement of this goal is obviously also an outcome. Suppose, because of the intervention, the female partner finds she is getting along better at work. The stronger relationships at work were not a goal set by the social worker or client but, like the improved marital relationship, are an outcome of the therapy.

Process evaluation is an evaluation of the method that the client–social worker team used in attempting to achieve the goals. Usually process evaluation answers such questions as the following: How satisfactory was the relationship building? What ups and downs were evident during the course of intervention? What were the actual methods of intervention? Was the intervention applied as intended? What steps did the worker do right? What steps need improvement? Responses to these questions tend to be qualitative by nature.

The following three steps put these ideas and assumptions together into a working model that practitioners can use to monitor everyday practice:

1. *Establish a clear reference point.* This step ensures a starting point or baseline against which to assess progress. Probably a key to professional practice is experience in judging the difference between goals that are achievable and those that are hopeless or extremely risky. Good assessment helps ensure that goals are appropriate.

   The reference point is a statement of a current problem, in measurable terms, that the client and social worker intend to solve. It is the current state—that is, where the client and social worker are currently in the relationship as opposed to where they want to be.

   The idea of establishing a clear reference point borrows from the concept of baseline as used in *single-subject designs* (see Bloom, Fischer, and Orme, 2003, Part 3) and *goal attainment scaling* (see Bloom, Fischer, and Orme, 2003, pp. 102–5). Both are generally *quantitative designs*. The reference point is often part of the *narrative* of the client's story and is frequently expressed in qualitative, or descriptive, terms. Often the reference point is in-depth information about the client's perception of her or his problem and the implied goals of intervention.

   The reference point is usually derived from the connection between goals and problems. In the problem-solving model, goals usually imply a solution to a problem. For example, Ann defines her major problem as losing her job. Ann and Kim agree that this is an important problem and develop two related goals. The first is to upgrade Ann's education and, when this is accomplished, the second is to find her suitable employment. Both of the identified problems of lack of a job and limited formal education are obvious reference points.

   In this example, both the reference points and the goals are stated in reasonably specific and measurable terms. Such clarity and specificity make evaluation possible.

   Sometimes, however, the problem is not identified in clear and measurable terms. Suppose Kim wants to evaluate progress related to the stress Ann feels in trying to be both mother and worker. Kim, along with Ann, needs to identify the specifics of the role strain that pose problems. For example, Ann may tell Kim that demands at work make Ann so tired that she has no time for the children. However, this may not be specific enough. Ann may need to be clear about what demands she is referring to and articulate what she means by "no time for the children." When the general problem is abstract, it needs to be restated in terms that both worker and client understand. Once clearly stated, the problem becomes a reference point against which change or progress is measured at a later time.

2. *Clearly articulate goals connected to the reference point(s).* In the problem-solving process, if client and worker cannot clearly understand stated goals, then the goals are essentially worthless. In part, this means that the social worker and the client will be unable to figure out whether intervention has been successful.

   Techniques such as goal attainment scaling and small sample designs sometimes require quantifiable (measurable in numbers) indicators. While quantification is not necessary and often not appropriate for evaluating everyday practice, the language used to describe the goals must be sufficiently clear for the social worker and the client to know when they have or have not reached their goals, and so each will have the same understanding of both baseline and goals.

3. *Evaluate progress: evaluation time-outs.* A social worker should always build into the problem-solving process a way to evaluate the progress being made. Every intervention session should include time-outs to evaluate progress. This may include beginning with, "Where are we today?" and ending with a summary of progress. At the end of each session, the social worker and client should agree on issues to work on at the next meeting or follow up on later.

A direct practitioner should use the evaluation time-outs, whether at the beginning, middle, or end of sessions, in at least three different ways:

1. To evaluate progress on goals in the relationship to the established reference points. This is central and will help both social worker and client determine whether the interventions are working.

2. To evaluate the process or method. The social worker and the client might ask questions such as, "How satisfactory is communication? Are there better ways to achieve our goals? Does the process seem to be achieving our goals?"

3. To decide whether the intervention is having effects other than helping to achieve goals.

Case Example

Kim and Ann ▼

Kim and Ann have not developed a formal evaluation process. When Kim first began working with Ann, she did not see the need. However, it has quickly become clear that evaluation will be important.

A clear and easy-to-state reference point is Ann's lack of education. However, when Kim began to connect the goal of "upgrade education" to the reference point in measurable terms, the goal suddenly seemed less clear.

What did they mean by upgrading Ann's education? Together, Kim and Ann begin a process to determine what they mean by "upgrading."

Both realize that, at a minimum, Ann must develop better reading and writing skills. But how long will this take? What level of skills does Ann need? Kim helps Ann to develop a process that leads to making a decision regarding the level of educational upgrading. This involves talking with employment counsellors, administrators of the adult education program, and the local welfare department. This time Kim knows that she must pay more attention to evaluation.

In effect, Kim and Ann identified two new problems. The first was the need to redefine the goal of upgrading Ann's education, and the second was the related lack of needed information. The two new reference points thus became "lack of information" and "no clear definition of upgrading." Kim helps Ann devise a plan to talk to the appropriate people to get the needed information. However, since Ann cannot write well enough to keep notes, they have to schedule several meetings to monitor her progress. Together they lay out the information supplied, the alternatives available to Ann, and the pros and cons of each. By monitoring this process and taking evaluation time-outs, Kim ensures that Ann makes a good decision.

If evaluation is informal, as it often is, the evaluation time-outs may simply be discussions of progress between social worker and client. While it is not necessary to put the evaluation in writing, some find this useful. For instance, a simple way is to list all of the reference points and goals. Then, during each evaluation time-out, chart or write down the progress. This is really a form of ordered recording. If it is made part of the intervention progress, the client should participate. However, the social worker can also record progress for agency purposes after the client has left, and to prepare for the next meeting.

Results of the evaluation time-outs can lead to redefinition of the problem (and by implication a new or different reference point), a different assessment, new or revised goals, a new means of intervention, and help in making a decision for ending the relationship. The process will work if the social worker (and client) consciously builds it into the helping process as an ongoing procedure.[1]

An important yet difficult part of any evaluation research is to link process with outcome. It is usually easy to describe process and measure application against some model. Specifying clear goals usually results in the ability to measure outcomes.

Evaluation in Short-Term and Involuntary Relationships

So far we have assumed that the client and the social worker can agree on goals and that the contact extends over at least several sessions. However, similar principles of evaluation apply in short-term contacts.

Crisis intervention is a good example of short-term contacts. In crisis situations, such as calls to a suicide hotline or a mobile crisis team, the social worker may need to act quickly to try to prevent a suicide from occurring. Nevertheless, identifying the problem implies the existence of a reference point. Goal setting may emerge quickly, as does formulating a contract for and an ending to the relationship. For instance, a call on a hotline or a request for face-to-face help from a crisis team worker may primarily be a plea for help (which is always taken seriously). The goal of both client and worker is help. This may never be clearly articulated, yet is usually understood by both parties. Evaluation time-outs may serve to restate difficulties in getting help or to review specific plans for referral to a helping agency, which may include such details as transportation to the helping resource.

In involuntary contacts, the social worker's primary role may be to monitor the behaviour of an offender or to protect an abused child rather than to provide personal helping. However, evaluation is still required in these instances, maybe even more so than with voluntary clients. The principles of establishing a reference point, setting goals, and determining outcomes remain important. The differences are that the reference point and goals are from third parties, usually mandated by an agency or the courts, and evaluation is usually done by the social worker alone. However, when possible, it remains important to share the evaluation with the client even though he or she may not agree with it or with the process.

Endings

All problem-solving processes must eventually end. Usually either an explicit or implicit goal of the process is to help the client learn how to engage in his or her own problem solving without further need for social work assistance. When accomplished, ending of the helping process should take place.

Ending is a general concept that means closing the contact between social worker and client. There are many possible endings, including referral, a decision that no further help is needed or warranted, termination, unplanned endings, and combinations of these.

Referral

Referral means connecting the client with a needed resource or service. It may or may not end the professional relationship. However, for many social work interventions, referral does become an ending for the referring source. Referral after first contact is a frequent outcome of many social work interventions.

Sometimes, however, referral is not an ending but simply a need for further service. For instance, Kim referred Ann to an employment counsellor but did not end her relationship with Ann.

Referral involves several important tasks. The social worker must make sure that the referral instructions are clear and the client has the capacity to carry them out. If not, the worker needs to help the client complete the referral. This may range from simply giving verbal instructions to actually taking the client to the referral agency. It is equally important that the client understand the reasons for the referral. Like all parts of social work intervention, the referral process is really a form of contract. Referral is most successful if both client and worker agree not only on why the referral is important but also on the type of referral, the expected service, and the goals of the referral.

Often, the social worker must prepare the referral agency for the client. This may involve arranging an appointment and, with the client's agreement, sending information about the client to the new agency. It is important that the worker's professional responsibility go beyond simply giving the client a referral source. Further follow-up ensures that the client takes appropriate action. If the referral falls through, the social worker can also intervene.

Termination (Planned Ending)

The process of termination is used to end the intervention after the client and worker have completed the agreed-upon work. It is a planned process that should take place when the worker and the client believe that the client's problem solving can continue without the worker's assistance.

The significance of termination is a direct function of the strength of the relationship between client and worker, their attachment, and the length of service. Often, the process is an emotional one. Sometimes obvious change has taken place and both client and worker readily agree that there is no longer a need for continued service. Other times, progress is less apparent but it seems that the worker has done all that is possible. The social worker sometimes thinks it is time to terminate the relationship while the client does not. The reverse may also happen, when the social worker feels that there is more work to be done but the client disagrees and wants to end the relationship. Termination is a process fraught with issues, most of them specific to the particular client–social worker situation.

Successful planned endings often take place when worker and client have met their goals. Goal completion signals the time for them to consider termination. It is important that both agree to end intervention.

The decision for termination should be based on ongoing evaluation. If a client and a social worker have established a process for ongoing evaluation, then the decision for termination should occur as a result of the evaluation.

Brill (1998) suggests that the client and worker must deal with unfinished business and feelings about ending the relationship and plan for the future. Often both agree that termination should occur, but other issues remain. Possibly the client has become dependent on the worker. Maybe, in the process of helping, they have discovered other areas that call for professional assistance. Sometimes both feel a loss when termination occurs, and both need to address this issue and take action to resolve it. Sometimes, when dealing with unfinished business, the social worker refers the client to another needed service.

Unplanned Endings

Unplanned endings occur for many reasons. A client may move, get sick, or even die. She or he may feel there is no longer a need for service or may submit to pressure from a family member or friend not to seek the services of a social agency. A social worker may get transferred or quit his or her job.

The social worker has at least two important functions in unplanned endings. If the ending is the result of the worker's action (e.g., job transfer), then she or he has the responsibility to go through a termination process that will likely include referral. Often the referral is to another practitioner within the worker's own agency.

Most unplanned endings are the result of client action. In such cases, the social worker should try to find out the reasons for the client leaving. If the worker believes that service is still required or advisable, then she or he should take appropriate action. There are no real principles to guide "appropriate action," because the reasons for unplanned endings tend to be unique to each situation. Referral is a possibility. Working through some of the issues identified in the above section on termination is advisable. In many instances the worker should accept the client's judgment that service is not needed or not helpful.

Difficulties of unplanned endings occur when client–social worker interaction is not voluntary. If, for example, the court requires a youth on probation to visit his probation officer weekly and the youth stops the visits without court permission, the worker probably must report that action to the court. Even in such instances, the worker has the responsibility to ensure that he or she extends all possible services to the youth.

IMPLICATIONS OF THE PROBLEM-SOLVING APPROACH

Individual Orientation: A Limited Scope

The problem-solving approach tends to be individualistic in practice due to its focus on helping people solve specific, articulated life problems for themselves. The individual is the centre of the process. In the case example about Ann, the problems are Ann's, not her sister's or her social worker's or even society's. This means, much like the medical model, that Ann as an individual becomes the focus of expert attention aimed at solving her problems. While the model does not exclude interventions related to larger systems, problem solving in social work primarily focuses on the individual's behaviours and her or his adjustment to the environment. The problem-solving model generally does not question or challenge current social structures and institutions but implicitly accepts them as part of life. Nor can the paradigm be easily used to address social change. It offers instead a kind of blueprint of logical steps and procedures that can be applied and adapted to different problems in which interventions can be devised and outcomes measured.

The individual orientation of traditional problem solving encourages the tendency to place people in categories, a professional kind of shortcut that tends to pigeonhole. Saleebey (2006a) puts it this way: "When we transform persons into cases, we often see only them and how well they fit into a category. In this way, we miss important elements of the client's life—cultural, social, political, ethnic, spiritual, and economic—and how they contribute to, sustain, and shape a person's misery or struggles or mistakes" (p. 6) (also see Holmes, 1997). For example, when youths are convicted of crimes, helpers and others may define them as delinquents. By doing so, these youths are put into a category of people who are seen to share similar characteristics instead of being understood as unique individuals. In the context of his or her own environment, the individual youth is partly defined in terms of characteristics that are associated with others labelled "delinquents." Usually this definition emphasizes deficits. The youth is typecast ("pigeonholed") by the category that has been assigned to him or her. The better the perceived fit to the category "delinquent," the more the youth has been typecast and defined by the helper's conception of delinquents. The placement into categories does not help the problem-solving process.

Restorative versus Promotional Approach

The problem-solving approach is essentially restorative. Restorative—sometimes called *residual*—in this context means that action (intervention or treatment) takes place only after the social worker and client have identified a problem that requires solution. Intervention is restorative because it is an action taken to alleviate an identified and existing problem.

Generally, a person must experience a problem before helping takes place. Kim helped Ann only after she left her children unattended. If there had been no problem in the eyes of the Child Protection Agency, there would have been no intervention. Most social and health agencies focus their efforts on residual problem solving: mental health agencies generally treat patients only after they are diagnosed with a mental illness; the criminal justice system usually works with people who are legally defined as offenders; and so on. All of these are examples of treatment after the fact. A problem-solving approach fits restorative programs because they have similar bases.

The flip side of restoration is sometimes called a *promotional approach*. This approach results in programs that are different from those intended to solve a specific problem. Promotional programs are aimed at addressing wider needs. For example, public health education programs are often designed to promote good health in a large population; the Canadian government's promotion of physical fitness and programs aimed at keeping teenagers in school are examples. Often one of the goals of promotional programs is prevention of problems.

Case Example

Kim and Ann ▼

As part of the effort to help Ann get her life back on track, Kim suggests that she needs to consider her own physical well-being. The local health centre has just established a top-notch wellness clinic that offers a physical fitness and mental health promotion program. Because the centre is government-funded, it is able to defray most of the costs for people on social assistance.

Ann likes the idea and enrolls in the program. The intent of both Kim and Ann is not to solve a particular problem but to help improve Ann's quality of life and possibly, as she feels better about herself, improve her ability to solve her own problems.

Continued

Kim also thinks it would be a good idea to put Ann's younger son, John (age 4), into a pre-kindergarten learning centre. First, however, Kim consults with Ann. Ann quickly agrees. All children are eligible to attend, and the purpose of the learning centre is to prepare them for the public school system. The purpose is not restorative but promotional. (If the intent of the centre were to help children "catch up," then one might consider the purpose restorative.)

Social Worker as Expert: An Issue of Power

The problem-solving model holds that a partnership between the social worker and the client is essential. The professional relationship is built on this partnership. However, this is a relationship with important power differentials.

Even in relationships that are entirely voluntary, the worker is presumed by both the client and the worker to be an expert with good practice skills. Certainly one reason people with problems seek out social workers for help is because they perceive them to have expert knowledge and skills. A marriage counsellor without specialized knowledge and skills would likely not be very effective or helpful.

Thus it is important *not* to assume that in problem solving the client–social worker partnership is one of equality of power. Social workers must know how to effectively, ethically, and judiciously use this power differential in order to engage and work effectively with clients. A major reason social work, and also most other professions, has a code of ethics is to regulate the potential power of the professional and help prevent the abuse of power.

Other approaches to practice are critical of power differentials in the helping relationship and suggest different ways to build helping relationships that minimize power differences. These are discussed in Chapters 11 to 14, on the strengths, Aboriginal, feminist, and structural approaches.

Involuntary Problem Solving, Social Control, and the Principle of Best Interest

The problem-solving process was illustrated using the case of Ann, a single mother, and Kim, a family social worker in a child protection agency. Although Ann was initially an involuntary client, she quickly formed a helping relationship with Kim. What might have happened if, as it often does, Ann had not wanted Kim's help? Ann would have been an involuntary client and the problem-solving process would have been very different.

The Canadian Association of Social Workers *Guidelines for Ethical Practice* (CASW, 2005b) (particularly Section 1.4, "Responsibilities to Involuntary Clients and Clients Not Capable of Consent") establishes an ethical framework for providing help when help is not wanted or not requested. The *Guidelines* urge a strong commitment to clients and their best interest, but provide for a wide range of exceptions that permit social workers in Canada to ethically make decisions against the will of their clients. If clients are presumed to be at risk to themselves or others, the right of clients to make decisions by themselves may be suspended, always assuring that such action remains in a client's best interest. Under these circumstances, social workers clearly act as agents of social control.

Suppose Ann did not want help from Kim but made it very clear that she wanted her children back. Kim and the agency would not agree to return them if they could clearly show that the children were at risk. A child protection agency is a mandated agency and is legally responsible for the safety of the children and must protect their interests. Their safety and well-being would have the highest priority.

In our case example, if Ann is an involuntary client, Kim still has an obligation to provide service to her. Kim can still follow the problem-solving process—by, for instance, clearly laying out to Ann the conditions under which the Child Protection Agency will return her children. She can also suggest alternative plans and resources that might be available to Ann. Kim may even make decisions that affect Ann without her consent. Another possibility is to show Ann that the quickest and best way to have her children returned is to problem solve with Kim. Kim may attempt to negotiate a helping relationship with Ann. In mandated practice, the social worker can intervene without the agreement of the client if the worker can justify that the action is in the best interest of the client.

Often probation or parole officers are faced with clients who are assumed to be a potential risk to society but who do not want help. They appear for interviews only because they are forced, by threats of penalty, by the courts. In these cases the best interest is often that of society as well as of the parolee. People in mental health hospitals may be treated against their will. This can occur even if the courts have not committed a patient to the hospital. Often patients are "voluntarily" hospitalized because a family member, public agency, or community entity threatens some form of action if they do not seek treatment.

Notwithstanding the intent, the principle of best interest sanctions the social worker to determine what is best for the client as long as the worker can clearly document the reasons for doing so. The principle holds the worker as expert with power over the client in both voluntary and involuntary relationships. Determining best interest is a judgment call made by social workers. Since such judgments profoundly affect the lives of others, the skills to make them are some of the most important that social workers need.

The principle of best interest permits suspension of the right of self-determination. The strengths perspective, Chapter 11, argues a different process called a *consumer-driven approach*. In this approach, the client is seen as the expert in "charge" of intervention. As will be developed in Chapter 11, there are some contradictions between a best interest and consumer-driven approach.

CHAPTER SUMMARY

This chapter has presented an overview of what is often considered the foundation of traditional social work practice. The problem-solving process in social work involves a number of elements, which are graphically displayed in Exhibit 8.2:

- Define the problem(s)
- Conduct an assessment
- Set goals and objectives
- Establish a contract
- Intervene
- Evaluate the process
- End the process

The formation of a practice contract between the social worker and the client is central to problem solving. Successful helping depends on agreement on the problems, their nature, and an understanding about them; the goals of intervention; and the action required to meet these goals.

In this chapter we suggest a workable, informal method that front-line social workers can use to evaluate their everyday work. The three basic steps are as follows:

1. Establish a clear reference point.
2. Clearly articulate goals connected to the reference point.
3. Evaluate progress and take evaluation time-outs.

Understanding implications of the problem-solving process is important. We have identified several of them:

1. The problem is usually that of the person and it is the person's responsibility, with help, to solve the problem.
2. Intervention is a restorative process.
3. The worker is seen as an expert and in a position of power.
4. The principle of best interest and how the principle is used is important to address in work with involuntary clients.

Much of the remainder of this book takes the reader beyond problem solving by critiquing, informing, and discussing enhancements to the traditional social work process.

NOTE

1 The logic used in this example is similar to the research strategy of goal attainment scaling and single subject designs. Goal attainment scaling is a formal and sometimes complicated process for evaluating the extent to which practice goals have been met (see Grinnell, 1993; Kiresuk, Smith, and Cardillo, 1994; and Tripodi, 1994).

chapter 9

The Broad Knowledge Base of Social Work

Theory and use of knowledge in social work is necessary to conduct assessments, set goals, plan, and carry out interventions. The goal of this chapter is to begin to articulate the theoretical foundations of social work and to connect these foundations to assessment.

This Chapter ▼

- begins to build the theoretical foundations of social work
- argues that social work practice requires theoretical diversity and a broad knowledge base
- shows the links to the social sciences
- develops ecosystems as an assessment framework
- uses ecosystems to organize a range of diverse theories basic to social work
- briefly describes a selection of diverse theoretical perspectives and links them to assessment
- is closely linked to Chapter 10, Application of Focused Assessment within a Broad Knowledge Base; Chapter 10 uses a diverse and broad knowledge base in the assessment of clients

Recap of the First Eight Chapters ▼

In this textbook, the first eight chapters of this book presented basic principles that form the foundations of the broad knowledge base of generalist social work practice. These are as follows:

- Social work practice is strongly influenced by an ideology that is based on a set of values.
- Generalist social work consists of a variety of roles.
- Social work is practised in the context of social and agency policy, legislation, and social welfare institutions.
- Forming professional relationships is a necessary part of social work intervention.
- Social workers must understand culture and cultural diversity and be able to practise cross-culturally.
- Social workers must understand oppression and practice anti-oppression.
- Traditional social work practice is built on a problem-solving approach.

THEORETICAL DIVERSITY

For about three-quarters of a century social work searched, to no avail, for a single, unified theory of social work. Historically there have been two main theories that held promise. Up until about the mid-20th century, casework adopted Freudian psychoanalytic or neo-Freudian theory. Emphasis was on the inner person. By the mid-1970s, emphasis shifted to person-in-the-environment, with many asserting the unifying power of systems theory.

Today most accept that derivatives of Freudian theory, such as ego psychology, and person-in-the-environment theories (e.g., ecological or ecosystems) are important, but there is no unified theory of social work practice or human behaviour that is useful to social workers (Forte, 2007; McMahon, 1994, pp. 85–86; Turner, 1999a, p. 26). Instead social workers use a range of diverse theories. Current thinking is that there is no unifying theory on the horizon and that this is a positive development, a step forward.

Francis Turner (2002) asserts, "If there is any single term that best describes the theoretical basis of contemporary Canadian social work it is that of diversity" (p. 47). Forte (2007) uses the colourful phrase "multiple theoretical languages" to articulate theoretical diversity. He (Forte, 2007, p. 29) quotes Turner, "the challenge for the field is to differentially draw from the spectrum of practice theories we are privileged to have and put together a profile of intervention that best suits the situations of various vulnerable individuals, dyads, families, groups and communities" (Turner, 1999b, p. 30).

Interestingly, Turner observes that Canadian social work has led other countries in accepting the principle of theoretical diversity. He speculates that this may, in part, be due to our acceptance of cultural diversity (Turner, 2002, p. 46). The world is diverse, and if so, so should be our theories that attempt to explain social and human behaviour.

"The social worker who speaks multiple theoretical languages can help his or her clients better than the no-language or one-language social worker" (Forte, 2007, p. 29). Having access to and working knowledge a wide range of theoretical views leads to more competent practice.

Theoretical diversity has two meanings. The first is that social work as a profession must embrace a wide range of theoretical perspectives. This range covers the breadth of social work practice: from micro to macro practice, from direct practice to social policy analysis, from conservative to radical orientations.

The second meaning is that each social worker needs to be able to incorporate a broad base of theory into his or her practice. This selection of theory is only a portion of the wide range of theoretical conceptions available to the profession.

BROAD KNOWLEDGE BASE

Knowledge used in social work practice is not based solely on theory. Theory constitutes only part of what social workers must know and incorporate into practice and to engage in assessment and intervention. Hence, the notion of diversity is included in the conception of a broad knowledge base.

Practice includes skills that are learned over long periods of time and are incorporated within one's total life experiences. One experienced worker has suggested such skills are often difficult to articulate, are intangible, and are learned by "osmosis"—a biological metaphor referring to an unconscious process of learning. Many of these skills are in the area of developing meaningful and helpful human relationships. Others rest in understanding, appreciating, and empathizing with the human and social condition.

The best way to acquire knowledge depends on the subject matter and the purpose of knowing. The following are five common sources of knowledge that we all use to learn about ourselves, our world, and our environment and, of course, social work.

1. *Diversity of theory*: As explained in the previous section of this chapter, theory that social workers use is wide ranging and diverse.
2. *Life experience (wisdom)*. Maybe the most common and important way that all of us learn is through our life experiences. For instance, what we learn as a child has an enormous impact on adult life. How social workers face adversity in their personal life will undoubtedly affect their approach to practice. So too will the nature of adversity. If one was abused as a child, for instance, then that experience will influence how the worker will approach work in child welfare.

   Age of worker is important. Older workers have more life experience and are more likely to have more experience in problem solving. Most certainly this will influence practice.

   We could continue with many more illustrations. It is sufficient to point out that life experience may be the most important source of a social worker's knowledge.
3. *Culture, tradition, and religion*. A critical part of life experience that shapes our understanding of the world is our culture and associated traditions. Culture is often intrinsically linked with spirituality or religion, and these reflect many of the values of a culture. All religions assert a foundation of truths, many of which are based on articles of faith. The social worker's culture shapes his or her knowledge base. As well, the social worker must understand how the views and knowledge of clients are products of their cultural background.

4. *Authority.* We often accept knowledge because an expert tells us something is so. This is particularly true if we know little about the subject matter. Thus we tend to accept the teachings of those we consider knowledgeable.

While depending on authority is a quick and easy way to acquire knowledge, it is fraught with problems when accepted unquestioningly; so, it is not a good way for professionals in any field to build knowledge. How can we be sure that the expert is correct? In professional practice it is up to each practitioner to have the tools to evaluate the validity and usefulness of information. Social workers must be able to make judgments about assertions, theory, research, and the like. Without observation and testing, reliance on authority can lead to accepting dogma and incorrect conclusions.

5. *Observation and testing.* Observation and testing are integral parts of life experience that are practised in all cultures. The process is a part of everyday life.

We all learn how to observe and test as small children. Observation is the process of perceiving something through one or more of the senses. It can be very simple; for example, a toddler just learning to talk who listens to a parent speak and hears a word that he cannot pronounce demonstrates a simple form of observation. The child then may then test the observation by attempting to speak the word.

Testing is an attempt to validate, or determine the truth of, an observation. The toddler's effort to speak the word is a type of testing. The child may test whether and how others respond when he attempts to pronounce the word. If the response is rewarding, the child will likely continue to use the word. Eventually it will probably become part of his vocabulary.

Now, look at an Aboriginal woman who is a BSW graduate and counsellor in a Saskatchewan reserve. She works with people who often have very low self-esteem, are despondent, feel hopeless, and place a lot of psychological blame on themselves. Sometimes the counsellor talks about colonization (see Chapter 12) and observes that often, as people begin to understand what happened to them in the past, they seem to feel a little better about themselves. The woman then begins to intentionally use, in her counselling, discussions of the past to help clients understand colonization and how it affects their lives. Again, as she tests her observations, she notes an improvement in self-respect and a reduction in self-blame. A process of observation and testing was used. In fact, many current direct helping techniques were actually developed by processes similar to this example.

Observation and testing can be very rigorous. The process is at the heart of science and most theory building. Science is a rigorous way to build knowledge by observing and testing. Scientists generate hypotheses from theory and then test them. Other times science draws generalizations from observations.

THEORY IN SOCIAL WORK

All theories address only parts, rather than the whole, of the human condition. Some are more useful than others, depending on the nature of problems, the setting, the culture, and a host of other factors. One of the important steps in becoming a professional social worker is learning how to select and use theory that best serves, addresses, and focuses the assessment and intervention problems at hand. This skill must be learned over time and honed throughout one's professional life.

The term *theory* is often used in several different ways and sometimes loosely. Sometimes it is used to speculate about an explanation for an event when evidence is not available, not known, or unclear. For instance, a friend notices that John feels blue. The friend may state, "It is my theory that John is blue because he did not do well in school," even though the friend does not actually know the reasons for John's feelings; the assertion is really an educated guess. This is not what is meant by a theory in the social sciences.

The purpose of a theory is to explain or predict part of the world. A theory consists of a network of concepts. These concepts are sometimes observable (empirical) and sometimes abstract. At least some of the concepts must be empirical in order to test the theory. Also, at least some of the concepts must be either logically or empirically connected to each other.

The above description of theory is accurate but rather technical and probably does not reflect everyday use of the term. Turner provides a definition that better reflects usage in social work: "Theory is the term that describes those efforts that have marked the history of the human race to explain various aspects of reality around us in a special way. … they are provided in a manner that can be tested and verified by others" (Turner, 2002, p. 48).

The terms *perspective*, *approach*, and *framework* are often used to describe theoretical ideas, and sometimes in place of the word *theory*. These terms sometimes seem to be used interchangeably, yet there are some differences. *Approach* tends to be used when the subject matter is primarily intervention—for example, an Aboriginal approach to practice. *Perspective* usually refers to a broad view about an area of practice with many very loosely related concepts but with a central theme—for example, the strengths perspective. A *framework* is similar to the use of perspective but defines the context of something. Person-in-the-environment is a framework that helps organize assessment and intervention.

LINKS TO SOCIAL SCIENCES

Social work is related to psychology, sociology, anthropology, economics, and other fields of study. Social work shares with these social sciences the interest in and need to understand human personal and social behaviour. For example, social workers, like economists, need to understand the effects of such factors as recessions or inflation. Like anthropologists exploring cultural beliefs, social workers are often required to know about individual and group perspectives on areas such as dating, marriage, and child rearing.

There are also substantial differences. Maybe the most obvious is the difference in emphasis between a profession and a discipline. The purpose of a profession is to provide a service, such as teaching, medical help, engineering service, or legal advice. The central purpose of a discipline such as sociology, psychology, or economics is to develop a deeper and better understanding of the world in which we live.

Medicine is a profession and essentially a human service. In order to practise, a physician clearly must possess a wealth of knowledge and skills. However, it is not the main purpose of medicine to develop new knowledge; rather, it is to provide medical services to people.

Yet new knowledge about health is very important to medicine, and many physicians spend their entire career in the pursuit of new knowledge. When they do, they make considerable use of knowledge developed in other disciplines. They may also be trained in a discipline such as biochemistry. Medicine uses biochemistry, a discipline, in order to help develop new knowledge to better meet its main professional goal of provision of health care services.

Social work is a human service profession. While developing new knowledge is important, it is not the main goal of social work. Social work, maybe more than most professions, uses theories and knowledge developed in disciplines. Most knowledge used by social workers to understand human behaviour and the social environment has been developed in such disciplines as sociology, economics, political science, and psychology.

Branches of some disciplines such as psychology provide human services. For example, clinical psychology and counselling psychology are two fields that provide therapeutic and counselling services to people. As in medicine, some social workers devote their careers to knowledge building. But, as in medicine, these social workers are in the minority. As a whole, the emphasis in social work is on providing human services, while in the scientific disciplines the primary, but certainly not exclusive, focus is the pursuit of knowledge.

ECOSYSTEMS AS A FRAMEWORK

Ecosystems can be conceptualized as a framework for assessment and intervention that connects a person with the environment. Ecosystems is a good way to conceptualize, understand, and map the relationships that a person, group, or even community has with their social environment.

Background

Up until the 1960s, theories that most social workers used, who worked with a person or family, focused on understanding the "inner person." The environment was merely seen as an external force that had an impact on the individual. There were few links that connected these domain-based theories of person and environment that social workers used (Turner, 2002, p. 47).

Some saw major flaws in using these theories. They argued that the person and the environment could not be separated. As early as 1958, Gordon Hearn began to apply systems theory to social work (Hearn, 1958). William Gordon (1969) laid some of the foundation for a new line of thinking. Gordon, a social work practice theoretician, suggested that the uniqueness of social work rested in the transaction between people and their environment—or, as he called it, the *interface*. What he meant was that the primary focus of social work should not be on psychological forces, the environment, or the social structure, but on the interface or relationship between the person and the social environment. This was very different from the commonly held view that the person and the environment were separate entities.

By the 1970s, an ecosystems perspective that captured the interface between people and the environment was articulated. This perspective has been developed and honed to the point that today it is frequently seen as fundamental to social work practice; to some, it forms the common base of all social work practice (Gitterman and Germain, 2008, pp. 5–70; McMahon, 1994; Meyer, 1983, 1988; Wakefield, 1996b).

Ecosystems

Ecosystems involves a combination of systems and ecological concepts (Meyer, 1988; Wakefield, 1996a, p. 4). Generally, a systems perspective examines the connection between a set of interacting elements. Systems theory in social work is a metaphor of a mechanistic model borrowed from the physical world. A system is seen as a whole with a number of parts that all, when working properly, contribute to the smooth functioning of the system. Interaction exists among parts of the whole, and between the system and other systems and with many feedback loops. For example, an individual may be viewed as the centre of that person's system. The person's system is all of the primary individuals and institutions (family members, school, work, social worker, friends, etc.) with whom the person interacts. Or the centre may be a family or agency or any other social unit.

An open system grows and develops by receiving and using input from outside sources as well as contributing to those sources. An open system reaches a healthy state when equilibrium, homeostasis, and steady state occurs (Forte, 2007, p. 197). Interactions are frequent and rewarding.

Equilibrium is a state of balance. Input and output operate smoothly with each other. An example in human relationships is that the reward that one gains from a relationship is roughly equal to what one puts in to it.

Homeostasis is a state "appropriate for a living organism." This state is considered healthy, and produces growth for the organism, and assumes a state of equilibrium (Forte, 2007, p. 197).

Steady state refers to an "open interchange with the environment." Human systems thrive on variety in the environment. Growth occurs through this interaction, particularly as new situations and goals are encountered (Forte, 2007, pp. 197).

All systems need attention. The organism must work at maintaining its health. Systems theory holds that organisms in healthy systems strive and work to maintain equilibrium, homeostasis, and steady state. However, an unattended system moves toward *entropy* (Forte, 2007, pp. 197–98).

In human systems, entropy is a state of disorganization and decreased interactions. A disorganized system that does not interact with other systems or parts of its own system, does not use input, or refuses input is a closed system and is fraught with problems (Payne, 2005, p. 144; Rodway, 1986, p. 517). They are unable to grow and be productive. According to systems, clients (individuals or families) who experience problems and seek help are often parts of closed systems.

To maintain homeostasis, a system must have some mechanism to achieve balance. The goal of intervention is to move from a state of entropy to a state of equilibrium, homeostasis, and a steady state. How this is accomplished depends upon the use of other theories, methods, or approaches.

The ecological perspective emphasizes the person-in-the-environment. Ecology is a biological concept that refers to the interrelationships between living organisms and their environments (Dubois and Miley, 1992, p. 58). Social work uses the biological metaphor of ecology as a framework. In biology, ecology refers to species relationship and adaptation to the natural world. The biological theory holds that a species will continue to survive and flourish if able to find suitable habitat.

Social work borrows concepts from biology and uses them as a metaphor to understand individual humans and their environment and how they relate and adapt to each other. "The ecological perspective makes clear the need to view people and environments as a unitary system within a particular cultural and historic context" (Germain and Gitterman, 1995, p. 816). The perspective emphasizes the unity of a person within his or her environment, and the focus of practice is on the interface between them.

Germain and Gitterman (1980, 1995; see also Gitterman and Germain, 2008) base their *life model of social work* on ecology. "In [the life model] human needs and problems are generated by transactions between persons and their environment, and through a process of continuous reciprocal adaptation, humans change and are changed by their physical and social environment" (Dubois and Miley, 1992, p. 59). Central to the ecological perspective is the concept of goodness of fit between the person and the environment (Wakefield, 1996a, p. 3). Clients experience problems when there is not a good fit with their environment. Causation is circular in that the environment and the person affect each other.

The ecosystems perspective accepts the broad principles of the ecological perspective while also drawing from the systems perspective ideas such as: systems are sets of interacting elements; systems can be open or closed; and systems possess states of equilibrium or disequilibrium (Meyer, 1988; Wakefield, 1996a, p. 4).

Following are some principles that are drawn from ecosystems theory (Germain, 1979, 1991; Germain and Gitterman, 1980, 1995; Gitterman and Germain, 2008; Payne, 2005) that are useful to generalist practice. The first two are derived from a systems perspective and the remainder from ecology.

- *Open systems.* An open system is a functional system, while a closed system is dysfunctional. Change and growth tend not to occur in closed systems.
- *Transactions are reciprocal.* Resources are exchanged among systems, with all systems both receiving and sending resources. This reciprocal exchange is necessary for the well-being and growth of systems.
- *Habitat.* This is a central concept that nicely illustrates the ecological metaphor. As the name implies, it is the place where people (or any biological organisms) live. Habitat must be a place where growth can take place and people feel secure. A good habitat must have productive resources that people can use. When resources are deficient, social, economic, and personal problems often develop.
- *Niche.* This is the position that an organism (in biology, a species) occupies in the environment, including the habitat. For people, it is the position that they occupy in order to experience self-esteem and to feel wanted. A niche is where a person grows and prospers. This concept is also very important in the strengths perspective. The ecosystems principle of niche hypothesizes that if people cannot find a good niche, social, economic, and personal problems often emerge.

- *Person/environment fit (goodness of fit).* There must be a fit between the person and his or her environment so that both mutually experience benefits and growth. Fit (or the lack of it) occurs through social exchanges. When social exchanges become predominantly negative, development, growth, and general functioning often become impaired.
- *Stress.* Stress in ecosystems theory is similar to the general use of the concept. It is an emotional, personal, or inner response to an internal or environmental stimulus or source and can be either functional or dysfunctional.
- *Coping measures.* These are, in a sense, the ecological equivalents of defence mechanisms in ego psychology. Instead of entirely focusing on internal psychological processes, the ecological view of coping measures is a combination of personal and environmental resources used to deal with life's stressors. A person experiences a stressor, assesses it based on her or his knowledge and experience, and reacts. Stress is normal, and all of us face it in our lives. Sometimes the reaction to a stressful event or situation might put a person into crisis, where emotions cloud clear thinking. The kinds of coping measures used depend on how the person perceives the seriousness of the situation and the resources available to her or him. Some coping measures that people might use to reduce or eradicate stress include seeking information, taking no action at all, drawing on personal resources such as self-esteem, taking time to think things through, denying the problem, and making changes in the environment to deal with the stressor (Germain, 1984).

Summary of Essential Principles

Ecosystems is a framework (not a theory) borrowed from biology that shapes practice. Many claim that it is a comprehensive, unifying, and generic perspective that underpins social work (Dubois and Miley, 1992, p. 60; Meyer, 1983; Wakefield, 1996a, p. 6). Herein lies the source of much debate: is ecosystems really a generic, unifying perspective? Is it even useful in practice? This debate is important because the perspective is very widely accepted in social work.

Jerome Wakefield (1996a, 1996b, and 1996c) wrote three thoughtful articles that were highly critical of ecosystems. His work questions the widespread use of this perspective, even its usefulness. Alex Gitterman (1996), well-known for his work on the ecological perspective, responded. While we do not summarize the debate here, we use it to focus on four principles that guide this book's view of the ecosystems perspective.

Ecosystems is not the common or generic base of social work or even a foundation of social work in the sense that traditional practice is based on problem solving. This view agrees with part of the argument put forth by Wakefield (1996b). Like Wakefield, we question whether social work even needs a common theoretical base.

In fact, we argue the merits of multidimensional practice. Social work practice involves too wide a range of fields to even attempt to bring all practice together under a single theoretical umbrella. While common values, principles, knowledge, and practice skills are shared among generalist social workers in widely disparate fields, it is not reasonable to assume that all should share the same theoretical base.

Ecosystems is a combination of related concepts drawn metaphorically from general systems theory and ecology. Ecosystems is a combination of ideas from general systems theory and ecology that does not have any real explanatory power (Payne, 2005, p. 158; Wakefield, 1996a, p. 4). It can be used to map and understand social relationships and helps us understand the nature of human relationships.

It is a useful framework that helps us organize assessment and acts as a lens that focuses assessment on the person-in-the-environment (Gitterman, 1996). Ecosystems spawns many useful ideas, concepts, and hypotheses that are testable. See Forte (2007, pp. 117–208), Gitterman and Germain (2008), and Payne (2005) for detailed discussions of systems, ecology, and ecosystems in social work.

One important way this perspective organizes assessment is by helping us conceptualize broad knowledge bases along a micro to macro continuum. This helps us link *domain*-specific theories ranging from personality theories on the one hand to structural theories on the other. This can be aided by an eco-map (Gitterman and Germain, 2008, pp. 118–21).

THEORETICAL DIVERSITY AND ASSESSMENT

This section on theoretical diversity and assessment begins to connect theory to the process of assessment and carries over into Chapter 10. We maintain that making this connection is one of the most important skills that social workers need to develop. In order to begin to address this connection, we need to select and summarize a variety of theories.

This book is about social work practice, not human behaviour and the social environment (HB&SE). While HB&SE theoretical content is an important part of practice, we can only briefly summarize each selected theory. We recommend reading Forte (2007) and Payne (2005) for more detailed content on theories social workers use.

One of the challenges that we faced in writing this textbook is how to select and present from the extremely wide range of social work and social and behavioural science theories that are useful to Canadian social work practice. Different authors organize differently, and theory selection varies.

Turner suggests there are five theories that are basic to Canadian social work. These are development based theory, cognitive based theory, emergency or crisis theory, problem solving–task theory, and systems based theory (Turner, 2002, pp. 52–54). We agree these are important for social work practice.

Forte (2007) argues that theoretical diversity leads to multi-theory practice. To him, multi-theory practice requires use of applied ecological, systems, biological, cognitive science, *psychodynamic*, behaviourism, symbolic interaction, social role, economics, and critical theories.

Payne's (2005) selection is long: psychodynamic, crisis and task centred, cognitive-behavioural, systems and ecological, social psychology and construction, humanism, existentialism, social and community development, radical to critical, feminist, anti-discrimination and cultural sensitivity, and empowerment and advocacy theories, models, and views.

Accepting the principles of theoretical diversity and multi-theory practice, we choose to use the ecosystems conception of micro, mezzo, and macro practice to organize theories important to all of social work practice.

ORGANIZATION OF DIVERSE THEORY: THE MICRO TO MACRO CONTINUUM

We have argued that social work practice, including assessment, needs to draw upon a diversity of theory. However, there needs to be a way to selectively use or focus use of this diversity. One of the ways this can be done is to frame theory used in practice by means of ecosystems. Exhibit 9.1 shows a listing of theory by system size—micro, mezzo, and macro—which helps workers select appropriate knowledge accordingly.

Consistent with the ecosystems perspective, diversity of theory can be classified into three interconnected system sizes: micro, mezzo, and macro (Kirst-Ashman and Hull, 2009). Micro social work practice focuses on work with individuals or primary groups, such as the family. Micro assessment uses knowledge derived mostly from psychology and is mainly concerned with inner psychological functioning or relationships between individuals and small, usually primary, groups. The focus in macro practice is large social institutions, such as the health or welfare system, or work with communities or large neighbourhoods, including social policy issues. Macro assessment usually uses theories from economics, political science, and sociology. Between micro and macro systems is work that is carried out with secondary groups, task groups, and small local groups, which is called mezzo practice. Mezzo assessment is drawn mainly from theories from sociology and social psychology.

Exhibit 9.1 organizes and lists a selection of theoretical perspectives that are basic to social work. There is considerable overlap with Turner's, Forte's, and Payne's lists outlined above. Some of the areas listed in the exhibit are fundamental to the major theme of this book, a problem-solving approach and beyond, and will only be briefly summarized in this chapter. Two of these, culture and anti-oppressive practice, are more fully developed in earlier chapters of this book. Strengths-based practice, Aboriginal practice, feminist theory, and structural approach are addressed in detail in Chapters 11 to 14. You may choose to read or scan Chapters 11 to 14 before reading the next section of this chapter.

Exhibit 9.1 ▼ Theoretical Perspectives Used in Social Work

Micro Orientation: Focus on Person
• Cognitive theory • Ego psychology • Crisis theory and intervention
Mezzo Orientation: Focus on Groups
• Group work principles • Family intervention and principles
Macro Orientation: Focus on Large Systems
• Principles of community development • Structural social work
Micro to Macro Orientation: Focus on Range of System Sizes and Connections between Systems
• Principles of anti-oppressive practice • Culture

Continued

- Ecosystems
- Role theory
- Labelling theory
- Strengths-based practice
- Aboriginal approach
- Feminist theory and practice

The following sections briefly describe each item listed in Exhibit 9.1. We then show how a series of questions can be used in assessment that flow from the respective theoretical perspectives. Over time and with a wide selection of cases, many or even most of the questions would lead to valuable information. However, in a single case, only some will yield useful information. Thus, assessment can be focused partly by asking appropriate questions suggested by each of the following theoretical perspectives.

For instance, in some situations, principles and questions that emerge from ecosystems may be more useful than those of structural social work to focus assessment. Or a combination of strengths and feminist theory may be more appropriate than person-in-the-environment conceptions such as ecosystems, role, or labelling theory.

Cognitive Theory

Cognitive theory is aimed at individuals (micro systems). As its name implies, cognitive theory emphasizes the thinking process. Central to the theory is the idea that if people can think about their problems in constructive ways then they may be able to do something about them. The theory assumes that behaviour and emotions are products of cognition. Therefore, if people change the way they think, they can also change the way they behave and feel (Goldstein, Hillbert, and Hillbert, 1984; Payne, 2005, pp. 119–41).

Cognitive theory is closely related to behavioural and learning theory. Payne (2005) suggests that in 1977 Albert Bandura, a learning theorist, opened the door to cognitive theory by "arguing that most learning is gained by people's perceptions and thinking about what they experience" (p. 121). Cognitive theorists hold that how people perceive the world around them is instrumental in determining how they feel and behave.

In the past 30 years or so, a number of cognitive approaches have gained importance in social work. Payne (2005, p. 226) suggests that *cognitive restructuring* is probably the best-known cognitive intervention used in social work. It is assumed that irrational beliefs often dominate the client's thinking. Burns (1990) calls some of this type of thinking "cognitive distortion." For example, a young man who feels discomfort and freezes during social situations, such as parties, likely freezes because of misperceptions about himself, the other people, the nature of parties, and subsequent distortions of thinking. The task of the social worker is to challenge this thinking and help the young man find ways to structure a new, productive way of thinking. In this example, the hope is that the freezing will end.

Cognitive therapy is a specialty often used for phobias, depression, and anxiety. It is also controversial, mostly because it seems to reduce human behaviour to almost a mechanistic, computer-like machine.

Using Cognitive Theory in Assessment

Assessment that uses cognitive theory focuses on the thinking processes, particularly irrational or distorted thinking. Generalist social workers without special training do not implement cognitive therapy. However, many principles of cognitive theories have use in generalist practice.

General assessment questions that emerge from cognitive theories might be: How does the client perceive the world around him or her? Is part of this perception distorted? Does it lead to irrational thinking? What is the nature of the distorted or irrational thinking? How did distorted learning occur? How does it affect the client? By answering these and other, similar questions, social workers attempt to devise a plan whereby the client learns new ways of perceiving the world and restructuring thinking into productive channels.

Case Example

Kim and Ann ▼

Let's return to the story of Kim and Ann that was introduced in Chapter 4. Recall that Kim is a family social worker in the Child Protection Agency (CPA). The nightshift worker has placed Ann's three children in temporary custody.

Kim explores with Ann how Ann perceives herself as a parent. Unfortunately, Ann currently thinks that she has very little to offer her children as a mother and gives an example that depicts failure. Kim, however, is convinced that Ann deeply cares for her three children and is really a loving mother with the capacity to develop good parenting skills. Kim has seen evidence of this in a home visit with Ann. Using cognitive theory, Kim could help Ann to identify the ways in which Ann has strived to be a good mother and the hopes she has for her kids in the future. Kim counters Ann's view of herself as a poor parent, offering an alternative perspective. In this way, Kim helps Ann restructure her thinking about her capacities as a mother and encourages Ann to recognize that she has the capacity to be a good parent.

Comment   Kim most certainly would not attempt cognitive restructuring. The problem does not lend itself to such an approach and Kim does not have the training. However, the principle that people can solve problems by a rational, thinking process is a principle important to all of social work practice.

Ego Psychology

Ego psychology, a contemporary theory, is part of a family of theories often called *personality* or *psychodynamic theories*. The theory assumes that behaviour is a product of both rational and irrational processes. While some behaviours occur because of cognition, others are related to the "irrational" emotional world. It is about how ego adapts to the person, including the person in his or her environment (Payne, 2005, pp. 85–91).

One of the best definitions of ego: "The ego is considered to be a mental structure of the personality that is responsible for negotiating between the internal needs [of the person] and the outside world" (Goldstein, 1986, p. 375). "The ego is the part of the personality that contains the basic functions essential to the individual's successful adaptation to the environment. Ego functions are innate and develop through maturation and the interaction along bio-*psychosocial* factors" (Goldstein, 1984, p. 9). While ego psychologists have developed a number of concepts that are useful to social workers, one of the most important of these is the concept of defence mechanisms. A defence is a mechanism that the ego uses to protect itself from anxiety by keeping intolerable threats from conscious awareness (Goldstein, 1986). Defence mechanisms are often healthy and important ways that people handle stress. However, sometimes stress overwhelms defences and pathology occurs.

Some of the early ego psychologists were Freudian or neo-Freudian psychoanalysts. Erik Erikson is one of the most famous. In his important book *Childhood and Society* (1950), Erikson argued that successful maturation in adulthood depends on mastery of eight stages of child development. Erikson's approach is psychosocial, meaning that he sees both inner forces and the environment shaping child and adult development. (It is recognized that Erikson's framework has its shortcomings because it is based solely on the study of males and a male norm of human development.)

While Freud held that early conscious and unconscious experiences shape almost all of personality, most ego psychologists believe that personality is also determined by interaction with the environment throughout life and that social interaction is crucial. Both Freudians and early ego psychologists thought environment was important, but the latter elevated it to a more prominent position.

White (1963) broke from the Freudian tradition by arguing that, along with innate drives such as sex and hunger, people are also driven toward mastery and competence. This need to explore the world, according to White, is a powerful human motivator.

Ego psychology and other psychodynamic theories are widely used in social work but not without controversy. Probably the most common criticism is that the theory mostly ignores the environment and assumes that the locus of problems is in the person and not in the social structure or social environment.

Using Ego Psychology in Assessment

Assessment using principles of ego psychology focuses on understanding the inner person. How does the client protect herself or himself from psychological stress? What defence mechanisms are used? Do the defences lead to pathological behaviour? Can the client learn how to use adaptive defences? How does the client deal with stress? How does the client view herself or himself? What is the client's level of self-esteem? How does the client view her or his self-competence? How does the client attempt to achieve mastery? What developmental stages have been successfully completed? Were some of the stages incomplete? What effect does this have on the person's current life?

> ### Case Example
>
> #### Kim and Ann ▼
>
> Kim recognizes that everyone uses defence mechanisms, but some that Ann uses are counter-productive (some ego psychologists would say pathological). Ann tends to rationalize away her problems. All of us sometimes do this, but Ann tends to deny that she neglects her children's care needs. This denial is one of the reasons why the child protection agency has placed her children in temporary custody.

Comment   Workers in child welfare settings might sometimes find ego psychology useful in understanding the problems that Ann faces. However, intervention based on ego psychology often involves long-term therapy and is seldom the preferred choice of action in child protection situations, such as neglect of children and parenting difficulties. A more likely use of ego psychology is in clinical practice in mental health.

Crisis Theory and Intervention

Elements of crisis theory have been considered for over a half-century. Unlike most of the theories used by social workers, crisis theory addresses a particular life event. The life event can be traumatic and unexpected (such as a sudden death in the family), or natural events, like marriage or the first day of school.

Encountering a person in crisis is a likely occurrence in most social work settings. Many student social workers in Canada find volunteering in a crisis centre is an excellent learning experience. Few theories about the individual are more important to understand than crisis theory.

Crisis theory holds that people who experience a crisis go through a predictable process until the crisis is resolved. Kanel (2007) suggests that there are three parts to a crisis: "1) a precipitating event; 2) a perception of the event that causes subjective distress; and 3) the failure of the usual coping methods" (p. 1). Kanel further shows the formula for increased functioning: "Change in perception of the precipitating event and acquiring new coping skills," then "decrease in subjective distress," and then "increase in functioning" (p. 2).

People in crisis often respond to either a stressful situation they face or some existing condition that appears during a crisis (Zastrow, 1995, pp. 452–53). The precipitating event is important and understanding it is often critical in the helping process. The event may be developmental or situational (Johnson, McClelland, and Austin, 2000, pp. 314–15). Birth of a child, first day at school, puberty, marriage, menopause, and so forth are examples of developmental crises. A situational crisis is often sudden and unexpected. A traumatic event, a suicide attempt or fear of suicide, and sudden death are examples.

Most crises are relatively short term (Kanel, 2007, p. 4). Crisis theory holds that resolution always takes place and usually within a few weeks. Resolutions can be either dysfunctional or functional (Wicks and Parsons, 1984). Kanel (2007, p. 3) calls these opportunities and dangers.

Growth that emerges from crisis is a usually a healthy part of human development. A healthy response to a crisis leads to increased skill in other and future stressful events. For example, the birth of a child usually leads to increased family bonds and psychological and social growth of parents, or, in a situational crisis, grief from the unexpected death of a spouse may lead to increased coping abilities and a sense of independence.

Sometimes a crisis leads to dysfunctional behaviour and emotions. For example, unresolved grief can lead to depression or even a suicide attempt. Help is often required in such situations, and, if left unattended, can lead to long-term dysfunction.

People who are undergoing a crisis are particularly vulnerable but also are often ready to make constructive use of help. Because of this element of readiness to receive help, crisis theory is very important to social workers in some settings (Germain, 1984; Golan, 1986). Since crisis resolution begins soon after the crisis event, early intervention is important.

Crisis theory does not stand alone. For instance, crisis workers draw heavily on cognitive theory. According to Kanel (2007),

> Every crisis model is based on a behavioural problem-solving model:
> 1. Define the problem.
> 2. Review ways that you have already tried to correct the problem.
> 3. Decide what you want when the problem is solved.
> 4. Brainstorm activities.
> 5. Select alternatives and commit to following through with them.
> 6. Follow up. (p. 19)

Kanel (2007, pp. 69–96) also developed one of the most used models of crisis intervention, which has been dubbed the ABC mode:

A: Developing and maintaining contact: This includes developing rapport. Help depends upon being able to maintain contact with client.

B: Identifying problem: This depends upon building rapport and is the most crucial stage. It includes understanding the precipitating event and the therapeutic intervention.

C: Coping: This step examines the past, present, and future coping mechanisms of the client. The worker attempts to ensure future coping mechanisms are functional. Often the client can be helped to use past coping methods that were functional to address current crises.

In social work, much can be done during a crisis period to help clients function again in a healthy way. Assisting people to draw on their own capacities and strengths, when possible, is an important part of this work.

Using Crisis Theory in Assessment

Crisis theory focuses attention on a specific life event. Crisis theory holds that people who are experiencing crisis are often in great need of help and are willing to make constructive use of it. Examples of assessment questions that flow from this theory: What precipitating event led to the problem or crisis? What precipitating event led to seeking help? Were the events the same? What are their dynamics? How did the events affect the client and others close to the client? What immediate steps can be taken to begin resolution?

Case Example

Kim and Ann ▼

Ann is not in a serious state of crisis even though the removal of her children has caused her considerable stress. Suppose, however, that after a few days Ann realizes all of the implications of the recent events and becomes depressed and potentially suicidal as a result. Afraid of what she might do, she calls a crisis hotline. The hotline workers would be responsible for assessing her state of crisis, helping her manage it, and intervening in other ways if needed.

Comment   Crisis theory does provide useful concepts that Kim might use. For example, what precipitated Ann's parenting problems? How can Kim develop rapport and maintain contact?

Knowledge about suicide risk is important for all social workers, since it can save a person's life. Assessing risk of harm to persons requires considerable preparation and guidance. Social workers assess risk of harm in client situations through (a) the identification of risk (dangers, hazards, and threats to safety); (b) risk prediction (whether the existing risks are likely to lead to danger, based on collected information and professional knowledge); (c) planning for risk management (action to minimize risk of danger, determination of greatest and least risk in possible courses of action, and possible consequences of selected actions); (d) review of the plan for action, and (e) back to other steps as needed (Bailey, 2002, "Mental Health." In Robert Adams, Lena Dominelli, and Malcolm Payne, eds., *Critical Practice in Social Work*, published 2002, Palgrave, p. 175. Reproduced with permission of Palgrave Macmillan.)

Knowledge about Family Relationships and Processes

The knowledge that underpins family-focused intervention and family therapy is important to social work, since families are often the focus of practice in numerous settings. The family is an interdependent group in which members' needs and interests are addressed. It can also be the centre of many problems (e.g., parenting issues, child maltreatment, substance abuse, illness, and financial strain) (Zastrow, 1995, pp. 220–24) and the context in which members grow, develop, care for one another, and participate in memorable occasions together (e.g., weddings, vacations, births, anniversaries, and funerals).

Systems theory has shaped thinking about family assessment and intervention, in which the family is seen as a system interacting with the environment (Hepworth, Rooney, and Larsen, 1997, p. 277). Family members all interact with one another within the family system, which has effects throughout the family system and beyond it. Helping a person within the family means working with the whole family, since other members are affected by an individual's change efforts and can help by supporting these efforts.

There are many related, specific areas of knowledge, such as *family life cycle* tasks and development, culture, family structure, emotional expression, *family norms* and rules, roles, communication, decision making, strengths and capacities, resilience, power, functions, and boundaries.

Working with families is a specialty and requires training. Family therapies include family systems, structural (not to be confused with social structure or structural social work), experiential, psychoanalytic, and cognitive-behavioural family therapy. Some of these therapies adapt more general theories to working with families. These include systems, psychoanalytical, and cognitive theories, each of which are introduced in this chapter. (Ego psychology emerges from *psychoanalysis*.)

Ridgely, (2002, pp. 271–73) points out that in Canada types of family treatment range from neo-Freudian developmental theories to systems and, more recently, feminist theories.

Exploring knowledge development in family therapy since the 1940s, Becvar and Becvar (2000) include in their review a description of the social construction of meaning and truth, multiple views, the importance of language as a vehicle of power, the use of a story or narrative, and the role of the therapist as impartial actor (see also Freedman and Combs, 1996).

Using Knowledge about Family Relationships and Processes in Assessment

Assessment questions might include: How are individuals' needs for care and attention met in the family, and is this satisfactory? How do family members communicate with one another? How does culture play a role in the family? Are there problems in communication? How is power distributed in the family, and is there conflict about it? How are decisions made? What are the family's strengths? Is the family resilient in the face of problems or change? What rules does the family set (e.g., regarding chores, children's bedtime, and dinner times)? What are individual members' views of the family and its situation?

Case Example

Kim and Ann ▼

After much work, Ann finally has her children returned to her. Kim continues to work with Ann to ensure that she is able to apply the learning from her parenting classes to caring for her three children. In home visits with Ann, Kim sees that Ann's oldest child, Jim, takes on many adult tasks such as cooking and minding the younger children. Ann speaks to this 9-year-old as though he is an adult. Perhaps she copes by relying on him when she feels tired or depressed. However, this is having an impact on Jim, who seems to find it difficult to play with other children his own age and spends much of his time with his mother. Ann feels that Jim is being a really good son and rewards him with special treats from time to time. Ann has few friends from whom she can seek support and companionship, and finds that Jim sometimes offers her these.

> In Kim's assessment, there is a problem in the boundary between mother and child. She wants to make a referral to a family therapist in a local family counselling agency because she knows that this kind of problem can create difficulties for everyone in the family. Jim will someday resent not having his own life in activities with his friends. He might also begin to view his mother as weak and without authority. Ann consents to the referral since she wants to help her children and herself. She states that she can see how much she relies on Jim and wants to explore how she can help him while helping herself, too.

Comment Family therapy or counselling is a specialty. However, many generalist social workers work with families in a variety of capacities and can draw upon family theory to help their practice.

The family counselling agency could include both Jim and Ann in family counselling, or, in this case, include only Ann. If they define the problem as parenting issue, then most likely Ann alone would be the client. If the agency believes that the problem is interaction between mother and son, then it would be more likely that the family (particularly Jim and Ann) would be defined as the client.

Group Work Principles

Group work in social work is increasing. Many Canadian agencies that previously provided services to individuals are cutting back on this type of intervention, either encouraging or requiring participation in group treatment instead. Much of this seems to be motivated by cost cutting.

There are a number of ways to categorize groups. A few are listed below.

- *Primary:* Close friends, family. Primary groups are often the most important groups in people's lives.
- *Reference:* Groups to which one wants to belong. Reference group theory, a derivative of role theory, holds that groups that individuals want to belong to can be a powerful determinant of behaviour of members (e.g., peer groups, family, and youth gangs).
- *Task:* A task group has as its purpose engagement in an activity, for example, a second language class, women's or men's club or group, a card-players' group, and so on. Sometimes social workers lead task groups with a secondary purpose of treatment or intervention. For example, people who are depressed may join a women's group for the primary purpose of socialization but also to support each other in battling their depression.
- *Support:* These are also often self-help groups. The purpose of such groups is for members of the group to help each other, often in the quest to address a serious problem such as schizophrenia or depression. Probably the best-known support and self-help group is Alcoholics Anonymous.
- *Treatment:* Groups in which the only purpose is treatment. Such groups could address anger management, socialization skills, or discharge planning for patients leaving a hospital.

Several theories used in this book can be used to help explain small group behaviour. Role theory (discussed later in this chapter) addresses the relationship between expectations of others, usually a small group, and an individual or even a group. Systems and ecosystems also help explain group functions. Labelling theory helps explain how groups can be oppressive to others as well as their own members.

Theory pertaining to groups reflects such areas as group development, tasks and goals, process, bond, growth, dynamics and interaction, cohesion, roles, skills and strengths, power, conflict, norms, and values (Brill, 1998, pp. 182–83). Working with groups involves understanding group structure, bond, leadership, group purpose, and composition. (See Mesbur, 2002.)

A family is a kind of group. So too are groups that have been formed or that come together for therapy, education, self-help, program planning, community projects, or some other reason. Usually a group is formed in response to a need, which shapes its purpose and goals. Social workers, if they are leaders of or consultants to groups, require knowledge of theories about groups in order to be helpful. In feminist group work, for example, the social worker must understand the interest in affiliation (connection) among women and the importance of emotional maintenance (see Butler and Wintram, 1991).

Using Theory about Groups in Assessment

Assessment questions might include: What is the interest of group members in participating? What is the level of cohesion among the individuals? What roles have individual members taken on, and are these satisfactory? How can the group's development be described? What are the dynamics in the group's relations? How does the group deal with conflict? What skills and strengths exist in the group, and how are they used? Do certain members hold more power than others? If so, how does this affect group maintenance? What norms and values are present in the group?

Case Example

Kim and Ann ▼

Suppose, after the return of her children, Ann loses her new job. This is due to the increased stress that Ann is having a difficult time handling. She also experiences low self-worth and isolation at home with the younger children.

Kim, after phoning Ann, is concerned that Ann is not doing well and needs some help. Kim knows of a local community centre that has started groups for women who are raising children on their own. She knows that such a group could enhance Ann's growth and provide her with a supportive environment in which to realize her skills and strengths. Kim also knows that childcare is available and that the centre is close to Ann's home. When told about the resource, Ann agrees to join the group.

In the group, Ann meets other women and takes part in discussions about caring for children, managing on a fixed income, and community organizations that offer resources. At first the group members wait for the facilitator, a social worker with the community centre, to lead discussions, but soon members begin to interact more with one another and set their own agenda for each session. The social worker encourages these efforts and supports the group's development.

Comment   Group work could be quite effective in the above example. It is not only an efficient form of intervention, but Ann can be helped through learning from the experiences of others.

Principles of Community Development

Community development is focused on work with community groups or voluntary organizations, usually in a small geographic area (community-based). The Internet has broadened this definition through the electronic linkage of people who form communities bound by common interests and goals (e.g., websites and chat rooms set up for environmental, antiwar, and other activists). Community development is difficult to define precisely and may be seen as social work that is community-based, carried out in a community or "street-front" organization, and involves community members or occurs as part of community outreach, action, or organizing activities. It is often framed as beneficial or positive (Popple, 2002).

However, community organizations and/or their activities are not all good or harmless. Some community development and organizations may, in fact, include activities that are racist and harmful to immigrants, children, or women (e.g., neo-Nazi groups, child pornography rings, and others). In social work, the CASW *Code of Ethics* is applied to all practice, and any community organization efforts that contravene professional values, principles, and guidelines cannot be supported.

Some forms of community development may be promoted by the state and conducted in top-down fashion, while other kinds of community development can be termed bottom-up or collective community action. Bottom-up community organizing may represent a direct challenge to the state and some groups in society (Popple, 2002). Some methods used by bottom-up community organizations may be perceived as a threat (e.g., occupation of government buildings or other forms of protest).

Community development has been a part of social work since the settlement house movement and continues to respond to local needs not met by governments or other social service agencies. Community development may be seen as a process involving "the process of establishing, or re-establishing, structures of human community within which new ways of relating, organising social life and meeting human need become possible" (Ife, 2002, p. 2). Community development work can involve a range of projects or initiatives that are aimed to improve community life for members. Examples include a local playground and green space for children to play in, community drop-in centres for youth and older persons, and a petition to city government for better policing or street lighting.

In community work, it is important that social workers act as facilitators of community members' efforts, advocating for them and fostering skills in leadership and other capacities among them rather than taking the lead themselves. Without the active participation of community members, there can be little ownership of change efforts by the community. Colleen Lundy (2004) suggests that empowerment occurs through community members' active participation in the decisions that affect them. Their voices and pooled experiences, skills, and knowledge are critical in the process of change.

Using Knowledge about Community Development in Assessment

In community development work, knowledge encompasses perspectives on locality and neighbourhood development and social planning; group work (Rothman, 1996); organizing approaches and methods in mobilization of individuals and groups; running community meetings; collaborating with other staff and volunteers; problem solving; conflict mediation; and, often, grant proposal writing and fundraising (Homan, 1999).

Case Example

Kim and Ann ▼

Suppose that Ann, with other mothers in her neighbourhood, decides to ask a voluntary organization's social worker to help them establish a play area for young children. Little park or play space is available in the poor inner-city neighbourhood area where they live, and families can not afford the recreation programs available elsewhere. One local home had been gutted by fire and was awaiting demolition by the city. The women thought that the empty lot could be developed into a green space with play equipment for children.

The community social worker, Lilo, was asked to respond to the women's request and began to work with them. He asked about their backgrounds and experiences, finding that some women knew how to write letters and make phone calls to local politicians. Others had organizing skills and connections with local businesses and schools. Lilo wanted Ann and her neighbours to build their capacities and utilize their collective skills to gain the attention of the city council. He advocated for them and supported their efforts. He also acted as a consultant to the women and arranged for meeting space and fax, photocopier, and phone access at the community organization office where he worked. The women needed money to print flyers and Lilo helped them to write proposals for funding.

Comment   The above is a good example of how principles of community development can be utilized when working with individuals in a community context.

Structural Social Work

Chapter 14 addresses structural social work. A structural approach to social work emphasizes inequality and social injustice. It suggests ways to address these issues in everyday practice with individuals, families, groups, and communities. In structural social work practice, macro analysis is connected to working with individuals.

The goal of structural social work is to help people regain control of their lives. The approach makes the assumption that people's problems are often caused by, or at least closely related to, failures in social institutions such as the economy, or, at a lower level, difficulties in understanding a bureaucracy or unfair treatment by an agency such as the court, the police, a child welfare agency, or the mental health system. Such problems are common. The task of the social worker is to help people gain control in their dealings with social institutions.

Using the Structural Approach in Assessment

Assessment that uses a structural approach focuses on the institutions of society, including political institutions. Examples of assessment questions include: Is injustice evident? How do existing inequities and injustices of programs or institutions affect people whom the programs or institutions are meant to serve? What is their power? How do they use this power? Is this use of power unfair or unjust? What resources exist to address these problems?

If the client is an individual or a family, similar assessment questions can be asked, but with the focus on the effect of the institution on the client. For example, how fairly has a social agency dealt with a client? Does inequity affect the client's situation? How can the client take charge in dealing with the agency? A social worker might also ask how power relations play a role in family relations (e.g., gender or age) and whether an individual or a family faces social discrimination that impedes access to jobs or housing.

Case Example

Kim and Ann ▼

A week after the court granted temporary custody of her children to foster care, Ann learns that her social assistance payments will stop. While she expected a decrease in the payments, she did not expect complete denial. Both Kim and Ann believe this is very unfair and probably against the policy and related rules of Public Social Services. The lack of assistance is a major problem for Ann and is compounded by her belief that powerful institutions have taken control of her life and that she can do nothing about it. Ann has always deferred to their decisions without questioning them, but often with considerable anger.

Continued

> With Ann, Kim examined the real power of Public Social Services and the workings of its bureaucracy, as well as Ann's ability to make the bureaucracy work for her. A general goal of this assessment was to help Ann take charge of her relationship with the agency so that she was treated fairly; the specific goal was to have her assistance payments reinstated.

Comment   All too often we hear social workers asserting, "We can't use structural social work in our practice! It only deals with the big society things and it takes too long to change." This statement is not entirely true. Yes, structural social work centres on macro issues and social change does take time. But macro issues greatly affect the lives of individuals. Often social workers can help clients overcome system and bureaucratic problems by using principles of structural social work. The above example demonstrates this principle.

Unlike the other areas that we have covered in this section, which refer to specific theories, perspectives, or approaches, the section that follows refers to a set of principles that shape and help filter assessment.

Principles of Anti-Oppressive Practice

The significance of anti-oppressive social work was discussed in some detail in Chapter 7. We noted that this perspective is important when working with clients who have experienced discrimination, marginalization, or oppression and also with everyone we encounter in social work. In recent years, there has been renewed concern with oppression as a fundamental focus of social work practice. Anti-oppressive practice is emerging as an important form of social work intervention that has come to represent good social work.

"Oppression is generally understood as the domination of subordinate groups in society by a powerful (politically, economically, socially, and culturally) group" (Mullaly, 2002, p. 27). Personal oppression occurs when individuals are singled out for oppression by the more powerful. Examples are personal discrimination against an immigrant family in search of adequate housing or attacks on people who are gay. Cultural oppression involves a society's general attitudes, assumptions, and ideas that help to sustain the oppression of a particular group of people; for example, men living on the street. Believing that such people are all addicted to alcohol or drugs, are (or have been) engaged in crime, and have no interest in work represents cultural oppression by our society. Oppression at the structural level is evident when policies and practices create and maintain economic inequality, favouring those who are wealthy and more powerful over those who do not have such resources. For instance, many argue that the large number of the working poor is largely due to our capitalist economic system.

Examples of oppression are numerous. The colonization of Aboriginal peoples, as discussed in Chapter 12, is a prime illustration. Members of non-dominant ethnocultural groups are often oppressed through institutional racism and other processes. People who live on the street are oppressed, as are women—who, as a collective, are often dominated by economic and social institutions shaped primarily for male interests. Those who are mentally ill frequently find themselves disenfranchised and dominated by the powerful health and legal systems. Those who are poor generally lack power and are at the mercy of the economic system. The list could go on and on. The key point is that oppression causes social problems (see Mullaly, 2002, for a detailed explanation).

We adopt Ann Bishop's view (2002) that class represents a major structural form of oppression, while other sources of oppression—such as sexism, racism, and those based on physical ability, sexual orientation, age, and others—cut across class. As Bishop explains, "on a structural level, class is different from other forms of oppression such as racism, ageism and sexism. Class is not just a factor in inequalities of wealth, privilege, and power; it *is* that inequality. Other forms of oppression help keep the hierarchy of power [class] in place" (p. 82). For example, oppression according to cultural background or skin colour can affect many, but if one has substantial financial resources, these factors may be mitigated to some degree. Those with the lowest income and fewest assets may experience the effects of racism according to cultural background and skin colour more keenly.

Using Anti-Oppressive Practice in Assessment

Anti-oppressive practice is social work practice that challenges oppression and subordination. Leonard (1997) and Mullaly (2002) argue that anti-oppressive practice must take place at both the personal and structural levels and that the interaction between personal and structural oppression is critical in its challenge. An example of personal anti-oppressive practice is to address, through counselling, the harm that oppression has done to a person. Another often cited goal is to help a client become liberated from felt oppression and subordination.

At the structural level, anti-oppressive practice attempts to change the social policies, programs, institutions, and structures that cause oppression. Sometimes clients who experience oppression may find it therapeutic and empowering to engage in social change efforts. For example, this may be the case with Aboriginal persons who, as children, experienced abuse in foster care. As adults, they attempt to help change the system that caused these problems.

Although we can readily identify groups of people that can be categorized as oppressed (e.g., those who are poor, Aboriginal, addicted to street drugs, etc.), it cannot be assumed that the persons within such groups will themselves feel oppressed. We need to acknowledge that people's own views about whether and how oppression affects them are important. All persons are unique and have the right to interpret for themselves their life experience, rather than having it interpreted for them.

At the heart of anti-oppressive assessment and intervention is the use of reflection and reflexivity by social workers. Understanding the role of class in people's lives and the effects of class with intersecting forms of oppression such as racism, sexism, heterosexism, and ageism is important in all client situations. This is because past experiences and current problems are often related to these effects. It is also possible that people have learned how to overcome or deal with such effects by drawing on supports or strengths. Assessment also needs to consider continuing oppression that is experienced by clients. Critical questions that emerge from a focus on oppression might be: Has the client experienced oppression? What is its nature? Was/is it personal, cultural, and/or structural? How does it affect the client? How does the client perceive the oppression? What can be done about it?

Case Example

Kim and Ann ▼

Ann has received social assistance for a number of years and has had frequent encounters with child welfare agencies. She is a single mother with limited education and employment skills. Because of these factors she does not have the opportunity to advance herself as do others with more skills, education, resources, and family supports. Because our social structure offers others more opportunities, Ann experiences oppression. Likely these events need further exploration because structural, personal, and perhaps cultural oppression may affect Ann's situation. Kim needs to know the perception Ann has about the effects of oppression in her life situation and make some decisions with Ann regarding what can be done about it.

The view Ann has about herself as a mother, fed for many years by verbal and physical abuse from her husband, represents a form of personal oppression and Kim should explore with Ann the need for counselling to address the hurt that remains from this abusive relationship. Also, Kim needs to explore in some detail with Ann to determine other oppressive situations that continue to affect her life and, if found, determine how to challenge these.

Comment   Oppression is often hidden. Social workers must look for it. Almost certainly Ann has been oppressed. It does remain unknown whether Ann perceives herself as oppressed. Also, Kim must be careful to not be an oppressor. She is in a power position over Ann. Use of power over Ann must be as little as possible. Further, Kim's action can be seen as oppressive if she does not strive to help make opportunities available to Ann. It is best for Kim to work with Ann to develop Ann's power, thereby helping Ann herself to become more empowered.

Culture

Please refer to Chapter 7 which is about social work and culture. Cultural factors can strongly affect how clients behave and how they interpret and understand problems, so they are central to social work assessment. Culture is important in all of our lives, not just those of our clients.

All interpretations of theory and assessment are culturally dependent. This means that the application of a theory is, at least to some degree, shaped by culture. For instance, in role theory, the definition of deviance or occurrence of role conflicts is different in different cultures. Likewise, what is seen as an appropriate use of power may also depend on cultural factors.

Using Culture in Assessment

It is important for social workers to understand how culture shapes the problems that people present. Questions to consider include: How are the problems interpreted? How do religious or cultural beliefs contribute to or affect the problems? What religious or ethnocultural resources are available that the client might make use of? Are there some cultural beliefs that constrain the client or cause harm? If the social worker comes from a different culture than the client's, the worker must attempt to understand how her or his own culture might cloud or colour personal perceptions. Often social workers, in assessing clients who share the same majority culture, take cultural beliefs for granted and do not explore their effects on clients.

Case Example

Kim and Ann ▼

Kim and Ann are both of Western European decent and are both from blue-collar families. Kim is both English and German, and Ann is second-generation Dutch. Both consider themselves Canadian, not members of an ethnocultural minority group, and generally share the same cultural beliefs.

Ann and her family share a strong work ethic that has deep roots in their Dutch heritage. This has made accepting welfare difficult for Ann. Kim also wants to explore how Ann's family views child rearing. For example, do they think it is acceptable for small children to be cared for by a 9-year-old sibling? The answer to this question might help Kim understand Ann's decision to leave her children alone.

Comment   All people have a culture; not just members of a minority group. While worker and client generally share the same culture in this example, it remains important for Kim to understand how Ann interprets the values and ideology reflective of their common culture.

Ecosystems

The ecosystems perspective was introduced and discussed earlier in this chapter. Ecosystems is an important framework that helps assessment. Unlike many theories that are used in work with individuals, families, and small groups that focus on psychological factors, the emphasis of ecosystems is on person-in-the-environment.

Using Ecosystems in Assessment

Maybe the most important question that ecosystems poses is: What is the person-in-the-environment fit (goodness of fit)? Are there problems with this fit? If so, are they sources of the client's problems?

Other questions are: Does the client have a positive niche? Habitat? Further examples of questions that flow from this perspective include the following: Does the client experience an open or a closed system? If open, what strengths can the client use? If closed, what factors make it closed? What can be done to help interactions? What is the quality of the client's habitat? What are the most important resources in the habitat? How can the client best use the habitat? What niches does the client find productive? Where are the problems with the niches? What niches might the client like to develop? What are the client's major stressors? Are these stressors internal or environmental? How does the client react to them? What coping measures does the client use? How can they be improved?

Case Example

Kim and Ann ▼

Kim wants to know about the key relationships in Ann's life and how they interact with one another. How does Ann fit in with her social and physical environment? Who are the important people in her life? Her children? Her parents? Her friends? The local pastor? Her ex-husband? The people at Public Social Services? Her son's teacher? What is the nature of Ann's interactions with these people? Who supports her, and who are the people she can count on to support her as she gets her life back together? With whom does Ann have conflict? How does this conflict affect her? Does anything need to be done about it?

Another question that Kim needs to address is whether Ann has a good social niche. The initial assessment has revealed that Ann feels that she does not really fit in anywhere. Ecosystems holds that all people need to feel that they belong. For most, life is empty and lonely if they feel unwanted and that they do not "fit in." Probably one of the most important things Kim needs to help Ann accomplish is to find a comfortable social niche. Carefully exploring Ann's relationships with others may help Ann and Kim develop and use a good social niche for Ann.

▲

Comment   It should be clear that ecosystems is a good assessment framework for Kim to use in her work with Ann.

Role Theory

Role theory is not an integrated theory but, like many others used by social workers, is a collection of related concepts. Role theory holds that behaviour is a function of social expectations. Groups at all levels of society—from small, primary groups such as families to large groups such as social institutions—set expectations that prescribe the behaviours of people. These expectations are called norms. Expectations or norms are usually grouped into categories called statuses. When people act in accordance with norms associated with a status, they are conforming to a role. Role theorists argue that norms become an important determinant of behaviour. (See Forte, 2007, pp. 411–52; and Payne, 2005, pp. 161–80.)

For example, societies set norms that prescribe what a father is supposed to do. A man's family of origin and current family likely also set norms for the father in a family. This combination of norms defines for that family the status of father. When the father acts in accordance with the prescribed norms, he is carrying out the role of father. Role theorists argue that social norms are powerful determinants of individual behaviour. This is particularly so when clear formal or informal sanctions exist for those who do not act according to these norms. In some societies, people who do not perform well in their roles are shunned by community members or denied certain resources (e.g., loans or social support).

If a person's behaviour violates the norms of a role and there is an attempt to penalize that person, then the behaviour of that person may be seen as deviant. For example, if a father abandons his family, he will likely be defined as deviant, and others, including the legal system, may attempt to force him to conform, at least to the role of provider. Deviance is a behaviour path or trait of an individual that does not conform to the normative expectations of others and toward which others take negative sanctions. Often these sanctions are forms of punishment.

Sometimes norms may conflict and cause strain in people who fill more than one role. Role conflict occurs when people experience incompatible expectations from two or more different sources (Davis, 1986). To illustrate, a teenage father may be expected to be a provider for his young family. His circle of male friends may also want him to continue to participate in their activities. These two different expectations may create conflict within the young father. He may have to choose which expectations to conform to and risk failure in either his role as father or as "one of the guys."

Other times roles are strained. This often happens when expectations are unclear or when a person cannot live up to what is expected of them (norms).

Another problem suggested by role theory is called *role ambiguity*, which occurs when expectations are unclear. Unclear expectations make it difficult for a person to conform because the norms are unclear. Members of one culture who live in another culture may experience role ambiguity because they have difficulty interpreting the social norms of the new culture.

Using Role Theory in Assessment

Assessment that uses concepts from role theory focuses on the relationship between norms and behaviours. Like ecosystems, the focus is on the person-in-the-environment. Usually the norms expressed by small groups, including primary groups such as the family, are the most relevant. Examples of assessment questions to pursue are: Does the client conform to important norms of relevant others? If not, do others define the client as deviant? If so, how does this affect the client? How does it affect the client's relationships with others? What are the client's most important roles? How well does she or he perform these roles? Does she or he feel comfortable in them? Are they rewarding? Does role conflict occur? If so, how does this affect the client? How can the role conflict be resolved?

> ### Case Example
>
> ### Kim and Ann ▼
>
> In some ways a role theory and an ecosystems analysis of Ann's situation are similar. Central to an ecosystems analysis are the questions: What is the nature of key relationships, and how do these affect Ann? Parallel to these queries, role
>
> *Continued*

theorists might ask: What are the key expectations of the major actors in Ann's life? Does Ann conform to or deviate from these expectations? Do the expectations cause her role conflict or role strain? Are they ambiguous?

Kim's initial assessment suggests that Ann may frequently feel role conflict in her role as mother and as sole provider. The only jobs that she has been able to find that pay reasonable wages require considerable evening work. This is also the time during which she feels she should be with her children. Ann's solution to this problem has been to seek public assistance. As a result, the family barely has sufficient income to survive, causing additional strain for Ann.

Comment   Like ecosystems, role theory is useful in many situations because it focuses on the person-in-the-environment. It helps explain Ann's situation.

Labelling Theory

Labelling theory, which is closely related to role theory, was introduced in Chapter 6. A person is seen as deviant when she or he breaks social rules. Usually this occurs when a person does not conform to role expectations. Sometimes the rules that are broken are formal ones, such as laws, but more often rules are informal. For example, we all have an expressed or implied understanding of how we are supposed to behave in a wide variety of social situations. If we break these codes, we may be perceived as deviant by others.

Labelling is the process that others use to help define behaviours as deviant. To labelling theorists it is not the tag or label—such as homosexual, schizophrenic, delinquent, and so on—that is important but the implications and consequences of the tag. For example, the damage occurs when a person who is tagged "schizophrenic" is ostracized, discriminated against, degraded, segregated, or otherwise treated in a negative manner and faces forms of social control because of the schizophrenia. Labelling theory suggests that these consequences can be devastating for individuals who are defined as deviant.

Using Labelling Theory in Assessment

Most perspectives and theories that social workers use are micro-oriented or, like role and ecosystems theory, centre on the person-in-the-environment. The primary unit of analysis in the first instance is the individual, and the second is the relationship between the environment and individual. Labelling shifts the focus of assessment to the analysis of groups and the larger social system. While intervention might be intended to help clients adapt to situations that label, the real intervention should be with those who do the labelling. Thus, the target of intervention is often not the client. To illustrate, suppose Ibrahim is having trouble in school and has been referred to the school social worker. The worker discovers that Ibrahim's teacher is treating him differently because he is a recent immigrant. The fact that the teacher has very low expectations of immigrants has contributed to Ibrahim's difficulty in learning at school.

In this case scenario, the social worker should target for intervention the teacher's labelling and her views of immigrants.

Examples of general assessment questions that arise from labelling theory include the following: Is the client perceived by others as breaking a social code or rule? Is the client defined as deviant, at least by some? If so, what are the labelling processes? How do these affect the client? What are the social and psychological consequences of the labelling for the client?

Case Example

Kim and Ann ▼

Ann's Dutch background has reinforced a strong work ethic. As far as her parents and siblings are concerned, Ann has failed in her efforts to provide for her family. An implied but clear expectation was that Ann would marry, have children, and be supported by a responsible husband. The marriage failed, and hence so did her main means of support. Ann's family also expected, after the marriage failure, that Ann would be able to manage both employment and parenting. These are the same roles in which Ann experiences major role conflict.

In the eyes of her parents and siblings, she is a failure. Her family's disapproval has contributed to the erosion of Ann's self-confidence and self-esteem. They have labelled her as a failure and as a consequence she is degraded, ostracized, and stigmatized by her family.

Comment   Kim wants to help Ann find ways to rationally and emotionally handle and defend against the labelling. Even as it occurs, Ann might find ways to mitigate its effects. Kim also, with Ann's permission, wants to target some members of her family for intervention, hoping to stem the labelling and improve family relationships.

Strengths Approach

The strengths perspective will be discussed in detail in Chapter 11. A strengths approach capitalizes on people's capacities, vitality, abilities, strong points, talents, courage, and power. The approach uses people's own resources to help them grow as human beings, improve their quality of life, and develop their own problem-solving skills. It is a developmental process that assumes that if growth and quality of life improve, improved problem-solving skills will follow. This approach incorporates ideas such as wellness, support, empowerment, and wholeness. It also assumes that improving a person's quality of life will often contribute to other gains.

There is a connection between the ecosystems and strengths approaches. For example, finding good habitats and niches are both strengths and ecosystems principles. Like the ecosystems approach, the strengths perspective emphasizes the connections that people have with their environment. Both perspectives view the relationship between the person and the environment as an inseparable, integrated whole. Both approaches also emphasize empowerment.

Using the Strengths Approach in Assessment

Assessment principles that flow from the strengths approach, as one would anticipate, focus on understanding strengths. What are the client's strengths? How does the client use his or her strengths? Does the client perceive that he or she has strengths? How does the client typically handle problems? Can the client muster sufficient inner or environmental resources to solve his or her own problems? Does the client have the capacity to solve these problems?

How can the social worker help the client develop his or her own problem-solving skills? How does the client empower himself or herself? What can the social worker do to help the client empower himself or herself? To what extent is the client resilient?

Some of the questions that flow from this perspective are similar to those from the ecosystems perspective. For example, what is the client's niche? Is the niche functional or dysfunctional? Might the client find self-help groups helpful? Can a self-help group become a comfortable niche for the client?

Case Example

Kim and Ann ▼

A central function of Kim's assessment should be a good understanding of Ann's strengths. Reference to some of the previous analysis may help illustrate this.

For example, from role theory, what roles does Ann find important? Which roles make her feel that she has or can gain control over her life? Ecosystems suggests that finding a productive niche is important. Who in Ann's life can and will be able to provide important social supports as she engages in the process of regaining custody of her children? If she succeeds in overturning the decision to cut off her social assistance, this should help her gain not only new skills in dealing with bureaucracies but also the realization that she has some ability to influence powerful social institutions.

In the past, Ann's parents have been important to her and have been good social supports. It is only after they began to define her as a failure that their positive relationships began to break down. Kim needs to explore in some detail the nature of these family relationships, particularly why the relationships were important to all family members and how to rebuild them. This rebuilt support system could be one of the most important resources that Ann can draw on.

Comment   In each and every case, understanding the strengths of a client is important. Often the worker and client can use these strengths to meet the client's wants, needs, and goals of intervention.

An Aboriginal Approach

Chapter 12 describes an Aboriginal perspective of social work based on the views and culture of the northern Plains peoples. The perspective emphasizes the importance of wholeness, harmony, balance, and the interconnectedness of all things. The goal of practice can be seen as the achievement of *mino-pimátisiwin,* roughly translated as "the good life."

Healing is an important process in Aboriginal perspectives, and while the concept is similar to social work's use of helping and treatment, it is also very different. Aboriginal healing includes restoration—fixing, reconciling, or resolving something that is perceived to be wrong. However, the goal of healing is *mino-pimátisiwin.* Thus, healing is really a developmental concept—a lifelong journey that is the responsibility of all people, not just clients. As achievement of *mino-pimátisiwin* gets closer, the person is better able to fix and resolve problems.

More so than in the ecosystems perspective, the Aboriginal view emphasizes the interconnectedness of all things, including people, the environment, the land, and all parts of nature. Nature is seen as part of the inseparable whole.

Using an Aboriginal Approach in Assessment

An Aboriginal perspective helps assessment in two different ways. First, it helps social workers understand clients who are Aboriginal, particularly those who adhere to traditional ways. Second, the perspective helps with focused assessment of all clients.

For example, what is the journey that the client is using to reach *mino-pimátisiwin?* Is the journey of healing taking place? To what extent does the client perceive her or his life to be in balance? How does the client connect (or not) with all aspects of her or his environment? What appears to be out of balance? Are some of these connections problematic?

Case Example

Kim and Ann ▼

Neither Ann nor Kim is Aboriginal. However, an Aboriginal perspective is relevant to Ann's situation because it can place the process that Ann will pursue in context. Ann needs to heal. Her ultimate goal is very much like the achievement of *mino-pimátisiwin,* the good life. Translated, this might mean establishment of a healthy social niche and caring relationships. Achievement of these goals might be seen as a step toward *mino-pimátisiwin.*

Continued

> Further, the process necessary to meet these goals is healing. Healing is not a short process but a lifelong journey. Neither the main goal of *mino-pimátisiwin* nor Ann's immediate goals will be achieved easily, nor will she find complete success in the short term. An important step in the healing process is for Ann to understand the interconnections between all parts of her life and her environment.

Comment   An Aboriginal approach is designed for a particular population of people. To use an Aboriginal approach as designed requires intimate knowledge of the culture of the Aboriginal clients. However, concepts such as *mino-pimátisiwin* and healing can be adapted to apply to other situations and other cultures. (Please refer to Chapter 12 to learn more about these concepts and their application.)

Feminist Theory and Practice

Feminist social work is consistent with structural social work in many respects. Much of the feminist focus is on issues of inequality and social injustice. Feminist social work is described in detail in Chapter 13 of this book. This approach is concerned with eliminating domination, subordination, exploitation, and oppression. In working with women, a belief in their innate health and ability to "identify and mobilize inherent individual and collective capacities for healing, growth, and personal/political transformation" (Bricker-Jenkins, 1991, p. 277) is important. Women's strengths must be acknowledged, applied, and built on in a context that stresses equality in the relationship between clients and social workers.

Feminist social work is as much at ease with micro practice as it is with large macro and political systems. Attempts have been made to apply structural social work principles to micro-level practice; however, feminist social work has seen greater development of its principles in micro practice applications. Feminist social workers also hold (as do structural social workers) that personal and political issues cannot be separated.

Two concepts that are very important to feminist social work practice are *empowerment* and *validation*. Empowerment refers to people being able to take control and ownership of their lives. This instills a sense of self-esteem and accomplishment that is necessary for personal growth. Validation is seen as a step toward empowerment. It is a feeling that the client is heard, understood, and listened to, and a belief by the client that her experiences and views are important and respected.

Using a Feminist Perspective in Assessment

Assessment that uses feminist principles focuses on understanding processes such as empowerment, validation, oppression, and human capacity for growth. Empowerment and capacity for growth are as important to feminist assessment as they are when using the strengths approach.

Questions that may be used in assessment include the following: Have exploitation and oppression taken place? If so, what are the dynamics? Does the client feel exploited or oppressed? If so, how does this affect the client's personal life and psychological functioning? Does the client understand the political forces that lead to oppression and exploitation? What does the client think can and should be done—if anything—about these inequities?

What are the client's strengths? How can she mobilize her capacity for growth? How can she empower herself? What does she need to feel validated? What helps her to feel that she has an important and respected place in her world?

Case Example

Kim and Ann ▼

Ann's ex-husband Jack has been refusing to pay child support even though the family court has ordered him to do so. A feminist analysis might suggest that this may be due to social policies that do not respond adequately to the realities of many women who are single parents. While the order for child support is on paper, neither the courts nor the enforcement authorities have chosen to ensure that Jack pays.

Kim wants to find a way to ensure that Jack resumes his child support—a feminist worker would search for ways to take necessary action so that payments are made. However, Kim also discovers that Ann feels the lack of child support is partly her own fault. Since she thinks she has failed as a mother, she feels that to some degree she does not deserve the payments. This view does not surprise Kim, but she holds a very different position. She believes that a major part of Ann's parenting problems are the result of the payments having stopped. Kim will tell Ann this but knows that simply telling her so will have little impact.

Thus, Kim decides on a different tactic. She is aware of a small group of women who are experiencing similar problems and have had one meeting to discuss whether they can take some collective action. They are being guided and assisted by a competent activist and feminist. Kim tells Ann about the group, and Ann decides that she will attend their next meeting. Kim has several goals in mind. (Note that structural analysis as well as other perspectives could also lead to the same or similar goals.) The first and obvious goal is to give Ann a way to regain the child support payments. Kim believes that this group has a good chance of succeeding. Second, and probably more important, the group provides a situation in which Ann might be validated. If she sees that others face the same problem she does, she may come to believe that she is not the cause of the problem. The women have a legal right to child support. This message, coming from peers who are experiencing the same problems, is likely to be much more powerful than anything Kim might say. Third, Kim strongly believes that Ann needs to empower herself. Both the validation process and the collective action to regain child support should go a long way in Ann's empowerment.

▲

Comment   Like an Aboriginal approach, feminist theory and practice were intended for a specific population; in this instance, women. However, many conceptions of feminist theory have carried over into other areas of social work. Examples are validation, empowerment, the idea that the personal cannot be separated from the political, and more.

CHAPTER SUMMARY

The main theme of this chapter is to show that generalist social work uses a diversity of theory and a broad knowledge base both in assessment and intervention.

For much of the past century, social work searched for a single or limited range of theories that could unify the profession. In the past 25 years or so and as generalist social work matured, Canadian social work, in particular, accepted the importance of a broad knowledge base.

Theoretical diversity has two meanings. The first is that social work as a profession must embrace a wide range of theoretical perspectives. This range covers the breadth of social work practice. The second meaning is that each social worker needs to be able to incorporate a broad base of theory into his or her practice. This selection of theory is only a portion of the wide range of theoretical conceptions available to the profession.

However, theoretical diversity is not the only source of knowledge that social workers use. The base is even wider. The broad knowledge base of social work embraces theoretical diversity but also includes life experience (wisdom), culture and tradition, spirituality or religion, authority, and observation and testing.

Social workers draw from this broad knowledge base and diversity of theory in order to engage assessment and intervention. However, it needs to be focused. One of the ways this can be done is to frame theory used in practice by means of ecosystems. Exhibit 9.1 shows a listing of theory by system size (micro, mezzo, and macro), which helps workers select appropriate knowledge accordingly.

Another way that practice can be focused is that, from each theoretical perspective listed in Exhibit 9.1 (and then briefly described), a set of questions emerge that a worker can consider. Over time and with a wide selection of cases, many or even most of the questions would lead to valuable information. However, in a single case, only some of the theoretical perspectives of Exhibit 9.1 will yield useful information. Thus assessment can be focused partly by asking appropriate questions suggested by each of the theoretical perspectives.

Chapter 10 further addresses diversity and focused assessment.

10

Application of Focused Assessment within a Broad Knowledge Base

To articulate principles of assessment and then apply them to the assessment process.

This Chapter ▼

- articulates the road to assessment
- shows how social work assessment applies a diversity of theory and a broad knowledge
- argues that while ideally assessment should be an inductive process, in reality it is a blend of inductive and deductive thinking
- articulates determinants of assessment
- demonstrates that social work assessment is focused by determinants of assessment including a professional lens
- demonstrates, by case example, how in practice focused assessment within a broad knowledge base can be applied in the context of agency mandate and reality of practice situations

INTRODUCTION

Please note that this chapter makes reference to several concepts that are more fully explained in Chapters 11 to 14. You may want to read or skim ahead to one or more of these chapters.

THE ROAD TO ASSESSMENT

Social work assessment is an ongoing analysis and interpretation of information (sometimes loosely called "facts") collected by the worker about the client and the client's situation. The primary purpose of assessment is to set goals and determine a strategy for intervention usually designed to meet those goals. In voluntary relationships, the worker and client must agree not only on the assessment itself but the plan of intervention.

Assessment is *multidimensional*. Human problems are connected, and sometimes one problem affects another. Often a problem has psychological consequences, but it also is almost certainly connected to the environment and probably affects other people. The problem may also affect other needs of the client. Multidimensional assessment in problem solving is a holistic approach. This means that social workers need not only understand the "narrow" problem but also the wider biological, social, cultural, psychological, and spiritual dimensions. (See Hepworth, Rooney, and Larsen, 1997, Ch. 8, pp. 194–229). To engage in multidimensional assessment, the worker must use diverse theories and a broad knowledge base as articulated in chapter 9.

Diverse theories (multiple theoretical languages) are the range of practice theories in social work and theories about human, social behaviours, and the environment that social workers use.

A *broad knowledge base* embraces five sources of knowledge: diversity of theory; life experience; culture, values, and ideology; observation and testing; and, to a limited extent, authority.

Conversely, assessment needs to be focused. Without a narrowing process, use of a broad knowledge base, diversity of theory, and multidimensional assessment would be an eclectic quagmire. We have suggested that organizing theoretical perspectives according to system size (micro to macro) and using theory to generate assessment questions help to direct assessment. More importantly, in this chapter we show how assessment is also *focused* by *determinants of assessment*. Focus helps assessment to become manageable in a diverse world.

So then how do we continue to travel the road to assessment? This chapter addresses this important question.

INDUCTIVE VERSUS DEDUCTIVE ASSESSMENT

Assessment may be approached deductively or inductively. In deductive assessment, the worker fits the case to theory. To illustrate a purely deductive approach, a social worker may learn and master a theory, say role theory. Then the worker uses role theory to analyze every case the worker is assigned whether or not the case situation fits the theory. In its extreme form, a deductive assessment would likely use a single theoretical language. This process is common in some kinds of specialized practice. For example, a family counsellor may base all of her practice on a single approach, for example, structural family therapy.

In an inductive approach, the worker would first study and understand a situation, the client's story. Then she or he selects, from the worker's repertoire, theoretical perspectives that fit the case. The first step for newly assigned cases is to collect information, study, and comprehend the presenting situation. Then the worker selects from her or his theoretical repertoire those that are most appropriate and useful in engaging assessment. An inductive approach is important in most social work, particularly generalist practice.

The above approaches to assessment are polar extremes. In real life, workers develop preferred ways and means of assessment that blend inductive and deductive approaches.

DETERMINANTS OF ASSESSMENT[1]

Determinants are the factors that structure an assessment; they determine the boundaries. They focus an assessment and include much more than a theoretical understanding and analysis of a case situation. Every assessment is highly influenced by a wide variety of determinants.

Here we address determinants that we consider essential for generalist social work. No doubt there are other determinants; many depend upon the setting and specialized practice. All of these determinants shape every assessment and focus use of diverse theories, broad base knowledge, and multidimensional assessment. Exhibit 10.1 lists the key determinants in generalist social work practice.

Exhibit 10.1 ▼ **Key Determinants in Generalist Social Work Practice**

1. The social worker

a. Theoretical repertoire (diversity)
b. Professional lens
   i. Selective use of theory
   ii. Worldviews, ideology, and personal values of worker
   iii. Interpretation of social work values and ideology
   iv. Practice wisdom; experience gained over time
   v. Social worker's culture and life experience

2. The client's situation
a. Nature of problem(s) b. Strengths c. Nature of person d. Nature of social environment
3. Risks of and to client
a. Of client to others b. Of client to self c. Of intervention to client

Continued

4. The workplace
a. Fields of practice/types of service
b. Agency
i. Mandate
ii. Relevant social policy
iii. Agency policy
iv. Agency procedures

The Social Worker

Assessment in generalist social work selectively draws upon broad-based knowledge and theoretical diversity in order to understand the client and situation, set goals, and plan for interventions. How we use and interpret this wide knowledge base is filtered and influenced by factors such as the worker's personal culture, life experience, worldview, ideology, and personal interpretation of professional values. This means that practice knowledge differs from worker to worker in varying degrees. Generalist workers, as all social workers, develop their preferences and favourite sources of knowledge (See Forte, 2007, pp. 19–28). In reality, generalists learn from a wide range of knowledge sources but engage assessment through a lens with many filters. This is the worker's professional lens.

Professional Lens

Every social worker's professional lens is shaped somewhat differently. Hence assessment depends greatly upon social worker judgment and, most importantly, the social worker's understanding of how his or her professional lens affects understanding of the client and the client's environment. This makes assessment a blend of deductive and inductive approaches; inductive in the sense that the social worker draws from a wide knowledge base including diversity of theories in order to understand the client's situation, and deductive because the worker's professional lens filters, shapes, focuses, and limits the worker's approaches to assessment.

To illustrate, let's use two social workers. Both Ingrid and Jim are generalist social workers and have worked for the past 18 months for the same child protection agency. They are familiar with agency mandate, policy, and procedures. Each has a good understanding of current thinking and literature on child abuse and substance abuse. Both workers have experienced the same generalist social work education at the same university.

Now pretend (so that we can compare the social workers' approaches) that both workers have been assigned to Sally. Sally is a single parent who lost her job a week ago. At the same time she stopped receiving support payments from her ex-partner. As a result, she has been dinking rather heavily and is now at risk of having her child apprehended because of two incidents of leaving her 6-year-old alone while she was at a bar.

Both workers begin by understanding Sally's story and situation. Independently, each draws upon their understanding of diverse theories and decide that crisis theory (loss of job and income was traumatic and is a crisis) and understanding of strengths is important in their assessment. The process used is consistent with assessment in generalist practice and is mostly inductive.

Now, in reality the two workers also are quite different from one another. Each has a different professional lens and each will interpret crises and strengths differently. Further, their approaches to Sally will likely be different.

Ingrid, a single mother, considers herself a strong feminist, is politically active, and a socialist. Her heritage is Danish and she has a blue-collar background. She is a social activist. Ingrid advocates a consumer-driven approach.

Jim, unmarried with no children, would consider himself a political conservative with a strong compassion to help people. He has a background in psychology. Jim identifies with his Eastern European heritage. His career goals are to be a counsellor or therapist. Unlike Ingrid, he generally accepts a best interest approach, particularly in his work in child welfare.

Both workers clearly understand the risks to the child and are prepared to recommend apprehension if drinking and neglect continues. However, Ingrid is likely to see the roots of the problem as societal and gender-related. Men usually do not have responsibility for child care. Women have more difficulty obtaining good-paying, quality jobs. They also often have less access to educational funding necessary to find high-paying jobs. While she would address Sally's immediate needs, she would expand her assessment to include understanding the wider social structure and how they can adapt to meet the client's needs. She may use intervention techniques such as consciousness-raising, validation, and affirmation, probably by emphasizing strengths of client (see Chapter 14). Ingrid's feminist and socialist professional lens helps focus her assessment.

Jim, on the other hand, has a very different professional lens. He will likely emphasize personal and psychological factors in his assessment. Jim also likes to balance person and the environment. He may conclude that Sally suffers from a stress or anxiety disorder that compromised her job performance. As a result she lost her job and turned to drinking to help alleviate the stress. Assessment and intervention may emphasize how Sally can find ways to handle her stress. Like Ingrid, he also may see strengths as important but from a different lens.

While both workers understand that crisis theory and understanding strengths offer important ways to help Sally, the filters in their professional lens are very different. The steps that Ingrid takes to help may be different than the steps Jim takes.

The obvious question, when working with Sally, is which lens is better? Jim's or Ingrid's? Our answer is that both can be appropriate. However, you must answer this question for yourself, though you can be guided by some of the following principles:

1. Assessment is built on a wide knowledge base but is focused by determinants of assessment. One of the most important determinants is the social worker's professional lens.
2. A professional lens is a reality of all social workers.
   a. Generalist social work permits—and even encourages—the development of professional lenses.
   b. Because of the diversity between social workers in life experience, culture, personal values, religion and spirituality, and so on, every social worker will develop theoretical preferences—a professional lens.

3. Assessment and intervention must be *appropriate* to the nature of the client and the client's situation. Assessment is a blend of the following:
   a. An inductive approach, which generally assures that the use of knowledge and theory fit the case. Good assessment should always understand a situation and then draw upon a wide knowledge base to engage assessment.
   b. A deductive approach; the worker must be able to adapt her or his professional lens to meet the *needs and goals of a client.*
   c. Social workers must know the limits of their professional lenses and judge the situations in which it is appropriate to use or not to use them.
4. The professional lens is shaped by many factors and differs widely amongst social workers.
5. The professional lens helps focus assessment. It narrows the range of use of diverse theories and multidimensional assessment.
6. Social work assessment and practice is based on making informed decisions and judgments. The process is a human process based on human decisions. Usually there are many ways informed decisions can be made. A social worker's wide knowledge base and professional lens helps guide making important decisions.
7. Each worker needs to clearly understand her or his own professional lens and how this informs their practice. This includes understanding how the social worker's culture, personal values, and life experiences affects her or his assessment of clients.
8. Social work values are *interpreted* by a social worker and become part of the professional lens. For instance, Ingrid's acceptance of a consumer-driven approach reflects a strong commitment to democratic ideals and principles of self-determination. Jim's emphasis upon best interest grows out of the principle of client safety.

The Client

A generalist approach to assessment requires that clients be understood in the context of their social environment. The social worker must have the knowledge and tools to assess and help clients. In short, in order to complete an assessment the social worker must know what to assess.

When working with individuals and families, social workers need information not just about the client, but also about the client's basic needs and the client's environment. To engage assessment, social workers need information about the person, the environment, and how the person connects with the environment. This includes the problem(s) and strengths. Sometimes this package of person, environment, connections with the environment, problem(s) and strengths is referred to as the client's story or, in ecosystems terminology, the client's situation. *A broad knowledge base and the social worker's professional lens are used to help understand and analyze the client's story.*

Exhibit 10.2 is a list of important areas of the client's story (client's situation) that a social worker needs to be able understand. Often the important areas to understand are determined by the purpose of the service and mandate of the agency. Only some of the areas will be important in each situation.

Exhibit 10.2 ▼ **Important Areas of the Client's Story**

Person
• Health and mental health
• Emotional functioning and coping
• Wants and needs
• Reason for service; includes precipitating event(s)
• Social skills
• Past experiences relevant to current situation
• Client understanding and perspective on problems
• Strengths
• Coping efforts
• Obstacles
• Effects of age and life stage
• Gender issues
• Spirituality
• Ideology and worldview
• Individual identity
Environment and Connection with Environment
• Material circumstances such as income and assets
• Available support systems and resources
• Shelter
• Safety of surrounding community
• Salient aspects in cultural background
• Family relationships and family life cycle
• Experiences of stigma, discrimination, marginalization, and/or oppression

Risks

Most social work intervention involves risk. This is particularly so in mandated agencies. Thus most assessments need to consider risk.

There are several different kinds of risk. One is that the intervention itself might prove to be damaging to the client. A second is the possibility that client could harm himself or herself or others.

Intervention as a Risk

How can intervention be risky? One way to understand this is to use an analogy from medicine. Iatrogenic medicine is an adverse or negative reaction from medical treatment. Frequently news outlets report on problems caused by a medical treatment. For instance, on March 28, 2007, CTV News reported that "nearly one in every 13 Canadian patients experiences a preventable hospital-related infection or incident" (CTV News, 2007, March).

Intervention-related mishaps are common in social work. Let us explain by use of examples. A couple in marriage counselling finds their problems have magnified after therapy. An apprehended child is severely injured or dies from neglect in a foster home. A school social worker attempts to help a boy who is constantly bullied. The bullying increases after the bullies find out that the boy has sought help; he is further stigmatized simply because he has sought help and is considered a "wimp." A counsellor sets unattainable goals and the client's failure to reach them causes a setback. A client who is a member of a minority ethnocultural group and feels oppressed is told by her social worker that since she lives in Canada she must accept Canadian values. Implied is that she must give up her own values; hence, the client feel even more oppression, as the practice is oppressive. Examples abound.

A different type of social work mistake is connected to assessment and involves labelling. Putting people into categories can and often does have a harmful outcome. Labelling can become stigmatizing, degrading, and oppressive. An important principle is to *use categories only if the category aids the helping process.*

One of the most important skills that a social worker must learn is when *not* to intervene. Too often social workers seem to want to help when help is either not wanted or needed. There are some guides that can be of use to determine whether intervention is warranted. Also see the Canadian Association of Social Workers *Guidelines for Ethical Practice* (2005b).

Normally intervention with adults should take place under the following circumstances:

- A client asks for help.
- There is clear evidence of risk of the client harming herself or himself and/or others.
- Intervention is required by legislation. (This is sometimes called *mandated practice.*)

There are exceptions to these principles. An example is social work with young children. Another is in the case of an outreach worker whose "clients" are drug users in the core of a city. Sometimes social workers may attempt to encourage or cajole clients to get help. They intervene without asking permission from the client. If none of the three above conditions apply, social workers need to carefully ask themselves the question, "Am I really going to help or will I make things worse?"

Risk of Client to Self or Others

In many settings it is important to assess client risk. The most common of these are child protection, crisis work, family violence, mental health, and criminal justice. Many generalist social workers are employed in these settings, particularly in child protection. Unfortunately, this type of risk assessment is too complicated and too specialized to cover in this book in any detail. However, we will introduce the topic by offering two illustrations. (See Chapter 5 for more on risk assessment in the child protection field.)

Risk to self illustrated　Generalist social workers often work as volunteers or paid employees on crisis telephone hotlines. The purpose of the hotline is often to give immediate help with a secondary yet important task of assessing suicide risk. Crisis agencies usually provide specialized training to employees and volunteers. Every phone call may require a judgment about suicide potential.

There is no standard or diagnostic form that predicts suicide. Prediction of suicide is a judgment call of the worker. There are a number of ways that a social worker can make a prediction. An excellent introduction to the topic is Kanel (2007, pp. 97–113).

Kanel (2007) summarizes a list of typical signs of potential suicide:

- Giving things away.
- Putting things away.
- Writing a will.
- Withdrawing from usual activities.
- Being preoccupied with death.
- Experiencing the recent death of a fried or relative.
- Feeling hopeless, helpless, or worthless.
- Increased drug or alcohol use.
- Displaying psychotic behaviour.
- Giving verbal hints such as, "I'm no use to anyone anymore."
- Showing agitated depression.
- Living alone and being isolated. (p. 99)

The intent of this section on risk assessment has been to establish it as an important determinant of assessment and to introduce the reader to the topic. Risk assessment is complicated and depends upon the setting and purpose. Risk assessment in mental health is different from risk assessment in child welfare, and both are different from risk assessment used in drug abuse situations.

The Workplace

The workplace of most Canadian social workers is in a public or private agency.[2] Agencies can be grouped according to field of practice or type of service. Examples are health, child and family social work services, criminal justice, marriage and family counselling, mental health, school social work, immigrant and refugee services, crisis work, substance abuse, and so on (See Hick, 2006). The service of each agency is limited to a specialization. It is within such specialized agencies that most generalist social workers practice.

This text is about generalist social work. Most BSW university degree programs in Canada use a generalist curriculum. The Canadian Association for Social Work Education (CASWE, 2009) sets standards for a generalist BSW degree. Is it not, then, a contradiction that by far the greatest majority of generalist workers are employed by specialized agencies whose mandate is located within a specific field of practice or type of service?

The answer often given to this question is that the generalist skills and theory that are the foundation of social work can be applied across all or most fields of practice. We accept this answer as only partially true and with qualifications.

The agency, its mandate, and the social policy from which the mandate flows greatly influence practice (including assessment and intervention) for work within the auspices of the agency. The agency policy and mandate is an important determinant of assessment. Thus, a better way to answer the posed question is that generalist practice must be and almost always is anchored within specific agency policy and mandate. Practice does not take place in a vacuum. In the end, generalist social workers need to have considerable knowledge about the field of practice in which they work and be able to adapt their generalist skills to the agency in which they are employed.

Thus, the generalist principles of social work practice are always *anchored* in a field or type of practice that is conducted under the auspices of a specific agency. One of the important products of this reality is that assessment is influenced greatly by agency mandate and policy.

Let us illustrate. Assessments in mental health agencies or organizations require social workers to have a working knowledge of psychosocial functioning, psychiatric diagnosis, prognosis, level of functioning, patients' rights, provincial mental health acts, etc. Contrast this with child welfare and child and family social work services. In such work places, social workers need to know about parenting, child abuse, parents' and children's rights, risk, child welfare legislation, and more.

Beginning generalist social workers often find that there is a steep learning curve as they begin their first social work job. They need to know the details of practice that are specific to their agency of employment and to the related field of practice.

APPLICATION OF THE ASSESSMENT PROCESS

In the classroom a frequently asked question is; "I think I understand the theory of assessment but I have never done one. What does a real assessment look like? How do social workers apply an assessment?" Or a student with agency experience might say, "I have done assessments but not applied theory. How can you do this in real life?" We address these questions here.

In this textbook we have assumed that principles of generalist practice are applicable across most fields of practice. However, each social worker must anchor these principles in their employing agency and related field of practice.

Usually programs have specific and limited goals. Assessment questions, often organized by a form developed by the agency, are designed to help determine the best ways that clients can reach these goals. For example, in a supportive housing program for those who have a persistent mental illness, the assessment would include need for housing, degree of support required, income level, obstacles that client faces in locating and maintaining housing, client strengths and abilities in locating and maintaining housing, and so on. On the other hand, a well-baby program for first-time mothers would focus assessment on mothers' and babies' health, the growth and development of babies, parenting abilities and skills, and so on. So the type of necessary information varies greatly according to agency mandate and goals.

Partly because of this specialized character of the workplace, there is no common assessment form or even outline for generalist social work. If there was, we would include it in this text. However, there are principles that we can address.

The form that an agency uses for assessment is important and needs to be carefully thought out. While the form itself should never drive an assessment, the content of it does. It must permit the worker to get information sufficient that appropriate planning and intervention can take place. Therefore, professionals in the agency need to give careful thought to the content and structure of the assessment form that social workers in the agency use. Updating needs to be frequent.

Eligibility assessment   Some assessments are used to determine eligibility for a service or program. An example is a child's eligibility for a publicly funded daycare program. Or an older person's requirements for and needs in a personal care home. Very often such assessments are completed using a checklist, *rating scale*, or some other similar instrument that require professional judgments. For example, a five-point rating scale might be used to rate an older person's mobility or ability to dress herself or himself. Or a similar scale could be used by a school social worker to rate a child's level of aggression on a school playground.

Risk assessment   As developed earlier, a risk assessment is an attempt to predict probability of a client harming self or others.

Problem-solving assessment   Problem-solving assessments (introduced in Chapter 8) are probably the most commonly used by social workers. Problem-solving assessments are designed to analyze collected information so that an intervention plan can be developed. The purpose of such assessments is to develop a plan that meets a client's needs, often expressed as goals.

Strengths-based assessment   This is a variation of a problem-solving assessment. A key difference is that rather than assessing problems, analysis focuses on a client's wants and needs. So instead of problem solving, the emphasis is upon using a client's strengths in order to achieve needs and wants (See Chapter 11).

Most problem-solving and strengths-based assessments should be (and are) divided into two parts:

1. Facts: Facts are information necessary to understand the situation. Facts may be observations, opinions, reports from clients as well as significant others and other agencies, etc. The facts form the basis of a dynamic analysis.
2. Dynamic analysis: The assessment is an analysis and dynamic understanding of the facts and the situation and to engage planning and intervention. It requires the judgment of the social worker and is based on the determinants of assessment with particular emphasis upon the broad-based theoretical perspective and knowledge frame of generalist social work practice, the social worker's professional lens, and agency mandate.

Most agencies use an assessment form appropriate to their mandate. Most are primarily organized to gather information or facts either by use of a checklist, a narrative format, or a combination of these. Sometimes agency assessment forms include a section called "impressions," "summary," "goals," or "plan." The intent is to summarize a dynamic assessment often based on a problem-solving method and/or a strengths-based approach. Most agencies also require record keeping that includes elements of a dynamic analysis, usually emphasizing planning, intervention, and charting of progress.

Exhibit 10.3 illustrates an agency problem-solving/strengths-based assessment using a dynamic analysis based on "facts." The agency used in the illustration provides a service to immigrants and refugees. If it provided different services, such as those in mental health or child welfare agencies, the headings or topics used in the form would be different. However, regardless of the facts or how they are obtained, social workers must be able to carry out a dynamic assessment.

Exhibit 10.3 is a composite assessment form. The attempt is to make a problem-solving/strengths-based assessment as realistic as possible. The form has been constructed from a review of assessment forms and processes from a wide variety of social service and health agencies.

Assessment Illustrated: A Case Example

The example in Exhibit 10.3 was introduced in Chapter 1. It uses a fictitious agency called City Immigrant and Refugee Services (CIRS), funded by the United Way and provincial government grants. CIRS's mandate is to help immigrants and refugees adjust to Canadian life. The agency has several programs, including employment services, a housing program, counselling services, English as a second language service, a crisis hotline, and easy referral access to specialty programs such as parenting programs and legal help. The agency also has a large community hall, which is used by a variety of immigrant and ethnocultural groups for educational and social activities.

Omar, aged 28, is a generalist university-educated social worker who has worked for CIRS in the counselling service as a case manager and counsellor for just over three years. He emigrated from a West African country 15 years ago and received a BSW five years ago. Omar's professional lens emphasizes a culturally competent strengths approach in the context of ecosystems. He is a strong advocate of a consumer-driven and anti-oppressive practice.

The following is Omar's initial assessment of Alberto and his situation after one interview with him and a brief interview with Alberto and his wife, Maria. Agency practice is for the intake worker to assume the role of case manger and to complete an initial assessment after the first or second interview. Omar and Alberto seem to respect each other and Omar can easily empathize with Alberto because he also had a difficult adjustment after immigration. Omar draws upon his experience of immigration to help understand Alberto and his predicament.

The left column of the exhibit is the form itself. Content in regular type is the agency's assessment categories that each worker must fill out. In italics is the social worker's (Omar's) assessment. In the right column are some comments and explanations about the assessment.

General comments   This is an initial assessment. The case manager has not yet formed a contract with the client but will do so as the intervention plan proceeds. Omar's next step is to very quickly meet with Alberto and begin to implement the plan.

Omar used a broad-based knowledge base including a diversity of theory. His assessment was mostly inductive in that he selected theory based on his understanding of facts. Yet his professional lens was clear particularly in his emphasis upon determining the client's wants and needs (strengths) and social relationships (ecosystems).

In this example, Omar's client was Alberto, not Maria. Given what Maria has experienced, and the stress she also faces in her marriage, her needs and wants are also important and cannot be ignored. Maria would also be a client should she seek help to deal with the abuse she has experienced and/or marital problems that affect the relationship between her

Exhibit 10.3 ▼ Case Example

CITY IMMIGRANT AND REFUGEE SERVICES	
INITIAL ASSESSMENT AND PLANNING FORM	DISCUSSION
Identification Information Name Alberto Age 46 Time in Canada 2 years Employed No English Use Fair Marital Status Married Spouse's Age 38 # Children 1 Age 12 Origin Peru Religion Catholic Education Gr. 12 equiv. Profession/Trade Electrician Spouse's Name Maria Name(s) Carlos	• The categories are not exhaustive; the intent is to illustrate. • Most of the responses to each of the categories could be a checklist.
Reason for Service: Describe reasons, self-referral or from other source. *Self-referral but came under pressure from wife.* *Alberto broke leg by fall on ice in front of grocery store and as a result lost job as a construction worker. Employment Insurance benefits about to expire. Still unemployed.* *Client is discouraged and has talked about returning to Peru. Needs: A source of income and "to feel better."*	• Alberto is the client since he has asked for help for himself. However, Omar does have responsibilities to both Maria and Carlos, particularly when safety is an issue. • Sometimes reason for service is called the *presenting problem*. CIRS uses the term *reason for service* because sometimes the need for service is not for problem solving and to help ensure that their lexicon is not that of deficits. • In this instance there is a clear and immediate problem but probably not a crisis. • All problems should be translated into needs. The loss of job is quickly translated into a need. Both Alberto and Omar agree on both problem and need. • The feeling of being discouraged needs more exploration.
Nature of Immigration: What were the circumstances that led to immigration? *Brother-in-law, Paulo, and family had immigrated to Canada 5 years earlier, liked Canadian life and encouraged Alberto to follow. Brother-in-law sponsored Alberto and family.*	• There is nothing unusual about the immigration nor was Alberto escaping an adverse situation. • Omar wonders if Alberto wants to move back to Peru but decides to wait to approach the topic.

Continued

CITY IMMIGRANT AND REFUGEE SERVICES (Cont'd)

INITIAL ASSESSMENT AND PLANNING FORM	DISCUSSION
In Peru, Alberto and family lived a reasonably comfortable life. He was an experienced tradesman but cannot find skilled work in Canada due to limited English. Maria and son are happy in their new country.	• If wife and son are happy in Canada and Alberto is not, then potential for major family difficulties; needs further exploration.
Cultural Background. Description. *Lived in small city in Peru. Family is closely knit. He is a Catholic. After immigration, family did not feel comfortable in Canadian churches and, even with support from Spanish-speaking friends, lost interest in church activities.*	• Omar, given his emphasis on strengths and ecosystems, realizes that Alberto feels that he does not belong. He does not have a niche and membership may be a need that he and Alberto should address. • Omar is still attempting to understand Alberto's situation but begins to think that ecosystems and strengths might help in the analysis.
Family History. Events of family of origin that affect current problems.	• Good practice and the Canadian Association of Social Workers *Guidelines for Ethical Practice* (2005b) require that information should be collected only when it helps address client problems. Family history may or may not be relevant to explore. Settlement experience in Canada is relevant and may be useful in helping to solve current problems that Alberto faces. The social worker can return to family issues topic if warranted. • Family history can be important in fields such as mental health or child protection.

Current Family Situation *The source of much of the family information is from Maria, Alberto's wife. Maria has worked as a full-time sewing machine operator for two years. Maria's English is adequate. She learned at work and by talking to neighbours and people at their church. Alberto is frequently angry. Feels his brother-in-law, who is a manager at a department store, looks down on him. Serious arguments with his wife. Sometimes slaps or pushes her. Had huge argument with her about how his education in Peru hadn't helped him. She has fewer years of education than he does, but has a steady job. Alberto couldn't control his anger. He hit his wife and bruised her so badly she did not want to go out in public. Maria packed her clothes and, with her son, left to stay with a friend. Did not make police report.*	• There are important problems other than the original request for service.
	• Understanding family dynamics is important. Omar needs an understanding of role, ecosystems, and feminist theories as well as family dynamics.
	    For example, what are the roles of each family member? Are they functional? Is there role strain? Is there role conflict?
	    Further, feminist theory may help understand gender issues. How does power work in the family? Power differentials? Does Alberto feel powerless due to loss of traditional gender role in family (as main breadwinner); not in control? Does he feel disempowered due to unemployment? How does Maria experience Alberto's anger and need to control her? Is it unsafe for her to return home?

Marriage was stable and rewarding for both up until Alberto lost his job. Mario thinks her husband has lost self-confidence because he speaks poor English, has job difficulties, and feels inferior to her.

Alberto begged her to return home; three days later she complied. Family relationships remain tense and Maria continues to threaten to leave Alberto if he cannot control his anger. Alberto is very proud of his son, Carlos, who does very well in school, speaks good English, and thinks sun rises and sets on his father. Carlos is on local soccer team and has asked his father to coach it.

Work Skills and Work History
In Peru, Alberto worked as an electrician for five years before immigration.
Provincial officials would not license him as an electrician because of lack of suitable Canadian experience and lack of English language ability. Found work as a night custodian for Tower Insurance. Has been able to find part-time summer job on highway construction.

- Ecosystems can be used to map family relationships. An eco-map could be constructed. Likely it would show strain between Maria and Alberto.
- While Omar does not condone Alberto's behaviour, he accepts who Alberto is as a person and realizes that he needs help.
- Is Maria at risk? Maybe. History of family violence is short, very recent, and seems situational. But there are risks that require some safety planning if Maria returns home to Alberto, as she plans to do. Traditional gender roles of men and women in Peru differ from those in Canada. Immigration and settlement experiences challenge the family. Maria did not report incident to police and does not want to do so; this would be unacceptable in her culture. Charges were not laid. Maria has not asked for help, but there may be a need. She believes that husband's stress triggers the abuse and is prepared to forgive him.
- CIRS does not have applicable agency policy. The Canadian Association of Social Workers *Guidelines for Ethical Practice* (2005b) does not have clear guideline. If Alberto tells Omar that he does intend to harm Maria if he becomes angry with her, then *Code* requires the worker to inform target of threat. But at this time, there is no threat.
- Omar's action is a judgment call. He decides that he will take no action unless there is another incident or threat. If either of these occurs, then he will break confidentiality. If there is a threat, he will inform Maria. If there is another incident (or threat), he will be proactive and help Maria to secure help and choose from available options and resources, including police intervention.
- Is accreditation to practise his trade in Canada a structural issue? Omar thinks Alberto is experiencing oppression and discrimination because officials will not recognize Alberto's electrician credentials. Omar experienced a similar situation after immigration and learned that the Employment Services Program and CIRS could help.

Continued

CITY IMMIGRANT AND REFUGEE SERVICES (Cont'd)

INITIAL ASSESSMENT AND PLANNING FORM	DISCUSSION
Client is unhappy and discouraged because he cannot find job as electrician and is now unemployed. Employment insurance is about to expire and Alberto is having difficulty finding new employment. Poor use of English prevents him from entering training programs. Attempts to speak English causes some frustration, but wants to learn.	• Considers referral to Employment Services so Alberto can improve English and gain Canadian work experience.
Education Has high school equivalent in Peru. Learned to be an electrician in an apprenticeship program. Wife encourages Alberto to take Canadian training as an electrician so he can gain provincial licensing. Brother-in-law has offered to help fund this through a no-interest loan. Alberto is angry about provincial policy and refuses to enroll. Maria thinks husband is unreasonable.	• A dilemma for worker. Quick change of provincial policy re: accreditation for trade is unlikely. Will need to explore depth of client's lack of motivation. What prevents Alberto from upgrading English and training in chosen trade in Canada? Not sure that more education is appropriate solution if Alberto does not want it. • Omar needs to backtrack, use strengths perspective, and attempt to discover what client really wants and needs. • Is client depressed? Frustrated in his expectations? Unhappy in Canada? How does he see himself?
Social Relationships (friends, organizations, pastimes, hobbies, etc.) Family finds the Catholic church nearby to be very different from the one they attended in Peru. Maria attends but Alberto does not. In Peru, church was centre of their social life. Family expected the same in Canada. Main pastime of Alberto is watching television. Has made friends with fellow custodian at previous workplace. Normally Alberto makes friends easily but has had difficulty in the past year.	• Spiritual needs are not being met. • Social network seems very limited. • Difficulties in settlement and integration in Canada. • Eco-map would help clarify and maybe suggest solutions.
Current Economic and Living Situation Can make ends meet, but not easily. However, loss of income could result in crisis when EI runs out. Rents small home. Badly needs repairs. Cannot afford better housing. Source of embarrassment for Carlos; does not want friends to see house and lack of furniture.	• Living conditions add to the feelings of low self-esteem in Alberto because he feels that he is responsible for his family's poverty.

Summary of Strengths *Relationship with Carlos affable.* *Problems are recent and seem to be situational.* *Stable marriage up until a year ago.* *Wants to learn English.* *Completed immigration; not an easy task.* *Has trade skills.* *In past motivated to work but currently discouraged.* *Church was very important to him in Peru.*	• Searching for strengths is important. Every client in every situation has strengths. However, because social workers tend to emphasize problems and deficits, it seems that it may take more effort to uncover strengths. • Clearly Alberto has surmounted hardship and has numerous strengths that can be used in the helping process.
Summary of Obstacles *Anger.* *Deteriorating relationship with wife.* *English needs improvement.* *Low self-confidence and self-esteem.* *Job situation.* *Provincial policy re: lack of Canadian accreditation of trade skill and experience from Peru.* *Does not find church satisfying.* *Few friends.*	• CIRS uses the term *obstacle* instead of the word *problem*. The intent is to reduce the tendency to define a problem in terms of deficits. The obstacles listed by Omar are problems, in no particular order, that face Alberto.
Summary Assessment *What the client really wants and needs requires exploration. An assumption that Alberto wants more education and a better job may not truly reflect the client's own real goals and needs. Alberto is a resilient man who experiences difficulties as a result of immigration. Central problem, at this time, seems to be lack of employment and English skills, which are connected to a variety of other situational issues. Alberto's inability to find a job could cause escalation of client's difficulties and is one of the triggers of abusive behaviour and anger. Alberto has lost self-esteem and self-confidence as a result of job loss, stress of emigration, injury, and difficulty in adjusting to Canada. Result is psychological stress, discouragement, guilt, and possibly depression.*	Note: Comments below connect multidimensional theory to summary assessment. • Assessment and the resultant plan must be flexible and change as intervention proceeds (problem solving). • The format of the assessment is problem-solving process that applies a number of theories. • Omar recognizes that what Alberto really wants needs to be explored, so his needs can be addressed. Understanding this is central to a strengths perspective assessment. • Omar realizes that understanding of personality theory and ego psychology may help him explain the stress that Omar is feeling regarding job loss and under-employment. This includes the principle that psychological stress, loss of self-esteem and self-confidence, and depression can be a result of environmental factors. Transition to life in Canada poses challenges.

Continued

CITY IMMIGRANT AND REFUGEE SERVICES (Cont'd)

INITIAL ASSESSMENT AND PLANNING FORM	DISCUSSION
Alberto most likely feels guilty because of inability to, in his view, adequately provide for his family and find work as an electrician. He blames himself even though this is due to an oppressive government policy. *Family problems are probably not at the root of Alberto's difficulties but a result of his struggle to adjust to Canadian life. But if family relationships deteriorate, anger and stress will increase and motivation and self-esteem will deteriorate, adversely affecting the client. Therefore, family relationships will be crucial in client's life.* *Abuse of Maria and angry outbursts seem to be triggered by situational stress. If further stress appears in Alberto's life, then possibility of abuse increases.* *Alberto feels that, in relation to Maria, he is in a lesser position of power. For Alberto and in the context of male-dominance in his Peruvian culture, this loss of power is hard to take. Coupled with the other life stressors, power loss has probably led to some of the abuse and anger.* *Alberto's relationship with son, Carlos, is a very important strength and may be an excellent opener to help Alberto regain his self-esteem and sense of belonging.* *Since moving to Canada, Alberto has felt that he has not belonged. He experiences little membership and has not found a niche. Yet he has good social skills and is an affable man who can make friends easily. Lack of social contacts at church helps reinforce feelings of isolation and lack of belonging. He lacks a place to express his religious beliefs.* *If there is no additional income for Alberto and his family, a crisis will ensue when his employment insurance benefits run out.*	• Feminist use of power and gender differences can be used to understand some of the anger and abusive behaviour of Alberto. Loss of traditional gender role in family can also be used to help explain loss of self-confidence and self-esteem. Strategy to gain power over Maria (violence) is unacceptable. • Structural social work and anti-oppressive practice helps analyze the oppression caused by provincial licensing policy that marginalizes newcomers without Canadian experience like Alberto. • Culturally sensitive practice is necessary to understand how Alberto feels and behaves in his transition to Canadian life and even his anger. Maria may also need counselling due to the abuse she has experienced and gender issues faced in Canada. • Membership, need to belong, and niche are all strengths and ecosystems concepts. Of particular importance is his relationship with his son, Carlos. • Careful examination of each relationship in Alberto's life might help in understanding how they affect his life. This process is important in ecosystems and can be visualized by use of a diagram, such as an eco-map. (See Gitterman and Germain, 2008, pp. 118–21.) • Income loss may be on the horizon. This could initiate a crisis. Crisis theory is useful even though this event has not yet occurred.

Plan: (order of priority)

A. Continue as case manager:

a. Immediate: Understand what Alberto really wants and needs. Must make sure that he can express them. This will set priorities and maybe alter the remainder of this plan.

b. Immediate: Family relationships. Find out what Alberto wants and then help him pursue his own goals. Maybe possible referral to marriage counsellor but only if client believes this will help meet needs.

c. Soon: Explore what is meant by "discouraged." If related to situation of job loss, more training may be indicated. If client also feels blue, lacks energy, trouble sleeping, and so on, referral to a mental health clinic familiar with newcomers' issues may be in order.

d. Long term: Help Alberto find a niche and create experiences that help him feel he belongs. Start with two immediate steps.

    i. Immediate: Explore son's request to coach soccer team. Because of language difficulties, social worker may need to help client negotiate necessary bureaucracy.

    ii. Help validate client's feelings by sharing own (Omar's) experiences of adjustment to Canadian life.

    iii. Help validate that it is not Alberto's fault that he cannot find work as an electrician in Canada. It is due to the barriers in foreign worker accreditation in Canada and policies that marginalize those without Canadian training or work experience.

B. Referral:

a. to Employment Services with recommendations: To address immediate need of a job and to explore training possibilities and challenge to oppressive policy of denial of electrician credentials from Peru.

Worker intervention should be minimally intrusive. A very important skill to learn is when not to intervene. Omar is guided by this principle and it is clearly reflected in his plan.

- The plan illustrates the role of case manager. Note the mixture of direct action taken by Omar and the referrals.
- Each item in the plan is "do-able"
- Omar recognizes that what Alberto really wants needs more exploration and uncovering this takes priority. He may have made a mistake by not addressing this more in the first or second interviews, but it can easily be revisited.
- Generalist workers must have sufficient information about mental illnesses to make a referral if necessary. Omar does not yet have enough information to do this, but there may be a "red flag." It may be that Alberto is experiencing situational problems rather than mental health issues. Omar needs to be careful about intrusiveness.
- Omar needs to draw upon ecosystems and strengths-based practice to help Alberto create real membership and feelings of belonging.
- Omar recognizes centrality of family relationships and tenuous nature of Alberto's marriage. However, instead of defining this as a problem or deficit, Omar shifts, using the strengths perspective, to first learning what Alberto wants and then constructs a way to meet his needs.

Continued

CITY IMMIGRANT AND REFUGEE SERVICES (Cont'd)

INITIAL ASSESSMENT AND PLANNING FORM	DISCUSSION
b. Anger management: Possible: To be effective, help with anger management must be seen by client as a need. There is no evidence that client wants anger management. Abusiveness and anger is a recent behaviour and due to current situation. Solution to other problems is also probable solution of anger. Will explain anger management to client and find out if he wants it. Anger will be monitored. If there are threats, Maria will be contacted and options and resources will be made available to her. c. Suggest to Alberto that there is a small, but active group of immigrants from Peru that use the agency's community hall. If Alberto and Maria want, he will introduce them to the group.	• Marriage counselling will work only if all parties want it and if there is no active threat of violence in the relationship. Omar will not even mention it until he is clearer about client's wants. Such a referral may take place at a later time. • There is some risk that Alberto's anger will re-emerge, jeopardizing Maria's safety. • A niche and feelings of membership/belonging are important strengths and ecosystems concepts. Validation is a principle of feminist practice. Strength-based practice holds that solutions need to be taken in small steps. At least two immediate steps, coaching and validation are important. A skilled social worker should be able to use this as a springboard for further successes.

and Alberto. Perhaps most appropriate in her situation is a referral to an immigrant women's group or counselling agency. If she chooses not to accept such help, it remains important to ensure that she has access to social support, safe accommodation, and freedom from violence in her life.

CHAPTER SUMMARY

Generalist social workers weave together a number of principles in order to engage and guide assessment. A summary of these principles:

- Generalist social workers should use:
    - ° Multidimensional assessment: This expands assessment to include not only an understanding of the "narrow" problem but also the wider biological, social, cultural, psychological, and spiritual dimensions. To engage multidimensional assessment, the worker must use diverse theories and a broad knowledge base.
    - ° Broad knowledge base: This refers to the necessity of social workers using a wide range of knowledge. The conception encompasses diversity of theory, life experience, culture, worldviews, values, and ideology.
    - ° Diversity of theory: Social workers must be able to have working knowledge of and be able to apply to the process of assessment a wide range of theories. This diversity applies to practice theories in social work and theories about human and social behaviours developed in the social work and/or the social, behavioural, and/or biological sciences.
- Multidimensional assessment, diversity of knowledge, and a broad knowledge base are all expansive conceptions. Without some way to focus, assessment becomes too eclectic and unmanageable. Generalist social workers must be able to focus—zero in—in order to engage competent assessment. Determinants of assessment help provide the boundaries that make assessment manageable.
    - ° Determinants of assessment: These are the factors that structure an assessment. They determine the boundaries and focus an assessment, including much more than a theoretical understanding and analysis of a case situation. Every assessment is highly influenced by a wide variety of determinants that includes the knowledge, culture, and life experience of the worker, the client and the client's situation, risks associated with intervention, and the workplace in which the social worker is employed. Exhibit 10.3 lists key determinants.
    - ° Professional lens: The professional lens is a major determinant of assessment. Assessment in generalist social work selectively draws upon a broad base of knowledge. How we use and interpret this wide knowledge base is filtered and influenced by factors such as the social worker's own culture, life experience, ideology, and values. All social workers develop preferences and favourite sources of knowledge. In reality, generalists learn from a wide range of knowledge sources but interpret and use them through a lens with many filters: the social worker's professional lens. The lens differs from social worker to social worker and greatly influences assessment. Thus, the assessment process becomes partly deductive.

- Inductive and deductive assessment processes: In deductive assessment, the worker fits the case to theory. In an inductive approach, the worker would first study and understand a situation and then select, from a wide knowledge base, the one (or more) most appropriate theory (theories) to apply. We argue that, in an ideal world, the process should be inductive. However, in reality, social workers should emphasize an inductive assessment but will need to blend it with a deductive approach. This is accomplished through the social worker's professional lens.

The last half of the chapter applied these principles to a case situation. The case example attempted to address common questions that students often ask: "I think I understand the theory of assessment but I have never done one. What does a real assessment look like? How do social workers apply an assessment?" Or a student with agency experience might say, "I have done assessments but not applied theory. How can you do this in real life?"

NOTES

1 The use of determinants of assessment was put forward by Sid Frankel, Associate Professor, University of Manitoba.

2 A small minority of social workers in Canada work outside the structure of agency. Most of these would be therapists or consultants in private practice. Most all of these have advanced education or training and have specialized their practice.

c h a p t e r

Strengths-Based Practice as a Development Process

Chapter Goal ▼

To explain how the strengths-based practice is fundamental to social work.

This Chapter ▼

- stresses that helping should emphasize strengths and development rather than people's deficits and problems
- shows how a strengths-based practice emphasizes client growth, development, and quality of life
- demonstrates how a strengths-based practice can be used to solve problems
- emphasizes empowerment as a major goal of social work practice
- develops the concept of a consumer-driven approach
- connects the strengths-based practice to the ecosystems perspective
- suggests that one of the most important resources for helping people is self-help groups
- shows that one of the most important attributes of people is resilience and that social workers often underestimate resilience
- argues that all relationships, including professional helping relationships, are reciprocal and that in good helping relationships both client and worker should be seen as partners who both contribute and receive rewards

INTRODUCTION

This chapter and the following three chapters conclude a major theme of this book: generalist social work practice needs to be based on a variety of perspectives, approaches, and theories that cover the micro to macro range. This chapter is the first to present an approach that goes beyond problem solving. While the previous chapters developed a broad knowledge base for assessment, the remaining chapters, while not neglecting assessment, also focus on approaches to intervention.

Readers should be aware that there is some confusion in the literature between use of the terms *strengths-based practice,* the *strengths perspective,* and the *strengths approach.* Many seem to use the terms interchangeably. We use strengths-based practice and the strengths approach to mean any helping practice that makes extensive use of strengths concepts. Recently, strengths-based practice seems to have become the term of choice. The strengths perspective is a term for a paradigm of social work practice that emerges largely from the work of Dennis Saleebey (1997c, 2002, 2006b).

STRENGTHS, DEFICITS, AND PROBLEM SOLVING

The idea of focusing on strengths is not new. Since the time of early casework, practitioners have focused on working with clients' strengths, and there is widespread agreement in social work, regardless of the approach, that this is an important part of practice.

Social workers, like most helping professionals, tend to focus on problems. This was articulated in Chapter 8. Problem-solving practice by definition centres on the dynamics of the problem, including the causes, the context, and how the problem affects the client and the client's environment. The strengths perspective holds that the lexicon, underpinnings, and indeed the focus of the problem-solving process is on deficits of clients (see Cowger and Snively, 2002; Goldstein, 2002; Saleebey, 2006b; and Spearman, 2005). Far too often practice centres on deficits.

Emphasis upon deficits means that the worker attempts to understand problems by looking for and understanding "weaknesses" or "limitations." The focus is on "What went wrong?" Once the deficits (what went wrong) are understood, the worker can then begin to take steps toward problem solution, often by some correction of the deficit (Spearman, 2005).

The strengths perspective forcefully argues that social work practice is bad practice if clients are viewed in terms of their deficits. Practice that uses a deficit model not only is inconsistent with the ideology and values of social work but also is sometimes counter-productive.

Social workers following strengths-based practice usually engage clients with the intent to help them solve problems. However, instead of working directly with client problems—or even balancing work between client problems and strengths—the strengths perspective dramatically shifts the balance to strongly emphasize people's strengths. In general terms, strengths-based practice (and particularly the strengths perspective) assumes that a solution is more important than understanding and analysis of the history of the problem. This approach enhances the problem-solving model by providing both a constructive critique of and a way to rethink traditional practice. Further, and importantly, the strengths perspective is a direct, frontal attack on efforts to treat personal and social problems as pathologies or deficits.

There is not a theory of strengths. What exists is a collection of many concepts, ideas, and notions of practice based on the fundamental principle that helping can best take place if its focus is on strengths. Some of the most important principles are described in this chapter.

PROMOTION OF PERSONAL GROWTH AND QUALITY OF LIFE

All of the approaches that we cover in this book share the idea that working with strengths is important, but each comes at it a little differently. This chapter focuses on the strengths of individuals. Problem solving often draws upon people's strengths. Feminist and structural approaches tend to assume that people's problems are often not the result of individuals' shortcomings but are due to difficulties, including inequities and injustices, in our social institutions. The emphasis of practice in these approaches is often to mobilize individuals' strengths, sometimes in the form of collective action, to address these inequities and injustices and in turn help individuals. The Aboriginal concept of healing is like a journey where the goal is to find "the good life." It is like the strengths approach in that people mobilize themselves to reach their full potential.

The strengths approach is about personal growth, development, and quality of life. The central propositions of a strengths approach are clear and straightforward. Strengths-based practice uses people's own resources to help them meet four goals: (1) to grow as human beings, (2) to improve their quality of life, (3) to develop their own problem-solving skills, and (4) to deal with their stress and adversity. To meet these goals, the approach capitalizes on people's capacities, vitality, abilities, talents, courage, and power. Compared with problem solving, the strengths approach is ***developmental***—focused on growth—instead of restorative or correcting an existing problem. It incorporates ideas such as wellness, support, wholeness, growth, development, and quality of life. Growth and development, the approach asserts, will lead to increased problem-solving skills.

The action stage in the problem-solving approach is intervention to help people solve problems. The counterpart in a strengths approach is to help people solve problems themselves. While by definition the problem-solving approach is problem-based, strengths-based practice may completely avoid *direct* efforts to problem solve.

To illustrate, imagine a rosebush that is about to burst into full bloom. Sam the gardener has noticed that the bush is not progressing as he had hoped. He detects that the edges of a few leaves are dry and curled: the dreaded aphids. Sam grabs the pesticide can, and sprays the plant. He has used a problem-solving and deficit approach to attack the aphids. The approach is analogous to the medical model: he examined the rosebush (inspected the leaves), diagnosed the problem (figured out there were aphids), and prescribed a treatment (applied the pesticide).

Let us assume that, instead of using environmentally unfriendly pesticides, Sam released a large number of ladybugs in his garden. Within a couple of days, the friendly bugs have accomplished the same task as the pesticide by eating the aphids. However, the process is still one of problem solving and deficits; the medical model was used. The only difference is the acceptability and ethics of the mode of intervention.

Now Sam increases the loving care of his rosebush. He prunes some overhanging branches of a large tree to give the roses more sunlight. He adds a special blend of nutrients to the soil and gives the bush exactly the correct amount of water. Sam takes all the steps necessary to promote the growth of the plant. The promotion of growth helps the sick plant become healthy again so it can resist aphids. Sam is using a developmental approach: he draws on the natural strengths inherent in the plant to grow, bloom, and survive. (Of course, engaging in solving its own problems is impossible for a rosebush. At this point the analogy breaks down.)

Sam used only part of the strengths equation. Strengths-based practice focuses on helping people solve their own problems. To complete the equation, a social worker using strengths-based practice promotes growth and development through engaging clients to take charge of their own lives, which includes problem solving. The process is one of empowerment; the goal, one of development and growth. The strengths approach is a very human process.

In day-to-day social work practice, as did Sam the gardener, workers draw on both problem-solving and strengths approaches. A most useful way to help people problem solve is to use their strengths. The following discussion and related examples of the strengths perspective develop this important point.

STRENGTHS APPLIED TO PROBLEM SOLVING

To understand how to use the strengths approach to solve a problem, it is necessary to first understand that there is a difference between problem solving as an important part of everyday life and the social work process of problem solving. While the strengths approach critiques the social work problem-solving process, it recognizes that all of us need to problem solve. So, how can social workers use strengths to help clients problem solve?

Proponents of the strengths perspective point out that they do not mean merely working with people's strengths. It requires a paradigm shift; to understand, analyze, and implement practice not from a problem-based deficit view as does the problem-solving process but to search for and use clients' strengths. Identifying, understanding, and using clients' strengths is always possible but very often a difficult task.

To begin to understand the application of strengths to solving life's problems, let us begin with a case example.

Case Example

Linda and Mac ▼

Mac MacGregor is a 36-year-old man who was diagnosed as having schizophrenia at age 21. During the past 15 years, he has been hospitalized six times for his schizophrenia, for a total of 4.5 years. Mac's life and social skills are limited. Particularly when under stress or excited, he puffs his cheeks in and out when he breathes. This is an annoying habit that draws negative attention from others. He is shy to the point of being withdrawn and has never held a job for more than four months.

Linda Whitefeather is a community mental health worker with a BSW assigned to Mac. Linda began working with Mac before his discharge. She quickly discovered that Mac has been on medications for a number of years. The hospital staff believed that Mac triggered his last hospitalization by refusing to take his medication. All concerned, including Linda, believe that monitoring Mac's medication is an important part of discharge. But Linda, operating from a strengths perspective, clearly understands that a *restorative approach* is only part of the recovery of Mac.

While Mac has a serious mental illness and limited social skills, those who have worked with him have noticed that he seems to feel good about himself when he sets a goal for himself and then accomplishes it. One example of this is that, while hospitalized, Mac wanted to purchase a birthday present for his 7-year-old niece. A staff member, surprised that Mac was thinking about his little niece, offered to help Mac with the purchase. Mac rather clumsily refused, asserting that he wanted a pass to go to a downtown store to select and find the gift himself. When Mac returned to the hospital, he was beaming with pride. He had achieved his goal by himself.

Among other things, both Linda and Mac believe that the quality of Mac's living arrangements is inadequate and needs immediate attention (better housing). Linda weighs a couple of options. One possibility is to, without Mac's input, make necessary arrangements with the local housing authority. Her second option is to engage Mac in a process that would identify his needs and wants and then help him make his *own* arrangements. Both Linda and Mac realize that availability of suitable housing is scarce.

Linda chooses the second option. Linda sets about finding out what Mac wants. By asking a variety of questions, she helps him articulate his housing needs and goals. They include a small, affordable flat with an easy bus connection to his brother's home. Linda coaches Mac on how to use the newspaper and the Internet to find apartments. (Mac is very pleased with himself when he discovers that he can learn to use a computer.) She also helps him organize a budget so he can figure out exactly what he can afford. All of this leads up to ensuring that Mac has the skills to apartment hunt by himself. When he finds a place that he likes, he has agreed to consult Linda. The process takes two months but is successful. Mac is proud himself; he has accomplished a major task by himself. He feels empowered!

In this case example, monitoring Mac's medication is clearly a problem-solving issue. So is finding him suitable housing. However, the strengths perspective adds a new dimension. Linda understands that if Mac is to survive outside an institution, he needs to be able to make life decisions himself. She wants to use the experience of finding housing to help Mac learn how to make other decisions. The intent is to help Mac grow in his decision-making capacities. The use of decision making to promote growth is similar to the use of enhancers to encourage the growth of the rose. Facilitating Mac's empowerment is more important than finding him housing, because encouraging his growth and development offers him the potential for an enhanced quality of life.

Principles of Strengths-Based Practice Used to Problem Solve

In the above example, Linda used principles of strength-based practice to problem solve. These are as follows:

1. Identify the client's wants and goals. Sometimes this is called the client's vision. *(Mac wanted a small affordable apartment with good bus connections.)*
2. Identify and assess strengths that can be used to help the client reach his or her own goals and wants. *(Mac: Good motivation; desire to be independent; feels good (pride) about self when goals accomplished.)*
3. Identify and assess obstacles and barriers that impede goal achievement. *(Mac: Lack of social skills; low income; limited quality of housing; no experience in such a large task as apartment hunting.)*
4. Use strengths in effort to reach goals and wants and overcome barriers. This is a creative process and largely depends upon skills of the helper. *(Mac: Linda used Mac's motivation to live independently by coaching him on how to apartment search.)*

The design of the enabling process should promote generalized growth and development. For example, the success and skills that Mac learned should help him improve his overall problem-solving abilities. While an important part of strengths-based practice, generalized growth promotion may not always be possible and often success is difficult to measure. However, in the case of Mac, the process that he experienced in finding suitable housing will likely have improved his general problem-solving and decision-making skills. It is but one step in his overall recovery. While strengths-based practice assumes a holistic approach, problems need to be addressed in small chunks. The sum of these chunks becomes a holistic approach.

EXAMPLES OF TYPES OF STRENGTHS-BASED PRACTICE

The word "based" in the phrase *strengths-based* is important. In this chapter we emphasize the principles and elements of a strengths approach in generalist social work practice. There are also more specialized types of practice that are clearly strengths-based. We will briefly discuss two of these: a recovery approach to mental illness, and solution focused brief therapy. Each of these requires training beyond beginning practice. However, all social workers can adapt some of these principles to their own practice.

Recovery in Mental Health

Recovery is a relative new concept in the field of mental health that has gained creditability and challenges the medical model. The medical model (a problem-solving and deficit model) assumes that the illness can be managed by medical intervention (treatment). If not, then the condition becomes chronic. Often medical practitioners see the person as the illness. The person becomes defined by the illness. For example, the person who has schizophrenia is defined as a schizophrenic and everything that the schizophrenic does is seen as determined or influenced by the illness.

The recovery model parts company with the medical model. Developed first at the Boston Center for Psychiatric Rehabilitation and articulated by Anthony (1993), it has become an underpinning of many programs of the Canadian Mental Health Association. The model argues that while mental illness is real and may be very debilitating, it should not define the person. Instead, the illness is a factor with which the person must contend. People can and do lead quality lives even though they have a mental illness. The recovery view is much like that of people challenged with a physical condition, such as loss of use of legs. Many people lead quality lives even though they are bound to a wheelchair (See Sullivan, 1994.)

Sullivan and Rapp (2002) connect the concept of recovery with the strengths perspective. With both physical and mental health challenges, people can use their strengths, capacities, and assets to build quality in one's life in spite of the fact that they face the challenge of a debilitating illness. Hence, recovery does not mean cure or elimination of symptoms or even symptom reduction. Instead it refers to a process by which people use their strengths to build their own quality of life, recognizing that sometimes medical treatment may be necessary to treat the illness. The role of the professional is not to treat but to support clients in building their own lives.

Solution Focused Brief Therapy

As the name implies, solution focused therapy is based on the principle that, in the end, the key factor is that a solution is found. The history of a problem or the past is unimportant. Even the presenting problem is seen as a secondary concern. The focus is on the present or future: "What a client is left with [in a problem-solving approach] is a more sophisticated definition of their problem, based on the professional helper's knowledge, biases, and favourite theories" (Weick, Kreider, and Chamberlain, 2006, p. 117).

The therapy, intended for a wide variety of personal problems experienced by people, assumes that all have experienced a lifetime of solving life's problems. Sometimes people are unable to solve these problems by themselves. Rather than focus on the problem that brought the client to the therapist, the therapy centres upon finding out what people want in the future and then helping to find a means to meet the clients' visions. Solution focused therapists assume that problem solution will take place if people can move forward in meeting their own goals. The process of moving forward to meet their own visions of life draws, by definition, upon people's strengths and capacities. While developed by psychotherapists, the principles of solution focused brief therapy draw upon many of same principles that social workers articulate in the strengths perspective (Weick, Kreider, and Chamberlain, 2006), as outlined previously in this chapter. See Berg and Nolan (2001) and De Jong and Berg (2007) for detailed descriptions of solution focused brief therapy.

KEY ELEMENTS OF STRENGTHS-BASED PRACTICE

Empowerment

The concept of empowerment has attracted considerable attention in the past number of years. Social work has embraced the idea to such an extent that it is the core of most practice that deals with individuals, families, groups, and communities.

The strengths approach sees empowerment as a process. People use their own resources, abilities, and power to take charge of their own lives. Empowerment applies to individuals, families, groups, organizations, and communities (Saleebey, 2006a).

To illustrate, often social workers are faced with a decision between doing something for the client or supporting the client in her or his own initiative. Usually, if the social worker decides to support the client's initiative, a goal is to help the client empower herself or himself. This is important whether the task at hand is simple or complex.

The following example illustrates empowerment of a collective. Suppose a group of people in an inner-city community may feel overwhelmed and frightened by the number of deliberately set fires in their area. They have little sense of community spirit. A social worker employed by a neighbourhood organization hears their concerns and encourages them to come to a local meeting. The residents tell him that they are worried for their families and afraid that an arsonist could target one of their homes next. Many are afraid to speak out publicly until they are at the meeting. They feel powerless to do anything and want to move to another part of the city. If people come together to protect their neighbourhood by speaking out, raising people's awareness about the problem, and seeking support from other community members and the municipality, then they are doing something. They also feel less fearful, more in control, and thus empowered as a group. In this case, the social worker encourages the residents to participate in the meeting in the hope that they will become empowered through joining forces with others to seek solutions. Had he tried to direct the group's actions, they would likely not have found their common voice, nor would they have attempted to take on neighbourhood change.

The strengths view of empowerment also holds that the act of intervention can be and often is a way of disempowering people. Social workers who make decisions for clients reduce the ability of clients to make their own decisions. Intervention itself implies a power differential between social worker and client. Too often, social workers use this power differential to expedite treatment without considering the need to let people take charge of their own lives.

In the case example, Linda would probably find it easier to find an apartment for Mac. Mac may even be appreciative of and very comfortable in his new home. Or Linda can decide that Mac needs a group home and can arrange accommodation for him. Either action is acceptable using a traditional problem-solving approach. However, the strengths approach would concentrate on Mac taking charge of his own life to the full extent of his abilities.

Helpers cannot empower others—empowerment is not something someone can give. It is, however, something that everyone can strive for. In this sense, empowerment is like human dignity and self-worth. Children, adults, and people who are mentally ill, homeless, and disenfranchised all have inside them the power to take charge of their own lives, but to varying degrees. The role of the social worker is to encourage and support the inner strengths of clients so that, to the best of their ability, they take control of their own lives. While few would disagree with the importance of empowerment, the strengths approach makes this idea central to social work practice.

Professional Relationships and the Strengths Approach

Increasingly, scholars and social workers alike are raising questions about approaches that place the helper (therapist, counsellor, etc.) in control of the helping process. The traditional problem-solving model tends to view the social worker as the expert in charge of the helping process and generally assumes that it is up to the worker to act in the best interest of the client (see Chapter 8). Even though the social worker–client relationship is a partnership, it is a partnership of unequal power. In involuntary relationships, the social worker may have varying degrees of control over the client. In voluntary relationships, the social worker is generally viewed as an expert with helping skills.

A Consumer-Driven Approach

A consumer-driven model of practice suggests a significantly different emphasis. A consumer-driven approach starts with the deeply held value, closely related to self-determination, that adults have the capacity and strength to make life decisions by themselves without interference from professional helpers. This is so even if the social worker believes that the client is making the wrong decisions. Among other things, this means that clients can choose whether they need help, who is to provide the help, and how it is to be provided. The social worker, while still an expert, acts more as an advisor or consultant. A similar principle is articulated in both the Aboriginal (Chapter 12) and feminist (Chapter 13) approaches. A consumer-driven approach implies that the nature of the helping process should be client-oriented rather than social worker–directed. While the approach still advocates a partnership, there is an active effort to reduce the power differential. The client is seen as in charge of the helping process. In a sense, this approach tips the emphasis of control in the partnership from that of the social worker to that of the client. The social worker's roles often become that of advisor and consultant. Other roles such as counsellor, enabler, or advocate may be offered, but the choice for their use is solely that of the client.

Unfortunately, the consumer-driven approach is not absolute, particularly when clients are involuntary or the function of the worker is mandated, such as in the criminal justice system. The section "Involuntary Problem-Solving, Social Control, and the Principle of Best Interest" in Chapter 8 presents guidelines for situations that require social workers to act in the best interest of clients even without their consent. Consumer-driven approaches have emerged primarily in such fields as physical disabilities and mental illness.

Sometimes conflicts between a best-interest approach and a consumer-driven one have important consequences for a client. The following case example illustrates this.

Case Example

Linda and Mac ▼

It has been eight months since Mac was discharged from the hospital. He is beginning to complain that his medication is causing him to feel "dragged out," and he cannot think clearly. He reports this to both his psychiatrist and Linda. The psychiatrist cannot find a reason to change the medication and leaves the dosage and type unchanged. Linda suspects that Mac might be trying to find an excuse to stop taking his medication. But she has also previously thought that maybe Mac does not really need it, and together with the medical team and Mac they should begin to plan to reduce or even eliminate his medication.

Linda expresses her doubts about Mac taking his medication, and he vehemently denies doing so. He counters with a request for a second opinion from another psychiatrist. Even though Linda is beginning to question the medication, she is reluctant to help Mac with his request because her agency has a good relationship with the psychiatrist and does not want to upset her. However, Linda also feels that Mac has the right to make such decisions by himself and this takes priority over her reluctance.

Following the principles of a consumer-driven approach, Linda would agree without qualification that Mac has the right to a second medical opinion. Mac has the power to make this decision. To thwart this request would be completely counter-productive in empowering Mac to make his own life decisions. This is so even though Linda may feel that Mac is really looking for an excuse not to take his medication.

In a best-interest approach, Linda might resist helping Mac in his request. Her reasoning may be that consistent use of medication is necessary to prevent hospitalization. Surely a trained psychiatrist knows what is best for Mac, a chronically ill, withdrawn, sometimes paranoid man with schizophrenia. It is in Mac's best interest to abide by the expert's decisions.

Now assume that Mac threatened to stop taking his medication if he did not get it changed. A consumer-driven approach would still assume that he has the right to make this decision even though Linda feels it is the wrong one. Further, Linda should continue to help Mac despite his decision, respecting Mac's judgment. The best-interest model, on the other hand, might lead Linda to take action to prevent Mac from stopping his medication. She might, for instance, refuse to provide her services (a common practice in some mental health centres) or might even warn him that he might be re-admitted to the hospital if he refuses his medication.

Note that probably most social workers would agree that direct protective action must be taken if the professional staff believes that Mac is at risk to himself or others by not taking the medication. Again, the social work codes of ethics help address this issue. (Although not explored here, if Mac decided to go off his medication on his own, Linda could explore with him ways that he could do so safely.)

Reciprocity

Case Example

Linda and Mac ▼

After a couple of months Linda and Mac are at ease with each other. They have met half a dozen times, and Mac has found reasonably good living accommodations, even though rent is high. Both of them have discussed Linda's commitment to empowerment (of course, using different words than those used in this book). Mac has expressed, in his own abrupt way, appreciation that Linda truly encourages him to make his own decisions, and he likes her position of noninterference. This gives the social worker a feeling of accomplishment.

Linda decides that they are ready to talk about how Mac's Scottish upbringing might have an influence on his life today. Earlier she had thought this might be important when he spoke briefly about what he wanted from life. (Note: Even though Linda is suggesting they explore the past, her focus on understanding Mac's wants remains consistent with the strengths perspective.)

At first Mac has a hard time responding. He is not used to discussing his background and does not really like talking to anyone unless necessary. Linda knows that people who experience schizophrenia and paranoia can sometimes be very sensitive to overtures from others. Mac could easily misinterpret her questions as prying. Mac begins by describing his parents, children of immigrants, as hard-working, poor, Presbyterian farmers. Soon, as Linda listens carefully, he begins to describe their strict discipline and puritanical beliefs.

Then, out of the blue, Mac blurts, "How can you help me explore my background? You're Indian. I'm not anything like you!" Linda is taken aback a bit but not surprised. She could, as some might do, attempt to turn the question back to Mac by asking, "Why is this important to you?" If she does this, Mac will likely become defensive and withdraw from her question. This response would be a conversation stopper.

Linda takes a few minutes to describe her urban Aboriginal background and her decision about 10 years ago to learn much more about her Ojibwa

Continued

culture. At that time, she was also engaged in her social work education. She describes her deep commitment to the Aboriginal value of noninterference in the lives of others. Linda relates how this position is similar to the strengths perspective views of empowerment and self-determination. Linda tells Mac that this approach allows her to work with people from many cultures even though she does not fully understand each person's culture. Mac likes this response.

The client–social worker relationship is shared or reciprocal. Human relationships that are rewarding are usually reciprocal. In a professional social work relationship, there may be rewards for both client and worker. Mac is rewarded by knowing that he has met some success in his own problem solving; Linda feels good because Mac acknowledges that her approach has contributed to his successes.

The example illustrates another principle of reciprocal relationships. When Linda chooses to tell Mac something about her Aboriginal background and culture, she is sharing experiences with Mac. Mac is rewarded in at least two ways. First, Linda is giving Mac more information so that he can better understand her background. This implies trust and openness, important ingredients in human relationships. Second, and maybe unrecognized by Mac, he is learning something new about a culture that is perhaps foreign to him.

Linda is also rewarded. She likes the fact that Mac was open enough to talk about his background. She knows this is difficult because it probably hurt and he has fears associated with his illness. She also learns a little more about Scottish culture.

In summary:

- Successful human relationships, including professional relationships, are reciprocal and shared experiences.
- One way to encourage reciprocal relationships is for the social worker and client to share stories related to their own lives and culture, as appropriate. Exchanging selected information can be useful to both parties.
- The strengths approach is compatible with cross-cultural practice.

Membership and Belonging

The principle that everyone must have a sense of belonging and membership is also central to strengths-based practice. The approach assumes that people are social beings and therefore need to feel that they are an integral part of a family, a culture, a society, and relevant groups. A number of related concepts emerge from this belief.

The problem-solving approach may address issues of membership by focusing on alienation. Alienation occurs when people feel dispossessed and not part of essential elements of society. The problem-solving approach tends to view alienation as a deficit or pathology and a problem that needs a solution.

While a strengths approach does not deny the importance of alienation, the focus of practice can be radically different. Instead of emphasizing what is wrong with the client, this approach shifts the focus to enhancing the client's sense of membership and belonging. As illustrated previously, practice that uses a strengths approach may never deal directly with or focus on the problem itself.

Case Example

Linda and Mac ▼

Several weeks after his hospital discharge, Linda notices that Mac seems a little down. After exploring his feelings with him, Linda realizes that when Mac was in the hospital he actually had a sense of belonging. She discovers that Mac took some pride in keeping his part of the ward tidy and enjoyed compliments that others gave him for his efforts. He also spent time watering plants in a small greenhouse and cleaning the day room connected to "his" ward. The hospital staff told Linda that Mac considered the day room his own space. Mac had created a ***personal niche***, a place that was his.

Since his discharge, Mac no longer has a niche. He also does not receive compliments from others that are uplifting. He feels he is not contributing anything and even feels alienated.

Personal Niche

A personal niche is an area in the environment that a person carves out that gives him or her a sense of belonging and ownership. In the case example, in order for Mac to remain outside the hospital, he needs to find a new personal niche. Part of Linda's job could be to help him find this niche.

The example also raises another important membership issue. By taking care of the ward and day room, Mac, in his own way, was contributing something to the hospital, to something bigger than himself. The appreciation shown by others and Mac's own sense of contribution raised his self-esteem. Belonging is a perceptual and reciprocal process. It is perceptual because what really counts for Mac is how he feels about doing his part. His contribution (input) brings him a feeling of self-satisfaction. To him it signifies a job well done. The process is reciprocal because for Mac to feel good about himself, he had to both give and receive. By contributing, Mac received cues from others that they appreciated his efforts. His perception that others liked what he was doing gave him some sense of satisfaction. The contribution (tidying), no matter how small it appears, became for Mac as important as the reward (praise from others) itself.

Now Mac feels that he is doing nothing that others consider constructive, so he does not consider himself useful. Linda has her work cut out for her. How can she help Mac engage in activities that he considers productive and useful? This is so important that Mac will likely need to return to the hospital if he cannot re-establish a sense of belonging and membership outside the institution.

A Social Niche and a Macro Connection

The ecosystems perspective (see Chapter 9) is compatible with the strengths approach. Recall that ecology, a major contributor to the ecosystems perspective, is a biological concept. Biologists have recognized that studying individual species alone is not adequate to understand life. To fully understand life, we must comprehend how each lifeform relates to others and to its environment. Biologists are particularly interested in the interdependence of species. The study of ecology thus includes the interactions among and dependence of different plants and animals on other plants and animals (for example, see Strickberger, 1990).

A biological niche is a position that a species holds in relationship to other plants and animals in its environment. It is the place in the environment that a species has carved out for itself (Germain and Gitterman, 1995, p. 818). Understanding niches includes knowing what the species can contribute to the ecology and what the species requires from the ecology in order to prosper.

Taylor (1997) has suggested an analogous concept, the social niche. A social niche, unlike a personal niche, applies to a category of people. Taylor defines a social niche as "the environmental habitat of a category of persons, including the resources that they utilize and the other categories of persons they associate with" (p. 219). For example, academics establish a social niche. They contribute to society through their research and scholarship, often funded by granting agencies; they work in universities; they relate to others, often those in the same or similar fields outside the university, by sharing their work; and so on. A social niche, according to Taylor, is conceptually more similar to a biological niche than a personal niche because, like a biological niche, the reference is to the environment of a grouping (of academics) rather than of individuals (individual professors). A biological niche refers to a species, while a social niche refers to a particular category of people. The social niches that people belong to can be functional and empowering or dysfunctional and oppressive.

Another way of putting this is that niches can be enabling or entrapping. An entrapping niche is a dysfunctional niche in which one gets caught and there seems no way out. In our case example, Mac is in an entrapping niche that is largely defined by his schizophrenia and lack of social skills and social supports. This type of niche is shared by many others who suffer from schizophrenia.

Mac has been and is labelled both schizophrenic and mentally ill. He is not personable and has an annoying puffing habit. He has been categorized and negatively labelled. Partly because of the label and associated stigma and partly because of his limited social skills, he cannot find a job, his financial resources from social assistance payments are very limited, and others in his community do not like to associate with him. All of these factors serve to further bury him in his entrapping niche. He feels that he does not belong and is not wanted. Mac has found himself in an entrapping niche that is very difficult to escape, prohibits his growth, and reduces his quality of life. Mac's habits exacerbate his problems, but his problems are also due to the wider social system, which has defined the entrapping niche for people who are labelled mentally ill or schizophrenic. Mac and most others who are defined as mentally ill are often powerless to escape their entrapment.

An enabling niche (Taylor, 1997), on the other hand, is one that fosters personal development and quality of life. A goal of intervention in the strengths perspective is to help clients find or develop enabling niches, and to target entrapping niches for change.

Self-Help: An Enabling Niche

Finding an enabling niche can be difficult. It must be one in which the person is accepted and where the person is seen for who she or he is rather than as representative of a category. The person must perceive this niche as rewarding and providing opportunities to grow and learn skills (Taylor, 1997, p. 223). One possible enabling niche that might be overlooked by practitioners operating out of an expert, best-interest model is the self-help group.

The self-help movement is at least 60 years old. Probably the most well-known self-help group is Alcoholics Anonymous. In recent years, self-help groups have flourished and include cancer support groups, survivors of abuse groups, anxiety and depression groups, to name only a few.

Self-help groups can be empowering because they help people address their own problems in the company of others who have had or are having similar experiences. Members generally empathize with and understand the fears, emotions, difficulties, experiences of stigma, and disabilities that others in similar situations face. Probably most importantly, self-help groups can be enabling social niches. People who suffer from the same kinds of problems often find a safe, comfortable, rewarding, and respectful environment in such groups (of course, not everyone feels comfortable sharing their problems in a group setting nor are all group experiences helpful or supportive).

Case Example

Linda and Mac ▼

Linda realizes that Mac will likely have to return to the hospital if he cannot find a comfortable social niche. She mentions to Mac that she knows a member of the local schizophrenia association, a self-help group. She recounts what she knows about the group and asks his permission to contact her friend. Linda will ask her friend to speak to Mac about the association and the possibility of his joining. Mac likes the idea. Linda is sure the association will help Mac feel wanted and respected, even with his quirky habits. She hopes that this will be an enabling social niche that may even help Mac open doors to other enabling niches.

Resilience

Resilience is the ability to bounce back from traumatic and difficult life experiences. Far too often, social workers believe that their clients do not have the capacity to recover on their own from these experiences. Much literature (e.g., Bernard, 2006; Masten, 1994; Saleebey, 1997a; Shulman, 1999, pp. 67–73) suggests that professionals generally underestimate people's ability to cope with adversity.

It is easy to explain after the fact why some people exposed to risk factors react with deviant and antisocial behaviours. For example, we may explain why James is a drug addict by understanding James's background of poverty and physical and sexual abuse as a child. Explaining why people become deviant has been the preoccupation of many scholars and researchers. However, now researchers and others are turning the question on its head: Why do many people who are exposed, for example, to poverty and physical and sexual abuse go on to lead productive and fulfilling lives? While the answers to this question are far from complete, what we do know is that resilience seems to be a very widespread and important human trait, and it is present in children right up to elderly people (Shulman, 1999).

Another implication of resilience can be understood by using major disasters as an example. During disasters like serious hurricanes or chemical spills, many people experience psychological trauma. Some respond to the crisis with symptoms of depression, anxiety, nightmares, and the like. We can attempt to understand these as pathologies, but we can also take a different viewpoint—why do the great majority of people who experience such events respond with resilience and strength? Unfortunately, this question is seldom asked.

Case Example

Linda and Mac ▼

Every day, Mac is reminded of his seemingly uncontrollable habit of puffing his cheeks out when he breathes. People sometimes stare; others refuse to make eye contact with him. Mac is very sensitive to such responses. One day when he is walking to a shopping centre, a group of teenagers jeers at and taunts him. Two of them mimic him. Mac is devastated.

Linda thinks this experience will be a big setback for him, and that he is too fragile to handle the humiliation. However, the next morning Mac appears to be himself again.

Frequently, we expect clients to be frail and unable to handle adversity. The strengths perspective holds that we underestimate our clients. Sometimes our expectations for such underachieving lead to a self-fulfilling prophecy, because people tend to live up to others' expectations.

In retrospect, Linda realizes that she needs to understand and appreciate the resilience that Mac has demonstrated in response to the disrespect that others have shown him and to the stigma he has experienced. Despite his illness and symptoms, Mac still lives his own life. He continues to go for strolls even though he knows others will look at him in odd ways. He enjoys his coffee at the local café, although he sits in a corner where he cannot readily be observed by others. Rather than doubting his capacities, Linda should have expected that Mac would react with resilience. The strengths approach promotes those activities that will improve Mac's resilience and coping capacities.

Culturally Sensitive Social Work Practice and Strengths-Based Practice

Strengths-based practice has embedded in it a number of principles that are useful in working with people of diverse cultures. Chapter 7 suggested that in order to be part of a culture one has to be an insider, to live as a member of that culture. An outsider can learn, appreciate, and understand much about a culture but cannot become part of it unless he or she becomes an insider. When a social worker and client have different cultural backgrounds, cross-cultural practice skills are useful. The social worker, by definition, is an outsider to the client's culture. A strengths approach offers some principles that help a social worker who is not part of the same culture as a client work with members of that culture in a productive and sensitive manner. Several of the ideas from the strengths perspective can be adapted and blended into some important practice foundations for working with people whose cultures are different from the social worker's.

Reciprocal Relationships in Cross-Cultural Practice

One of the reasons the strengths perspective is particularly useful in cross-cultural social work, as discussed earlier in this chapter, is because the approach, like a feminist view, is built on a partnership of reciprocal relationship in which the client directs the action. If the client wants to use the social worker as an expert (e.g., counsellor, advocate, enabler, mediator, negotiator, or other roles), the choice is that of the client, as long as the client is aware of and can make such choices. It may be necessary to first discuss the purpose and role of social work services with the client, since these may not be familiar to her or him. This approach shows respect and acceptance of the client's culture; it does not imply that the worker's culture is somehow superior.

Part of reciprocity is that both client and social worker gain from the relationship. This involves give and take from both parties. One thing a client can offer the social worker is a better understanding of the client's culture. This benefits the worker not only in that more about the client is understood, but also in that she or he should develop a deeper and better understanding of the other's culture. Taking the time to learn about another's culture is also a way to show respect and appreciation of that other culture and its customs. The social worker's own culture requires her or him to reflect on and be aware of culturally shaped beliefs, assumptions, and practices and how these might be experienced by clients and colleagues who are not part of the same cultural group. Sometimes culture can be drawn upon in helpful ways when sharing perspectives and experiences with others.

The Importance of the Client's Story

The social worker must listen to the client's story very carefully. It will be cast in the context of his or her culture, not the social worker's. Fully understanding it may be difficult.

The social worker's understanding of the story will be filtered by the worker's culture. As we have argued previously, if the social worker does not understand her or his own culture, the worker will have even more difficulty in understanding that of another person. Assessment must be based on understanding the client in the context of a client's own culture.

The strengths perspective holds that the client's own description and interpretation of his or her problems are the most important of all the sources of information. Part of this story is the client's aspirations and goals. We not only must take these very seriously, but also must understand that these goals are cast in terms of the client's cultural orientation and probably her or his understanding of the dominant culture.

Cultural Support

An important intervention that flows from the strengths perspective is *support.* Clients need to live their own life, a life that is not controlled by professionals. Often, however, clients' growth and capacity for problem solving can benefit considerably from formal support, such as that of a professional helper, and informal support, such as that of family. Supporting people's desires and goals is enabling and not intrusive. This includes supporting another's cultural expression. It is a way to build strengths.

While support is important in all of social work, it is particularly necessary in cross-cultural work. Direct intervention by the worker may be not only ineffective but also inappropriate because of her or his lack of understanding and because the worker is an outsider. Furthermore, people generally accomplish more if they are in charge; for example, non-Aboriginal social workers can support such issues as self-government and an Aboriginal justice system. They can even act as advisors. But negotiating, designing, and implementing such new programs are best done by Aboriginal people themselves and within the context of Aboriginal cultures.

Social workers and clients may be able to access important cultural resources. For example, suppose a social worker is helping an Aboriginal family prepare for the return of their recently disabled father. As part of the helping process, the father has shown that he wants to return to his cultural roots and live life in a more traditional manner. By doing so, he uses traditional Aboriginal practices to enhance well-being and seek spiritual fulfillment. Elders from the family's community may be able to assume the responsibility of helping the family prepare for the father's return home. In such cases, a social worker must be prepared to support a client's use of cultural resources even if this means relinquishing what were formerly the worker's responsibilities.

As another example, consider a Chinese teenager who speaks little English who has been convicted of shoplifting and put on probation. The probation officer is a middle-aged man of Ukrainian descent with little knowledge of Chinese culture. However, the officer does understand that the boy has had a tough time adjusting in Canada and that he will need support if he is to develop a productive adult life. Instead of the probation officer taking direct action by himself, he helps the boy find resources in the Chinese community. Through a program that uses volunteers, they find a young Chinese man who will act as a role model—something like a "big brother" for the client. The probation officer is still responsible for establishing the rules of the probation and monitoring progress, but he has turned much of the helping role over to a cultural resource.

Cultural Membership and Belonging

Membership can mean belonging to a family, a group of friends, and so on, but cultural membership may be equally important. Individuals who belong to minority cultures frequently feel that they do not belong in the dominant culture. They may even feel that their culture does not belong in the larger, dominant culture. Practitioners working with members of diverse cultures need to be aware that clients may lack a sense of belonging because of cultural factors.

Linda and Mac ▼

The fact that Linda chooses to use a strengths approach is not an accident. She traces her background and culture to the Ojibwa First Nation. Over the years Linda has achieved a good sense of understanding of who she is, her Ojibwa culture, and her connections with the pluralistic society in which she lives. Her culture emphasizes principles that are consistent with a strengths approach. Therefore, she naturally gravitated toward practice strategies that fit her values.

Linda knows that Mac's Scottish heritage has been an important part of his life. She does not yet know how it influences his current life.

However, Linda knows enough about the Scots to assume that, for many, a strong sense of personal independence is likely very important, and Mac probably feels he does not live up to this standard. Further, many cultures value an ability to take charge of one's own life and prize discovering ways to increase the quality of life. Linda also knows that in some other cultures, an individual's independence is second to family well-being and community harmony. Generally, the principles of strengths approaches can apply across cultures with differing values and practices.

Note that social workers should use practices that are consistent with their own culture, beliefs, and values. If they use a therapy or intervention that their cultural and personal values do not support, social workers tend to be ineffective. This is because they experience conflict between what they believe and how they behave.

Social workers must also be sure that whatever approach they use is consistent with the cultural values and traditions of clients. Because strengths-based practice focuses on principles accepted by many cultures, it is an important approach in cross-cultural social work practice.

CHAPTER SUMMARY

Strengths-based practice uses people's own resources to meet four goals: (1) to grow as human beings, (2) to improve their quality of life, (3) to develop their problem-solving skills, and

(4) to deal with stress and adversity. The approach capitalizes on people's own capacities, vitality, abilities, strong points, talents, courage, and power. Compared with problem solving, strengths-based practice is developmental instead of restorative and does not focus on deficits. It incorporates ideas such as wellness, support, wholeness, growth, development, and quality of life instead of focusing on problems. The approach asserts that growth and development lead to increased problem-solving skills.

Strengths-based practice is particularly consistent with the ideology and values of social work (see Chapter 3). It is an approach that maximizes client self-determination and helps achieve the twin ideals of equity and social justice. In traditional social work practice, the importance of values and principles such as self-determination, acceptance of all people and belief in their intrinsic worth, empowerment, and commitment to self-realization, growth, and healing is mitigated by the view that the worker is an expert who is in charge of the helping process.

Strengths-based practice can be used to help clients problem solve. Action or intervention of the social worker does not depend, as in the problem-solving process, upon assessment and analysis of the "problem." Action or intervention centres on finding ways to help the client meet her or his own goals and wants.

The principles of strength-based practice used to problem solve are as follows:
1. Identify a problem. Usually this is reflected in the client's search for help.
2. Identify the client's wants and goals. Sometimes this is called the client's vision.
3. Identify and assess strengths that can be used to help clients reach goals and wants.
4. Identify and assess obstacles and barriers than impede goal achievement.
5. Use strengths in an effort to reach goals and wants and overcome obstacles. This is a creative process and largely depends upon the skills of the social worker.

With the strengths perspective, the focus shifts from the best interest of the client to a consumer-driven approach. The social worker acts more as a consultant whose expertise the client can access. The client is in control of the process and decides whether help is necessary, who should provide it, and what kind of help is needed. The relationship is still a partnership, but with a different emphasis in roles. The professional helping relationship is seen as reciprocal, meaning that all parties must perceive the relationship as productive and beneficial. In good helping relationships, the client and social worker are partners who contribute and receive rewards.

Too often, social workers think that the people whom they serve are completely consumed by their problems. In reality, clients have many dimensions to their lives. The strengths approach emphasizes the development of the quality of people's lives, particularly in non-problem areas. This is particularly true in areas such as mental health, where the problem may be chronic. Strengths-based practice helps people build lives around long-standing problems.

Similarly, social workers often underestimate the capacity of clients. We tend to assume that because people are clients their capacities are limited. Strengths-based practice strongly challenges this assumption and argues that most people are remarkably resilient. Further, they may be "clients" for only a very brief time, for example, until a crisis situation becomes manageable for them.

An ecosystems view of practice is often consistent with the strengths approach. For example, an important goal of intervention can be to help people find enabling niches, an ecological concept. A self-help group might, for some, be an enabling niche. One of the ways that workers can help some people find enabling niches is to connect them with self-help groups.

Finally, in the strengths approach the primary emphasis should be on helping people to empower themselves. A social worker cannot empower others, but can help people strive to empower themselves.

An Aboriginal Approach to Social Work Practice

by Michael Anthony Hart

Chapter Goal ▼

To summarize an Aboriginal approach to social work practice, with an emphasis on how such an approach can inform, enrich, and enhance generalist social work practice.

This Chapter ▼

- shows how an Aboriginal approach incorporates historical factors, particularly the social and psychological effects of colonization on the person
- explains the medicine wheel as one of the models that guides an Aboriginal approach and describes some of the teachings that flow from it
- suggests that the concept of *mino-pimátisiwin,* roughly translated as "the good life," is both a life goal of all and the highest-level goal of the helping process set by client and social worker
- explicates a set of key concepts and values that guide an Aboriginal approach
- describes the healing and helping process and the helping relationships of an Aboriginal approach
- compares an Aboriginal approach with conventional social work

MAKING CONNECTIONS

Many Aboriginal people[1] utilize the services provided by social workers. Although there are an increasing number of Aboriginal social workers, most social workers tend to be from dominant North American cultures. Earlier in this book we introduced two concepts, both connected to an Aboriginal approach: the use of strengths in helping (Chapter 11), and the emic perspective of cross-cultural social work (Chapter 7). In this chapter, we show how Aboriginal concepts and practices can inform helping, offering possibilities for all social workers to enrich practice in unique and culturally supportive ways.

The position taken here explicitly avoids imposing specific treatments and cultural values—including professional social work values and beliefs—on clients. Helping takes place within the culture of the client and in the context of the client's own background. People are supported to use the capacities and strengths that flow from their own culture and life experience. Helping and healing take place in the context of one's community. For an Aboriginal client (or any client), helping occurs within that person's own culture, according to the needs and wishes of the client. This perspective contributes to the whole of social work practice.

At the same time, helping takes place in a political and historical context. What has occurred in the past in the name of helping cannot be changed now, but it can provide rich teaching material and lessons to use today. It is not easy for those who have experienced difficulties as a result of events related to colonization to recall memories that create distress and alienation. By studying the process of European colonization and the policies and practices that resulted, we can better understand the impact of structures and events that work to oppress people (see Alfred, 2005; and Bishop, 2002, 2005). We can also benefit by understanding our own and others' feelings, ideas, and experiences of oppression so that in our work we strive for relationships that are supportive, caring, and mutually respectful.

UNDERSTANDING ABORIGINAL PEOPLES' HISTORICAL CONTEXT

To be prepared to work with Aboriginal peoples, a social worker needs to understand the history of colonization that the peoples have faced. Since this history is well outlined by several authors (Dickason, 2006; Mawhiney, 1995; Miller, 2000), a few points are highlighted here to demonstrate the experiences that have led to the destruction of Aboriginal peoples' social institutions and internalized oppression.

Among the first dynamics that led to the oppression of Aboriginal peoples were the changes to their economic systems. At one time, all Aboriginal nations were self-sustaining while actively trading with one another. They brought their economic skills and abilities into the Euro-Canadian fur trade economy. However, when the fur trade collapsed and European wars in North America ended, they found the settlers treating them as hindrances instead of economic partners and military allies. Laws were passed by the settlers that outlawed fundamental aspects of Aboriginal peoples' economies, such as those banning the potlatch and the give-away ceremonies. Even when Aboriginal nations attempted to adopt the imposed system and made further alterations to their economic systems, new laws were introduced to keep them from fully participating. This is readily seen by reviewing the law that stopped Aboriginal farmers and ranchers from selling their produce for anything more than subsistence (Carter, 1990).

Oppression also occurred on a political level when the Canadian government imposed systems for Aboriginal peoples to govern themselves. For status First Nations peoples, this meant the oppression of their traditional forms of governance and the imposition of the *Indian Act* Chief and Council system. It is important to realize that this imposed system did not allow for a truly representative government that could address a wide spectrum of concerns. Instead, under the *Indian Act* system all matters to be discussed had to be approved first by the government-appointed Indian agent before a Chief and Council could address the matter. Once matters were discussed, any resolution had to be agreed upon by the appropriate federal minister before being enacted. When people attempted to address grievances they had with the government and the *Indian Act* system, laws were passed to stop them from organizing and effectively dealing with the issues brought forward. These laws included one that would fine and/or imprison anyone receiving monies for the prosecution of claims on behalf of a First Nations band—in other words, a person could not legally represent a First Nation and receive payment for services rendered (Canada, 1927). Another law fined and/or imprisoned any person who attempted to organize three or more First Nations people to make any request or demand of any agent or servant of the government in a riotous, disorderly, or threatening manner or in a manner calculated to cause a breach of the peace (Canada, 1884). Other barriers were also in place to stop people from organizing, such as the need for a pass from the Indian agent to leave a reserve (Miller, 2000).

These types of laws have also carried into other matters. There were attempts to directly attack the cultures of various Aboriginal peoples. Laws were passed that outlawed some of the peoples' spiritual ceremonies, such as the piercing and give-away ceremonies, without the non-Aboriginal peoples' understanding of the significance and role of these ceremonies. By encouraging and enforcing the pass system, Indian agents, priests, ministers, and law enforcement officials also attempted to stop the people from gathering to fulfill their spiritual obligations vis-à-vis the ceremonies. Indeed, aspects of Aboriginal peoples' cultures were deemed as evil, barbaric, and uncivilized. As a result of this view, many non-Aboriginal people—including government officials such as Deputy Superintendent General of the Federal Government Duncan Campbell Scott—took significant steps to eliminate Aboriginal cultures and control the activities of Aboriginal people (Titley, 1986). One example that demonstrates how far this control went was the banning of a First Nations person from public poolrooms by fining and/or imprisoning the Aboriginal person and/or the poolroom owner (Leslie and Maguire, 1978).

Aboriginal social institutions were also attacked. Aboriginal peoples had well-organized means to address such matters as education, medicine, justice, and family issues. However, the people's ways of addressing each of these areas were suppressed and denied for many decades. Multiple generations of Aboriginal children were forcefully removed from their families to attend residential schools (Milloy, 1999). Access to lands that held key medicinal plants used for healing and ceremonies was hindered, if not stopped. The communities' ability to deal with justice issues was undermined as a foreign justice system was imposed, with laws and consequences that followed non-Aboriginal peoples' perceptions of justice and met their needs. Families that had been able to deal with issues such as adoption and security through their extended kinship and community were torn apart and restructured through government laws, policies, and practices.

THE PRESENT CONTEXT

The examples above reflect the overall attack Aboriginal peoples have faced. However, we must recognize that while these examples are historical, many similar events continue to occur today. For example, in 2005, the First Ministers of Canada met with Aboriginal leaders in Kelowna, British Columbia, for the First Ministers Conference on Aboriginal Affairs. The result of the meeting was a five-year, $5-billion plan to improve the lives of First Nations, Métis, and Inuit peoples to the point where Aboriginal health and well-being would move toward that experienced by the general Canadian population. However, shortly thereafter, the Federal Liberal minority government was replaced by a minority Conservative government. With the change in Government came a change in policy, specifically the dropping of the agreement reached in Kelowna, despite the reality that study after study of almost any disease has found that Aboriginal people are much more at risk of developing a serious health problem.

Aboriginal peoples also continue the struggle to exercise their Aboriginal and treaty rights. For example, most recently, six leaders from Kitchenumaykoosib Inniuwag First Nation were imprisoned for interfering with a mining company who were staking claim to the traditional territory of the First Nation. While Federal court has stated that First Nations must be consulted when First Nations territory is to be affected by activities of governments or businesses, the mining company followed Ontario's century-old Mining Act, where the companies actions were perfectly legal. When the leaders peacefully protested the actions of the company, they were imprisoned by an Ontario judge for contempt of court after they followed the federal court ruling and ignored the provincial judge's order not to interfere with the mining firm. As stated by a representative of Amnesty International Canada (2008), "We're deeply concerned about the double standard at play in these cases. On the one hand, individual and communities are being punished to the full extent of the law for doing what they feel is right. On the other hand, the province is creating these conflicts by ignoring their own legal responsibilities" (Amnesty International Canada (ES), Mining Watch Canada & CPAWS Wildlands League, "Groups call for comprehensive reform of Ontario's outdated-mining laws", March 17, 2008. Available online at http://www.amnesty.ca/resource_centre/news/view.php?load=arcview&article=4254&c=Resource+Centre+News). Clearly, the plans of business continue to be upheld over the rights and well-being of First Nations.

Another recent act that clearly reflects the oppression First Nations face is that of the Federal government in relation to the United Nations (UN) Declaration on the Rights of Indigenous Peoples. On September 13, 2007 the general assembly of the United Nations voted on the Declaration, which addressed the following points, amongst others (United Nations Declaration on the Rights of Indigenous Peoples, March 2008. Available online at http://www.un.org/esa/socdev/unpfii/documents/DRIPS_en.pdf. Used with permission):

- The establishment of a universal framework of minimum standards for survival, dignity, well-being and rights of the world's Indigenous peoples;
- Collective and individual rights;
- Rights to educations, health, employment, and language;
- Outlawing discrimination against Indigenous people;
- The right for Indigenous people to remain distinct and to pursue economic, social, and cultural development; and

- Encouraging harmonious and cooperative relations between States and Indigenous peoples. (United Nations, 2007)

The Declaration was passed by the General Assembly, but four countries voted against it, namely New Zealand, Australia, the United States, and Canada. As reported by CTV and CBC News, the Minister of Indian Affairs for the Government of Canada stated at the time that the Declaration could not be support by Canada because it conflicts with the Canadian Charter of Rights and Freedoms, and is inconsistent with the Canadian Constitution, several acts of Parliament, and existing treaties (CBC News, 2007; CTV.ca, 2007, Sept.). Yet, human rights and Aboriginal groups, including a group of academics, lawyers, and social advocates, have reviewed the Declaration and found no credible legal rationale substantiating the Government's claims. They stated, "We, the undersigned, have researched and worked in the fields of Indigenous rights and/or constitutional law in Canada. We are concerned that the misleading claims made by the Canadian government continue to be used to justify opposition, as well as impede international cooperation and implementation of this human rights instrument" (Abel, Aiken, Alexander et al. 2008). Instead, the view was espoused that the intent of voting against Indigenous rights was more about maintaining control of the vast resources on land claimed by aboriginal communities (CBC News, 2007). Regardless of the intent of Canada's vote, what is clear is that the present Canadian government continues to work against the aspirations of Aboriginal people in Canada and internationally.

At an institutional level, Aboriginal people continue to face oppression. For example, the Government of Canada's Corrections Ombudsman reported such oppression in 2006: Correctional Services of Canada routinely classifies Aboriginal inmates as higher security risk than non-native inmates, release Aboriginal offenders later in their sentences than other inmates, and is more likely to revoke the conditional releases of Aboriginal offenders for technical reasons than other offenders (Sapers, 2006). At the individual level, Aboriginal people continue to face acts of racism, whether it is from police officers callously leaving individual Aboriginal people at the outskirts of a city in severe winter weather, or a court that objectifies an Aboriginal woman who has been killed but that views her killers in a sympathetic light (Brass and Abbott, n.d.; Razack, 2000).

As a result of such social inequity and continuing discrimination, Aboriginal peoples remain the poorest group of people in Canada and often face the worst social conditions. For example, off-reserve First Nation and Métis peoples have attained lower levels of education, lower average household incomes, and are less likely to have worked the entire year when compared to non-Aboriginal populations in Canada (Statistics Canada, 2003). They also have a higher incidence of chronic health conditions, particularly diabetes, arthritis, long-term activity restrictions, and major depressive episodes. They are more likely to smoke, be obese, and drink heavily than non-Aboriginal people (Statistics Canada, 2003). Further, the proportion of Aboriginal individuals with AIDS has been rapidly rising (Indian and Northern Affairs Canada, 2002).

Similar conditions are reported for the on-reserve First Nations population (Sibbald, 2002; Indian and Northern Affairs Canada, 2002). In addition, it is reported that status First Nations peoples have higher rates of suicide. In particular, the suicide rate for First Nations male youths is five times greater and for female youths is eight times greater than the rate of their non-Aboriginal counterparts. When compared to the general Canadian population, First Nations individuals experience tuberculosis at a rate 6.6 times greater, are three times as likely to have diabetes, and are twice as likely to report a long-term disability. Most Aboriginal people live at or below the poverty line, and 62 percent of First Nations people over the age of 15 consider alcohol abuse a problem in their community (Sibbald, 2002). In a report that compared First Nations community well-being (CWB) to that of non–First Nations well-being, McHardy and O'Sullivan (2004) stated that "the descriptive statistics contained herein illustrate clearly the marked disparity in socio-economic well-being between First Nations and other Canadian communities. The CWB index has also revealed that living conditions in a great many First Nations communities are appallingly low—much lower than the aggregate scores produced by previous studies have ever suggested." With a comparable measuring tool, the Assembly of First Nations cited that for that year the United Nations' Development Index ranked Canadian communities eighth in the world for the well-being of its citizenry. However, First Nations communities rank 76th out of the 174 nations (Assembly of First Nations, 2006).

The conditions Aboriginal people face in relation to institutions does not draw a better picture. For example, Aboriginal people are incarcerated at a rate nine times greater than the non-Aboriginal population (Sapers, 2006). The adult prison population is as high as 76 and 59 percent Aboriginal in Saskatchewan and Manitoba, respectively (Statistics Canada, 2001). The number of Aboriginal women who have been incarcerated has been increasing, while those for Black and Caucasian women have decreased. Aboriginal women make up 44 percent of maximum-security federally sentenced women, 41 percent of the medium-security female population, and only 18 percent of the minimum-security female population (Correctional Services Canada, 2002).

Regarding the well-being of children, while only one out of every 200 non–First Nation children are in care, a much higher one in every 10 First Nations children are in care; as many as 27 000 First Nations children are in care (Assembly of First Nations, 2007). Blackstock (2003) estimated that this number represents as many as three times more Aboriginal children in the care of child welfare authorities than was the number of Aboriginal children placed in residential schools at the height of those schools' operations in the 1940s. In the 2008 report of the Auditor General of Canada, it was noted that Indian and Northern Affairs Canada, First Nations Child and Family Services Program funds child welfare services in an inequitable manner for on-reserve First Nations children and families and that it cannot assure that services are culturally appropriate and reasonably comparable with those services normally provided off reserves in similar circumstances (Auditor General, 2008).

SOCIAL WORK'S PARTICIPATION IN THE OPPRESSION PROCESSES

The social work profession has not been an innocent bystander to the colonization of Aboriginal peoples in North America. For example, in the 1960s, child welfare workers began entering Aboriginal communities in significant numbers. In following their own white, middle-class values and child-rearing practices, they did not consider the colonial context and the significance of Aboriginal values and life practices. As a result, Aboriginal children were apprehended from their families and communities and adopted out to distant places, including countries abroad. While this event is referred to in Canada as the "sixties scoop" (Johnston, 1983), it continued into the 1980s and resulted in the loss of thousands of Aboriginal children from their home communities.

When conventional social work was practised, it often took the form of authoritarian control and regulation by external agents who had little understanding or appreciation of Aboriginal cultures and realities. As Collier (1993) has stated, "[T]he social worker was sent in with a job defined in an urban agency bureaucracy, not one defined or even informed by the needs or interests of the community in which the work was done. As a result, the social worker may have actively helped to dislocate people due to her/his adherence to policies and regulations which negated the unique situation of the community" (p. 44).

The social work profession has also contributed to the oppression of Aboriginal peoples through the reliance on theories, approaches, and practices based on and developed from non-Aboriginal perspectives. Privileging these perspectives, social work practice has often ignored the significance of Aboriginal peoples' historical and present colonial context in the situations they face. Without a critical historical and social analysis, the application of such theories and approaches tends to lay responsibility for the effects of the colonial oppression squarely on Aboriginal individuals. It also leads to the trivialization of Aboriginal perspectives and practices, the continued use of non-Aboriginal ways of helping by ill-prepared social workers, and a continued distancing between social work and Aboriginal people. Nor do cross-cultural practice concepts and practice methods help when it is assumed that social workers are white, non-Aboriginal people and those they help are not.

Given the history of Aboriginal peoples in North America, the impact of colonization on individuals and communities, and the limited manner in which social work has addressed Aboriginal perspectives, we can understand why social workers usually employed by government departments and non-Aboriginal organizations have problems in being accepted by the communities. The authority that a social worker is given by her or his employer to carry out certain work (e.g., child protection) may pose a threat. Thus, social workers are viewed as oppressors, or agents of social control sent by an agency that does not appear to represent the Aboriginal community's interests. Even when Aboriginal organizations are delivering services, the policies and/or laws they are required to follow often reflect the values, beliefs, and practices of non-Aboriginal peoples, thus making the delivery of services questionable. According to this view, social workers' primary obligation and loyalty is to the agency, an extension of the colonization that they represent, rather than to a caring, helping process. The social worker may have never intended to affect Aboriginal peoples in such a way, but as Mullaly (2007) aptly explained, oppression is not usually intentional. Whatever the reason, there is no doubt that this common perception of social workers is absolutely the polar opposite of the values and principles of social work practice.

AN ABORIGINAL APPROACH

Aboriginal peoples have been utilizing their own approaches to helping one another for centuries. Many Aboriginal social workers have incorporated these approaches or aspects of them in their professional practice. However, such approaches have not always been respected on their own merits by the social work profession. In recognition of this concern, the Canadian Association of Social Workers (1994) has long acknowledged the need for greater understanding and respect of Aboriginal practices. This need continues to exist today. In order to contribute to the development of this understanding and, in turn, respect for these approaches, one approach is outlined here. While this approach was developed in the 1990s, it continues to evolve.

It is important to note that Aboriginal peoples vary extensively in their worldviews. This becomes readily apparent when you consider the diversity of Aboriginal peoples throughout the territory now called Canada. There are more than 50 nations, including the Innu, Mi'kmaq, Maliseet, Odawa, Kanien'kehaka, Anishinaabe, Cree, Dakota, Blackfoot, Salish, Haida, Tutchone, Dene, Inuit, and Métis nations. There are over 630 First Nations communities throughout Canada (Assembly of First Nations, 2008), more than 50 Inuit communities (Inuit Tapiriit Kanatami, 2008), and numerous Métis communities and settlements. Aboriginal people live on reserves, in settlements, small rural communities, remote isolated locations, and large urban centres. Further, the cultures of the many peoples are a direct reflection of their traditional lands and environments. The diversity of the peoples is considerable given the great diversity in the land and environment throughout Turtle Island.[2] From this great diversity it is easy to understand that there is also a variety of Aboriginal helping approaches (for examples, see Bruyere, 2001; Morrisseau, 1998). The approach in this chapter is based on Aboriginal helping practices with a focus on Aboriginal peoples in Canada, particularly the prairie provinces. With these points in mind, this is *an* Aboriginal approach, not *the* approach.

Background of This Approach

One of the models that guides this approach and that is frequently mentioned in the literature is the medicine wheel (Absolon, 1993; Bopp et al., 1985; Bruyere, 2001; Garrett and Myers, 1996; Regnier, 1994; Young, Ingram, and Swartz, 1989). The medicine wheel is an ancient symbol of the universe used to help people understand things or ideas we often cannot physically see. It reflects the cosmic order and the unity of all things in the universe (Regnier, 1994), but it can be expressed in many different ways as there is no absolute version of the wheel (Bopp et al., 1985; Calliou, 1995). Indeed, many Aboriginal peoples, such as the Anishinabe, Cree, and Dakota, have utilized the medicine wheel and given it their interpretations (Regnier, 1994). As a central symbol used for understanding various issues and perspectives, the medicine wheel reflects several key and interrelated concepts that are common to many Aboriginal approaches to helping. Many of the following concepts help explain the medicine wheel. These concepts are outlined here as the foundation to this Aboriginal approach. They are wholeness, balance, relationships, harmony, growth, healing, and *mino-pimátisiwin*. But even before we can consider these concepts, the significance of spirituality to Aboriginal people must be highlighted.

The Central Pillar and Frame of This Approach

Since the outlining of this approach, spirituality has been outlined as a key concept and a value. Spirituality, as distinct from religion, has been implicit and continues to be in all aspects of Indigenous life, including our ontologies, epistemologies, methodologies, and axiologies, as well as our social, political, cultural, and economic interactions. It is a core characteristic of many Aboriginal cultures and is evident in many aspects of Aboriginal helping practices. Spirituality is highlighted here as a central concept in this approach.

Spirituality can be understood as the "life force" (Deloria and Wildcat, 2001). It is "grounded in our experience of the natural world as full of creation's power" (p. 14). Instead of the dichotomies and reductionism central in Amer-European worldviews, it emphasizes the understanding that we are all related, including being related to the land, life of the land, and the many, many cyclic processes of life. Many Aboriginal people hold a deep sense of spirituality and express it in a variety of ways, including through traditional ceremonies, meditation, prayer, incorporation of dreams in one's daily life, and more assimilated means, such as through Amer-European religious expressions. And, even though you will find individual Aboriginal people who do not demonstrate such a sense of spirituality, to ignore their sense of spirituality is to deny a part of them as Aboriginal peoples.

The centrality of spirituality in this approach is also reflected in two aspects of Indigenous worldviews that are highlighted here as the frame that holds the approach's key concepts. To understand these two aspects, it is important to note that Aboriginal worldviews tend to high- light a strong focus on people and entities coming together to help and support one another in their relationship. Reiterating Terry Cross, Thomas Crowfoot Graham (2002) called this a *relational worldview*. Key within a relational worldview is the emphasis on "communitism" and respectful individualism. Communitism is the sense of community tied together by familial relations and families' commitment to it (Weaver, 1997; Weaver, 2001). Respectful individualism is a way of being where an individual enjoys great freedom in self-expression, since it is recognized by the society that individuals take into consideration and act on the needs of the community as opposed to acting on self-interest alone (Gross, 2003). This Aboriginal approach should be seen where spirituality is central to each concept, value, and perception and where the concepts, values, and perceptions are framed within the under- standings of communitism and respectful individualism.

KEY CONCEPTS

Wholeness

In order to understand the concept of wholeness, it is important to recognize that the medi- cine wheel (see Exhibit 12.1) has been used to illustrate many teachings that can be expressed in sets of four and represented in the four cardinal directions: east, south, west, and north (Bopp et al., 1985; Calliou, 1995). For example, the medicine wheel has been used to explain the four aspects of humanness. According to this teaching, every individual comprises four key aspects, namely the emotional, physical, mental, and spiritual. Individuals are not whole unless they recognize and actively develop each aspect of their humanness. Other teachings that are addressed through the medicine wheel include the people of the four directions (identified as the red peoples, yellow peoples, black peoples, and white peoples), the four cycles of life (birth/infancy, youth, adulthood, and Elder/death), elements (fire, water, wind, and earth), and the four seasons (spring, summer, fall, and winter) (Bopp et al., 1985; Hart, 1992; Regnier, 1994) (see Exhibit 12.2). Wholeness is directly related to these and other teachings. Each of these teachings is part of a single whole. We can come to fully understand

Exhibit 12.1 ▼ **Common Structure of the Medicine Wheel**

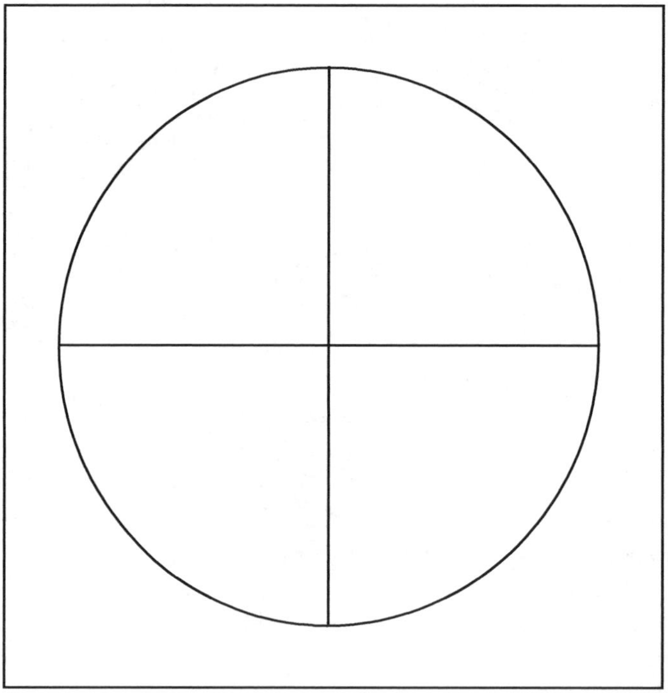

one teaching only if we can understand how it is connected to all other parts and teachings reflected in the medicine wheel.

Wholeness in the cycle of the year requires movement through all seasons; wholeness in life requires movement through the phases of a human life; and wholeness in human growth requires the development of all aspects. The year life (all the cycles that evolve during one year of life) and human growth can come to completion through this movement to wholeness. This movement is natural and fundamental to all living things (Regnier, 1994, pp. 132–33).

Thus, wholeness is the incorporation of all aspects of life. In order to focus upon the whole it becomes necessary to give attention to each part. This attention is reflected in the next key concept.

Balance

The concept of balance implies that each part of the whole requires attention in a manner where one part is not focused upon to the detriment of the other parts (Clarkson, Morrissette, and Regallet, 1992). Balance occurs when a person is at peace and harmony within and with all other living things, including the earth and natural world (Longclaws, 1994). It also includes paying attention to both positive and negative aspects of people (Absolon, 1993; Nabigon and Mawhiney, 1996). While balance is periodically achieved, it is never truly achieved for an indefinite period of time. As in all living systems, it has to be strived for continuously. When there is an unequal focus on one part of the medicine wheel there is an imbalance. Such imbalance is considered the source of a

Exhibit 12.2 ▼ **Examples of Teachings of the Medicine Wheel**

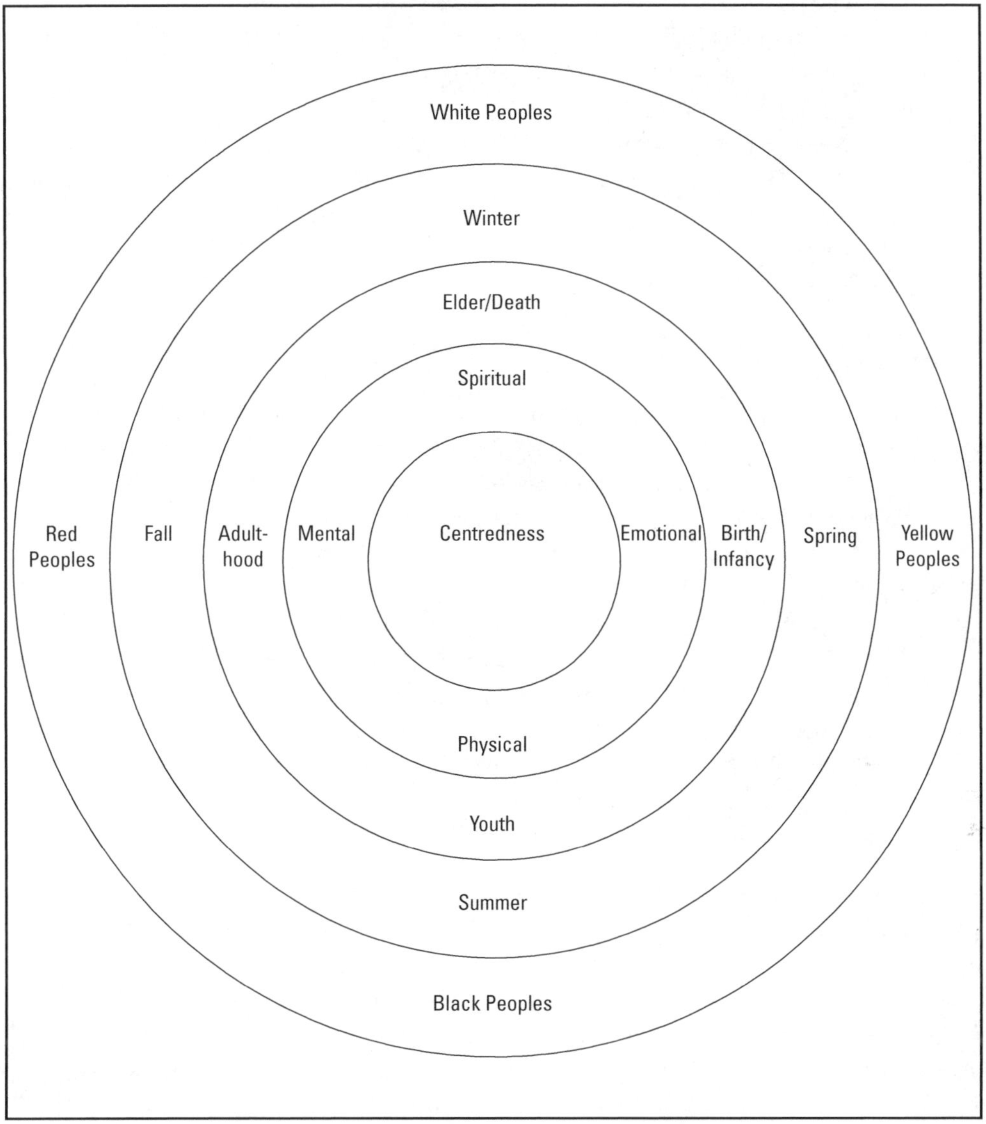

person's disease or problems (Canda, 1983; Garrett, 2003; Malloch, 1989). A person who does not strive for balance will not be able to develop his or her full potential. In order to restore balance, each part of the medicine wheel must be addressed in relation to all of the other parts (Peat, 1994).

Relationships

Balance involves more than just paying attention to each and every part of the medicine wheel. If it did, one could take a reductionistic view of only giving equal time to each part so that balance could be achieved. Balance includes giving attention to what connects each part of the medicine wheel; in other words, the relationships among all the parts.

Relationships between people characterize human life and are essential to people's well-being. Attention must also be given to the relationships within a person. Dion Buffalo (1990) states that "the traditional Cree approach is also holistic, concerned with and giving equal consideration to an individual's mental, physical, emotional, and spiritual well-being within the Sacred Circle of the universe" (pp. 118–19). People also are in relationship with entities surrounding them, including the earth, plants, animals, and the universe as a whole. Thus, in order to achieve balance people need to constantly foster the relationships between entities outside, as well as within, themselves. It is this fostering of relationships that is central to the next key concept.

Harmony

Harmony is frequently mentioned as a state to be sought after, whether it is harmony within oneself (Odjig White, 1996), with others (Brant, 1990), in the world (Canda, 1983), or in the universe (Regnier, 1994; Johnston, 1990). The concept of harmony not only is a state of being, but also leads to a good life (Dion Buffalo, 1990; Longclaws, 1994). Harmony involves the relationships of all the various powers, energies, and beings of the cosmos; when everyone—human, animal, plant, and planet—fulfills their obligations and goes about their proper business, then they are in harmony (Peat, 1994). There is also the notion that harmony includes respect for our relationships with others, within oneself, and in the give and take between entities (Nabigon, 2006). Overall, harmony requires finding a good fit between the components of life through collaboration, sharing what is available, and cooperation and respect. It involves peace, respect, and establishing connections. Through this harmonizing process one fosters the next key concept, growth.

Growth

Growth and learning involve developing the body, mind, heart, and spirit in a harmonious manner. People have the capacity to grow and change, and their growth is dependent upon using their volition to develop their physical, emotional, spiritual, and mental aspects (Bopp et al., 1985). Thus, growth is viewed as a lifelong process that leads people to their true selves. Growth can be seen as movement through life cycles toward wholeness, balance, interdependence or connectedness, and harmony within oneself and with other living things; it is the movement toward the centre of the wheel (Longclaws, 1994; Nabigon and Mawhiney, 1996; Regnier, 1994). The centre is the place of optimum growth and healing.

Healing

Within an Aboriginal perspective, healing is not defined as something that is done when an illness or a problem is present. Instead, healing is viewed as a journey; it is something that is practised daily throughout our lives (Absolon, 1993; Ross, 1996). Illness and problems are viewed as disconnections, imbalances, and disharmony (Malloch, 1989). Thus, "healing is the transition that restores the person, community, and nation to wholeness, connectedness, and balance" (Regnier, 1994, p. 135). In this sense, healing is developing centredness.

From this perspective, an individual's healing not only is necessary for that individual, but also is important for all people around that person since they are all interconnected (Longclaws, 1994, p. 32). However, healing for an individual begins with that individual. As such, healing involves individual responsibility for one's own well-being and growth.

Mino-pimátisiwin

It is through the taking of responsibility for their own personal healing and growth that individuals will be able to attain **mino-pimátisiwin** (in Cree, pronounced mi-no-pi-maa-ti-si-win)—the good life.

The good life is the goal of living life fully, learning, and healing. This growth and attempt to reach the good life is not just an individual focus—it also involves the family and community. Herring (1996) speaks of self-actualization in a manner that reflects the idea of reaching *mino-pimátisiwin*. He suggests that "Native cultures emphasize cooperation, harmony, interdependence, the achievement of socially oriented and group goals, and collective responsibility. Thus the goal [of self-actualization] is more akin to family and tribal self-actualization" (p. 74).

KEY VALUES

To reach *mino-pimátisiwin,* particular values have been emphasized.

Sharing

Among the values emphasized, sharing takes a central place. The many things shared among people include practical and sacred knowledge, life experiences, and food (O'Meara, 1996). Sharing with others tends to be a natural way of developing human relationships. Sharing promotes equality and democracy in that everyone is considered as valuable as any other person and treated accordingly (Brant, 1990). It also reduces feelings such as greed, envy, and arrogance that may cause conflict within the group. It is believed to be so fundamentally important that any breach would result in sickness (Zieba, 1990).

Respect

Another value that is extensively emphasized and believed to be one of the foundations of many Aboriginal cultures is respect (Briks, 1983). Calliou (1995), providing a First Nations explanation, states that "we unconditionally respect all beings because we all begin as seeds from the same materials of this Mother Earth. In the circle no one individual (two-legged, four-legged, mineral, or plant, etc.) is deemed 'more than' or 'less than' another, so that treatment which elevates or denigrates one or the other is ruled out" (p. 67). Respect means to treat someone or something with consideration; to show honour, esteem, deference, and courtesy; and sometimes to yield to another's wishes out of politeness. It is a central responsibility in all relationships, including spiritual relationships (Hampton et al., 1995).

PERCEPTIONS OF PERSONS

View of Human Nature and Activity Orientation

Human nature in an Aboriginal approach is seen as good, although the existence and expression of bad attributes by people are also recognized (Absolon, 1993; Waldram, 1997). According to Longclaws (1994), "it was believed that people were born good but that throughout life the teachings of the medicine wheel provided guidance and therefore protection from evil forces present in the universe that could lead people astray and off the good, or red, road" (p. 26). Further, while everyone has a direction and purpose in life, they have to actively strive to develop themselves positively toward *mino-pimátisiwin* (Bopp et al., 1985; Longclaws, 1994; Regnier, 1994). At the same time, "while people develop to come to know their true nature, the traditional Native also nurtures the experience of being alive" (Hampton et al., 1995, p. 259). Thus, while an Aboriginal approach mainly views people in a state of being (Nelson, Kelley, and McPherson, 1985), it also includes them in a state of being-in-becoming (Regnier, 1994).

View of Individuals, Time Orientation, and Relationships

As previously noted, all people have a purpose and are active as they strive to grow toward *mino-pimátisiwin.* This growth and development take place through people's own actions in life. This does not mean that they are oriented only to the future. As Brant (1990) states, "the Native person has an intuitive, personal and flexible concept of time" (p. 536). Life experiences and events that take place in the past and in the present time are all important, especially in terms of how future generations will be affected. Indeed, past personal and generational experiences are important to the present time, as well as how present events will affect future generations (Benton-Banai, 1988; Clarkson, Morrissette, and Regallet, 1992). For example, when considering the effects of a child being removed from a family, they will reflect on the aspirations of past generations and how such a move will affect future generations, as well as how the future generations will be able to carry on the past generations' aspirations.

Relationships are central to each person's well-being and life goals, and in each person's life relationships are made and remade. Individuals are deeply influenced by and influence the relationships in their lives, including relationships between and within entities (people, spirits, and things). To "try to accommodate those relationships instead of dominating the things within them—seems to lie at the heart of a great many Aboriginal approaches to life" (Ross, 1996, p. 63).

Relationships are guided by good conduct, since good conduct leads to *mino-pimátisiwin* (Hallowell, 1992). Good conduct in relationships involves not interfering in and not judging the affairs of others, since interference and judgments limit a person's self-determination (Good Tracks, 1989; Janzen, Skakum, and Lightning, 1994). Relationships that enhance harmony and avoid coercively directing others' behaviour are promoted. Overall, positive relationships are central to an Aboriginal approach.

Among the many relationships that are present, the relationship between women and men is key. Within this approach it is recognized that both genders have purposes as part of the whole of life. There has to be balance between women and men. One cannot be focused upon to the detriment of the other. Instead, both have to harmoniously support one another as they strive for *mino-pimátisiwin*. This support is enhanced through the sharing between genders, not the domination and oppression of one over the other.

PERCEPTIONS OF FUNCTIONING

Role of History

The process and effects of colonization have to be understood, not only as a structured relationship, but also as a personal experience (McKenzie and Morrissette, 2003; Morrissette, McKenzie, and Morrissette, 1993). The spiritual aspect of Aboriginal peoples has suffered great stress due to colonization, and this aspect requires special attention. The human service professions, such as social work, come face to face with the current problems stemming from harmful past events and practices. Duran and Duran (1995) discuss colonization in relation to psychology. Their statement applies equally to social work:

> The past five hundred years have been devastating to our communities; the effects of this systematic genocide are currently being felt by our people. The effects of the genocide are quite personalized and pathologized by our profession via the diagnosing and labelling tools designed for this purpose. If the labelling and diagnosing process is to have any historical truth, it should incorporate a diagnostic category that reflects the effects of genocide. Such a diagnosis would be 'acute and/or chronic reaction to colonialism.' (p. 6).

This quotation emphasizes that human service professions need to seriously consider impacts of the politics of colonization in North American history. Thus, an Aboriginal approach incorporates historical factors such as the effects of colonization on the person, family, and community. This makes real the popular social work slogan, "The personal is political," often attributed to feminist social work practice (see Chapter 13).

Individual Development: The Cycle of Life

Equally important as the effects of colonization on people's functioning is the cyclical nature of life. This cycle has been viewed in relation to the medicine wheel, where life is seen as having four key phases; within each phase tasks are developed, but not necessarily in consecutive order (Bopp et al., 1985; Calliou, 1995). These four phases are often referred to as the birth/infant phase, the child/youth phase, the adult phase, and the Elder/death phase. Thus, while it is possible to describe particular developments and achievements in relation to particular life phases (Longclaws, 1994), these phases are significant to people as individuals so that they can best understand their own development.

Importance of Consciousness and Unconsciousness

Dion Buffalo (1990), in identifying the importance of the unconscious, stated that the Plains Cree heal individuals by bringing the unconscious conflict and resistance to a conscious level where issues can be worked on. Often this process incorporates spiritual dimensions that are reached through dreams and visions. Among the traditional Plains peoples, dreams are held in high regard and are seen as a source of knowledge and power (Irwin, 1994). It is believed that spiritual beings—*pawakanak* in Cree—can offer guidance to people. They are contacted through dreams, and it is these contacts that enhance a person's ability to reach *mino-pimátisiwin* (Dunsenberry, 1962).

Ermine (1995) reviewed this process of learning, securing power, enhancement, and help through such events as dreams and visions. He stated,

> In their quest to find meaning in the outer space, Aboriginal people turned to the inner space. This inner space is the universe of being within each person that is synonymous with the soul, the spirit, the self, or the being. The priceless core within each of us and the process of touching that essence is what Kierkegaard called inwardness [1846]. . . . Aboriginal people found a wholeness that permeated inwardness and that extended into the outer space. Their fundamental insight was that all existence was connected and that the whole enmeshed the being in its inclusiveness. In the Aboriginal mind, therefore, an immanence is present that gives meaning to existence and forms the starting point for Aboriginal epistemology. (p. 103)

In this activity it is essential to note that this inward-looking process is important not only for individuals, but for the community as well. Overall, Aboriginal philosophy is a spiritual philosophy that strongly incorporates the unconscious and the conscious (Aitken, 1990).

Nature of Change and the Role of Motivation

Change in an Aboriginal approach is tied to balance, relationships, and harmony. Aboriginal peoples see the universe in a constant state of movement in which there is an order of alliances, compacts, and relationships among the energies and spirits of the world (Peat, 1994). This order, being in continuous motion, is always in a state of transition between order and chaos. As such, balance in the universe occurs in an environment of movement, transition, and change. Another way to view change, according to Chief Simon Baker, is to see it in terms of cycles (Baker and Kirkness, 1994). To illustrate, people are always involved in transitional processes, either directly or indirectly. Change occurs due to actions that occur outside an individual—say, when a winter storm strikes or a family member moves away. Such occurrences are part of the cycle of life. Change can also happen as a result of inner processes, such as feelings of fear, or a new understanding of oneself after a meaningful experience. When individuals are not balanced within, are disconnected in their relationships, or are in disharmony with their environment, then change is required. It is necessary to regain one's balance. At other times, when individuals feel they have achieved balance and attempt to remain "stuck" in that particular state, their growth is hindered since the world around them continues to change. Therefore, the nature of change is that it is an ongoing transitional process of balancing and connecting relationships within the individual, between individuals, and between individuals and their environment (Longclaws, 1994; Regnier, 1994). This process is not limited to the individual, but also involves relationships at a familial, communal, and tribal or national level (Briks, 1983; LaDue, 1994).

The primary motivation for growth and change lies in the desire to reach *mino-pimátisiwin* (Aitken 1990; Hallowell, 1992); therefore, the onus is on the individual to pursue change in her or his life. Emphasizing this personal responsibility for change, Ross (1996) stated,

> Only you can find the will to take those first steps towards trusting others, towards taking hold of the hands that reach down to help you. The healers can show you how they trust each other, how they don't let go of each other, but they can't force you to reach out yourself. They can only demonstrate, teach, encourage and receive. Everything else must come from the individual who needs the healing (p. 190).

Power

Power exists in all living entities. For people it is tied to their ability to imagine something or to make a choice and then implement actions so that the imagined something or the choice becomes a reality. Ideally, power should be used to help oneself and others to strive for *mino-pimátisiwin*. It is used to help people learn, heal, and grow, which in turn can lead to greater access to power. People's access to power is not evenly distributed throughout any society. What becomes highly significant is how the power that is available to an individual, group of individuals, or part of a society is used by them. A variation in the distribution of power may be acceptable as long as the power is used to contribute to the creation and maintenance of balance, relationships, and harmony for all individuals and entities. Therefore, the more power a person or group has access to, the greater the responsibility that person or group has to contribute to the well-being of others.

Power is abused when an individual, a group, a society, or an entity, for its own gain, hinders or attempts to hinder another person, group, society, or entity's learning, healing, or growth. Abuses of power result in imbalances, broken relationships, and disharmony. While it may appear in this situation that the individual or group with the power is growing stronger, in the larger picture there is little growth, and the likelihood of deterioration is great. As in trickster stories of various Indigenous nations, this deteriorating state is unlikely to remain, as a change will likely come either from within those abusing their power or by force from an external resource that will result in a redistribution of the power to a more balanced state.

THE HELPING PROCESS

Focus of Helping

In an Aboriginal approach to helping, emphasis is given to the relationships held by the people being helped. It is especially essential to nurture the relationship between a client and worker and to enhance its development and growth as a part of helping.

The focus of the helping process is restoring relationships that have become out of balance (Malloch, 1989; Ross, 1996). From a holistic perspective, it could be said that "an intervention will need to restore physical well-being to the body and harmony to the damaged social and spiritual relationships" (Ellison Williams and Ellison, 1996, p. 148). As in all social work practice, work with clients can be focused at the individual, family, community, or broader level of relationships. In addition, the level of relationships can be further extended to include people's relationships with the Creator and Mother Earth (Clarkson, Morrissette, and Regallet, 1992). In an Aboriginal social work approach, those providing assistance to clients are required to focus on maintaining their own balance, connectedness, and harmony—in other words, centredness—since they are in relationship with the people receiving help (Nabigon and Mawhiney, 1996; Nelson, Kelley, and McPherson, 1985). Indeed, it is emphasized that "before you can reach out to help the people around you, you must first understand how to help yourself" (Antone and Hill, 1990, p. 7).

The Helping Relationship and Specific Techniques

The helping relationship is one in which the helper and the person receiving the support are involved in a shared experience of learning and growing. There is no distinction in terms of status or position. In this shared experience the helper is fundamentally a supporter involved in an interdependent relationship with the person receiving the help (Nelson, Kelley, and McPherson, 1985). In order to respect individual autonomy, those offering help are required to be indirect, nonjudgmental, and noncoercive in their methods of practice (Longclaws, 1994; Nabigon and Mawhiney, 1996). As Boldt and Long (1984) point out, no human being has control over another's life. In the end, it is up to the individual what direction she or he takes. While some healers have been noted to be very direct and have used direct interventions (Malloch, 1989; Young, Ingram, and Swartz, 1989), most interventions that are parallel with social work practice involve a relationship of interdependence and support, and tend to remain fairly indirect. For example, when working with people, Aboriginal helpers do not direct action. Instead, they may share their own or others' experiences in the same or a similar situation. The person listening to what was said would be free to use the information in the manner he or she wishes to use it, including not at all. Of course, when the safety of another is at risk direct intervention may be required, such as in situations where someone is physically abusing another or attempting suicide.

Specific techniques reflect this relationship. In an Aboriginal approach, storytelling is frequently used as a method of addressing issues (Bruchac, 1992; Dion Buffalo, 1990; O'Meara, 1996). Some situations may call for the helper to share experiences that directly relate to the situation being addressed. Other situations may call for the sharing of stories in a general manner, thus allowing individuals to personally discover the meaning in the story that relates to them.

The use of humour is another important technique. According to Aitken (1990), "humour to our people is probably one of the greatest medicinal strengths" (p. 29). He considered it as an indirect nurturing approach that is both nonconfrontational and noninterfering. For example, the use of humour can help individuals to see the situations they are experiencing from a new perspective, and perhaps a lighter point of view.

Role modelling is another technique that can be indirect, nonconfrontational, and supportive (Brant, 1990; McCormick, 1995). The role-modelling process, or "teacher as healer," requires that a person live life as it is to be taught and wait for the student to come seeking knowledge (Katz and St. Denis, 1991, p. 31).

In an Aboriginal social work approach, the referral to or support of Elders is often highlighted. Significantly, Elders are often seen as people who have learned from life and are able to transmit the culture (Malloch, 1989; Stiegelbauer, 1996; Waldram, 1997). Transmitting the culture is considered a key aspect of the healing process for Aboriginal peoples (LaDue, 1994; McKenzie and Morrissette, 2003). Elders also provide counselling, offer spiritual guidance, and conduct ceremonies (Couture, 1996; Stiegelbauer, 1996; Waldram, 1997).

Conducting ceremonies and following rituals are significant techniques utilized in an Aboriginal approach. There are many ceremonies, and these are carried out in varying ways depending upon the practices of the First Nations peoples involved. They include smudging, prayer, naming ceremonies, pipe ceremonies, sweat lodges, feasts, and fasting. Despite the variability, "[C]eremonies assist individuals in centring themselves and give them strength to participate in a lifelong learning process" (Longclaws, 1994, p. 26). Ceremonies are not referred to as rights to be exercised, but as obligations to be fulfilled for one's renewal in the life cycle. They are ways to facilitate healing and to discharge emotions through crying, yelling, talking, swearing, singing, dancing, and praying (Ross, 1996). The discharge of emotion in and of itself is in fact seen as a healing method (McCormick, 1995).

Specific Knowledge and Skills of the Helper

One reason Elders are respected as sources of help is because of their experiences and how they have learned from those experiences (Couture, 1996; Stiegelbauer, 1996). They have reached the point of living the life they wish to teach. People who conduct healing ceremonies go through a learning process that incorporates years of intense study, acquiring the knowledge needed to fully work as an Aboriginal healer (LaDue, 1994). Utilizing an Aboriginal approach in the helping process at least requires the ability to appropriately use the basic knowledge and skills that reflect and respect Aboriginal worldviews and the ways of life that stem from these views. These include eliminating the expert role, maintaining humility, demonstrating centredness, acknowledging the spiritual, listening, being patient, using silence, and speaking from the heart.

People offering help cannot see themselves as experts in the healing process since "there is no inherent distinction between the helper and the helped" (Nelson, Kelley, and McPherson, 1985, p. 241). Humility, not judgment, needs to be emphasized (Nabigon and Mawhiney, 1996; Ross, 1996). Helpers need to incorporate personal experience to demonstrate alternatives for healing and therefore should be active in developing their own centredness (Nelson, Kelley, and McPherson, 1985; Ross, 1996).

Since centredness involves the spiritual aspect of people, and since the helper role includes acting as a mediator between the physical and spiritual aspects of creation, helpers need to acknowledge the spiritual (Absolon, 1993; Malloch, 1989). The need to be patient and a good listener are also necessary, since nondirective approaches take time. "The professional may need to alter his or her communication style, learning to sit patiently through long pauses and to listen rather than to be directive or to interrupt the speaker" (Broken Nose, 1992, p. 384). Related to listening and patience is the use of silence. Peat (1994) states that "coming-to-know arises out of silence. It is this same quality of silence that strikes so forcefully when you meet with a Native person" (p. 75). Silence is related to another skill that should be developed—the art of speaking from the heart:

Out of this power of silence great oratory is born. When Native people speak they are not talking from the head, relating some theory, mentioning what they have read in some book, or what someone else has told them. Rather, they are speaking from the heart, from the traditions of their people, and from the knowledge of their land; they speak of what they have seen and heard and touched, and of what has been passed on to them by the traditions of their people. (Peat, 1994, p. 75)

Speaking from the heart also includes the attempt to reach and touch the listener's heart. This process is important because such actions honour the listener by having the speaker share something that is truly meaningful, and not just information. Thus, it is by reaching inward and speaking from their own heart that people are able to reach others. In social work, speaking from the heart shows genuineness, empathy, and concern. It brings worker and client together in their common humanity.

Goal Setting

Since the Aboriginal approach outlined here espouses personal responsibility, goal setting is to be determined by the person being helped (Aitken, 1990; Nelson, Kelley, and McPherson, 1985). Unless the person has approached a traditional healer or Elder asking for a particular problem to be cured, the assessment of what goals are to be sought is also determined by the person being helped (Nabigon and Mawhiney, 1996; Nelson, Kelley, and McPherson, 1985). Due to the fact that for many people following an Aboriginal approach the central goal is to achieve *mino-pimátisiwin,* the good life, goal setting is a personal responsibility. Helpers utilizing an Aboriginal approach can only act to support the person being helped to develop her or his goals. In this way, the people seeking help direct their own actions and take responsibility for reaching their own goals.

APPLICATION

In utilizing an Aboriginal approach in practice, social work helpers begin with themselves. They need to prepare themselves by being aware of their own emotional, mental, spiritual, and physical well-being, how these aspects are balanced and connected, and how they move to establish harmonious relationships within themselves and with others. Social work helpers then need to recognize that they are role models of positive growth and well-being, and as such are required to demonstrate respect and be prepared and willing to share their experiences of growth. Those who take on the job of social worker begin on a kind of journey, one in which they learn about themselves as people and as participants in a relationship with people seeking help. They will see the difficult situations, problems, and pain created by the structures in our society and by people in distress. They will also see the beauty of discovery, healing, and growth within themselves and in the universe around them. In this way, it is important for social workers to be centred themselves and to maintain their well-being and balance as they take up this challenging and rewarding work.

In working with people seeking help and/or support, social work helpers need to develop understandings of each person's personal, family, community, and national histories and how these histories may be brought into play in the present, including how they may relate to the colonial oppression Aboriginal peoples face. To develop this understanding, the helpers need to listen to the life stories that people share. They are required to hear about and support the people seeking help to consider all the relationships they have. Awareness of each internal component of the people seeking help should be developed by the helper and the people themselves. There must be consideration of questions such as: Is the person able to express a full range of emotions appropriately, to take physical care of himself or herself, to meet cognitive challenges and actively learn, and to feel and express his or her sense of spirituality? There must also be awareness of the external factors influencing this person, in particular the oppression she or he has experienced and the strength that can be derived from her or his identity and culture. Some questions that should be considered are as follows: How may this person's life experience be an individual reflection of the oppression Aboriginal peoples have faced? Are the actions of this person a consequence of internalized oppression? What aspects of his or her culture can be tapped into as a source of support and growth for the individual? The relationships between internal and external elements should be considered in relation to each other—in other words, holistically.

The positive growth of these components and relationships should be focused upon as the helper supports the individuals to develop her or his own goals. An outline of how centredness can be achieved should be shared between the helper and the person seeking help. There may be use of ceremonies within some sessions. For example, a smudging ceremony in which cleansing plant medicines are burnt and the smoke is used to wash oneself may be conducted. Alternatively, there may be ceremonies conducted outside the sessions that may become part of the healing journey. People seeking help and possibly the helper may participate in ceremonies, such as sweats or sharing circles, carried out by healers or Elders.

Finally, and importantly, the social work helper and the person seeking help will have to decide on how to best utilize the support of Elders. Elders may be sought by the helper to give advice and direction on how to proceed or points to consider. Alternatively, the person seeking help may wish to be referred to an Elder for support. The case example describes the situation of Aboriginal clients seeking help for their problems. Consider the details given and, applying an Aboriginal approach, reflect on how you would try to help.

In following this approach to helping, some questions might arise, specifically:

1. To what degree does the approach apply to different Aboriginal peoples and/or different Aboriginal cultures across Canada?
2. To what extent they can be applied to non-Aboriginal people?
3. Can the principles of Aboriginal practice be used by social workers of different cultures?

It is important to remember that the source for this approach lies mainly with the ideas stemming from central Turtle Island, particularly the Cree, Anishinaabe, and Dakota peoples. Some of the ideas that established the approach are from other Aboriginal nations and writers as well. Further, the worldviews of Indigenous peoples can be seen to hold more in common with one another than with Amer-European worldviews. Certainly, our experience with oppression has many commonalities with other groups who have experienced oppression. With these points said, it is important to remember that there are differences between Aboriginal peoples, particularly when their lands are dissimilar, since the peoples' cultures are so closely tied to the land. As such, we cannot assume that the approach is automatically relevant for all Aboriginal peoples. Indeed, there are some Aboriginal people who are firmly against relating to their own culture and traditions, to the extent that such an approach may be considered "evil."

As with any approach, model, and/or theory, it is important to come to an understanding of how best to serve the people with whom you are working. As you develop this understanding, you will gain a greater awareness of which approach, model, and/or theory will provide the best support for the people you are serving. This point extends beyond Aboriginal people. There are some non-Aboriginal peoples who share similar understandings of the world and hence may benefit from an Aboriginal approach. It will be up to you as the social worker to come to an understanding of the people you are serving and determine whether the approach is an appropriate way to support them. Finally, whether this approach is utilized by Aboriginal or by non-Aboriginal peoples is not the key question. More appropriately, the approach has to fit with your personal way of practice and, ideally, the worldview in which you are based. Remember, worldviews are not exclusive, as there is always overlap between worldviews. Thus, the better the fit between the approach and your practice and understanding of the world, the better you will be able to follow an Aboriginal approach.

Case Example

Debbie, Eddie, and Tom Caribou ▼

Debbie Caribou (née Yellowtail), 23 years old, is married to Eddie Caribou, 23 years old. They are the parents of three children, Sikwan, 5; Keystin, 4; and Cheyenne, 18 months. Debbie and Eddie met in high school in Kihcikeesik First Nation. Debbie's parents are Métis from the neighbouring community of Big Sky. Eddie, like his parents, is a citizen of Kihcikeesik First Nation and has lived there all his life. Debbie previously lived in the largest city in the province where the communities are located. She lived there from the ages of 3 to 7, and again from 10 to 11. Her parents had moved from Big Sky to the city during those times in order to find work and returned after her father was unable to obtain any work other than a series of part-time positions. After many racist confrontations with employers in workplaces, where Debbie's father was regarded by them as a "lazy half-breed," Debbie's parents are now adamant about never returning to the city. This city is approximately 300 kilometres away from Kihcikeesik First Nation and Big Sky. Debbie's father now works seasonally fishing. Her mother stays at home. Eddie's father works for the First Nation's lumber company, while his mother cares for two foster children, ages 3 and 5, as well as Eddie's two younger siblings, ages 21 and 13.

Like Debbie, Eddie has three siblings who have moved back and forth from various cities to Kihcikeesik. One still lives in the largest city in the province.

This sibling, Tom, is five years older than Eddie, has type 2 diabetes, and lives alone in the city so that he can have dialysis treatment three times a week. Tom has been informed that he will need to have his leg amputated below the knee. Eddie's parents were gravely concerned about Tom and asked Eddie to move to the city to live with Tom during this time. Since Eddie and Debbie were living in Eddie's parents' home, and since they saw no chance to locate alternate living arrangements in the near future, they viewed this as an opportunity to make some positive changes. However, Debbie's parents expressed their dismay at the idea and have been encouraging them not to move to the city.

Upon moving to the city, they were turned down for several apartments, despite initially being told the apartments were available. They did find a three-bedroom apartment in one of the poorest parts of the city and had Tom move in with them to share the living expenses. Before moving their belongings into the apartment, Eddie had the home ceremonially cleansed by an Elder who is well-known to the family and who lives near the city. Now that they have moved into their home with their children and Tom, their focus is on getting Sikwan into school, finding employment for Eddie, and supporting Tom. However, both Debbie and Eddie are feeling overwhelmed with the city and are struggling with the stress of their situation. As a result, they are not supporting Tom and the children well and are often yelling at one another.

You are a social worker at the Aboriginal Health Centre connected with the hospital where Tom will be going for the operation and which serves a large Aboriginal clientèle. While Tom has kept his appointments and has been joined on occasion by his brother, it has been noted by the physician and nurses at the Centre that he has begun to complain about not sleeping, being quite sad and frustrated, and feeling like a burden to the family. While he is not suicidal, they are concerned that he is not preparing well for the operation that will occur in a month's time. You have been asked to provide support to the family so they can help Tom prepare for the operation and for the rehabilitation period that will follow.

In reading the case example about Debbie, Eddie, and Tom, think about the values, concepts, and principles you have read about in this chapter. How might you incorporate the historical and present colonial reality that influences them? How might the concepts of wholeness, harmony, and balance be important to the family? How might these concepts relate to you in this situation? What might you be bringing into the relationships that you will be trying to establish with Debbie, Eddie, and Tom? What role could relationships, growth, and healing play in each family member's life? What might *mino-pimátisiwin* look like for each of them individually and as a family? How might you find out? If Tom, Debbie, or Eddie spoke to you of dreams or visions, what importance do you think these might have for them? If any of them spoke of a relationship to the spirits and to the universe as a whole, how might you understand these? What techniques in helping could be useful (e.g., social worker–client relationship, use of Elders, ceremonies and rituals, setting goals)? How might you raise their awareness of the colonization Aboriginal peoples face so that it relates to each person?

Some might say that you must be of their culture (Métis, Mi'kmaq, Innu, Cree, Anishinabe, Stö:lō or other Nation) to help them. While it could be an asset, we do not limit the potential of others from being able to help them. We recognize that there are resources within their culture that might be very important to them and that a non-Aboriginal social worker or an Aboriginal social worker who does not identify with that culture may not be able to make use of. These include ceremonies and practices such as sweat lodges, traditional healing circles, and use of Elders. While you may not be able to gain access to these resources, you could support the family's use of them. In learning about Debbie, Eddie, and Tom's cultures from them, you may be indirectly supporting them in their growth and healing.

The overarching principles of relationship and helping through support are important. As shown in earlier chapters, support has many dimensions. Besides the support you can offer, there may be some support in the city and their home community that can be utilized. When you begin to work with each member of the family, you can support them first by listening and being patient. You might then be able to help them in learning to relate to their families and community again or support them to discover what it means to be a family from their cultural perspective. But these possibilities must be client-directed. Each family member may ask your advice, but that may come after they are ready to trust you. This may take time. The challenges they are facing, such as possible racism in the city may cause them to move away from the changes they are making. They will need to know who to contact should any problems arise. Sharing such information with each of them, as needed, will likely be necessary. On another level, you may be able to utilize their past experiences as a means to introduce concepts of colonization, systemic and internalized oppression, and the need for oppressed peoples to connect with others at a community level. You may also consider incorporating these concepts into the services you provide.

Each of the family members may want information from you about yourself, as well as what you know about them and their problems. In promoting a relationship that is egalitarian, you would likely want to tell them what you know. If this is not admissible by your employer, how would you deal with the situation without losing your job?

You cannot force the family members to take a course of action that they are not ready for or do not want at all. The support you provide must demonstrate respect for their own search for healing and growth. Unless you are able to build mutual respect in your relationship with them, it will be nearly impossible to engage in an effective helping process. Once you have developed a sense of mutual respect, you will be able to utilize your power as a social worker to support them in their growth and healing. In this situation, support will mean allowing them to identify how you can best help from the information you share about yourself, your role, your abilities, and your connections.

The well-known social work mantra, "Start where the client is," comes to mind. It is best not to impose your understanding of the family's problems on them, but to find out what they think they need. Some of this may be specific to their cultural orientation or other features of their lives (such as their desire to reconnect to their culture in the city). Listening for a while before speaking is a good idea. Try to understand their life experiences from an emic (insider's) perspective. Your cultural background may or may not be different from theirs, so you will filter what you learn through your own culture and background. This is true for any helping encounter. The family members can tell you about their lives, their home, and their community, and this will give you a good sense of what it is like to live in their world. You must be prepared to share aspects of yourself to facilitate this exchange, if that is what is wanted by each of the family members. The information will also be useful to you as their social worker. Once you have developed a connection with the family, you do not want to avoid talking to them about their experiences with racism and institutions that perpetuate such oppression; however, you will need to learn how to comfortably address these with them. Until trust is developed in the relationship, this approach is likely the best.

From an alternative perspective, what if you were a child protection services worker responsible for ensuring the safety of the children? How would you work with the family in light of your mandate? How would you incorporate an Aboriginal approach when you are required to ensure certain goals are met? A key to answering this question is to remember whose goals are whose, and how power is to be used. Try to remember each of the points outlined in relation to the previous scenario.

AN ABORIGINAL APPROACH AND CONVENTIONAL SOCIAL WORK

This book has explained that conventional social work is formulated around the problem-solving process. An Aboriginal approach, as described in this chapter, is one of four approaches that this book argues informs, critiques, and enriches conventional practice. While an Aboriginal approach is particularly suited to working with Aboriginal peoples, its concepts and ideas enrich all of social work.

Conventional social work is organized around a problem-solving process. An Aboriginal approach is not. Instead, an Aboriginal approach centres around the abstract goal of *mino-pimátisiwin*—a good life and the lifelong journey of growth and healing. Problem solving is but one part of this journey. The emphasis on this journey is on wholeness, balance, connectedness/relationships, and harmony. Like the strengths approach (Chapter 11), an Aboriginal approach emphasizes people's vitality and capacities. In an Aboriginal approach, people need to be able to solve their own problems, and as the journey toward *mino-pimátisiwin* continues, problem-solving capacity increases and improves.

In an Aboriginal view, helping and healing are connected but are not the same thing. Healing is viewed as a journey and something that is practised daily throughout everyone's life. Illness and problems are viewed as disconnections, imbalances, and disharmony. Healing is the journey to *mino-pimátisiwin,* which is achieved through maintaining centredness. As such, healing involves an individual responsibility for one's own well-being and growth.

As stated earlier, the focus of the helping process is on restoring relationships that have become out of balance. From a holistic perspective, it could be said that "an intervention will need to restore physical well-being to the body and harmony to the damaged social and spiritual relationships" (Ellison Williams and Ellison, 1996, p. 148).

Helping is not seen as a direct solution to specific problems as in problem-solving processes. Instead, helping is often viewed as but one part of the healing process. Helping, in this sense, is assisting another in his or her process of healing.

The helping relationship is one in which the helper and the person receiving the support are involved in a shared experience of learning and growing. Both conventional social work and an Aboriginal approach see the helping relationship as central to helping. They also view the relationship between social worker and client as a mutual partnership. However, an Aboriginal approach carries this view further, in that the helper and the person being helped are in an interdependent relationship where they can both learn and grow. Ideally, a helper using an Aboriginal approach is to have experiential knowledge of centredness and the issues she or he is addressing. Goals are determined by the person being helped in an Aboriginal approach and connect to lifelong processes of healing. In the ecosystems approach, as in problem-solving processes, goals are specifically related to the problem and are usually determined mutually between the helper and the person being helped.

AN ABORIGINAL APPROACH AND ECOSYSTEMS

Ecosystems was introduced in Chapter 9 as a person-in-the-environment perspective. Central to an ecosystems approach is the interaction and connections between the person and the environment. It is not much of a stretch to suggest, as some do (see Longclaws, 1994), that an Aboriginal approach bears some resemblance to a person-in-the-environment perspective and to an ecosystems view. It is true that an Aboriginal approach focuses heavily on relationships, including the relationship between people and their environments. In this sense, it is a person-in-the-environment perspective. Further Aboriginal concepts such as balance and disharmony share similarities with the ecosystems principles, like equilibrium and disequilibrium. However, as was shown throughout this chapter, the Aboriginal perspective is both much broader and more inclusive.

Neither ecosystems nor an Aboriginal approach is, as such, a theory. Instead, both are used in social work as perspectives and approaches and provide frameworks for practice. Ecosystems is drawn from biological ecology. There is no social ecological theory, although many testable hypotheses can be drawn from ecosystems. An Aboriginal approach has been developed over many centuries by North American Aboriginal cultures and represents a worldview that has only some similarities to ecological ideas. In this context, an Aboriginal perspective and ecosystems are not of the same order; ecosystems is a framework borrowed from biology. An Aboriginal perspective is a broader worldview with a very wide range of principles and teachings.

Central concepts in ecosystems are transaction and interface. Transaction generally refers to the interactions and connections between systems, including a person and the person's environment. Ecosystems holds that all systems have abstract boundaries or, metaphorically speaking, edges that distinguish and separate a given system from other systems. Often, however, systems connect with one another and overlap. The interface is the point at which systems come into contact with one another. An ecosystems approach holds that social work assessment and intervention should focus on these twin concepts of transaction and interface.

In the ecosystems approach, social workers seek to restore the fit between the person and the environment (Sheafor and Horejsi, 2008).

An Aboriginal approach is similar but also very different from an ecosystems approach. In an Aboriginal approach, as in ecosystems, the connections between parts are emphasized. Similar to the ecosystems' concentration on fit between person and environment, an Aboriginal approach focuses on restoring relationships that have become out of balance. However, an Aboriginal approach goes much further in that it also centres on the wholeness of everything, including the person, the environment, the spiritual and physical worlds, the universe, and the connections among all of these parts. Thus, wholeness is the incorporation of *all* aspects of life. To focus on the whole, it becomes necessary to give attention to each part.

Further, an Aboriginal approach includes understanding the conscious and unconscious, with an emphasis on spirituality. Spirituality is vitally important as the basis of all connections and beings. As such, healing involves the spiritual aspect of people.

The focus of ecosystems is narrower and centres on maximizing individual growth and development through people's transactions and fit with the environment. Mutual causality between environment and person, stress, adaptation, and goodness of fit between person and environment are emphasized. The ecosystems approach avoids inner-self factors such as the unconscious and spirituality, and if addressed at all they remain at the periphery of the approach.

In summary, it is important that social workers not confuse an Aboriginal approach with ecosystems even though they have some important similarities.

CHAPTER SUMMARY

This chapter has articulated a range of ideas and concepts that together make up an Aboriginal approach to social work. This approach is based on a broad worldview that has important implications for all of social work. As an approach to social work, it both challenges and informs conventional ideas and practices. In many respects, an Aboriginal perspective is the product of adapting a centuries-old helping and healing process to modern society and conditions.

The history of Aboriginal peoples in North America is one of colonialism, involving a process of attempted cultural assimilation, subordination, and economic exploitation. Conventional social work is often seen as part of the colonization of Aboriginal peoples, as in the past it took the form of authoritarian control and regulation by external agents who had little understanding or appreciation of Aboriginal cultures. The healing and helping process with Aboriginal peoples must often address the personal and social wounds of colonization.

Aboriginal peoples vary extensively in their worldviews. The approach developed here is based on a few of these Aboriginal worldviews, thus it is *an* Aboriginal approach, not *the* approach. One of the models that guide this approach and that is frequently mentioned in the literature is the medicine wheel. As a central symbol used for understanding various issues and perspectives, the medicine wheel reflects several key and interrelated concepts and teachings that are common to many Aboriginal approaches to helping and may be seen as the foundation to the Aboriginal approach described in this chapter. These concepts are wholeness, balance, relationships, harmony, growth, healing, and the important goal of *mino-pimátisiwin*—the good life.

The Aboriginal approach described in this chapter is one of many that are being used in various helping professions, including social work. Its focus is on relationships within and between beings, with the ultimate goal of growing toward *mino-pimátisiwin.*

NOTES

1 A legal term used to refer to First Nations, Métis, and Inuit people. In this chapter, "Aboriginal peoples" refers to people who have family connections to First Nations ancestry, including individuals referred to as American Indians. "Aboriginal people" has been used to refer to individuals, and "Aboriginal peoples" to groups.

2 Turtle Island is the name used by some Aboriginal peoples to refer to North America.

chapter

13

A Feminist Approach to Social Work

Chapter Goal ▼

To discuss the nature and significance of feminism in social work and the practice principles that comprise a feminist approach to social work and to explore the place of feminism in generalist practice.

This Chapter ▼

- questions why women, rather than men, are most often social work clients and social workers
- defines feminist social work from the perspective of women scholars who first brought it to the attention of the profession
- describes three main orientations in feminism that can be applied to social work
- presents the views of diverse groups of women regarding the relevance of feminism to them
- sets out key principles for a feminist approach to social work practice
- discusses how a feminist approach can be integrated with generalist social work practice

INTRODUCTION

This chapter promotes an approach to feminist social work that appreciates and affirms the diversity and commonality among women. The range of women's strengths, knowledge, and lived experience is acknowledged and highlighted. The core values, principles, and practice methods of feminist social work can be applied to generalist practice when these fit with an individual practitioner's orientation and client situations.

The principles of feminist social work practice have been developed over several decades. Social workers have increasingly applied feminist principles in practice settings that have adopted feminist approaches, such as women's shelters, health clinics, and counselling centres for women. It is also possible for a social work with a feminist orientation to apply the principles in generalist practice when the situation calls for it; for example, in a general hospital where women who have been physically abused seek treatment or in community organizing work with single parents whose financial assistance benefits are being threatened. A feminist approach to social work is useful because it enables a gender analysis of how societal and individual problems and situations differentially affect women and men. Women form the majority of our clients, and examining their unique circumstances as clients of social service agencies and as the targets of social and agency policies can help us to more effectively tailor strategies and interventions with them. Even if a social worker does not specifically apply a feminist practice approach, some of the principles can be integrated in generalist social work to enhance assessment and intervention. It also needs to be pointed out that problem solving is not generally discussed as part of a feminist social work practice approach, nor is a gender analysis part of problem solving. Nevertheless, if the principles of feminist social work practice are applied, problem solving could fit when conditions call for it. Both client and social worker need to work together so that the client is heard, that her wishes and views are respected and acknowledged, power is shared, and there is genuine support and collaboration in the process.

While there is no single theory of feminist social work practice, a collection of powerful social work practice principles, values, and interventions have emerged from feminist thinking and ideology (see Dominelli, 2002; and Dominelli and McLeod, 1989). For example, feminists have contributed to social work's understanding of the importance of power and empowerment in assessment and intervention (Dominelli, 2006; Yoder and Kahn, 1992).

It is also important to note that not only men and/or male-influenced institutions oppress women. Women can oppress and mistreat other women. Women are part of the same society with men, and are affected by the same structures. The divisions between women related, for example, to class, cultural background, sexual orientation, age, and physical ability can be factors that lead to marginalization and oppression of some women by other women and by society in general (see Dominelli, 2002, p. 23). Feminist social work principles that address intersecting oppressions are, thus, important. Recent work on *intersectionality* and feminism (Symington, 2004; Yuval-Davis, 2006) indicate that gender is only one social feature that oppresses or marginalizes women and that many women's lives are shaped at different times and places by social structures such as ageism, racism, classism, and/or other features. For example, a Black newcomer woman living on a low income in a Canadian city may not perceive discrimination that is related to her gender as a key issue when she seeks housing. Experiences and effects of marginalization or oppression may differ due to the overlay or intersection of these features.

Many feminist principles are consistent with the strengths and structural social work approaches, and present some challenges to more conventional practice, particularly problem solving. However, feminist social work differs from these due to its creation by women social workers and its focus on women and their concerns.

Few social agencies—aside from those that provide services solely or primarily to women—adopt, as policy, a feminist approach. In this sense, feminist practice is not mainstream social work. However, many of the feminist ideas of practice can be integrated by individual social workers into day-to-day social work. For example, the feminist practice principle of validation of a woman's experience may be followed when women clients seen in any social service agency narrate difficult stories of abuse or street life to social workers. It may also be appropriate for social workers to promote consciousness-raising in a group with other women who live with similar circumstances.

There is no question that feminist principles, and new applications and strands of feminist theory, will continue to influence social work. Social workers may view themselves as feminists or pro-feminists or might instead identify themselves in some other way, applying some feminist ideals and practice principles in their work with clients. At the same time, feminism may have little currency with women social work clients who have found their own strategies to survive (Lundy, 2004, p. 51) and give voice to their struggles, without identifying as feminists. For others to use the word "feminist" to refer to them would not be appropriate.

WOMEN AND SOCIAL WORK

Why is it that most social work clients tend to be women? And why are most social workers, especially at the front line, women? Lawrence (1992) has pointed out, "By understanding that women share a common developmental experience, as social workers we have to contend with the fact that we are very much like our clients" (p. 40). This may be so, but social workers have usually had the benefit of a university education and a professional income, which many social work clients have not. Baines (1997) has pointed out that that social workers need to be wary of drawing from middle-class experiences when applying a feminist practice approach.

An examination of the construction of social work practice and social policies, including the underlying assumptions about, and expectations for, women and men, is helpful for all social workers in reflecting on their practice experiences with clients in order to make improvements. Exploring the importance of gender both in the client–social worker relationship and as a feature that shapes a person's experience is critical for enhancing practice. It is also important to examine the roots of assumptions, ideas, and perspectives we take for granted about the social roles and responsibilities of women and men, and how these contribute to the way we view clients and their situations. It is our responsibility to carefully reflect on our position in relation to assumptions and viewpoints in social work and to practise reflexivity in our work.

In social work, just as in society, women tend to be responsible for childcare and health. Women take responsibility for the care and nurturing of others, especially family members and friends. Many women also face considerable stress at various times in their lives when they need to earn an income and at the same time ensure the well-being of children, spouses, parents, and others. Daughters or daughters-in-law, often with their own families to care for and other work to do, come to mind. Why? Day-to-day caring for the sick is the sort of work that is divided according to gender, and always has been. What is different about providing caring work now, if anything? If your answer is that nowadays many women hold down jobs outside the home (or work in their homes) and have other responsibilities without sufficient societal supports, you have identified a key problem that places substantial pressure on many women. Yet, as a society, these issues have not been adequately recognized or dealt with (see Baines, Evans, and Neysmith, 1998; Neysmith, 2000; and Neysmith, Bezanson, and McConnell, 2005).

Women who wish to stay in the home to care for children and/or family members while their spouses earn an income to support the household receive very limited support from social policies and programs. Many women receive no compensation for performing important caring labour and are disadvantaged in their old age due to reduced pension benefits. Some Nordic countries, on the other hand, have paid attention to the important role of care provision and have made provisions for those who take time away from paid work to raise children or care for other family members.

Social workers might find themselves offering support and other resources to help women who face difficult caregiving responsibilities. The goal may be to try to alleviate some of the stress, arrange for respite care, or explore other sources and types of care. For example, when a hospital patient is due to be discharged after surgery, often a social worker is given the task of ensuring that a care provider will be available at home to assist with changing dressings, monitoring medication, preparing meals, and other work. More often than not, the person performing this work is a woman, whether a paid homecare nurse or homemaker, or an unpaid family member or friend (Grant, Amaratunga, and Armstrong, 2004). Sometimes a combination of paid and unpaid services is used. Increasingly, the health care system demands and relies on informal help as shorter hospital stays and more complex care needs become more common (Simmons, 1994; Williams and Crooks, 2008). Some women may have developed intricate networks of help and support in their communities to draw upon when a crisis or other need arises (see, for example, Crooks et al., 2008; and Migliardi, Blum, and Heinonen, 2004).

FEMINISM AND SOCIAL WORK: BACKGROUND AND CONTEXT

A feminist approach is not only for women, but also for all people in society. Referring to Charlotte Bunch (1983), Van Den Bergh and Cooper (1986) in their important early work point out that feminism "is a vision born of women, but it addresses the future of the planet with implications accruing for males as well as females" (p. 2). This statement suggests that feminism should be seen as holding promise for a better society that benefits everyone.

Current forms of feminism began in North America during the 1960s along with radical student and civil rights movements. As a relatively new movement, feminism has continued to undergo challenges and changes. The social work profession has been slow to incorporate feminist principles, although Canadian scholars, such as Mary Valentich and Helen Levine, and American scholars, including Mary Bricker-Jenkins, Nan Van Den Bergh, and Lynn Cooper, pointed out in the 1970s and 1980s how feminism can be used to critique, enrich, and transform social work (Valentich, 1986). Feminism has played an important role in establishing the need for women's shelters, alternative health programs, and counselling services focused on women's needs. Feminist ideals influence social work practice with women who are facing abusive relationships, poverty, problems in providing care to others, concerns arising from life transitions, a need for reproductive health care, body image problems, and other issues (Baines, 1997; Dominelli, 2002; Hanmer and Statham, 1988; Russell, 1989).

In some organizations, such as women's health centres and feminist counselling agencies, programs are aimed specifically at women, and policies and mandates based on feminist principles guide workers' practices (Russell, 1989; Van Den Bergh and Cooper, 1986). However, in the organizations in which most social workers are employed (e.g., child protection), a feminist approach tends to be less evident. Day (2007) and Hanmer and Statham (1999) point out that in child protection and income security areas, women as mothers are scrutinized and judged, often without due consideration of the considerable demands on their time, energy, finances, and other resources. Individual generalist practitioners, however, may abide by and apply feminist principles in their work by striving to avoid mother blaming and acknowledging and fostering women's resilience and strengths in difficult circumstances.

Hanmer and Statham (1999, pp. 141–42) also stress that it is important for social workers to prepare themselves to be woman-centred practitioners. Methods include gaining clarity on our work; contributing to ongoing examination of emerging issues of concern to women as part of practice; ensuring accuracy of facts in research we use; continuing to enhance our practice skills to challenge sexism in society's institutions; requesting supervision and training to assist us in becoming better practitioners; bringing to light policies and practices that do not include voices and experiences of women and/or do not help them; and maintaining records of current and helpful resources for women.

Generally, key feminist principles include linking the personal to the political through consciousness-raising, validating women's strengths and experiences, reducing power differences, promoting self-disclosure and sharing of knowledge, and creating supportive environments (Russell, 1989; Van Den Bergh and Cooper, 1986). These combined are aimed at the empowerment of women, an important goal in a feminist social work approach to practice. In relation to community action, Dominelli (2006, p. 18) also points out that feminists highlight the contributions made by women to society, the various responsibilities of women in paid and unpaid work, women's development and provision of services for women including community work that advances the welfare of all, and connections women have made to environmental issues and quality of people's lives.

Feminist principles are not necessarily in conflict with other practice approaches. Some concepts appear similar to a structural approach, such as seeing women's problems as situated within their broader social contexts (Lundy, 2004) and recognizing people's strengths as assets and resources in the client–social worker relationship (Saleebey, 1997b). There are, however, some key differences. These ideas will be taken up later.

FEMINIST RESEARCH

Feminism has also challenged established conventions in research design and methods, the roles of the researcher and those studied, and the nature of knowledge (see Fonow and Cook, 1991; and Reinharz and Chase, 2003). Feminist perspectives have promoted ethical practices that respect participant needs, demystify and share the research process, and make improving women's lives a goal of the research (see Eichler, 1997; Fonow and Cook, 1991; Naples with Clark, 1996; Reinharz and Chase, 2003; and Stanley and Wise, 1993). Feminist researchers have pointed out that social research is not a neutral process, nor can it claim to be objective. Research that is conducted by a female researcher may differ from research that is carried out by a male researcher (Smith, 1990). Methods and processes in research using feminist viewpoints often see those researched as active participants in the study rather than as passive subjects responding to a researcher's questions (see Ristock and Pennell, 1996).

Let us illustrate some of the above concepts with an example drawn from research conducted on women who have experienced physical violence at the hands of their spouses. First, a feminist researcher would consider where she stands in relation to the research topic and the participants. The life experiences and understanding that bring her to study women survivors of violence would likely inform her position as researcher in the context of the topic and the research process. She would also want to reduce the power difference between herself and the research participants. One way to do this would be to acknowledge that many women experience violence in the home, whether they are professional women with a university education, refugees fleeing war, lesbian women, single mothers on welfare, or women living with disabilities. Other ways would be to participate in common activities together such as sharing food (e.g., during discussion about the research), and working with research respondents in data analysis, in validation of findings, and in writing about the research findings.

A feminist researcher would want to make sure that, in conducting the research, the participants are treated with respect, care, and concern. The ethics of such research would need to be well considered beforehand so that the women participants are given the information they need to make an informed choice, are provided with opportunities to ask questions, and are given access to counselling services if they experience distress as a result of the research process. This distress could occur, say, when the researcher conducts face-to-face interviews with women who have lived through violence. The feminist researcher takes responsibility for the participants' well-being in the research and ensures that any difficulties they experience are addressed. The researcher would be also interested in the ways she could help to promote the empowerment of women—for example, through bringing to light not only problems women have had but also the resources they found and used to survive. Research methods might be designed to validate the women's experiences and uncover strategies for improving policies or services that could benefit women experiencing violence in the home. This would be an example of making the personal political. When the findings are written up in a report, the researcher would offer participants an opportunity to be a co-author or comment on the research and/or findings.

LIBERAL, RADICAL, AND SOCIALIST ORIENTATIONS

Although there are many common threads among feminist perspectives and practice, there is no single perspective or practice that is used in social work. Instead, there are three main orientations: liberal, radical, and socialist (Nes and Iadicola, 1989; Saulnier, 1996). There are also challenges to these feminist orientations that have emerged from Black and minority ethnic women, disabled women (Hanmer and Statham, 1999), and Aboriginal women. Each orientation offers its own perspective on human nature, society, causes of inequality, and how relations between women and men need to change. The orientation adopted by a feminist social worker influences how a client's issues or problems are identified, assessed, and treated. There are differences across the orientations, but also some core principles common to all.

Liberal Orientation

Liberal feminists stress the need for women to have equal rights with men. They point to the inequality of opportunities available to women, and call on them to become more competitive and assertive in meeting their own needs. The aim is not to challenge the nature of society but to remove the barriers that stand in women's way. In the liberal feminist orientation, the public sphere is the focus rather than the private domain (Saulnier, 1996). Individual choice and self-determination are valued as the means for women to improve their lives and reach their full potential. Social work intervention is geared toward helping people with individual solutions, facilitating support groups (e.g., for assertiveness training), and advocating for women to gain equal access to programs and services. A social worker guided by liberal feminist ideals advocates or lobbies for change at the societal level where she sees obstacles to women's equal access to social services, employment, or education (Nes and Iadicola, 1989). Liberal feminists have been active mainly in childcare and pay equity issues (Dominelli, 1997).

Notably, according to Code (1993), liberal feminists acknowledge that if equal opportunity for women in society is actually achieved it will not be enough to create true equality. She maintains that existing rules, structures, and institutions in society, built primarily by men and according to their worldviews and interests, cannot be easily changed to accommodate women. Without these broader changes, women's social inequality will continue, supported by current legislation, employment practices, and welfare programs that inadequately consider many women's experiences, interests, and needs. Instead, injustice toward women will continue (Code, 1993; Saulnier, 1996, p. 20).

Radical Orientation

A practitioner applying a radical feminist approach views society, which is largely shaped and ruled by men (patriarchy), as the root cause of women's oppression. Drawing from radical feminist writings, Nye (1988) points out that these authors view the power of men over women as always having been present in human history. Acts such as rape and wife beating are seen as evidence of abusive male power. These have adverse effects on women's health and mental health (Humphreys, 2007). Relationships between women and men are affected by sex-role socialization; for example, boys generally learn more about how to compete and be assertive while girls learn more about developing relationships and caring about others. Institutions are seen as dominated by male-centred viewpoints, and decision-making responsibility is accorded to males over females in such areas as the legal system, politics, the economy, and so on.

As an illustration, consider how violence against women was once viewed. Spousal abuse was seen as an individual act that took place in the privacy of the family home. In effect, the notion "A man's home is his castle" was accepted. This meant that it was difficult for abused women to obtain help. Only recently has the issue come to be treated as a crime and raised to the public level (Hoff, 1990).

The power differential between women and men in many relationships and in most societies has consequences that, in the extreme, can lead to violence against women. Women who experience abuse in the home may not feel that it is unusual, especially if they have lived in violent homes throughout childhood (see, for example, *In Search of April Raintree* by Beatrice Culleton, 1992). In many cases, it may be difficult for a woman to leave a violent home if she has no economic resources, has nowhere else to go, or hopes that things will get better. Hearing from abused women about their particular experiences is necessary to understand how they view and cope with their lives. By doing so, social workers can better understand the effects of the abusive relationship on the woman client's self-esteem and her capacity to act in her own interest.

Radical feminists believe that biological reproduction and the institution of motherhood have been cast to reflect men's interests; women, therefore, need to resist male control and focus on "moving toward a full affirmation of woman-centred values. It is a voyage toward a separate and self-affirming women's culture" (Code, 1993, p. 42). The chosen methods of intervention are consciousness-raising for women and men—increasing their awareness of structural and social realities and the effects of these on their personal lives—self-help groups, and women-only group initiatives and activities (Nes and Iadicola, 1989). The aims of such methods are to raise awareness of how personal problems are rooted in the patriarchal nature of society, which affects us all, and to transform people and society itself to become more caring and nurturing, qualities seen as common among women (Saulnier, 1996).

To help women who have experienced oppression in our male-dominated society, alternative ways of living in communities with other women is encouraged. The role of a radical feminist social worker is to promote individual and political change with the goal of eliminating patriarchy and its oppressive effects on everyone (Nes and Iadicola, 1989).

A problem with radical feminism is its view that male dominance has always existed and is expressed in similar ways around the world. This assertion has been questioned by Black and Third World feminists, who disagree that there is a universal kind of patriarchy that affects all women in the same ways (Dominelli, 1997, p. 35). In fact, racism, rather than sexism, may be a more prevalent form of oppression experienced by women who are immigrants, refugees, and members of visible minorities (Baines, 1997; Bannerji, 1995). How these social structures intersect in each client's unique situation needs to be understood so that services are appropriate (Symington, 2004). Structural issues, besides sexism, affecting women are poorly addressed by radical feminism (Dominelli, 2002). One could also question the radical feminist notion that women possess particular female qualities—for example, caring and nurturing capacities—that men do not, at least not to the same degree. The extent to which women's and men's behaviour is determined by biology or social learning is not known.

Socialist Orientation

Socialist feminism has some features in common with a radical feminist perspective. However, it focuses on an analysis of the forms of work done by women and men, and it recognizes that capitalism oppresses both sexes (Dominelli, 1997). Men, however, are seen to gain from women's labour in the home through the relegation of childcare, household chores, and other service work to women. This household labour is not paid for, nor is it included in national calculations of the gross domestic product (Waring, 1996). At the same time, women are treated as a reserve pool of labour available at lower wages for part-time employment that offers few employment benefits (Saulnier, 1996). Even when women are employed full-time in the labour force (productive work), they are still expected to take primary responsibility for maintaining households and children (reproductive work). There is a need to compensate caring work in the household, whether the care is provided to children and/or other family members, so that women outside the wage work system are also seen as economically productive.

Socialist feminists acknowledge that the effects of oppression based on sex and class reduce the choices people have about how they can solve problems and live their lives. Some of the contradictions in capitalist economic systems (e.g., accepting some level of unemployment in order to guarantee a reserve supply of workers) are seen as contributing to individual and family problems, especially when a family member is unemployed (Nes and Iadicola, 1989). Socialist feminists emphasize the use of consciousness-raising activities and coalition building to eradicate all forms of oppression and injustice in society. Dominelli (2002) explains that some men have used a pro-feminist analysis to create facilities for men. These kinds of facilities may be helpful to groups of men who wish to examine and counter abusive behaviours they have used, discuss their concerns about child rearing, and many other topics.

Both the radical and socialist views focus social work intervention on structural and institutional change over individual change, although problems of an individual nature are not ignored. In this sense, feminist social work practice shares commonalities with structural social work. Stressing that the personal is also political and that individual problems and situations are connected to or created by societal structures and institutions are common themes. Another feature that runs across feminist and structural approaches is the need to do more than work with individual clients. Social workers can help by bringing women together, promoting community and collective action (Van Den Bergh and Cooper, 1986) and woman-centred community services (Hanmer and Statham, 1999, pp. 153–57).

Illustration of Differences in Orientation

To illustrate the differences in orientation, suppose a social worker is employed in a women's centre in a middle-class neighbourhood. Semareh, a client, approaches the worker and relates how she has worked in a large, nonunionized company for more than 15 years as a junior accountant. At any one time, the company employs 30 to 40 people in similar positions. For the past several years, Semareh had been raising two children, liked her job, and was content not to seek advancement to senior levels.

A few years ago, Semareh found out that her male colleagues who were doing exactly the same job were consistently paid higher wages than she was. When Semareh first noticed this differential, she did not think too much of it. Then she began to see younger, more recently hired, men being paid substantially more. Semareh did not want to make waves and possibly jeopardize her job. However, a week ago she got up enough nerve to approach her supervisor about the discrepancies and was told that the new men were hired under a different job title and at the "going rate" for new accountants. The company could not afford to pay anyone else more. Semareh was angry—very angry! She had worked there for 15 years, was a highly competent and skilled worker, and for 15 years had been rewarded with low pay. Now she asks the social worker what she should do.

Probably, feminist workers of any orientation would attempt to at least help Semareh find ways to establish pay equity. They would attempt to support her views and feelings, likely through validation. Certainly they would help her define alternative courses of action and then select from them.

Semareh would learn from the social worker that what the company was doing was illegal. With support from the social worker, she could engage a lawyer to begin legal action against the employer. This is an individual-focused problem-solving approach cast in a liberal feminist perspective. The liberal feminist approach would also be to help Semareh break down the barriers that prevent fair wages. Her individual situation could be brought to the attention of a lawyer and conflict resolution with the company might be sought. Although more likely from a radical or socialist feminist perspective, the social worker might even explore the possibility of helping Semareh take the first steps toward organizing other women workers in the company and elsewhere who have been similarly treated. This, of course, would entail risk for Semareh. However, if pay equity is achieved, a liberal feminist would consider her work completed.

Both a socialist and a radical feminist would be more likely to advocate further action. They would view Semareh's situation not only as discrimination by the company but also as a reflection of the values of society, including workplaces, about the value of women workers. The socialist feminist would emphasize the problems with capitalism and acknowledge how capitalism uses women as cheap sources of labour. Unionization, with a focus on ensuring women's representation and rights, and other public action would be potential strategies. The radical feminist would tend to see the problem as a reflection of male social domination and patriarchy. She might attempt to help by involving Semareh in a women's consciousness-raising group to explore the ways that patriarchy affects women in the workplace and to collectively advocate and rally for justice for women employees.

Socialist feminist workers might set up a program of class advocacy in the women's centre to advocate on behalf of groups of women who experience pay inequity and are not aware of their legal right to equal pay for work of equal value. Or they may begin some other form of social action, such as taking steps to assert women workers' rights in the company or the accounting profession and demanding that women be better supported to participate in workplace hiring decisions. Semareh might want to hear from other women in her line of work to see whether they too have experienced discrimination in the form of lower pay. Socialist feminists might work to enable Semareh to identify and organize other women workers to take action against companies where women accounting staff face direct or indirect discrimination. Or they could consider the issue from a broader perspective and organize protests to ensure women workers' rights and involve women workers from all walks of life.

A radical feminist orientation might involve advocating for fair pay on behalf of Semareh and other female employees whose jobs have been reclassified, but underlying any social work practice strategy would be the idea that the sexist society and all its institutions need to be transformed to eliminate male domination and hierarchies. This is clearly a fundamental and long-term goal. Radical feminist social work would then focus on raising consciousness and supporting women through creating alternative, female-organized groups and institutions to counter the existing male-dominated institutions (Dominelli, 2002, 2006; Nes and Iadicola, 1989). Unfortunately, this may not be a suitable personal solution for Semareh.

The socialist feminist might use coalition building as a strategy to change the workplace practices that foster pay inequity. However, both a socialist and a radical social worker would address and attempt to change the unjust policies and practices that allow pay inequity between women and men to occur. This strategy would involve fundamental and long-term change efforts, requiring significant resources and commitment to sustain them.

DIVERGENT MEANINGS AND SIGNIFICANCE OF FEMINISM

Feminist models that are based on the experiences of white, upper- or middle-class women have been countered by writers who stress that sexism and racism, or other structures, can work together to oppress women (Anthias and Yuval-Davis, 1992; Baines, 2007). Writers speaking about women of Asian background (e.g., Bannerji, 1995; George and Ramkissoon, 1998; Ng, 1993) also provide compelling arguments against universalizing women's social subordination. The effects of race and class, difficult and often significant parts of life experience, are reflected in feminist social work (e.g., Baines, 2004; Guttiérez, 1991). Studies that focus on the experiences and views of immigrant women help to enrich social work literature, bringing out the effects of "interlocking relationships between race-ethnicity, class and gender" (George and Ramkissoon, 1998, p. 103). Language and other barriers exist for immigrant and refugee women in seeking help for problems related to unemployment, stress, housing, health care, and physical abuse. Such barriers may also keep them away from social workers. Therefore, it is especially important to recognize that simply approaching a social worker may be a very difficult and major step for some women. The worker who has some understanding of ethnoculturally competent practice and settlement issues of newcomers may be better prepared to provide help (George and Ramkissoon, 1998, p. 116). Further, alternative ways of responding to difficulties by women within cultural communities need to be explored because they add much to social workers' knowledge about the range of interventions useful in a situation (Migliardi, Blum, and Heinonen, 2004). The effects of race, ethnocultural identity, and class, as daily features of many women's lives, might be seen not as individual problems but as issues needing wider attention.

Aboriginal women have questioned how the term "feminism" fits their lives. Some believe that feminism does not fit with Aboriginal women's vision of a society in which women's place is at the centre of the community, as it was in the past (Osennontion and Skonaganleh:rá, 1989). They point out that the feminist movement was primarily developed by white women to respond to their realities and needs, excluding the voices and ideas of those women whose lives had been more significantly affected by other forms of oppression. The North American feminist movement has been criticized for not considering the adverse effects of a history of racism and European colonization on Aboriginal women (Aboriginal Women's Roundtable on Gender Equality, 2000; Monture-Angus, 1993). Lucille Bruce (1998) describes how Aboriginal women leaving abusive relationships in isolated communities where English is not widely spoken and Native tradition and culture are practised face numerous barriers to getting help. Unless culturally sensitive and appropriate assistance is available and accessible, Aboriginal women trying to leave abusive situations will not find the help they need. Aboriginal women social workers, like social workers from other backgrounds, differ in their acceptance and use of feminist social work practice principles.

Women who live in rural areas, particularly on farms, have not been given adequate consideration in social policies that often affect them differently from urban women. For example, in the calculation of women's contributions to family farms, women often do not receive their fair share of income or benefits (Waring, 1996). The image of a male farmer sitting astride his tractor takes centre stage, hiding the female partner in "women's work," such as raising the chickens and tending the family garden. Lack of access to childcare, women's shelters, counselling services, and other help is often a problem. In addition, the possibility of taking part in local and higher-level policy processes and decision making can be an obstacle for rural women with primary child- or elder-care responsibilities.

Women with disabilities have brought attention to the particular challenges of living in a society that discriminates against females and those who have a disability. The different realities of women with disabilities, which may involve greater potential for being poor, abused, or receiving insensitive treatment by health care practitioners, and negative social attitudes about physical or developmental differences, have only recently been described (Asch and Fine, 1988; Barile, 2003). Wendell (1993) points to the need for a feminist theory of disability that acknowledges diversity among women: "[W]e will need to know how experiences of disability and the social oppression of the disabled interact with sexism, racism and class oppression" (p. 225). The issues facing women living with disabilities have not been adequately integrated into feminism, and there is room for further work. For their voices to be central, research studies that will shed light on the experiences and views of women with disabilities need to involve study participants as visible partners who design research questions and methods, analyze data, and interpret findings.

According to Diane Driedger (1993), women who have disabilities face obstacles in participating with men in groups for people with disabilities and in women's organizations. Driedger describes how she was unable to attend meetings of well-known Canadian women's groups due to the lack of accessibility. She was told that there were stairs to climb, an impossibility for a person in a wheelchair. To counter these barriers, women with disabilities formed their own organization, the DisAbled Women's Network (DAWN) (Driedger, 1993). There are, of course, variations among women with disabilities in terms of the type of disability and how it shapes quality of life, the availability and success of accommodations such as adaptive technology, and other features of daily life, including income and employment, access to a supportive social network, and satisfactory care provision. Women living with disabilities have formed groups to advocate for themselves and to raise awareness of the effects of various forms of oppression in their lives. The need to break stereotypes and promote understanding of women with many kinds of disabilities is a central concern (Asch and Fine, 1988; Williams, 1992; Wendell, 1993). Cuts to funding in 2007 for women's organizations, including those which conduct research and raise awareness about issues affecting women with disabilities, are expected to seriously challenge such groups to continue their work (see National Association of Women and Law, 2007).

With increased interest in women's aging, and the impact of chronic and disabling conditions, more attention will likely be given to disability as a feminist issue.

> Most of us will live part of our lives with bodies that hurt, that move with difficulty or not at all, that deprive us of activities we once took for granted or that others take for granted, bodies that make daily life a physical struggle. ... Encouraging everyone to acknowledge, accommodate and identify with a range of physical conditions is the road to self-acceptance as well as the road to liberating those who are disabled now. (Wendell, 1993, p. 227)

The concerns of lesbian women are beginning to emerge in social work (see, for example, the *Journal of Gay & Lesbian Social Services*). The heterosexist basis of social policy and social work practice can be seen, for example, in assumptions about the composition of families, the gender of parents, health care directives, pensions, and the capacity of lesbian couples to raise children. Difficulties in gaining acceptance from parents and other family members who may not recognize the legitimacy of same-sex co-parents can create problems in families (Epstein, 1993, p. 21). Issues affecting lesbians as they age, such as care preferences in old age and advanced directives (instructions for care in case of imminent death), are also of concern (Healey, 1994; Hughes, 2007). When a lesbian is in need of a personal care home due to increasing frailness, her partner can advocate on her behalf to ensure that a bed at the desired facility is secured. In the event of an accident or serious illness, a lesbian woman's partner can make health care staff aware of the patient's wishes regarding efforts to sustain her life artificially.

As social work clients, lesbians no doubt receive a great deal of inappropriate help, whether or not practitioners know about the women's orientation. As Brown (1992) states, "In practice, social agencies tend to deal with lesbians in one of two ways. Either the woman's specific needs as a lesbian remain unrecognized and ignored, or her lesbianism becomes the central preoccupation, the prism through which her every word and action is interpreted" (p. 201). The kind of help that responds to the specific needs of an individual is required. It must not focus solely on sexual orientation, because there is a danger that this will be accompanied by intervention based on assumptions and prejudice. A social work response that includes a broader and richer understanding of women's—including lesbian women's—health, parenting, individual life transitions, and family life cycle issues would be most helpful (Brown, 1992, p. 205).

As women age, the issues they face often involve the legacy of discrimination experienced in earlier years. Poor pension benefits, for example, are a direct result of low pay, inadequate workplace policies for women employees, part-time employment benefit limitations, and lack of pension programs for women who perform unpaid work at home (Barnwell, 2006). Women, who tend to live longer than men, also face fewer state supports in health care and social services due to the continuing trend to cut costs and limit services (Cox, 1998). Poor housing and health care and limited access to transportation may await many. Until recently, most feminist writing made little mention of older women or the issues that affect and interest them. Feminist social work literature also reflected this gap, focusing instead on women prior to mid-life (Hughes and Mtezuka, 1992). The growing numbers of people living to an advanced age means that more attention now needs to be given to protecting health and well-being and to ensuring that support is available to all of us as we age.

Various forms of oppression, such as those based on sex, disability, sexual orientation, age, ethnoculture, and class, can operate at the same time and intersect at different times and in different places (Bishop, 2002). Think of how being an immigrant and an older woman with a disability, for example, might present barriers in seeking housing and social services. Of course, it cannot be assumed that being oppressed means that women are always victims. It is evident that when difficult situations arise, women use whatever resources they have to deal with them. A feminist social work approach that attempts to understand these intersections and their effects is needed. So too is an approach that builds on individual and collective capacity and resilience. Such developments hold the promise of a richer, more inclusive feminist approach to social work.

APPLYING FEMINIST PRINCIPLES IN PRACTICE

Feminist social work practice, based on a core of principles, is concerned with eliminating domination, subordination, exploitation, and oppression of women. In working with women, a belief in their innate health and ability to "identify and mobilize inherent individual and collective capacities for healing, growth, and personal/political transformation" (Bricker-Jenkins, 1991, p. 277) is important. Such an approach would also be applied in feminist social work with men, especially to help them gain awareness of the effects of constraining gender role ideals on men and women. Women's and men's strengths are to be acknowledged, applied, and built on in a social work relationship that aims to reduce the difference in power between clients and social workers. Some ways that feminist social workers establish more egalitarian relationships with clients include discussing with them the practice approach and methods, sharing client records when possible, promoting non-hierarchical relationships, building connections among women, encouraging women's overall development, and self-disclosing in appropriate ways (Russell, 1989; Van Den Bergh and Cooper, 1986).

Situations can arise in which it may be inappropriate to apply some feminist methods. For example, you would likely not choose to use consciousness-raising about women's oppression as a method with a woman who is in deep mourning over the sudden death of her husband. The most important intervention in this situation is listening to and supporting the woman in her grief, and validating her experiences and feelings. Social workers must exercise judgment to select the practice methods that best suit the situation and time. This is true for any social work model or approach.

Validation

Practice principles help to anchor feminist social work with clients and provide a framework to guide activities. Bricker-Jenkins (1991) refers to these as methods for personal and political transformation, stating that women need validation of their experiences to feel that they have been believed and heard. This validation enables women to make sense of what has happened to them and tell about it in their own way. For example, reflect on the experience of an Aboriginal woman who was sent to an Indian residential school in childhood:

> The effects of children being forced into residential/mission schools is still being felt today. Generations of aboriginal people had their lives and culture disrupted, which resulted in a people growing up with no parents, no home life, no language of their own and not much in the way of love, comfort or security. These displaced children were unable to grow, unable to parent. (CCSD and NWAC, 1991, p. 2)

No one except a woman who has experienced it can really know what it was like to have lived and been educated in a residential school. The memory and perception of the experience may change over time, but it still needs to be understood as coming from the individual's unique experience. The significance of these events becomes more clear to the client as she tells her story to the social worker. The process of listening and validating to make sense of what happened may be far more important than any actions taken to resolve a specific problem. As Saleebey (1997a) writes, "[O]ur voices may have to be quieted so that we can give voice to our clients" (p. 10).

Clients need to be seen as resilient and possessing the capacity to make changes in their lives. Enabling them to give voice to their own experiences and views can begin the process of consciousness-raising for growth and healing. Validation honours clients' stories of their life experiences and is especially helpful when clients disclose traumatic experiences such as abuse. Feminist group work can help women face what happened to them and reconstruct their experience and their lives differently (Butler and Wintram, 1991). Further, when a group shifts "from individualist explanations to social, structural, and political analyses, they find that personal as well as collective empowerment ensues" (Naples with Clark, 1996, p. 179).

Consciousness-Raising

Social analysis, according to Russell (1989), involves making connections between the personal and the political and exploring how individual distress or problems have roots in unequal access to the resources that improve people's quality of life in society (p. 73). This process of analysis can also take place through consciousness-raising activities. For example, a woman trying to raise three children alone may experience personal feelings of failure and be given a prescription for antidepressants. Her situation is not an uncommon one. Could it be rooted in the current expectations that society has of women as mothers? Perhaps knowing that public assistance is deliberately kept low, that childcare is expensive and often inadequate, and that good jobs are scarce might help in explaining how this woman's individual situation is not of her own making. An acknowledgment that the personal is political—that individual failings or problems have social causes and connections—can help to free her from feeling personal blame. Of course, such acknowledgment is not enough. Further action is needed to address and improve the situation. What would you suggest that might help?

Consider the situation of a woman living with a physical disability who faces certain barriers in trying to secure a job. She may feel distress and frustration and be referred to a social worker to help her deal with her feelings, but it is also evident that she lives in a society where there are prejudices against people with disabilities, and many workplaces are not accessible or accommodating. The social worker would want to know about the individual woman's feelings and experiences to help her strengthen her self-esteem and confidence to approach potential employers. Although this might be helpful, it would also be necessary to offer the client a way to understand the bigger picture, to see that she is not to blame for her situation. The woman living with a disability needs to know that the social and physical environments are disabling due to obstacles that are yet to be dismantled. By joining with others who face or have faced similar problems in trying to live independently, she might feel more empowered personally. In a group, she can work collectively with others in identifying ways to eliminate social and physical workplace barriers that block women with disabilities from finding employment. While the example illustrates principles of the feminist perspective, the focus, as in the strengths approach (see Chapter 11), is on helping the client to use her own resources and abilities. Like the structural approach (see Chapter 14), the intervention includes addressing structural problems, the broader social barriers that hinder women with disabilities in meeting needs that are required for a good quality of life.

The views of the client and social worker may be far apart with regard to the impact of gender on their circumstances and life chances. Perspectives can be shared, however, for mutual learning. It is not the job of the feminist social worker to change clients' thinking to conform to feminist principles when these are not accepted by clients, or when it is inappropriate in a situation. Feminist social workers interpret and use feminist principles in helping clients to work toward the goals they have set. This does not mean that only by convincing a woman that she has been socially oppressed because she is female will there be any chance that she can deal with her situation or problems. Clients must be free to choose their own perspective and make their own decisions, not forced to adopt those of the social worker.

If a feminist social worker cannot work with a client whose views she sees as an obstacle to change, it would be best to locate another social worker with a different practice orientation for the client.

Transformative Action

Moving from consciousness-raising to action that is transformative beyond the individual level is a key concern in feminist social work (Bricker-Jenkins, 1991, Levine, 1989). As an example of transformative action, women who have experienced discrimination in pay due to their gender may move from an individual counselling situation to work together as a group where they can publicly demand compensation. As a result of their actions, it will be more difficult for employers to pay women less than men for the same type of work. Again, believing that the personal is political is a central principle in feminist social work; there is a recognition that individual problems are often connected to broader social structures and the limitations these impose (Van Den Bergh and Cooper, 1986).

Affirmation

Russell (1989) includes as a principle of feminist social work practice the affirmation of the worth of traditionally female characteristics and work. This affirmation is necessary in countering past discrediting of women and the work women have traditionally carried out in caring for children, cooking, and doing other domestic tasks and the perspective that household work is not important work. This, as in the strengths approach, also means that a woman's strengths and resilience in difficult situations need to be recognized (Saleebey, 1997b).

One effect of oppression is that those who experience it may internalize beliefs that contribute to maintaining the oppression. For example, a woman who is repeatedly told by an abusive partner that she cannot perform adequately in any job may soon come to believe it and to doubt herself. Self-esteem and confidence are often affected, and self-determination is undermined when women are undervalued. Thus, feminist practice includes affirming the worth of the individual in the context of the larger society.

Development of the Whole Person

The need to ensure that basic needs such as food, safety, and security are taken care of is highlighted in feminist social work practice (Bricker-Jenkins, 1991), as in all social work practice. Abraham Maslow's (1970) hierarchy of needs, illustrating that basic survival needs must be addressed before higher-level needs, directs the social worker to make fulfilling basic needs the first priority. A client who has not had a meal in two days needs to be nourished, and a client who fears that her partner will kill her needs to feel safe before any other work can begin.

Encouraging total development, including personal growth and exploring and integrating new behaviours that are free of gender stereotypes (Russell, 1989, p. 75), can also enhance feminist practice. This might occur when a male client chooses to leave a highly paid professional job to concentrate on childcare. More generally, promoting caring and respectful relations that support an environment that allows this kind of personal change is a feature of feminist social work. The man who makes the choice to stay at home with his children while his partner works should be supported in his aims. Loosening the bonds of rigid gender expectations helps to create flexible and more humane social environments.

In Chapter 7, the situation of Lola, an immigrant from a South American city, was described. Below we discuss a similar situation, that of Belita, someone Lola came to know through taking the course on family violence. We use Belita's situation to illustrate how feminist principles apply to a group situation, addressing partner abuse and how Belita's life was changed as a result of her participation in the course.

Case Example

Belita ▼

Belita, a 43-year-old woman who had emigrated two years ago to join her husband in Canada, was six months pregnant. She had a few female friends who had left the same South American country some years ago due to civil war. Belita was fearful, distressed, and ashamed to let these friends know that her husband had been beating her regularly. Sometimes it happened after a night spent drinking with his friends. At other times, it occurred because he was unhappy with her cooking or cleaning. She worried about what would happen when the baby came.

Belita was taking an English as a Second Language course at a local community centre. There were many other immigrant women and men in the classes and she enjoyed her time with them and looked forward to the day she could speak, read, and write well enough in English to be a travel agent. She had been a travel agent for five years before she came to Canada. Other class members provided her with baby clothes and information about hospital birthing and breastfeeding. Some offered to babysit when she needed respite time. In the class, a special training program was to be given to all women. These would be in separate classes and in English. The course instructor said that it would help develop their English vocabulary and provide some important information to them. There would be 10 classes given on violence in the family, with guest speakers, videos, and discussions. Belita was very curious about what would be presented, but also did not want people to know what was happening to her. She hoped that she could learn from the sessions.

In the family violence sessions, Belita learned that she was not alone. Many women in the class had similar experiences, even those who had lived in Canada longer. Some of them talked about how their in-laws in Canada abused them verbally or forced them to work in their businesses. Others told about brothers or partners who physically and psychologically abused them, sometimes with such force that they had to go to a walk-in clinic or emergency department. During all these incidents, the women claimed they had fallen or had an accident. They were terrified of speaking up about what had really happened, because most thought they would be deported.

Belita was profoundly affected by what she learned in the sessions. She cried, told her story, and was comforted and supported by the women in the class. She learned about her rights, about laws, about the cycle of violence, and about immigration policy. Belita found the courage to tell her woman friends about the abuse, now that she knew there was help in the community for her. Her friends, at first hesitant to believe her, admitted that they had heard about what her husband had done from their own partners. Theirs was a tight-knit community, one where men and women had many separate social activities.

After the next beating, Belita ran from the house and went to stay with a woman she had met in the course. One of the instructors also provided information about resources and helped Belita to lay charges. Although it was difficult, Belita's move had opened up new opportunities to her. She realized, importantly, that she was not alone, that she had help and support from friends, and that she could help others in similar situations too.

The case situation above demonstrates feminist principles in a group setting. Validation of Belita's experience by other women helped her to feel acknowledged, believed, and heard. The affirmation that she received helped her feel supported and valued. Consciousness-raising helped Belita learn that the violence was not her fault and that she had a right to be safe in her home. She also understood how the cycle of violence had been a factor in her situation. From consciousness-raising, Belita was determined to use her new learning to educate and help other women in her cultural community who were being abused. This resulted in transformative action, moving Belita to take action for change. During her time in the course, Belita felt that she developed as a person in other ways, not just in terms of the content she learned. She experienced a sense of empowerment, agency, self-fulfillment, and accomplishment as a result.

The Role of Power

Power in feminism is seen as a flexible resource that enables people's empowerment, and it can be extended and shared. The focus is on power within a person and power in collaborative relations with others rather than on power over people (Bishop, 2002). This concept challenges the definition of power as a purposeful method or outcome of domination and control. The need to give value to process, not only to product or result, is important in feminist social work (Van Den Bergh and Cooper, 1986). How people conduct their work and build relationships with others requires just as much attention as the result of their efforts. This idea fits well with social work in general, where there is a focus on building caring, respectful relationships with clients as a necessary part of practice.

Working with Men

Feminist social work is not only for women (Bricker-Jenkins and Hooyman, 1983)—men, families, groups, and communities can also be helped by an application of these principles. Clearly, a central idea in feminist social work is that the effects of male privilege and female subordination must be critically examined and challenged. Such analyses necessarily involve both the client and the social worker. A client shares her or his perspective, meaning, and understanding with the worker, and the worker in turn offers her or his view of the situation. Using good communication skills, the social worker presents information and ideas with care and concern for the client's well-being, paying attention to the process in the relationship and moving toward specific goals. These goals are established as much as possible through mutual discussion and consensus. A social worker cannot impose her or his own ideas on the client, but can explore these with him or her.

Whether men can or should refer to themselves as feminist or pro-feminist has also been a subject of discussion (Schact and Ewing, 1997). Many women who are feminist social workers prefer that men who ascribe to feminist ideals and apply feminist principles in their work use the term *pro-feminist*, reserving feminist practice for women alone (Valentich, 1986). In this way, men are identified as supporters of feminism at a time when feminist social work practice still needs to be developed further by women, who bring to it their gender-specific practice experience and knowledge. Mary Valentich (1986) has pointed out that there is clearly a need in social work for men who practise using feminist approaches. In working with men who abuse women, or even with women who are lone parents, for example, male practitioners will find that feminism can offer valuable resources. There are, however, some circumstances in which a male social worker, pro-feminist or not, may be unacceptable. Likely many women clients who have survived sexual abuse or rape by male perpetrators wish to work with a female practitioner. Thus almost all—if not all—workers in women's shelters and rape crisis centres are women.

Early family therapy models have been criticized for their assumptions about families and ideas about what a family ought to be, ignoring the many forms and variations that exist. Feminists have observed the inequality between men and women in families, seeing how idealized family roles trap women. The systems-based explanations of families as interacting parts divert attention away from power differences and their effects on male and female relationships in families (Laird, 1995), effectively minimizing responsibility in situations where a woman is abused, and blaming mothers when children exhibit problems (Hare-Mustin, 1978). Feminist family therapy, drawing on core principles of feminist practice, can be used in work with families to promote egalitarian gender relations and problem solving that avoids blaming women and assuming acceptance of traditional gender roles and tasks.

Recognizing Diversity

The diversity among women is highlighted in current feminist writing thanks to critiques by women who questioned why their lives were not reflected in earlier feminist works. In practice, women's unique histories, including the strengths they have developed and drawn upon in their lives, need to be "discovered and engaged by practitioners" (Bricker-Jenkins, 1991, p. 283). This means beginning where each woman is and assisting her in identifying where she wants to be and how she might get there.

CHAPTER SUMMARY

This chapter has discussed why the majority of clients and social workers are women, not only today, but also from the early days of social work.

Feminist social work focuses on critically evaluating the individual and collective choices that shape women's lives. It also seeks to challenge barriers that block women and others who are oppressed from realizing their full potential (Bricker-Jenkins, 1991, p. 285). Emphasizing strengths, rather than focusing on weakness or pathology, is important when working with clients. These features are not unique to feminist social work; the strengths perspective in social work (Saleebey, 1992, 1997b), for example, also stresses client strengths as resources for dealing with current problems. A feminist social worker needs to be prepared to reflect on her practice, creating safe spaces and supportive environments for clients. She is also required to provide women with resources that will help them and challenge sexist policies and practices in her workplace (Hanmer and Statham, 1999). The fact that feminist social work centres on women's experiences and realities, linking the personal to the political, makes this approach relevant and necessary for social work and is also consistent with the structural approach.

The various forms of feminism shape ideas about the causes of women's problems, what needs to be done about them, and what practice methods might be used. Although the major orientations in feminist social work are liberal, radical, and socialist, there are a number of other views about the place of feminism and its relevance for particular groups of women. Essentially, it has been argued that feminism needs to acknowledge and include diverse groups of women, such as older women, Aboriginal women, women with disabilities, lesbians, and women from non-dominant ethnocultural groups. The impact of different, intersecting forms of oppression, not only those based on gender, also needs to be understood.

Feminist principles in social work practice include valuing client strengths and resilience; emphasizing process, even over outcome; reducing power differences and sharing knowledge for empowerment; recognizing that the personal is political; creating nurturing and caring environments; valuing diversity; and using consciousness-raising for personal and collective empowerment (Bricker-Jenkins, 1991; Russell, 1989; Van Den Bergh and Cooper, 1986). These principles echo some similar ideas in the strengths (Chapter 11) and structural (Chapter 14) approaches.

In choosing to practise according to feminist principles, a social worker may be challenging conventional practice but, depending on the situation, the way that a worker applies feminist principles may fit well with generalist practice, for example, in a group for women care providers. Problem solving may also be appropriate at some point in the intervention when the social worker and client agree to it and collaborate as equals during the process. The organizations in which social workers are employed have their own culture, which may present challenges for feminist practice (Hooyman, 1991). There may be disagreements between social workers and their colleagues or employers, for example. There are, of course, many variations in how feminist principles and practice methods are applied. Depending on the workplace environment and culture, the degree of support for feminist social work will vary. This does not necessarily mean that social work agencies and organizations discourage practice that uses feminist principles. Even when they do, there may be room for change.

Structural Social Work and Social Change

To describe the structural approach and demonstrate how structural social work can effectively be used in everyday direct social work practice to effect social change.

This Chapter ▼

- connects structural social work with radical social work and anti-oppressive social work
- presents a social work approach that directly confronts all forms of discrimination, oppression, repression, and subjugation
- stresses the need for reflection and reflexivity in social work
- identifies and describes some of the practice applications of structural social work
- describes and discusses the importance of collective action
- shows that structural social work, unlike person-in-the-environment approaches, centres on the environment itself
- connects social work practice with the socioeconomic and political environments
- identifies and articulates a number of useful roles in structural social work
- demonstrates how a structural analysis and intervention can be used in everyday practice

FOUNDATIONS OF STRUCTURAL SOCIAL WORK

Structural social work has its roots in a radical perspective of practice. *Radical social work* focuses heavily on a *conflict perspective* and analysis of the existing social order. The worldview of radical social workers has been based on eliminating injustice and inequality, redistributing economic resources, analyzing power, and working toward a society that is based on cooperation and sharing (Burghardt, 1986, pp. 590–617; Payne, 2005, pp. 227–50). This approach to social work focuses on a socialist analysis of state control and oppression, and advocates changing the existing social order and related structures that oppress people. Traditional social work is seen as a form of social control that maintains social problems. Classism, imperialism, patriarchy, racism, ageism, sexism, heterosexism, and ableism are seen as oppressive forces (Davis, 1991; Mullaly, 2007, Chapter 10). Radical social work has also been characterized by its flexibility and openness in responding to the demands and issues of various groups that experience discrimination and oppression (Langan and Lee, 1989). Mullaly's newer work (2007), in addition to deeper analysis of social structures and society, includes a strong focus on anti-oppressive social work. Iris Marion Young (1990) offers an excellent analysis of oppression in society and how it cuts a wide swath across society, privileging a few while keeping most others disadvantaged. Mullaly's writing (1997, 2007) draws from her idea that it is not enough to emphasize a better distribution of wealth and other resources in society because the roots of injustice penetrate deeper and wider. Power, influence, rights and entitlements need also to be examined and redistributed.

Connection between Radical and Structural Social Work

Radical social work theory, in the past, has not offered much to frontline practitioners working with clients (Mullaly, 1997, 2007). Structural social work, a perspective articulated in Canada by Moreau (1979) and later championed by Mullaly, offers a direct practice application of radical social work that leads to social change.

There are, however, other examples of attempts to link radical thinking to practice. Janis Fook, in her book *Radical Casework: A Theory of Practice* (1993), provides examples comparing how client situations are approached from conventional and radical social work orientations. Her book illustrates how radical casework is essentially good social work practice. Colleen Lundy (2004), likewise highlights day-to-day social work practice using a structural approach. She demonstrates how an analysis and understanding of the effects of social structures on people who come to be our clients gives shape to a reflexive, ethical, and just social work practice. Reflexive practice is discussed and defined in a later section of this chapter. A website developed by Carolyn Campbell (2003) at Dalhousie University states that anti-oppressive practice is "generally understood as an umbrella term that encompasses a variety of practice approaches including, but not limited to, radical, structural, feminist, anti-racist, critical, and liberatory frameworks" and is inclusive of a number of other approaches in social work practice. These other approaches also fit well with structural social work as it is currently conceptualized (e.g., Lundy, 2004; Mullaly, 2007) because they involve a critical analysis of social structures; social change in which injustice, inequality, domination, and oppression are challenged and confronted; and the aim of a reflexive, caring, and ethical social work practice with individuals, groups, and communities.

Social workers daily face the difficulties of people who are poor, ill, lonely, in conflict with the law, or otherwise troubled. Bailey and Brake (1980) said, "social workers, *unlike other workers,* confront daily, as their job, the victims of an economic and political structure that creates poverty and humiliation" (p. 8). This statement remains true today.

Structural social work tends to focus on applications at the level of front-line practice. It is not only concerned with the oppressive features of social structures, but also responds to those who are oppressed. This chapter articulates ways to understand and apply structural social work.

Anti-Oppressive Social Work

In Chapter 7, we introduced oppression and anti-oppressive practice. We view anti-oppressive social work, not as an established approach with a unique base of theory and methods, but as a way of working with people that values people's differences, hears and validates their experiences, works for social justice with and for people who have been socially excluded, gives voice to those who have had few chances to be heard, and has as its goal ***social transformation,*** where a fair distribution of social, political and material equality can be realized.

According to Mullaly (2002), oppression is dynamic, affecting differently social relationships between individuals and groups, at different times and in different situations. As evident in the story of Tom (Chapter 6), a boy who experienced labelling and discrimination, oppression may also be internalized by those who feel its effects. It is not simply a matter of one group oppressing another. Also, people or groups who see themselves as oppressed often attempt to fight against oppressive practices by taking action (e.g., letter writing, lobbying politicians, organizing marches, and performing street theatre). Their dissatisfaction may also take destructive forms toward themselves or others, for example, violence or self-harm. As discussed in Chapter 7, social work seeks ways to eradicate discrimination, subjugation, and oppression of individuals and groups. Anti-oppressive social work practice counters the effects of these processes through intervention at individual, group, and community levels, recognizing that diverse forms of oppression have always existed and continue to exist in our society.

Structural features in society may be experienced negatively, contributing to or creating problems for people. Discrimination and oppression adversely affect many people's lives. Consider a young boy who is often teased by his classmates because he has a hearing impairment, or a Muslim woman whose style of dress is met with disdain at work. Bishop (2002) explains that there are many forms of oppression besides that related to socioeconomic class. Racism, sexism, and heterosexism, as well as discrimination due to disability, national origin, religion, age, and others, can oppress people whether they are rich, middle class, or poor. Discrimination cuts across classes, but people who have more money and other resources are better able to protect themselves from it or to confront it directly. With reference to disability, for example, Bishop (2002) states,

> You will find more people with disabilities the lower you go in the class strata, because discrimination based on disability affects the education and employment opportunities of people with disabilities. Also, a disability limits the life of a person in a lower class more than it does someone who has wealth and power. (p. 83)

From the quotation above, it is possible to understand that being poor and living with a disability means fewer opportunities to succeed in education or work. The accommodations that help to reduce barriers (e.g., computer technology, mobility devices, and other supports) can be costly to purchase or are subject to long waiting periods if subsidized or provided free.

Anti-oppressive social work should form a backdrop or frame for all of social work. In our view, it is primarily an ideology, not a model of practice. Social workers, as part of good practice, need to help clients handle oppression they have experienced and, in Mullaly's (2002) view, challenge personal, cultural, and structural issues that promote, cause, and maintain oppression. Anti-oppressive social work is particularly congruent with structural social work because both acknowledge and work to counter oppression based on class, race, sex, physical ability, sexual orientation, age, and others.

It is possible to integrate an anti-oppressive framework into generalist practice by bringing to one's work a critical analysis that involves questioning, being open to unpopular explanations, and adopting a reflexive stance. Through these methods, a social worker can work toward justice and fairness for all. If we aim to practise in anti-oppressive ways, we need to be prepared to be mindful of the need to take action when we encounter discrimination or domination of people we work with, whether they are colleagues or clients. One way we can do this is by challenging racist or sexist comments and practices, whether these stem from individual interaction, such as racial slurs made in a high school toward an immigrant student, or practices in organizations–for example, when an organization gives the least desirable work to people who are from visible minority groups and saves the better jobs for those who are of from white and from dominant Anglo-Saxon backgrounds.

In order to challenge oppression and to practise from an anti-oppressive framework, it is not enough to understand oppression and what it means theoretically (in one's head). It is necessary to deeply appreciate, comprehend, and empathize with the depth of hurt that comes from being discriminated against, discounted, dominated, or excluded by society and to be conscious of its effects on those we work with. Many readers will have experiences in which they have felt oppressed and can recall their reactions. Some have witnessed the oppression of others and felt the pain of oppression experienced by our clients. These kinds of experiences can better enable us to "walk in another's shoes." It is useful for social workers to carefully listen to the accounts of people who have lived with, and continue to live with, one or more forms of oppression and to learn from them. Did they speak about these experiences to others? Were they supported and in what way? Did they take any action? If so, what was the outcome? Those who work in the field need to really know what it is like to be denied housing or a job or be belittled because of our skin colour, ethnicity, disability, age, gender, sexual orientation, and other features that make us feel different. However, it does not mean that we have to experience the same thing in order to work with people who are oppressed. The people who experience oppression are the people we spend our working hours with and whose interests we keep uppermost in mind.

Background of Structural Social Work

In the 1960s and 1970s, the feminist, civil rights, and peace movements, among other *social movements,* introduced critiques of social work practice as it existed at the time in North

America and Britain. Criticism was levelled at many professions that were seen as maintaining social inequality and protecting the existing relations of power by a few over many others. Professional helpers, working on behalf of the state, were viewed as perpetuating injustice by not initiating change to benefit those who were most disadvantaged or oppressed in society. Social work that was involved in service delivery under these conditions was regarded as supporting the status quo (Galper, 1975) and the continued oppression of clients. Social work was—and continues to be—caught in a contradiction because it served to control clients on the one hand while trying to help them on the other.

Radical social work ideas disagree with a singular focus on the individual as an architect of his or her situation, and stress how problems are caused by or related to social factors and events that are beyond individuals' direct control. However, without a social revolution it would be difficult to implement all of the goals of radical social work. Some suggest that social workers join with workers in labour unions and get involved in political parties to work for change outside their profession (Fook, 1993, p. 6; Lundy, 2004, p. 198). Few guidelines are available, however, for social workers to practise using a radical approach. Everyday social work practice, involving large caseloads and complex human problems, takes up much time and energy, leaving little for social action. How can social workers realistically combine the two?

Colleen Lundy (2004, pp. 63–67) identifies five goals of structural social work. The following activities are involved: (1) acting as allies of clients to promote their rights and advocate for their interests; (2) bringing people together to solve problems and effect social change; (3) analyzing the effects of poverty and unequal distribution of wealth to avoid blaming individuals; (4) working to enhance the power of clients in relation to social workers in practice situations; and (5) promoting and supporting clients' personal change goals. As Lundy describes, the goals and practices of structural social work in Canada have been advanced by an extensive study by Moreau and Frosst (1993) at Carleton University.

A Conflict Perspective

Structural and radical social work, based on the notion that society is characterized by conflict between groups of people, acknowledges differences in power, influence, and access to the good things in life. Traditional social work is based on an order perspective.

Simply put, the ***order perspective*** sees society as holding common values and sharing a similar culture. This view holds that, in general, people in our society have similar chances to succeed in life. However, some are better at succeeding, or are luckier, than others. This perspective also assumes a consensus among the majority of people regarding how social institutions function in society.

The conflict perspective rejects such a view, claiming that society consists of people with opposing views and interests who are continuously trying to have their ideas and wishes recognized. Society is not seen as held together by consensus but by "differential control of resources and political power" (Mullaly, 2007, p. 227). A critique of the present social order and capitalism is central to structural social work: "Social work is seen as both reproducing and able to undermine patriarchy, racism and class society" (Moreau with Leonard, 1989, p. 10). Agreement among people cannot be assumed, since diverse groups of people with varying views and interests constantly struggle to have their needs met through public channels. In addition, the interpretation of needs often differs among groups in society (Fraser, 1989).

Framing

Wharf and McKenzie (2004) state that how a problem is framed suggests the range of solutions being considered. Depending on the prevailing ideology of decision makers, the framing of a social problem will suggest how it will be seen and resolved. For example, poverty might be framed either as people's lack of desire to work hard, or as too few available jobs, or as complex factors related to broader social trends. The prevailing viewpoint on the problem (usually put forward by the current government) shapes the strategies and methods that are developed to deal with it. Pointing to possible outcomes of different framings of the problem, Wharf and McKenzie (2004) suggest that there could be increased incentives (or penalties) for not working, job creation measures, or broader policy initiatives.

The way in which these outcomes are created is complex and depends on many factors. Nancy Fraser (1989) explains how public debate about people's needs (needs talk) and how these needs are interpreted constantly shift. She refers to childcare, once considered a private, domestic issue but one that has now become the subject of public debate as governments and various groups strive to put forward their vision of what is needed. A perspective that acknowledges the influence of different voices (e.g., parents, childcare providers, the state, workplaces) in the public forum of policymaking can help us understand how alternate views or "framings" take hold at different times and in different places, affecting how problems are seen and resolved. Drawing attention to the experiences and voices of individuals who have not always been heard and who have knowledge to share can be useful.

The Place of Structural Social Work in Practice

By the late 1970s, structural social work was being taught in a number of North American and European social work schools, including Carleton University in Ottawa. Maurice Moreau was a strong proponent of structural social work (Bailey and Brake, 1980). He saw this work as addressing various intersecting forms of oppression, not only the class structure (Mullaly, 2007). His book *Empowerment through a Structural Approach to Social Work* (Moreau with Leonard, 1989) is a report of research on how social workers applied principles of structural social work and dealt with barriers and opportunities in their day-to-day practice. The social workers who took part in the study had graduated from Carleton University and had been exposed to structural social work, emphasizing an "analysis of power at all levels, a community approach and client empowerment" (Moreau with Leonard, 1989, p. viii). Findings from this study conducted in the 1980s suggest that social workers worked within their organizations and with their clients for change, but faced considerable difficulty in becoming involved in broader-level change, which was often seen as problematic for their organizations. The less autonomy and workplace support for social change that workers had, the more difficult it was to fully apply a structural approach. The results of the research point out that social workers thought that they could not act independently without risking the well-being of their clients or their job security. Although they strove to apply structural social work principles, they faced some limitations due to their professional and workplace environments. The study concludes that social work

> operates in a wider social context which delimits the possibilities open to its workers or to clients. In order both to understand and take effective action, structural social workers have to perceive and act outside the social framework *as well as within* it. To do so, they must protect themselves both within social agencies in which they work and outside their confines. (Moreau with Leonard, 1989, p. 277)

What this means is that structural social workers find spaces and opportunities for change in their own agencies and organizations as well as in the broader social environment, but do not do so without care and without weighing the consequences of their actions. However, opportunities to foster and support organizational and broader-level social change are available, and social workers do find ways to work toward these ends.

People's personal problems are seen as primarily caused by unequal socioeconomic (also referred to as "class") features, which control and exploit individuals in society. Material (food, clothing, and shelter) and personal needs must be separated in order to avoid "blaming the victim," so that clients are not held wholly responsible, for example, for their situation of poverty. As discussed earlier, it is necessary to look beyond the individual person or family to address the source of problems. Social workers must examine the social, economic, and political conditions that lead to or create poverty for some and wealth for others, rather than the reasons individuals and families fail to maintain themselves. Collective action (e.g., advocating for better wages in an industry, organizing a media campaign or community rally) is one way that structural social workers can address people's needs at a broader level.

Structural Social Work and Direct Practice

Most social workers are employed in ***direct practice*** positions. Only a few find jobs in which the primary function is based on collective action and activism. However, direct practice workers should still engage in efforts to bring about social change in their own work and take part in collective action, especially when it can help improve services for clients. For example, an agency policy that is unfair to a particular group of people (e.g., young single parents) requiring help needs to be challenged.

Often, direct practice workers acknowledge the importance of social change but go about their daily work without a hint of social change activity. Laurence Shulman (1999), not known as a structural or radical social work proponent, also agrees with this position, when he asserts,

> The client cannot wait for the major changes in our society that will be needed to modify institutionalized oppression. Thus, while we need a conceptualization of practice which reframes our way of viewing client troubles and requires us to act on injustices in our society (and agencies), we simultaneously must provide services to the victims of these injustices. (p. 27)

Most of direct social work practice is concerned with how to help clients adjust, adapt to, and make use of the resources of a system that we acknowledge as unjust. This is the nature of the problem-solving approach. As is common among social work practitioners, practice theorists frequently acknowledge the importance of social change and then dismiss it as something for someone else or another branch of social work to deal with.

Direct service practitioners are primarily responsible for providing services to clients even if the system is unjust. But this does not relieve these same practitioners of the responsibility to engage in social change, because social change is at the root of social work. The CASW *Code of Ethics* (2005a) emphasizes the importance of eliminating oppression and injustice and enhancing humanitarian and egalitarian ideals. All social workers have the responsibility to work toward these ends.

This task is not easy. Front-line workers cannot suddenly become agents of social change, but in almost all direct practice there is room to work toward social justice and equality. Much of the balance of this chapter addresses this type of work.

Reflection and Reflexivity in Social Work

A number of authors point out that social workers must critically reflect on their practice, which means unpacking its underlying ideology, assumptions, and values. Reflection requires a willingness to examine oneself and a desire to learn about alternative views on client situations and worker interventions. Reflection advances to reflexivity when insights are integrated into subsequent social work practice. As Payne, Adams, and Dominelli (2002) assert, "*Reflexivity* means being in a circular process where social workers 'put themselves into the picture' by thinking and acting with the people they are serving, so that their understandings and actions inevitably are changed by their experiences with others" (p. 3).

We believe that reflection and reflexivity help social workers to practise critically. The understanding acquired when these processes are part of everyday practice can lead to improved client assessment and intervention skills and greater satisfaction among social workers about the work they perform.

APPLYING THE STRUCTURAL APPROACH IN PRACTICE

Overview

Mullaly (1997, 2007) suggests that structural social work practice can take place inside and outside the sociopolitical system. However, he emphasizes that, in both instances, the goal of working for social change works against the system.

Working outside, and often against, the system is essentially a political activity. It entails social activism related to social movements and building coalitions to challenge established institutions. Union organizations and professional associations can be used as vehicles for social change. Frequently, working outside the system involves electoral politics, often at the local level (see Mullaly, 2007, Chapter 12). Relatively few social workers find paid employment in positions where the intent is to work outside the system.

In this chapter, we focus on how generalist social workers can use structural social work principles in their regular practice. In Mullaly's (2007) view, direct practice that uses such principles involves work within but against the system. As you will recall, social workers who use the problem-solving approach work with clients on problems within their environment, rather than on problems in the environment that negatively affect people. For example, think of the situation of a family living solely on social assistance benefits. They may come to see a social worker because they are not able to stretch the money they receive to pay for rent, groceries, and other needs. The family may be facing some crisis that creates additional financial strain, such as the illness of one member.

Problem-Solving Approach: Family Intervention

A social worker who applies the problem-solving approach will explore the above situation of how the family has been managing up until now. She or he will usually ask about supportive and stressful relationships within the family and with systems outside it, about the family's coping strategies, and how they have managed problems before. Once the need for help is clear, the social worker and clients plan what work needs to be done and agree on the goals and actions to meet these needs. One strategy might be to increase the resources of the family so they will have enough to eat. People differ in terms of their access to resources, backup systems, or supports that can be drawn on for help during tough times, and this capacity will also be a part of assessment. Based on mutual planning and goals, the social worker might then refer the family to a food bank, offer help in planning nutritious and economical meals, and suggest shopping strategies. She or he might also advocate on behalf of the family by contacting the social welfare department and asking whether the family's benefits can be increased. Essentially, using the problem-solving approach, the social worker does not initiate change beyond the clients and their current relationship with the social welfare department.

Structural Approach: Collective Action

Structural social work challenges the above approach through its focus on **_collective action_**—working together for change—beyond the client–agency boundary at the levels of community and society. Although the strategy of increasing people's resources so that they can meet their basic needs is an important one, other strategies aimed at broader changes must also be used. Making connections between the individual or family situation and the social, economic, and political context in which they are embedded is necessary. An assertion by Bailey and Brake, writing in 1980 (p. 8), still rings true; "No matter how well meaning a social worker, a criticism is justified if, as a result of dealing with a client, that client remains unaware of the public dimension of his or her problems."

For example, the social worker, aware that social assistance benefits, like many other social programs, are being steadily decreased by the government, might want to work alongside clients with a local antipoverty or welfare rights group to lobby the government, help organize a rally to oppose social assistance reductions or increase benefit levels, or write letters to government leaders. A structural social worker might also work in a local community to initiate projects to increase resources at the community level, such as community vegetable gardens or food co-ops, while also advocating for social change.

A structural approach must include at its centre the active search for and identification and use of people's individual and collective strengths. Coming together with others who face similar circumstances or problems can increase the pool of strengths, adding to its power and diversity. In community organizing, the need for representation from all groups makes for a richer breadth of ideas and talents that can be used in local planning and action. When common goals and working relationships are established in a group, a sense of direction and energy results. The stress on collectivities in structural social work makes it especially useful in social work in community organizations, or as Carniol (1995) and Mullaly (2007) term it, in *alternative social services,* where collaborative and cooperative work characterize the relationships between social workers and community residents who want to improve their lives. Some of the roles of such social workers have been discussed in Chapter 4.

One problem with the structural approach is that sometimes collective action will not, at least in the short run, actually help the individual client. How can one work in an agency that provides a mandated social service (e.g., child welfare, public welfare, or corrections) and still attempt to change the social structure so that the changes actually help individual clients? There are some ways to make this possible. For example, suppose you are working as a counsellor in a public welfare agency in the inner city. All of your clients are on social assistance. You and some of your coworkers recognize that food takes up a large proportion of the benefits they receive. Your group considers and then quickly rejects the idea of organizing public demonstrations and actively lobbying for an increase in welfare payments. You are civil servants and you could risk losing your jobs. Further, you recognize that, given the current government emphasis on reducing deficits and cutting taxes, increases are unlikely.

One of your colleagues has heard of community kitchens (adapted from a Latin American model), where ingredients are purchased at low cost to be prepared, cooked, and eaten communally or stored for the use of local families. This is really a kind of co-op that has worked well in many other Canadian cities. In these settings, not only can members benefit from cooking together, they can also learn about poverty and how they might work toward social change together. It might be possible for you to help clients organize a community kitchen that could be a good forum to make other individual and collective changes. This kind of project could also spur collective activities such as a community-directed video or performance about the rising cost of food and adverse effects on health and well-being. This kind of encouragement and facilitation by social workers is not only an application of structural approach, it is also simply good social work.

There are some similarities between how the problem-solving framework and structural social work are applied. Both address and attempt to solve problems. However, in structural social work the emphasis is on collective change and social action, while in the problem-solving approach the client is expected to have her or his needs met within the boundaries of the existing social structure.

Structural Social Work and the Environment

Social work practice tends to focus mainly on interpersonal relationship issues rather than on the social environment itself. The ecosystems approach (see Chapter 9), currently in widespread use in social work practice, emphasizes people's capacity for coping and adapting as well as reaching out to resources in the surrounding environment when help is needed. When resources do not exist or cannot be obtained, it is possible to work with environmental systems and processes so they will respond better to clients. This principle of the ecosystems approach, which encourages social workers to work toward changing structures and processes to respond better to client needs, resembles the ideals of structural social work. In reality, the approaches are quite different.

In ecosystems, the focus is squarely on the connections between the person and the environment and not, as in a structural view, on the environment itself. Another way of putting it is that in ecosystems the unit of analysis is the connection between the person and the environment, whereas in structural social work it is the environment. In practice, most social work is conducted with individuals and families and is not aimed at broader-level change. Improving the environment so that people can obtain material and other resources to improve their lives (e.g., jobs, financial help, housing, counselling, etc.) is often difficult. Most social workers, due to agency mandates and resource constraints, tend to focus more on working with people's personal or interpersonal problems and far less on environmental or structural ones.

Although they have the greatest stake in changing their situation, people who are most affected by structural problems often have the fewest resources and least influence in speaking out for change (Wharf, 1990, p. 23).

Case Example

Maria and the Low Family ▼

Kai Low is a 30-year-old man who took a construction job upon completing high school. He married at a young age and, with his wife, Linh, a newcomer to Canada, spent many difficult years trying to make ends meet. They have an 8-year-old son, Kevin, a quiet boy who is doing relatively well in the third grade at a nearby school. Last year, Kai injured his lower body while working on a non-union, private job when he was unable to find other work. He was not covered by workers' compensation or any other insurance. Kai decided not to sue because the company moved out of town and he did not know where it had gone. Besides, he had no money to pay a lawyer. He was hospitalized for a month, discharged home, and then referred for regular physiotherapy. Kai has had a long rehabilitation period as he has struggled to regain strength in his legs and back. He has been receiving some financial support from social assistance since his employment insurance benefits ran out a few months ago.

Linh works as a seamstress in her own home. The piecework wages she earns are too low to maintain the family. As a result, the family has had to move to a cheaper apartment and borrow money from relatives to make ends meet. Kai is upset and angry about his situation. He has begun to argue with his wife about money. He is also worried about how he can find a job again once he is well enough. He knows that he can't physically handle construction work

Continued

again. Feelings of failure dominate his thoughts. He feels ashamed when his parents visit because he thinks they are disappointed by his inability to work and his need to accept help from the government. He was raised to believe that providing financially for his family was his primary responsibility.

Linh has phoned Maria, a social worker whose agency is listed in the phonebook. Maria's agency offers job training and work placement for people who are unemployed. Linh tells Maria about the family's situation. Maria can clearly hear the stress and concern in Linh's voice. She asks Linh to talk to her husband, who is willing to meet with Maria provided she can help him get a job.

In thinking about the family's difficulties, Maria knows she'll want to help Kai with his personal concerns, but she also wants to consider his social situation—how he and his family have been affected by inequitable social arrangements (e.g., lack of workplace protection, low wages, and exploitive piecework). Maria reflects on her ideas about this couple's problems. She wants to carefully consider how her own assumptions about their relationship might influence her actions.

After she spends time learning from the couple about their situation, Maria changes the way she planned to work with the couple, because she realized that her assumptions were incorrect. Maria also acknowledges the couple's strengths as they struggle to maintain their family with little support and few rewards. She recognizes how distress and hardship can occur when people are not blessed with health and wealth. In this case, the family's coping capacity is seriously affected.

Consider the case example of Maria and the Low family. A problem-solving or strengths approach would frame this situation using an ecosystems, role theory, or another person-in-the-environment conceptualization that explains individual behaviours in an environmental context. The family's problems, while not their or the system's fault, are their responsibility. It is up to them to do something about the problems. The system will help them, within its capabilities, but in the end it is up to the Lows to make the best use of available resources.

A structural analysis takes a very different perspective. While Kai still needs to recuperate from his accident, the family's main problems are seen as structural rather than individual. The Lows' problems need to be understood in a political and economic context (see Mullaly, 2007). The Lows are victims of a social system that does not effectively meet the needs of people who experience difficulties in life or who are disadvantaged in some way. The economic system, based on industrial capitalism, works against people like Kai and Linh.

The social safety net has failed the Lows. Their income, after Kai's accident, is not enough to meet their needs. There is no built-in program or appropriate follow-up for him to begin preparing for a return to the job market or job retraining while he is receiving physiotherapy. The reasons for the limited programs are both political and economic.

Kai and Linh also have immediate needs that must be met. Although a structural analysis sheds an important and different light on the family's problems, any social change will likely be too late for them. Maria clearly has a responsibility to respond to Linh's urgent request for help concerning job training and placement for her husband. Maria probably has two immediate priorities: to ensure that the Lows are not going hungry and that their basic needs are being met, and to involve Kai in a helping process. From this point on, Maria and the Lows will need to negotiate the goals and next steps.

Nevertheless, Maria may still try to use this situation to engage in social change. In Kai's case, she may offer to look into regulations and standards of safety for short-term contract work. Kai may not have known that the company's lack of insurance coverage for injuries would mean that he would have no protection if something happened to him. It might be determined that the company was operating illegally and could be held liable for the accident. Social workers might advocate for better working conditions and benefits so people don't "fall through the cracks." Letters could be written on Kai's behalf to government representatives, unions, occupational health organizations, or a local newspaper. If he is agreeable to this, Maria could also help to bring people with similar experiences together with him to discuss their shared issues so they can consider taking action.

Maria would likely want to discuss Linh's situation, as it seems that her job is unsatisfactory. A feminist approach could be helpful in understanding her circumstances, especially as a woman employed in exploitative piece work that pays women newcomers poorly and keeps them isolated from one another. Feminist social work principles of validation and addressing how the personal is political (see Chapter 13) could provide support for Linh to find the strength to change her life situation. Perhaps the experience she has in sewing would help her to find a better job that includes employee benefits.

It is possible that the Lows may decide not to participate in these initiatives. Perhaps they do not want to "make waves" or they justifiably feel vulnerable in their current situation. Structural social workers take care not to coerce clients into becoming involved in social action, do not reveal clients' identity without their permission, and do not put their own desire to correct an injustice or change policies above the needs of the client. Although difficult decisions must be made in taking client situations to a higher level, the social work codes of ethics give workers a mandate to promote social change to better people's lives.

It is much easier to work with people at the individual or interpersonal level and aim for small changes in behaviour than to strive to change the structures or institutions of society. In carrying out any change effort, it is essential for social workers to carefully consider the risks and potential consequences for clients and themselves, asking questions such as: What effects might there be for the social worker, the client, and the worker's organization? What does the client have to gain or lose? Is the client prepared and able to take the risks that are involved?

Roles in Structural Social Work

Chapter 4 outlined a number of roles in generalist social work. Of these, at least three roles can also be used in structural social work: advocate (particularly class advocacy), enabler, and educator might be applied to effect system change.

Maybe the most frequent role that direct practice workers fill in using a structural perspective is advocacy. Sometimes the reason a social worker advocates on behalf of a client is because the worker's skills in accessing an important resource or influencing a decision are simply better than the client's, so the chances of success are better. At other times, the need for advocacy results when a client or group of clients wants to change an oppressive, discriminatory, or unjust policy. Most workers will, from time to time, face the need to address such a structural issue.

Usually advocacy is not thought of as collective action because it is the social worker who advocates. However, a structural approach particularly emphasizes class advocacy—action that is taken on behalf of a group of clients. The group, for example, must inform the worker and negotiate with him or her to ensure that the worker clearly understands the issues and can address the different views among group members. While the collective action is not a direct social change attempt, class advocacy does require collective group participation.

The enabler role can be used to facilitate collective action. In a sense, it is the opposite of advocacy by a social worker in that the attempt at social change is made by a collective of others. Sometimes a direct practice worker faces a situation in which a solution to a problem requires the worker to mobilize clients in order to deal with an injustice that unfairly affects them. At other times a social worker may be approached by a group of clients with a request for action.

Often, enabling requires that the social worker be an educator. In order for clients to engage in social action, including collective action, they need to be informed. The social worker may be in a position to provide clients with important information or to help them search out, find, and use such information.

In most social service programs, the government (in public agencies) or the board of directors (in private organizations) controls policy and determines programs. Alternative social services tend to arise in communities and groups where experiences of oppression are well-known. For example, a home construction and renovation project might be initiated where there is a lack of safe and affordable housing. In these kinds of alternative programs, the provision of social services is controlled by community members themselves.

Social action is the mobilization of people to put pressure on established institutions, using non-violent protests and demonstrations, to change programs or policy. Mullaly (2007) encourages social workers to become involved in labour unions to "advocate participation in and control over all aspects of one's living and working conditions" (p. 339). By forming *coalitions* with unions, structural social workers can be more effective in social action and change because coalitions bring together different people from diverse constituencies to work on a common problem. Thus, they greatly increase their resources and ability to bring pressure for change. For example, immigrant or Aboriginal women may need to organize in order to resolve an injustice. If both groups can form alliances with, say, each other or with labour unions, or women's organizations, then the likelihood of success is considerably greater.

Mullaly (2007) cautions that coalition-building may be based on single issues or be limited to one oppressed group (e.g., people with physical disabilities), rather than being inclusive of others whose oppression is seen as different or outside of their interests (e.g., refugee women). Divisions, conflict, and competition for funding may work against effective social change that could benefit many.

EXAMPLE OF STRUCTURAL SOCIAL WORK AND DIRECT PRACTICE

Some may think that the principles of structural social work are too esoteric and removed from daily life to be useful in generalist social work practice. They argue that it is difficult to put the principles into practice. To counter this criticism, the Low family case example illustrates the importance of understanding the socioeconomic environment of clients and how clients might engage in social change that benefits themselves as well as other members of society. In the section below, the case of Kenny is used to further articulate a number of principles of and approaches to social change that can be implemented by generalist social workers in their regular practice. This case example also demonstrates how the structural approach can be used in direct practice and complements other interventions, including the problem-solving and strengths approaches. The intent is to clearly demonstrate that front-line, generalist social workers cannot afford to ignore structural and social change skills.

In the case of Kenny and the boarding homes of Martins Grove, it will be seen that not only was it good social work practice for the case manager to help individual clients select a social change strategy over restorative intervention, but also that the social change strategy was easier and more efficient.

Case Example

Kenny and the Boarding Homes of Martins Grove ▼

Kenny was first admitted to the mental health centre 14 years ago. At the time, he was 27 years old. He had previously held a number of unskilled jobs and had never married. One day, when walking to work at a car wash, Kenny began to hear voices. These voices were sometimes loud but were usually just mutterings. The voices bothered Kenny, but he did not tell anyone about them.

At the same time, Kenny began to develop a deep fear of "catfish." Catfish are ugly, slimy fish with long whiskers that are often found on the bottom of muddy rivers. Kenny began to believe that there were huge catfish lurking at the bottom of nearby rivers, and he became obsessed with the fish.

One day a particularly loud voice told him that the owner of the car he was cleaning was evil and that Kenny must destroy the inside of the car. If Kenny did not, catfish would rise from the rivers. Before anyone could stop him, Kenny ripped the car seats with a screwdriver, broke the windows, and destroyed the dashboard. The police were called, and Kenny was arrested and taken to the hospital for assessment. Shortly after being admitted, he began to ramble about the huge catfish and how ugly and fearful they were. Kenny was diagnosed with schizophrenia.

Continued

For the next seven years after Kenny's first admission to hospital, he had periods of symptom remission followed by stays at the centre for up to six months. When out of the hospital, he would become lonely and stop taking his medication. Nightmares about the catfish would return.

Kenny felt safe in the mental health centre, mostly because of the routine. He particularly enjoyed his work in the garden and, during winter, in a small greenhouse. Generally Kenny could avoid the severe episodes if he took his antipsychotic medication. Both Kenny and the staff at the centre knew that he needed a supportive living arrangement, maybe for the rest of his life.

Danielle, Kenny's new case manager, learned that he liked the cottage and lake country and that there were some small, marginal farms that boarded mental health clients near several lakes in an area called Martins Grove. The farm that was selected for Kenny offered an opportunity for him to putter in a garden much as he did at the centre. Danielle suggested to Kenny that they take a drive to see one of the farms.

Kenny moved to the farm and was there, without incident, for eight months. He formed reasonably good relationships with the other boarders, and he liked Anna and Josef, the owners. His symptoms reappeared only once: Anna reported one day that when fishing, she happened to catch a catfish. This set Kenny off and the old fears returned. He began to babble almost incoherently. Luckily, however, Anna was able to calm him down. Kenny, amazingly, understood that catfish were commonly caught in the nearby rivers and that they were harmless even though very strange looking. Kenny, through this insight, seemed to have taken a very small step toward recovery.

Anna and Josef were also pleased. They were gratified that Kenny seemed to fit in, and the room and board fees from Kenny and the other clients provided the couple with much-needed income.

The community mental health workers were impressed by the environment that the farm couple provided. Over a few years, the number of residents had risen from two to four. Also, because of the success that Anna and Josef were having, 11 other families in the community began to house people who suffered from a serious mental illness. In total, 29 residents were boarded in affordable and supportive housing. The boarding-home program at Martins Grove not only had become an excellent resource for the mental health centre, but also was beginning to nicely contribute to the local economy. In a way it was a cottage industry. Then two events occurred at almost the same time, both of which could have spelled disaster for the program.

Kenny relied on social assistance to pay for his board. At first, the local welfare department agreed that Kenny was eligible for the boarding home. The total cost was far less than that of keeping Kenny in the hospital. The money he received was sufficient to cover the cost of his board, buy a few clothes, and give him about $35 pocket money per month. Since Kenny had few expenses, he usually managed to save a part of his pocket money.

The Martins Grove welfare department had a policy of requiring annual medical reports, including diagnosis and prognosis. From the report at the end of Kenny's first year at the boarding home, it was clear that Kenny was adjusting quite well. The welfare department had just introduced a workfare program that required able-bodied recipients to find work to cover at least part of their livelihood. If recipients could not find work in the competitive job market, they were required to work at a job to be determined by the department. Otherwise, their welfare benefits would be cut off. Since Kenny seemed to be improving, the local welfare department felt that he was now able-bodied and could work.

Kenny, Danielle, Anna, and Josef were stunned when they found out about these plans. Kenny was improving because he was in a safe environment. He was now 41 years old, and his last and highest-paying job had been washing cars over 14 years ago. The puttering he did in the garden and greenhouse could hardly be counted as real work. Kenny, in the opinion of Danielle, Anna, Josef, and his psychiatrist, did not have the work or social skills required for competitive employment. It was likely that if Kenny was required to find employment, the mere mention of it could cause the terrible catfish to resurrect themselves in his mind. He would probably require rehospitalization.

The second event was potentially even worse. Some of the neighbours had become alarmed at the growing number of boarding homes in the area. They formed an action group that called for a municipal bylaw restricting boarders to one per household. The effect of the bylaw would be to shut down the boarding homes. The rationale given was that the area was a quiet, rural neighbourhood and that allowing boarding homes to spring up would change the nature of the community for the worse. The action group was able to solicit support from two of the six municipal councillors. They tabled the bylaw before the Martins Grove Municipal Council.

For Anna and Josef and the other boarding-home operators, this was alarming. Taking in boarders had improved their standard of living and had allowed them to remain on their small, marginal farms. To all of them, operating a boarding home had become a small cottage industry that gave them a reasonable standard of living. If the number of boarders was cut to one, their future would be very uncertain.

Danielle and the boarding-home operators suspected that the action group actually had motives other than those stated. Many of the boarding-home residents looked "odd," and some had an "institutional shuffle." Others could be

Continued

seen talking to themselves in public. Almost none had found work, and most did not participate in local events. When they did take part, it was almost always as a group and as onlookers rather than as participants. A good example was at the local fastball games. The boarders would often come as a group and sit together in the bleachers. They kept to themselves. It annoyed the community residents that some of the boarders would sometimes cheer for the visitors.

None of the boarders was violent, yet many in the community seemed to fear them. Danielle and others believed that the real motive behind limiting the boarding homes was to rid the community of perceived "undesirables" and "deviants."

Direct Service or Social Change?

Danielle is a direct service, generalist social worker employed by a community mental health centre as a case manager. She is not a social activist, nor does she consider herself "political." In the example, not only is the hard work of Danielle and others at risk of collapsing, but, more important, the gains that many residents have made over the last three or four years are also in serious jeopardy. Danielle and her colleagues have two choices. One is to concede that their work as case managers has encountered a wall, and that the social workers and their clients will need to start over. The other choice is to become "political," to use their social action and social change skills.

Both options are considered. If the professional staff retreats, years of hard work will be lost. Clients who are doing fine in their boarding homes will likely experience major setbacks. A few may never again be able to make a satisfactory recovery. Further, the task of finding new boarding homes in another location is formidable. No one is sure that the homes can really be replicated.

The social change option is much more attractive. If successful, then the boarding-home program in Martins Grove could continue. Further, after careful analysis, the case managers actually think not only that there is a better chance for the success of social change than for the direct service option, but also that the social change option would be easier and more efficient. This is so because of the enormous amount of work that would be required to rebuild the program somewhere else. Further, if they fail, plan B—the direct service choice—would still be available.

Strategies of Action

A structural analysis holds that both events in the case example are forms of oppression. The first, the loss of social assistance, is a structural problem with a social institution—the welfare department. The second is oppression in the form of discrimination that is sometimes deep-seated in communities, often unspoken until a situation like the one at Martins Grove arises. People fear those who seem different from them. If Danielle began all over again to find Kenny a new home, according to a structural analysis she would become part of the oppression.

The Proposed Workfare Program

To ensure that Kenny and others do not lose their source of social assistance income because of a forced work scheme, the local welfare policy needs to be changed. A structural view would also contend that the entire social welfare system is oppressive and unjust. All people have a right to a decent standard of living. The means test, part of social assistance programs, is grossly unfair, as is the requirement to work (workfare) in order to receive welfare. (According to National Union Research [2000], welfare recipients in workfare programs do not enjoy the benefit of labour protection or employment benefits, need to accept less than the mandated minimum wage, and have no right to holidays.)

The mental health professionals at Martins Grove understood all this but, rightly, focused on only a very small part of the social welfare policy: the injustice of a policy that would require people who suffer from long-term mental illness and are placed in boarding homes to work in order to receive welfare. This suggests an important principle of social change for direct service workers: target something that is reasonable and that has the potential to be successfully resolved and managed given the skills and resources of the workers. In the case example, it would not have been wise for this group to attempt to change the overall policy on workfare. However, it is entirely possible, if they are successful at a more limited level, that this could open the door to reform of the entire system of workfare.

After some preliminary work, Danielle and her colleagues agreed that their target was clear—the Martins Grove Welfare Board. The board had the power to change the workfare policy. Two strategies were considered. One was for one or more of the professional staff to advocate on behalf of the group or for a professional advocate, possibly a lawyer, to be hired to do so. The group would need to build an argument based on the benefits that the boarding homes brought to the community of Martins Grove.

The second strategy was to enable the group of clients to collectively act on their own behalf. Several were quite capable of doing so. This strategy had the benefit of engaging and investing the clients in their own lives, a form of empowerment. Further, if the clients were visible, the chance of influencing the Welfare Board was increased. The clients' personal lives would take on political meaning.

As part of the empowerment process, the workers acted as educators to help the clients understand the social welfare policies that affected their lives, a process called ***consciousness-raising.*** This included helping them understand and reflect on the dehumanizing influences of the policies.

Consciousness-raising, used by structural theorists but borrowed from feminist theory and adult education, can increase an individual's understanding of his or her oppression or social injustice through reflection and new insights. A collective form of consciousness-raising takes place when a group of people reflect on and analyze the effects of social injustice and oppression on their lives and take action aimed at altering societal conditions. Sometimes, when an individual has her or his consciousness raised, she or he might join with others in collective consciousness-raising.

In the end, the clients as a group understood the issues and selected two of their members to act on their behalf.

Outcomes   Both strategies were implemented. Two case managers and two clients negotiated with the Welfare Board. The advocates persuaded the board that most of the boarders would not be able to work. However, they agreed that some could and would gain satisfaction if the work was consistent with their skills. While this was officially a compromise solution, the case managers considered that all of their clients were winners because they had, in the end, opened some community doors for clients who had work potential and wanted jobs.

The Ban-the-Boarding-Homes Movement

The second problem, the anti-boarding-homes movement, was very different because it reflected negative, discriminatory attitudes and an unreasonable view of the boarding-home residents. The case managers also thought the movement posed considerable risk to the boarding homes because they suspected that the discriminatory values were shared by some vocal people in the rural community and the "ban-the-boarding-home" movement might be able to generate wider support.

The case managers had two targets. The first was the anti-boarding-home movement itself. The ultimate goal was to get the members of the movement to reconsider their attempt to eliminate the homes. However, prejudices are hard to change. Therefore, a more realistic goal was to limit and reduce local support for this movement.

The second target was the Martins Grove Municipal Council. The professional staff was more optimistic about influencing the council than they were about the grassroots movement. They reasoned that the council was less interested in oppressing a harmless and benign community group and more interested in maintaining the economic benefits that such a group might bring to Martins Grove. The case managers believed the old cliché "Money talks." Thus, instead of making oppression their primary focus of argument, their main position was that the boarding homes were an important economic asset for the community. As such, why should the council discriminate against them and the clients they served?

Unlike the strategy of advocacy with the Martins Grove Welfare Board, the professional helpers believed that they needed a coalition (Mullaly, 2007) of boarding-home residents and operators. They thought that action needed to be taken by a collective rather than by individuals, and that the collective needed to include residents of Martins Grove, not the professional case managers. They needed to take the issue to the public.

Implied in this strategy is that success in maintaining the boarding homes, will, in the end, be determined by powerful interests. A structural view holds that societies, including communities, are made up of conflicting interests. If the ban-the-boarding-homes movement gains too much support, the balance of power might be tipped in their favour. On the other hand, if the residents and boarding-home operators developed a strong power base, then they could gain the upper hand, at least while their case was being heard. The strategy was to use the coalition in order to gain the needed power and, hence, the upper hand.

As a first step, Danielle called a meeting of boarding-home clients and operators. She used consciousness-raising tactics to help these groups not only to understand the problem and begin identifying how the coalition might operate, but also to understand the problem from the point of view of the anti-boarding-home supporters. During the meeting, one of the operators said that he knew two church groups that might join them. The coalition quickly expanded, gaining more support and power.

During the next meeting, which included members from the two church groups, two people, one from a church group and one boarding-home operator, were selected as spokespeople for the coalition. The church group representative, Ellen, had a little political campaign experience, and the boarding-home operator, Yves, was known as a good organizer. Danielle was pleased to see the coalition use its collective strengths. From this point on, the coalition operated on its own. Danielle and her colleagues worked behind the scenes doing tasks that enabled the coalition.

The coalition agreed that one important task was community education. They asked Henry, one of the case managers, to assume this role. His task was to provide information about mental illness in as many ways as possible, and in particular to attempt to allay the fears local residents had about the boarding-home residents. One of Henry's tasks was to frame (see Wharf and McKenzie, 2004) the problem to show that the boarding-home residents not only were harmless but also in fact contributed to the community, particularly economically.

Despite the importance of keeping the power base of the anti-boarding-homes movement small, the coalition's major focus was on influencing the Municipal Council. Only two counsellors had been swayed by the movement. The coalition believed that all of them were primarily interested in economic matters. The council really did not care whether the boarders were people with a mental illness as long as they were harmless and brought money into Martins Grove. The coalition decided to attack on three fronts. First, they circulated a petition supporting the homes. Second, Ellen and Yves prepared a written brief and submission for the council. The thrust of the brief was based on research undertaken by two of the case managers (information gained from mental health financial records and the tax returns of boarding homes and residents) that showed the homes were making a major financial contribution to the community. Third, Ellen, Yves, and another resident, Matthew, lobbied each councillor on an individual basis.

Outcome The result of all this effort was that the anti-boarding-homes movement remained small. The economic agreement won the day with the Municipal Council. The proposed bylaw failed in a four-to-nothing vote, with two councillors abstaining.

Note that throughout this scenario there should have been no risk to the social workers' employment. What they did was just good social work. However, in order to be successful they needed the support of their mental health centre. In this and similar situations, it is important that workers seek and gain the support of their superiors.

According to some, radical theory sets out a narrow view of power without really exploring the complex nature of power relations, especially at the interpersonal level (Payne, 2005, p. 247). Radical theory has tended to view power as static, as available to some but not to others. The dynamic nature of power can be seen when one political party in an election loses its following to another, only to rise again during a subsequent election campaign. Some writers (e.g., Bishop, 2002) have asserted that power needs to be seen not simply as a resource that is owned and used by those who have it over those who do not. Certainly, some have more claim to power than others due to their position, wealth, or kinship. Power can be given or taken. At the same time, power can be shared among people, and it can shift from one person to another at different times and in different places (Bishop, 2002).

CHAPTER SUMMARY

Structural social work is based on radical social work theory. The structural approach is an effort to put into practice the tenets of radical thinking. Collective action is central to this approach.

Collective action is a powerful political tool that can initiate change, often at the grassroots level. Social workers can often help clients work collectively. The collective as a whole can benefit, as well as the individuals, often clients, who initiate the action. Collective action can also be empowering when it gives people a sense of being in control of their lives. Structural social work has much in common with a feminist approach, since both apply a social critical analysis of the structures that create and maintain a social order that is oppressive for women or for other groups in society.

Social workers must not confuse the structural approach with a person-in-the-environment perspective. Person-in-the-environment perspectives, including ecosystems and role theory, and even an Aboriginal approach, focus on the transaction or connection between people and the environment. The structural approach focuses on the environment itself, defined as the social structure, and attempts to initiate social change. The ultimate goal is for individuals to benefit, but analysis and intervention are directed toward changing the social structure.

The socioeconomic environment is very important to structural analysis. For social workers, this means having a basic understanding of the economic system, particularly as it affects and shapes the circumstances of clients. More recently (e.g., Mullaly, 2007), an anti-oppressive framework has enriched structural social work so that poverty, ableism, classism, sexism, ageism, heterosexism, and others are included in the analysis of social structures and become targets of social work action.

The important goal of structural social work—to eliminate the social oppression of people—is not easily attained. Achieving social change is usually difficult and takes considerable time and energy. Influential groups in society will likely not give or share power and resources easily. Many social workers are unable or unwilling to risk frustration and failure given the odds against them. It is often easier to turn a blind eye to inequality and injustice. Nevertheless, even small-scale successes are important first steps toward a more just and caring society.

There are certainly situations where people have worked to change oppressive social conditions or structures and met with success—for example, the work done by women's groups and committed individuals in calling attention to domestic violence. These efforts have led to changes in laws, changes in social and agency policies and practices, and an increase in services. However, even these successes should not be taken for granted, as new moves for reducing programs and services threaten women's security and well-being. Social workers need to be aware and prepared to take action.

A major part of this chapter has centred on explicating a number of roles of social work that make use of structural analysis and intervention, but social workers in all settings need to consciously consider principles of structural social work in their everyday practice.

chapter 15

Putting It All Together: Problem Solving and Beyond

Chapter Goal ▼

To bring together the various approaches and perspectives discussed in this book and show how they compare with and enhance the problem-solving process.

This Chapter ▼

- provides an overview of social work approaches and perspectives
- explains how these approaches and perspectives inform and enhance problem solving
- reiterates the basic principles that form the foundation of all social work practice
- summarizes approaches to practice for comparison

INTRODUCTION

Good generalist social work practice is based on the fundamental ideals of promotion of social justice and equality, and a commitment to people's self-realization, growth, healing, and well-being. To reach these ideals, generalist social workers must apply a variety of approaches and perspectives that range from direct micro and mezzo practice to social change at the macro level. Problem solving is a foundation of generalist social work, but practitioners must learn and use it flexibly in conjunction with a variety of approaches and practice orientations. Whether a social worker's practice orientation is Aboriginal, structural, or feminist, the problem-solving process can be integrated or adapted to meet the needs of different client situations.

There is no single or unique approach to social work practice. While many principles of practice are foundational to all of social work (e.g., values, importance of helping relationships, contract with clients, and so forth), social workers must be able to use a variety of approaches and perspectives depending on many factors, including the current situation, nature of the problem, culture, and agency setting. The central theme of this book is that social workers not only must clearly understand the traditional problem-solving approach to social work practice, but also must be able to extend practice depending on the situation, and move beyond by using other approaches and perspectives, including strengths, Aboriginal, structural, and feminist. At the same time, social workers must critically reflect and be reflexive, learning from their work with clients and always striving to enhance their practice with new insights. This is particularly important in advancing anti-oppressive and antiracist social work practice.

We recognize that most social workers are employed in a field of practice. To do this, social workers must assume specialized roles that are defined by the respective field of practice. However, there is a core of social work that is generalized across fields of practice. The entire book addresses this core and is about generalist social work practice in Canada.

EXTENDING PROBLEM SOLVING

People in all cultures develop a process for solving problems, although methods and problem situations may differ across cultures. In most Western cultures problem solving is at the heart of how we think. Science and research make use of forms of problem solving that we come to know and understand. The medical model, discussed in Chapter 8 of this book, is a problem-solving method of practice. Western cultures emphasize problem solving; it is a process cast in the context of a technological society that stresses advancement and discovery in industry, medicine, engineering, and many other fields.

Due to its use in Western countries, it is not surprising that social work developed a problem-solving orientation. Richmond (1917) first articulated a framework much like the medical model, and Perlman (1957) refined, modernized, and broadened it. Compton and Galaway (1999) and Compton, Galaway, and Cournoyer (2005) cast the problem-solving process in a person-in-the-environment context, bringing it up to date and identifying its features. This model in social work and in our society works when social work is defined as a restorative process—one that takes action to solve a problem after the problem is identified. Social work probably cannot develop a model of practice that does not include a problem-solving component. Yet the problem-solving process or approach often does not fit neatly into the delivery of human services.

In the problem-solving process, defining the problem is often a professionally dominated activity, supported by referral information and existing records stating what client problems exist. The client's view of what happened, how she or he got into this situation, and what issues are of most importance to her or him at this time may not be fully considered. The context of the person and her or his capacities and resources may be overlooked or may be perceived as important only for the purpose of solving the problem. Using problem solving as the overriding framework in social work limits the possibilities for seeing people as actively engaged in growth, healing, and change in their own ways and with the resources they have available. By beginning with an assessment of client strengths, abilities, capacities, and means, we can widen our understanding of human functioning and resilience in difficult periods and in happier times. So, in the strengths perspective, the problem-solving process should not frame helping, but instead be used as a tool when appropriate.

The strengths perspective (Chapter 11) both compares and challenges the problem-solving process, particularly in the sections on resilience, self-help, and the central role of the consumer, and holds that helping can take place without focusing on the problem but by complementing problem solving. This perspective stresses that client strengths need to be at the heart of the helping activity. It is a holistic approach that focuses on the well-being, vitality, and resilience of clients.

An Aboriginal approach to social work (Chapter 12) stresses the importance of spending time listening to a client's story and developing mutual respect and trust, selecting the best time and circumstances to initiate problem solving—say, when a client requests guidance in implementing a change in his or her life. This is one way to adapt problem solving to an Aboriginal approach to social work. Problem solving in this approach remains mostly client-directed, with the social worker offering guidance and support as needed. It may also be possible that the problem-solving process is not used at all if it is not suited to the situation (e.g., where the helper acts as a cultural guide or support by listening and responding to the client's story).

Feminist social work (Chapter 13) and structural social work (Chapter 14) represent approaches that emphasize the connection between the personal and the political or an individual's situation and its social roots. In both of these approaches the macro, or societal, level is central. We can illustrate using a feminist social worker's view of a couple facing financial strain due to expensive childcare arrangements.

The social worker recognizes that our society and government expect women to provide childcare while men work outside the home. Although this notion is premised on traditional gender roles and an adequate income by one income earner, generally a man, today many women need and want to participate in the labour force. Despite the fact that most parents need to earn an income, existing social policies and service provisions to support families requiring daily childcare are less than adequate. Nor are there adequate provisions in cases where one spouse wishes to provide full-time childcare at home. As a result, families must seek out suitable and affordable services from a patchwork of facilities and providers. For parents whose incomes are low, childcare costs can be high in relation to income (see Ferguson, 1998, for a useful analysis of this issue). A feminist social worker would understand this dilemma and the stress it creates for parents, especially for women who feel pulled in several directions. The worker would help the couple see that the situation is not their personal failing but a failure of the current social welfare system. At the micro level, the social worker would listen to the couple's account, affirming and supporting their resolve to do what they feel is best for their children. In addition, some new strategies or resources might be suggested, and a problem-solving process might be used if appropriate. In using problem solving, the couple, with the worker, could explore options, plan and contract, take action, and evaluate the outcome. If a solution to the problem of high-cost childcare is found, then the client–social worker relationship may come to an end.

Macro-level work might involve a broader strategy for social change, one that addresses the gap in social policy. The social worker could support the couple in joining with a parents' group committed to changing current childcare provisioning, conduct research on the issue, and provide information about what has been initiated or is being suggested by governments. If appropriate, the social worker could join the clients in trying to improve current childcare provisions through community organizations or the social worker's professional association. In taking such action, a feminist social worker connects the personal to the political, helping to bring what is seen as a private issue to public attention.

A structural social worker would likely behave in a similar way in the same situation. Both a feminist and a structural approach acknowledge the need to see individual problems as having social roots, and both emphasize action at the macro level as an integral part of social work practice, however challenging this may be. A conscious effort to understand the experience of oppression and racism, and to challenge these whenever they arise, is also highlighted in the current structural social work approach and has also been embraced by many feminist social workers, particularly those from immigrant and non-dominant ethnocultural backgrounds. Structural and feminist approaches also stress connections between individual empowerment and collective fulfillment. By joining with others who have similar interests and ideals, strength and commitment can often be enhanced and relationships become richer. (One must be prepared for the fact that collective efforts may not always be successful, however.) Addressing social change is highlighted in both the structural and feminist approaches. Social workers are obligated to support social change that is aimed at eliminating discrimination, oppression, and other injustices.

CONTEXT AND FOUNDATIONS OF SOCIAL WORK PRACTICE

Traditional problem solving and the emerging approaches developed due to many historical events. Social work, as explained in Chapter 2, developed as a result of a number of social forces that began about 200 years ago and accelerated near the end of the 19th century. The most important of these forces, industrialization and urbanization, are still changing and affect all our lives. Social workers continue to practise in the context of ever-changing social and economic systems, in which alternative perspectives and methods such as those in the strengths, Aboriginal, feminist, and structural approaches are suited.

In our view, today's social work cannot be understood unless we also understand how the profession emerged. Social work has an exciting history and was in the forefront of social change that has led to our modern health and social programs, including health care and social insurance.

A central theme of this textbook is that social work's view (image) of the world is filtered by an ideological lens that most members of the profession share. This ideology shapes the way that clients are viewed and social policies are conceptualized, developed, and implemented, and it shapes the nature of practice, including assessment and intervention. A major part of social work ideology is a set of values based on humanitarian and egalitarian ideals and reflected in the Canadian Association of Social Workers' and the International Federation of Social Workers' codes of ethics.

USE OF A RANGE OF APPROACHES AND KNOWLEDGE

Social workers who embrace different orientations emphasize different values. For example, the strengths perspective is organized around the importance of the values of self-determination, empowerment, and commitment to self-realization, growth, and healing. This is not to say that the other values are unimportant to this approach. Structural and feminist social work practice also regard these values as very important, but centre on collective empowerment, the right to social justice, and the elimination of oppression, domination, subordination, and exploitation.

Social work practice takes place in the context of social and agency policy in a field of practice. We hold that all social workers need to understand social policy. The processes of policymaking involve social workers not only because they come to know the impacts on their clients, but also because they interpret policy every day in the work they do. In some settings, such as child protection (see Chapter 5) and criminal justice, the roles of social work are, in part, mandated by legislation and government policy. Social workers also have opportunities to participate in policymaking through the activities of their professional associations, workplaces, public meetings, and through research and writing.

In social work, a good relationship and formation of a mutual, working contract between clients and workers is essential. This does not mean that a client has to like a social worker or that a social worker has to like a client. Effective practice depends on a helping, mutual relationship between client and worker. In many situations, clients are not interested in building a relationship with a social worker. The practitioner must work hard to establish communication and reach out to such clients. All social workers must develop ways of working with clients who are unwilling to work with social workers.

Relationship is central to all social work approaches. The importance of building a respectful and trusting relationship is fundamental, for example, in an Aboriginal approach to helping, described in Chapter 12. The Aboriginal helper's aim is often not to be directive, but to offer support and help within a relationship that reflects culturally specific practices. The helper acknowledges the help seeker's own resources and views in the context of Aboriginal culture and the broader universe. Feminist social work practice emphasizes the need for reducing power and for mutual sharing in the relationship between worker and client. In a feminist approach, the relationship can be a means for mutual learning and support.

Social work practice is a personal endeavour. What is appropriate and workable for one worker may not be for the next. How the range of approaches and perspectives is used depends on the practitioner's personality, culture, ideology, experience, and education. This position does not mean that social workers have the right to impose their values, beliefs, and ideologies on clients—quite the contrary. The essence of this principle is that the social worker's primary helping tool is her or his "self"—a self that includes sensitivity, capacity to build helping relationships, personality, practice style, and beliefs. The worker must learn to use these qualities of self in helping others.

A social worker needs to work effectively across cultures, since practice is culturally based. This means that practice, regardless of approach, must be both culturally competent and consistent with the culture of people served. Techniques, skills, and knowledge differ depending on the cultural context. (See the discussion of ethnocultural awareness, antiracist and anti-oppressive social work practice in Chapter 7.) An Aboriginal social worker might feel competent in making use of the medicine wheel as a means of helping Aboriginal youth in trouble. However, a worker of non-Aboriginal background may not share the same competence. Yet, he or she can learn about the medicine wheel's significance in Aboriginal culture and for clients. The knowledge and skills of a non-Aboriginal worker may not allow him or her to use culturally specific methods, but would enable a worker to be sensitive to cultural beliefs and practices that are important to clients. Such openness and understanding can build relations in cross-cultural helping.

In our multicultural society, social workers and clients often work across cultures, including the workers' own professional culture and ethnocultural orientations. Being open to diverse ways of seeing and dealing with troubling issues and situations, respecting culturally specific beliefs and practices that are beneficial to clients and that differ from one's own, and appropriately using cultural resources to help clients are of critical importance. These features of good cross-cultural social work do not come easily to most, but need to be learned and nurtured. Sometimes the practice of social work itself is foreign to clients and we must explain what we do, how, and why.

Another important lens that filters practice is the selection and use of knowledge upon which we base assessment and intervention. Certainly the knowledge that is emphasized depends, in part, on the approaches used by the worker. Social work practice uses multiple approaches and diverse theories. Our profession has drawn from numerous disciplines and bodies of theory to define and shape social work practice. A theme of this book is that knowledge used by social workers needs to be broad based with a range of different theories available to social workers. By broad based, we mean that social workers need to be able to selectively draw on a wide range of diverse knowledge to engage in effective practice.

An important use of a broad knowledge base is in assessment. Assessment is multidimensional. Human problems are connected; sometimes one problem affects another, and we need to be holistic in our assessment of client situations. To engage in multidimensional assessment, the worker must use diverse theories and a broad knowledge base. While theory is broad based, there needs to be a way to focus assessment. Determinants of assessment, explained in Chapter 10, are important ways to focus the assessment process.

Social work practice needs to be able to draw from many sources as society, people's issues, and resources change. The ability to respond to change is crucial to our profession. Without such a capacity, we are poorly equipped to address current concerns such as occupational stress, youth in gangs, issues in same-sex relationships, isolation of older people living alone, inner-city transitions, and many others. Our profession also aims to build theory through research and writing, especially theory about practice. Social work research extends our knowledge of diverse aspects of social problems, policies, services, and practice methods.

Social work's history of direct practice and service to individuals, families, and groups is a cornerstone in our profession and continues to be at the core of social workers' daily activities. We believe that it is not enough to focus on micro and mezzo practice, important as they are; social workers must also confront the context in which we practise.

Further, as we have discussed in various parts of this book, social work as a profession is faced with a contradiction. On the one hand, social workers try to promote clients' well-being and help them care about themselves and others. On the other, we control clients by monitoring their behaviour to ensure that they are following laws and rules, and if they are not, we take appropriate action or report this to the courts or other authorities. Our professional education and training emphasize these functions in our work—for example, in corrections, social assistance (welfare), and child protection. The work we do in ensuring that clients follow stipulated rules aims to protect society and to help clients meet some of their own needs.

Our society is characterized by inequality and numerous social problems, some of which are addressed in varying degrees, while others are poorly addressed. The character of our society's policies and social provisions reflects how people's needs are seen and publicly provided for at the level of the state. In Canada, our chid protection system is based on the view that the best interest of the child needs to be a priority. However, there is less attention paid to preventing child abuse and neglect by supporting families, communities, and society to better care for children. It could be said that our society has been able to accept poverty and incremental and continued erosion of social welfare provisions.

It can be argued that social spending has to be contained even if this means greater inequality in society. While budgets do indeed have to be effectively managed, there is no guarantee that our society will be better off in the future if we focus on reducing spending on social programs today. Social workers can help in observing, documenting, and speaking out about the barriers and unmet needs faced by oppressed groups in society—for example, those who are elderly, Aboriginal, newcomers to Canada, disabled, jobless, ill, young, and others. This would represent a contribution to social change and a challenge to oppressive structures in our society.

COMPARATIVE SUMMARY OF FIVE APPROACHES TO SOCIAL WORK PRACTICE

Exhibit 15.1 sets out some key elements of the problem-solving process, the strengths perspective, and the Aboriginal, feminist, and structural approaches. For each, the elements that we have highlighted are as follows:

Exhibit 15.1 ▼ Social Workers at a Glance

OVERVIEW	PROBLEM SOLVING	STRENGTHS PERSPECTIVE
Strengths, Aboriginal, feminist, and structural approaches go beyond traditional problem solving.	Helps people find solutions to personal and social problems. The steps are (1) problem articulation, (2) assessment, (3) goal setting, (4) intervention, and (5) ending, with evaluation occurring at each step.	Helps people find solutions to problems but emphasizes personal growth and development so that people are able to do their own problem solving.
ABORIGINAL APPROACH	**FEMINIST APPROACH**	**STRUCTURAL APPROACH**
A general approach focusing on developing centredness and growth through the concepts of wholeness, balance, connectedness/relationships, and harmony.	Stresses connecting the personal to the political, empowering women, validating women's experience, and affirmation and transformative action to enhance women's lives.	Identifies the roots of people's problems primarily in the unequal distribution of resources, especially wealth, in society. Social change and collective empowerment are goals. Structures that create oppression of people who are poor, disabled, old, female, homosexual, and others need to be eliminated.

PROBLEM DEFINITION	PROBLEM SOLVING	STRENGTHS PERSPECTIVE
Working with people in social work almost always involves identifying problems. Each approach frames problems differently.	The process by which client and social worker identify and clarify the types and the nature of problems. The focus is on clarifying the problems to be worked on. Problems are often defined as individual limitations or often deficits.	Part of a wider process that includes clarifying and identifying all relevant facts of a client's life. The focus is on client strengths rather than deficits.
ABORIGINAL APPROACH	**FEMINIST APPROACH**	**STRUCTURAL APPROACH**
Part of the process of establishing wholeness, relationships, harmony, and centredness in the lifelong journey of healing and growth toward *mino-pimátisiwin*—the good life. The focus is thus on the relationships within and between individuals and entities.	Forms part of the process of consciousness-raising for women, in which the personal is made political and problems are named. Gender oppression, patriarchal relations, and confining social expectations create problems for women, men, and families.	Occurs within a context of work with clients in which the roots of individual problems are traced to social causes—especially, but not solely, class. Social workers advocate for clients, working collectively to identify problems and striving to resolve them.

ASSESSMENT	**PROBLEM SOLVING**	**STRENGTHS PERSPECTIVE**
Assessment is always an analytical process. Each approach emphasizes different theoretical, analytical, and sometimes ideological views.	The analysis of a problem in the context of relevant systems so that goals can be set and a treatment or preventive strategy can be developed. Emphasis is on understanding the nature of problems in the context of people's environments and interactions within them.	Focuses on people's capacities, vitality, abilities, strong points, talents, courage, and power, which help them grow as human beings, improve their quality of life, and develop their own problem-solving skills. Understanding the nature of problems and their effects is secondary to analyzing strengths.
ABORIGINAL APPROACH	**FEMINIST APPROACH**	**STRUCTURAL APPROACH**
Focuses on the whole person and whether and how the relationships between individuals and other entities are connected, balanced, growing, and in harmony, and what is needed for individuals, families, communities, and the surrounding world to move toward centredness and *mino-pimátisiwin*. Assessment is directed by the person seeking help.	Centres on the client as the expert of her experience. Assessment is conducted with the client's safety and needs in mind. Mutuality in the client–social worker relationship is important, as is the reduction of power differences between the client and practitioner. A feminist social worker does not impose her views on a client but may explore with the client to offer alternative explanations.	Takes place as the client's situation unfolds. The social worker does not play an expert role, but learns from the client about his or her experiences and understanding of his or her situation and how it came about. Mutual respect and reduction of power differences are important, as is fighting "victim blaming."

GOALS	**PROBLEM SOLVING**	**STRENGTHS PERSPECTIVE**
Goals are based on assessment and help determine how intervention will take place. If the client is voluntary, the social worker and client must agree upon goals.	Solving, in partnership with the client, identified problems.	Helping people harness their own resources to solve problems while promoting their growth, development, and quality of life.
ABORIGINAL APPROACH	**FEMINIST APPROACH**	**STRUCTURAL APPROACH**
Oriented toward seeking *mino-pimátisiwin*. Specific goals are determined by the individuals seeking help with the support of the helper.	Supporting the empowerment and fulfillment of women individually and collectively and eliminating gender oppression in society.	Assisting individuals who experience the effects of social injustice and eliminating social inequality and structural oppression due to class, gender, age, sexual orientation, disability, and other forms.

Continued

INTERVENTION	PROBLEM SOLVING	STRENGTHS PERSPECTIVE
Intervention is action that a social worker and/or client take toward problem solution. Each approach suggests a different emphasis of intervention.	Generally intervention flows from the assessment and from goals that have been established. Intervention emphasizes treatment—direct action by a social worker to alleviate a problem.	Promotes growth and/or quality of life. Empowerment is emphasized so that people can take control of their own lives and successfully do their own problem solving.
ABORIGINAL APPROACH	**FEMINIST APPROACH**	**STRUCTURAL APPROACH**
Focuses on supporting individuals to maintain, or regain, balance and spiritual connection in life so that they become more centred and in harmony with themselves and their surroundings. In other words, interventions promote growth toward *mino-pimátisiwin* and are not necessarily problem focused.	Based on the goals and needs of the client, and aimed at validating experience and knowledge, building self-esteem, and individual and collective empowerment. The centrality of feminist ideals and a supportive relationship enhance intervention. Client and social worker are allies in effective change.	Stresses the partnership between client and social worker. Advocacy and social action may be used, in addition to micro and mezzo interventions, when client situations require it. The social worker helps the client deal with the effects of problems attributed to social causes such as oppression.

SELF-DETERMINATION	PROBLEM SOLVING	STRENGTHS PERSPECTIVE
Self-determination is central to all of social work. Each approach has a different emphasis.	Best interest of the client is key. The social worker is the expert and in a clear position of power over the client. Accepts the principle of self-determination within limits, such as those spelled out by the code of ethics. Empowerment is in the context of best interest.	A consumer/client-driven approach with a very strong emphasis on a client's right to self-determination. The focus is on empowering clients and de-emphasizing client–social worker power differentials. Both of these are circumscribed in agency policy and social work mandates.
ABORIGINAL APPROACH	**FEMINIST APPROACH**	**STRUCTURAL APPROACH**
Self-determination in a manner that positively supports individuals' relationships is primary. In the helping relationship, both the individuals receiving help and the helpers are self-determining while respecting others in the relationship. Thus the focus is on the well-being of all involved.	Viewed as essential for clients as a means to build personal strength and empowerment. It is also recognized that self-determination can empower women to collectively act at the macro level to improve the economic, legal, and social position of women.	An important concept that reflects strength and direction in life. For people who experience oppression, being self-determining is powerful, building a sense of entitlement to the resources in society. Collectively, the self-determination of like-minded persons can lead to action against social injustice.

INVOLUNTARY CLIENTS	PROBLEM SOLVING	STRENGTHS PERSPECTIVE
In many fields of social work practice, clients are involuntary. Social work in fields such as child welfare, criminal justice, and mental health include mandated practice and social control.	Best-interest principle permits work with involuntary clients; that is, if "worker knows best" is assumed, then work with involuntary clients can be justified.	Using a consumer/client-driven approach, the consumer maintains control. Using this approach, as far as the legal mandate will permit, often assists in forming relationships with involuntary clients because the clients maintain control.
ABORIGINAL APPROACH	**FEMINIST APPROACH**	**STRUCTURAL APPROACH**
Involuntary clients are given control over the parameters of the relationship so that the balance between their needs and those around them are maintained. In other words, the general goal of *mino-pimátisiwin* holds not only for individuals but also for their families and communities.	Seen in the context of a patriarchal society characterized by unjust gender relations. The client is given a full opportunity to be heard and her or his experiences and feelings are validated. The power difference between social worker and client is discussed openly and reduced as much as possible.	Involuntary clients, survivors in a society characterized by injustice and inequality, are treated in a respectful and nonjudgmental manner. It is important to be open and clear about the involuntary nature of the relationship, and to recognize that client situations are often linked to events or circumstances beyond their control.

ROLE OF THE CLIENT	PROBLEM SOLVING	STRENGTHS PERSPECTIVE
The role of the client can range from passive recipient to active participant to self-help.	Relatively passive. While the client is expected to engage in solving his or her own problems, the social worker acts as the primary change agent.	Relatively active. The client is expected to solve her or his own problems. The social worker attempts to help the client maximize personal strengths to promote growth and enhance general problem-solving skills.
ABORIGINAL APPROACH	**FEMINIST APPROACH**	**STRUCTURAL APPROACH**
Active in that the client is expected to determine his or her own path and make his or her own movements toward healing and growth. The helpers are supports and models on the journey.	Active in that the client offers his or her account of the situation that is troubling, determines what he or she would like to see change, and works with the social worker to achieve his or her goals. The worker supports and guides the client in an egalitarian relationship.	Needs to be active to ensure that she or he will be able to determine her or his own needs and what changes must occur. The social worker helps in supporting and affirming the client, possibly joining with her or him in broader-level social change.

Continued

NATURE OF THE PROCESS

The principles behind the process of intervention range from restorative to empowering.

PROBLEM SOLVING

Restorative. Social worker action takes place only after the problem has been identified. Prevention relates to preventing future problems.

STRENGTHS PERSPECTIVE

Promotional. Social worker action helps promote general growth and development. A strong preventive component is stressed that is not necessarily problem focused.

ABORIGINAL APPROACH

Promotional in that the individual focuses on striving toward healing, growth, centredness, and *mino-pimátisiwin*.

FEMINIST APPROACH

Empowering not only for individual empowerment of the client but also for the collective empowerment of women.

STRUCTURAL APPROACH

Empowering in that individual empowerment is connected to broader-level empowerment of oppressed groups in society.

ROLE OF SELF-HELP GROUPS

PROBLEM SOLVING

Marginally supported and sometimes seen as a hindrance to effective therapy.

STRENGTHS PERSPECTIVE

Strongly supported and encouraged to form. They are seen as a step toward individual empowerment.

ABORIGINAL APPROACH

Likely taking the form of talking, sharing, healing, or spiritual circles. Are methods or processes that directly reflect an Aboriginal approach. As such, they are supported.

FEMINIST APPROACH

Seen as helpful resources for clients who have common experiences and problems, and can promote sharing and mutual help for growth, healing, and empowerment.

STRUCTURAL APPROACH

Seen as potentially useful for individuals to gain strength to change their situations and act to better their own lives and those of others with whom they share issues and challenges.

PROBLEM OWNERSHIP

Who "owns" or is responsible for a problem? The individual client? The social structure? Is it beyond the client's control? Is ownership shared?

PROBLEM SOLVING

The problem/deficit belongs primarily to the individual. Generally, the individual must adjust and adapt to the larger system and use the system to her or his advantage.

STRENGTHS PERSPECTIVE

The individual owns the problem and has the responsibility to solve it. A problem is not defined as a deficit.

Concept	PROBLEM SOLVING	ABORIGINAL APPROACH	FEMINIST APPROACH	STRUCTURAL APPROACH	STRENGTHS PERSPECTIVE
(continued)		Problems are those events/issues that move people away from centredness. Thus, problems may be viewed on an individual, family, or community level, particularly in the relationships within and between people. Responsibilities for problems lie at the level most directly affected by the movement away from centredness, since all are part of a whole.	Although experiences and events can create problems that affect individuals, families, and groups and are owned by them, the roots of such problems can be located in patriarchal society and unequal gender relations. An individual needs to be able to name the problem and take steps to change its impact on him or her.	Problems are experienced and felt by individuals, families, groups, and communities, but are seen as rooted in an unequal society in which some groups experience adversity and oppression. Individuals must actively participate in advocating for themselves and for others who face similar circumstances.	
RESILIENCE — Too often we do not appreciate the importance of a person's ability to "bounce back"; resilience.	Seen as an asset that all people have to help them through life.	Seen as lying not only within individuals but also throughout the universe. While people look within themselves for the strength to address those events/issues causing movement away from centredness, they can also use others for support, including those within the spiritual realm.	Seen as a human quality that is available to all people in many difficult situations. For women, it is used to survive violence, for example. Resilience is a strength that helps women to heal and make changes for themselves and others.	Seen as a resource used by all people in facing adverse situations in life. It helps those who are poor, ill, old, or otherwise challenged or oppressed, in a society that does not adequately care for all, to harness the resources and strengths to live.	Clients, like all people, are presumed to be highly resilient and possessing an inherent power and capacity for growth.
CONTRACT — A contract is simply an agreement between the social worker and client. This is a key part of all approaches.	The process of agreeing on problems, assessment, goals, and intervention strategies, which is seen as essential. It is also an outcome. The contract may be in principle or in writing. The client is assumed to want help.				Seen as essential. While not different in substance from that used in problem solving, its importance is elevated. The contract may be in principle or in writing. The client is assumed to want help.

Continued

ABORIGINAL APPROACH	FEMINIST APPROACH	STRUCTURAL APPROACH
Based on what individuals present and seek, and the individual's and helper's understanding of balance, relatedness, harmony, and centredness. Contracts may or may not be formalized, depending on the desires of the individuals involved.	Important because it represents an understanding that is accepted by both social worker and client. The process of contracting is open, mutual, respectful, and flexible, promoting sharing and support. The contract can take a verbal or written form.	Enables the social worker and client to be clear and directed in their work together. It is a mutual agreement, formal or informal, that can be changed as needed and offers a guide as to what is to come for both the client and worker.

CLIENT–SOCIAL WORKER RELATIONSHIP

PROBLEM SOLVING	STRENGTHS PERSPECTIVE
All approaches understand that the social worker must bring expert skill to the worker–client relationship, but reciprocity is also an important component. Each approach has a different emphasis.	A successful relationship is reciprocal and involves shared experiences. The client is an expert on her or his own life experience.

ABORIGINAL APPROACH	FEMINIST APPROACH	STRUCTURAL APPROACH
A positive relationship is paramount to the process. The relationship is reciprocal and interdependent.	A mutual and respectful relationship is highlighted. Sharing and reducing power differences promotes reciprocity between client and worker. The client is an expert on her or his own life.	By its very nature, structural social work strives for partnership in the relationship. The worker aims not only to engage the client in a mutual relationship, but also to bring people together for social action. The client is an expert on his or her own life.

CROSS-CULTURAL SOCIAL WORK

PROBLEM SOLVING	STRENGTHS PERSPECTIVE
Not specifically addressed, but the social worker must have knowledge of the client's ethnocultural background and the significance of his or her own.	This approach is useful in cross-cultural social work, particularly when one lacks knowledge of a client's culture. The client is an expert on her or his experience, including the significance and meaning of her or his ethnocultural background.

CROSS-CULTURAL SOCIAL WORK
Culture is an increasingly important component of Canadian social work practice.

ABORIGINAL APPROACH	FEMINIST APPROACH	STRUCTURAL APPROACH
An Aboriginal approach is compatible with cross-cultural social work practice, as it is a broad-based perspective that incorporates individual mental, physical, emotional, and spiritual aspects of life.	A feminist social work approach addresses the diversity of women, including, but not limited to, ethnocultural background. In cross-cultural social work relationships, as in all others, clients are viewed as unique individuals with diverse experiences and histories, including oppression due to culture or race.	Structural social work acknowledges forms of oppression related to race and cultural background. Culture is also seen as a potential resource for clients.

Overview

- problem definition
- assessment
- goals
- intervention
- self-determination
- involuntary clients
- role of the client
- nature of the process
- role of self-help groups
- problem ownership
- resilience
- contract
- client–social worker relationship
- cross-cultural social work

Summarizing these features helps to highlight key similarities and differences across the approaches. The table also ties together ideas that have been discussed earlier, some of which have been illustrated by examples from practice. It is important to note that this table presents an ideal or common situation, but in the real world not all situations are ideal, and there may be overlap between one approach or perspective and another in some features. For example, the role of the client in the problem-solving process is seen as relatively passive; however, this role may be active depending on the situation and other approach used. The strengths approach stresses active participation of the client in the helping relationship, but this may change if the client's life or someone else's is endangered. In such a situation, the social worker must take action to prevent harm to the client or another person.

CHAPTER SUMMARY

The non-traditional strengths perspective and Aboriginal, feminist, and structural approaches can be used to critique, inform, enrich, and enhance problem solving and, when used in combination, can meet the goals of generalist practice that range from direct practice to social change. These non-traditional or alternative approaches go beyond problem solving. As such, they expand social work in directions that help us meet our humanitarian ideals through interpersonal helping and the achievement of social justice.

In this chapter, we have summarized the main themes of the book. This includes a comparison between problem solving, strengths, Aboriginal, feminist, and structural approaches. It is the hope of the authors that this book has presented possibilities that can be further explored in practice. It is in the work of each social worker with his or her clients that practice is shaped and reshaped reflexively to meet the needs of the workplace, the profession, and our society.

Glossary

Acculturation: refers to a process whereby persons adapt or integrate in varying degrees to a new cultural context. For example, when newcomers arrive and settle in Canada, they experience acculturation over time as they interact with others in Canada and as they learn about living in their new country and culture.

Agency: (1) a common name given to an organization, private or public, that provides social services to people; (2) the capacity to act or to exert power.

Boundaries: an invisible line separating people's psychological, physical, and/or social space that, if crossed, can create discomfort. Boundaries can be permeable, allowing some movement across them, or rigid, not allowing others to cross. A person's culture, relationship with another, and situation can affect the setting of boundaries between her or him and others. Professional boundaries, family boundaries, subsystem boundaries, and personal boundaries are some applications of the concept.

Child welfare: policy and practice that focus on children's well-being in families, the community, and society. Social services in the child welfare field include counselling and related services to children, family supports that enhance a child's environment, placement of children in alternative settings such as foster homes and group homes, and others.

Clinical evaluation: a type of research that monitors or assesses the effectiveness of direct (clinical) social work practice.

Coalition: a broad-based alliance or group of people or organizations that have similar aims or ideologies and that usually engage in social change.

Cognitive restructuring: a set of techniques, drawn from cognitive theory—a cluster of theories that emphasize the rational or "thinking" abilities of people—that attempts to change distorted or dysfunctional thinking into constructive patterns.

Collective action: political action carried out by a group working together for change.

Conflict perspective: a view that assumes divergent and competing interests in society, based on differences in power and influence.

Consciousness-raising: a process of educating people about the political and social policies that affect their lives. The term comes from the work of Paulo Freire (1970), a Brazilian educator, and involves increasing the awareness of people as active and knowing agents in deepening their understanding about the social and structural realities of their lives, and searching for a way to transform their lives through active participation in social change.

Construction: an interpretation of meaning about some phenomenon in society, for example, what is a "typical family" or a "problem child." A social construction refers to a shared meaning or truth as formed by people in a certain place, time, and context.

Consumer: sometimes used to replace the word *client,* usually by agencies or social workers who view the person being helped as being in charge of the helping process. Another connotation is that the consumer is a user of selected services.

Developmental (theories): a broad class of theories that focus on the growth processes of people.

Direct practice (or services): sometimes called clinical practice, work that usually involves direct micro intervention with clients in a process of helping or therapy. Direct practice can be contrasted with policy practice, or macro-level intervention, in which broader systems, policies, or services are the focus of action. Direct practice might also be accompanied by intervention beyond the individual client or clients when change at other levels is sought on behalf of a client.

Discharge planning: often refers to work done by a hospital social worker in helping a client to prepare and plan for departure to home from hospital. The social worker generally assists by assessing the person's needs prior to discharge and after, and arranging for needed social services and resources in the community.

Domain (of social work): usually means the realm of social work that includes ideology, values, knowledge, and so on. In some instances, there is a more narrow usage, which refers to system size. For example, the domain of casework is usually seen as work with individuals and sometimes families, while the domain of group work is usually small groups.

Empowerment: enabling people to use their own resources, abilities, and power to take charge of their own lives.

Family life cycle: the stages or phases a family moves through over the life course (for example, becoming a couple, having children, raising children, launching children, retirement and old age, and death). The diversity in family forms contributes to variations in family life cycles.

Family norms: unwritten rules about what is acceptable and expected behaviour for people holding particular roles in a family. Family norms refer to standard patterns (e.g., Sunday visits, decision making about major expenditures).

Family therapies: forms of intervention that focus on the family and include a range of traditions and methods developed over time, such as strategic family therapy and structural family therapy.

Feedback loop: in the problem-solving process, the transmission of evaluative information to one or more of the earlier stages of the process so that, if necessary, new action or correction can take place.

Feedback mechanism: in the problem-solving process, the means of evaluation that helps to ensure that the evaluation is continuous and ongoing.

Fields of social work practice (or fields of practice): various broad areas in which social workers are employed—for example, child welfare, health, criminal justice, mental health, family services, social assistance (welfare), and so on.

Framework: an overall structure that holds different but related parts together. A framework can be composed of theories and concepts that fit together (e.g., a feminist framework can integrate theories about gender roles and concepts such as validation and empowerment).

Freudian theory: psychoanalytic theory as first postulated at the turn of the 20th century by Sigmund Freud. Psychoanalytic theory is a complicated theory of personality based on psychic determinism (mental functioning does not happen by chance) and holds that much of personality is motivated by unconscious forces.

Goal attainment scaling: a type of evaluation in which pre-specified concrete and measurable outcomes (goals) are measured against actual or attained outcomes. Goal attainment scaling is a specific form of goal attainment evaluation in which the goals are tailored to meet the needs of individual situations—that is, to measure the extent to which the specific goals of a particular intervention have been met.

Human service: a service provided for people for their welfare (education, nursing, social work, psychology, etc.). Social work is a human service profession.

Institution: (1) an abstract and often vague term used for a custom, principle, group, or element of a society that has a set of common characteristics. For example, the family is sometimes considered a social institution and consists of elements like mother, father, and children. The social welfare institution (or system) consists of such elements as child welfare, public assistance, and old age assistance. (2) A physical plant or building that is used to provide a social service or health program—for example, a hospital, a mental hospital, and a prison. See also **social institution**.

Intersectionality: refers to the intersections between social structures, such as class, gender, ethnoculture, age, physical ability, and others that reflect a person's social position and potential sources of oppression. Ann Bishop (2002) uses a chart or matrix to illustrate how these intersect; however, she cautions us not to assume that experiencing a number of the social structural features associated with oppression is worse than experiencing only one. For example, a disabled refugee man from Bosnia may not experience more oppression than an old, Canadian-born, Caucasian man. Although we might assume so, these persons themselves may prefer to determine and name their own experience of oppression.

Licensing: regulation of the practice of social work through legislation by professional organizations applies only in some jurisdictions.

Life model of social work: articulated by Carel Germain and Alex Gitterman in 1980, this model is based on the ecological approach. It stresses the transactions between people and their environments over the course of their lives.

Macro system: a community or neighbourhood. Macro social work practice deals with such large groups of people.

Mandated organization (mandated practice): An agency that has the responsibility to carry out a legislated function. Usually the legislation is protective. Examples of agencies that carry out legislated functions are **child welfare** (protect safety of children) and criminal justice agencies such as probation or parole (protect the public).

Mezzo system: a small group of people. Mezzo social work practice deals with such groups of people.

Micro system: an individual or an intimate small group, such as a family. Micro social work practice deals with individuals and families.

Mino-pimátisiwin: ongoing striving to live a good life by being a good person according to traditional teachings.

Narrative: a story told (orally or in writing) by a person or people. Narrative therapy refers to the use of stories as a means of helping.

Neo-Freudian theory: revisions of psychoanalysis that have been postulated by a variety of personality theorists. For example, ego psychology theorists are often considered neo-Freudian.

Niche: an environment in which a person lives or functions regularly. In biology, species each have a niche in which they live and survive, for example, grassy marshes for water birds. Niches may be supportive or unsupportive, and may change over time and place.

Order perspective: a perspective that sees society as holding common values and sharing a similar culture, thus giving people similar chances to succeed in life.

Organizational policy: can be written or inferred. The policies of an organization provide standards and guidelines for practice with clients. Often some flexibility is possible in day-to-day practice.

Paradigm: a fundamental framework that organizes a view of something. A paradigm in social work might be the view and theories that hold that helping is a restorative process.

Personal niche: an environment or place in which a person feels comfortable or fulfilled.

Philanthropy: the practice of charitable giving or helping—for example, by donating money annually to a community service organization.

Practice approach: a perspective (broad framework, based on ideology and knowledge, that guides social work) that is applied to a social work intervention.

Private practice: social work practice in which the worker receives a fee for service; it often takes place in a for-profit clinic or counselling group. Most private practitioners provide therapeutic or counselling services to individuals or families.

Process evaluation: a form of evaluation in which the methods or means of intervention are assessed and monitored.

Psychoanalysis: a type of psychotherapy based on a complicated theory of personality grounded in psychic determinism (mental functioning does not happen by chance) that holds that personality is presumed to be motivated by unconscious forces. Sigmund Freud was the founder of psychoanalyis, which is still practised today by some psychotherapists.

Psychodynamic: the interactions of and relationships among the complex, active, and continuously changing psychological forces (e.g., behaviour, cognition, motivation, drives, self, etc.) of individuals.

Psychosocial (and biopsychosocial): in social work, reflects the combination of psychological and social aspects of the person. The term "biopsychosocial" also includes biological aspects.

Qualitative evaluation: broadly, involves research methods in which the data are words, not numbers. There are a variety of traditions in qualitative research, each with different roots and methods. Qualitative methods can include participant observation, individual interviews, focus group discussions, archival research, and images.

Quantitative designs: research designs that involve the use of numerical data and statistical methods in data analysis. Quantitative designs might use surveys and experimental or quasi-experimental research.

Radical social work: a perspective of social work practice that focuses heavily on conflict ideology and analysis of the existing social order.

Rating scale: a means used to order or rank a set of questions used in a questionnaire. For example, a rating scale might be used to evaluate and order a consumer's view of the effectiveness of a social program.

Reflexive: in social work, being reflexive means reflecting on and learning from one's experience in practice, then applying or integrating what one has learned into subsequent work with clients.

Research methods: include participant observation, interviews, and mailed surveys that are used to collect information about research questions that are of interest.

Resilience: a person's ability or capacity to "bounce back" or return to a functioning state from a compromised state. Often when people experience a serious crisis in which they are very distressed or hurt, they show resilience because, in time and with some support, they begin to function normally again. A common image of resilience is a sponge that springs back to its usual form after being squeezed. It withstands the squeeze and takes on its former shape.

Restorative approach: as opposed to preventive, developmental, or promotional, an approach in social work that attempts to help correct or treat an existing problem, and restore the client to a prior state.

Safety planning: when someone is in a situation that might endanger her or his well-being, planning aimed at helping the person to remain safe and/or to escape the situation is needed. Safety planning is needed, for example, when women experience violence or abuse at the hands of partners or boyfriends.

Single-subject design: a research design commonly used by social workers in direct (clinical) practice that applies the reasoning used in the quasi-experimental design, called time series (repeated measures over time), to evaluate the effectiveness, impact, or outcome of interventions of single cases. Sometimes single-subject designs are used to evaluate programs.

Social control: the outcome or action of a professional worker, agency, representative of a court, or other legally mandated organization that is intended to regulate, govern, or restrict the activities and behaviour of a client. Usually the action is taken to protect a third party, such as children in abuse cases or the public when the client has been convicted of a crime.

Social institution: a collection of interrelationships among organizations and entities that serve a particular social purpose. One can refer to the social institution of marriage, the legal system, and education, for example. See also **institution**.

Social justice: an abstract and strongly held social work ideal that all people should have equal rights to the resources of a society and should expect and receive fair and equal treatment.

Social location: how a person locates or situates herself or himself within a social context and in relation to other people. For example, one might locate oneself by saying, "I am a white, middle-class Euro-Canadian immigrant female."

Social movement: a broad-based organized effort to create change. The women's movement, disability rights movement, and the lesbian and gay rights movement are examples.

Social (welfare) policies: guidelines, rules, and practices usually formed by governments to arrange or direct individuals in their interactions with other people, organizations, and society. Often social policy reflects a prevailing set of values and assumptions present in society, but these and the social policies on which they are based may be contested by different groups. Some social policies relevant to social work are those on child protection, health care, and social assistance (welfare).

Social safety net: the net or protective cushion consisting of programs, services, and allocations usually provided for by governments, but also by voluntary organizations, that ensure people's well-being. In recent years, the social safety net has been torn due to budget cuts and other factors.

Social transformation: refers to change that transforms relations in society so that those whose voices have been silenced are heard and acknowledged and the ideal of fair and equal social, political, and material equality can be achieved.

Social welfare: the well-being of all people in a society. Social welfare also refers to the set of publicly provided programs, services, and delivery systems in fields such as health, education, housing, child care, and income security that contribute to a better society.

Social work ethics: As outlined in the *Code of Ethics* (CASW, 2005a), social workers are expected to conduct their practice ethically and with the interests of their clients in mind. Most professions have a code of ethics that sets out expectations of ethical practice to guide practitioners.

Solution-focused therapy (or approach): a practice method involving brief therapy stressing client achievements and strengths. The solution-focused approach highlights positive growth by drawing on what has been helpful to the client.

Theoretical framework: the basic conceptual structure of a theory. Usually, when used in social work, the term refers to knowledge that is organized according to the structure of a given theory.

Theory: a network of concepts that are either logically or empirically related to one another. A theory either explains part of the world or predicts events. A practice theory helps social workers intervene with clients. A theory about human behaviour usually explains behaviour and sometimes attempts to predict behaviour.

Therapy: in generic use, refers to a remedial and directed process, usually the cure or treatment of an illness or disease. In social work, therapy generally has a somewhat broader meaning and includes the treatment of a problem. Some see therapy as interchangeable with counselling.

References

Abell, Alexander, Aiken, et al. (2008). General–Open Letter– UN Declaration on the Rights of Indigenous Peoples. Retrieved June 2, 2009 from http://www.nationtalk.ca/modules/news/article.php?storyid=9167

Aboriginal Women's Roundtable on Gender Equality, Status of Women Canada (2000). *Equality for Aboriginal women*. Ottawa, ON: Status of Women Canada.

Absolon, K. (1993). Healing as practice: Teachings from the medicine wheel. A commissioned paper for the WUNSKA network. Unpublished manuscript, Canadian Schools of Social Work, Ottawa, Ontario.

Addams, J. (1910). *Twenty years at Hull House, with autobiographical notes.* New York: MacMillan.

———. (1930). *The second twenty years at Hull House, September 1909 to September 1929, with a record of a growing world consciousness.* New York: MacMillan.

Aitken, L. (1990). The cultural basis for Indian medicine. In L. Aitken and E. Haller, (eds.), *Two cultures meet: Pathways for American Indians to medicine*, pp. 15–40. Duluth, MN: University of Minnesota–Duluth.

Akman, D. (1972). *Policy statements and public positions of the Canadian Association of Social Workers*. St. John's, NF: Memorial University.

Albert, J., and Herbert, M. (2008). Contemporary issues in child welfare. In J. Marsh, et al. (eds.), *The Canadian Encyclopedia*. Retrieved Nov. 3, 2008, from http://www.thecanadianencyclopedia.com/index.cfm?PgNm=TCE&Params=A1SEC818182.

Alfred, T. (2005). *Wasáse: Indigenous pathways of action and freedom*. Peterborough: Broadview Press.

Amnesty International Canada (2008, March). *Courts being used to punish people who peacefully oppose mining projects.* Retrieved Aug. 5, 2008 from www.amnesty.ca/resource_centre/news/view.php?load=arcview&article=4254&c=Resource+Centre+News.

Anthias, F., and Yuval-Davis, N., with Cain, H. (1992). *Racialized boundaries: Race, nation, gender, colour, and class and the anti-racist struggle.* London: Routledge.

Anthony, W. (1993). Recovery from mental illness: The guiding vision of the mental health system in the 1990s. *Psychosocial Rehabilitation Journal 16*(4): 11–23.

Antle, B. (2002). *CASW-ACTS project to research and develop a national statement of ethical principles, Phase 1: Critical appraisal of the literature.* Retrieved Nov. 17, 2008 from http://www.casw-acts.ca/members/phase1_e.htm.

Antone, B., and Hill, D. (1990). *Traditional healing: Helping our people lift their burdens.* London, ON: Tribal Sovereign Associates.

Apollo, A., Golub, S., Wainberg, M. and Indyk, D. (2006). Patient-provider relationships, HIV, and adherence: Requisites for a partnership. *Social Work in Health Care 42*(3/4): 209–24.

Asch, A., and Fine, M. (1988). Introduction: Beyond pedestals. In M. Fine and A. Asch (eds.), *Women with disabilities: Psychology, culture and politics*, pp. 1–37. Philadelphia: Temple University Press.

Assembly of First Nations. (2004). *Fact Sheet: First Nations & Specific Claims.* Retrieved June 28, 2004 from http://www.afn.ca/Programs/Treaties%20and%20Lands/factsheets/specific_claims_fact.htm.

———. (2007). *First Nations child and family services – Questions and answers.* Retrieved Aug. 6, 2008 from http://www.afn.ca/article.asp?id=3372.

———. (2008). *Description of the AFN.* Retrieved Aug. 5, 2008 from http://www.afn.ca/About%20AFN/description_of_the_assembly_of_f.htm

Auditor General. (2008). Report of the Auditor General of Canada to the House of Commons. Chapter 4: First Nations Child and Family Services Program—Indian and Northern Affairs Canada. Ottawa: Office of the Auditor General of Canada.

Bailey, D. (2002). Mental health. In R. Adams, L. Dominelli, and M. Payne (eds.), *Critical practice in social work,* pp. 169–80. Houndmills, UK: Palgrave.

Bailey, R., and Brake, M. (eds.). (1980). *Radical social work and practice.* London: Sage.

Baines, C., Evans, P., and Neysmith, S. (eds.). (1998). *Women's caring.* Toronto: Oxford University Press.

Baines, D. (1997). Feminist social work in the inner city: The challenges of race, class, and gender. *Affilia, 12*(3): 297–317.

———. (ed.). (2007). *Doing anti-oppressive practice: Building transformative, politicized social work.* Halifax, NS: Fernwood Books.

Baker, S., and Kirkness, V. J. (1994). *Khot-la-cha: The autobiography of Chief Simon Baker.* Vancouver: Douglas & McIntyre.

Bala, N. (2004). Child welfare law in Canada: An introduction. In N. Bala, M. K. Zapf, R. J. Williams, R. Vogl, and J. P. Hornick (eds.), *Canadian child welfare law: Children, families and the state,* 2nd ed., pp. 1–26. Toronto, ON: Thompson Educational Publishing, Inc.

Banks, K. (2002). Community social work practice across Canada. In F. J. Turner (ed.), *Social work practice: A Canadian perspective,* pp. 301–14. Toronto: Pearson Education Canada.

Bannerji, H. (1995). *Thinking through: Essays on feminism, Marxism, and anti-racism.* Toronto: Women's Press.

Barile, M. (2003). *Disablement and feminization of poverty.* Report for DisAbled Women's Network Ontario. Retrieved Aug. 7, 2008 from http://dawn.thot.net/mbarile1.html.

Barnett, H. (1950). The beginning of Toynbee Hall. In Lorne Pacey, ed., *Readings in the development of settlement work*. New York: Association Press.

Barnlund, D. (1988). Communication in a global village. In L. Samovar and R. Porter (eds.), *Intercultural communication: A reader*, pp. 5–14. Belmont, CA: Wadsworth.

Barnwell, G. (2006). *Women and public pensions: Working towards equitable policy change.* Report of the Women's Centres in the Western are of Nova Scotia. Retrieved Aug. 7, 2008 from http://women.gov.ns.ca/pubs2005_06/WPPExecSummary.pdf.

Bartlett, H. (1970). *The common base of social work practice.* New York: NASW.

Becker, H. (1963). *Outsiders: Studies in the sociology of deviance.* New York: The Free Press.

Becvar, D., and Becvar, R. (2000). *Family therapy: A systemic integration*, 4th ed. Boston: Allyn and Bacon.

Bellamy, D., and Irving, A. (1986). Pioneers. In J. Turner and F. Turner (eds.), *Canadian Social Welfare,* 2nd ed., pp. 29–50. Don Mills, ON: Collier Macmillan.

Bennett M., Blackstock, C., and De La Ronde, R. (2005). *A literature review and annotated bibliography on aspects of Aboriginal child welfare in Canada,* 2nd ed. Ottawa: First Nations Research Site of the Centre of Excellence for Child Welfare and The First Nations Child & Family Caring Society of Canada. Retrieved Jan. 25, 2009 from http://fncfcs.com/docs/AboriginalCWLitReview_2ndEd.pdf.

Benton-Banai, E. (1988). *The mishomis book.* St. Paul, MN: Red School House.

Berg, I., and Nolan, Y. (2001). *Tales of solution: A collection of hope inspiring stories.* New York: W.W. Norton.

Bernard, B. (2006). Using strengths-based practice to tap resilience of families, In D. Saleebey (ed.), *The strengths perspective in social work practice,* 4th ed., pp. 197–218. Boston: Pearson Education, Inc.

Bidgood, B., Krzyzanowski, S., Taylor, L., and Smilek, S. (2005). Food-banks: Food insecurity in a land of plenty? In T. Heinonen and A. Metteri, (eds.), *Social work in health and mental health: Emerging developments and international perspectives*, pp. 108–26. Toronto: Canadian Scholars' Press.

Biestek, F. (1957). *The casework relationship.* Chicago: Loyola University Press.

Bishop, A. (2002). *Becoming an ally: Breaking the cycle of oppression in people,* 2nd ed. Halifax: Fernwood Publishing.

———. (2005). *Breaking the cycle of oppression in institutions.* Halifax, NS: Fernwood Publishing.

Blackstock, C. (2003). First Nations child and family services: Restoring peace and harmony in First Nations communities. In K. Kufeldt and B. McKenzie (eds.), *Child welfare: Connecting research policy and practice,* pp. 331–43. Waterloo: Wilfred Laurier University Press.

Bloom, M., Fischer, J., and Orme, J. (2003). *Evaluating practice: Guidelines for the accountable professional,* 4th ed. Boston: Allyn and Bacon.

Blum, E., and Heinonen, T. (2001). Achieving educational equity in social work through participatory action research. *Canadian Social Work Review 18*(2): 249–66.

Boldt, M., and Long, J. A. (1984). Tribal traditions and European–Western political ideologies: The dilemma of Canada's Native Indians. *Canadian Journal of Political Science 17*(3): 537–53.

Bopp, J., Bopp, M., Brown, L., and Lane, P. (1985). *The sacred tree*, 2nd ed. Lethbridge, AB: Four Worlds Development Press.

Boyle, S., Hull, G., Mather, J., Smith, L., and Farley, W. (2009). *Direct practice in social work,* 2nd ed. Boston, MA: Pearson/Allyn and Bacon.

Brant, C. (1990). Native ethics and rules of behaviour. *Canadian Journal of Psychiatry 35*: 534–39.

Brass, M. (Reporter), and Abbott, H. (Producer) (n.d.). Starlight tours. *The National Magazine*. Retrieved January 11, 2004, from http://www.cbc.ca/news/indepth/firstnations/starlighttours.html.

Bricker-Jenkins, M. (1991). The propositions and assumptions of feminist social work practice. In M. Bricker-Jenkins, N. Hooyman, and N. Gottlieb (eds.), *Feminist social work practice in clinical settings*, pp. 271–303. Newbury Park, CA: Sage.

Bricker-Jenkins, M., and Hooyman, N. (1983). A feminist world view: Ideological themes from the feminist movement. In M. Bricker-Jenkins and N. Hooyman (eds.), *Not for women only: Social work practice for a feminist future*, pp. 7–22. Silver Springs, MD: NASW.

Brieland, D. (1995). Social work practice: History and evolution. In *Encyclopaedia of social work*, 9th ed., vol. 3, pp. 2247–57. Washington, DC: NASW Press.

Briks, M. (1983). "I have the power within to heal myself and to find truth": Tumak's cousin (fifty-five minutes with a Native Elder). *The Social Worker/Le Travailleur Social 51*(2): 47–48.

Brill, N. (1998). *Working with people: The helping process*, 6th ed. New York: Longman.

Broken Nose, M. A. (1992). Working with the Oglala Lakota: An outsider's perspective. *Families in Society: The Journal of Contemporary Human Services 73*(6): 380–84.

Brown, H. C. (1992). Lesbians, the state and social work practice. In M. Langan and L. Day (eds.), *Women, oppression and social work: Issues in anti-discriminatory practice*, pp. 201–19. London: Routledge.

Bruce, L. (1998). A culturally sensitive approach to working with Aboriginal women. *Manitoba Social Worker 30*(2): 1–10.

Bruchac, J. (1992). Storytelling and the sacred: On the use of Native American stories. In B. Slapin and D. Seale (eds.), *Through Indian eyes: The Native experience in books for children*, pp. 91–97. Gabriola Island, BC: New Society.

Bruyere, G. (2001). Making circles: Renewing First Nations ways of helping. In L. Dominelli, W. Lorenz, and H. Soydan (eds.), *Beyond racial divides: Ethnicities in social work practice*. Burlington, VT: Ashgate.

Buchanan, J. (2005). Problem drug use in the 21st century: A social model of intervention. In T. Heinonen and A. Metteri, *Social work in health and mental health: Emerging developments and international perspectives*, pp. 65–84. Toronto: Canadian Scholars' Press.

Bunch, C. (1983). *Going public with our vision*. Denver, CO: Antelope.

Burghardt, S. (1986). Marxist theory and social work. In F. Turner (ed.), *Social work treatment: Interlocking theoretical approaches*, 3rd ed., pp. 590–617. New York: Free Press.

Burns, D. (1990). *The feeling good handbook*. New York: Penguin.

Butler, A., Elliott, T., and Stopard, N. (2003). Living up to the standards we set: A critical account of the development of anti-racist standards. *Social Work Education, 22*(3), pp. 271–82.

Butler, S., and Wintram, C. (1991). *Feminist groupwork*. London: Sage.

Calliou, S. (1995). Peacekeeping actions at home: A medicine wheel model for a peacekeeping pedagogy. In M. Battiste and J. Barman (eds.), *First Nations education in Canada: The circle unfolds*, pp. 47–72. Vancouver: University of British Columbia Press.

Camilleri, P. (1996). *(Re)Constructing social work*. Aldershot, UK: Avebury.

Campbell, C. (2003). What is anti-oppressive social work. *Anti-oppressive social work: Promoting equity and social justice*. Retrieved April 9, 2009 from http://aosw.socialwork.dal.ca/index.html.

Campfens, H. (1997). *Community development around the world: Practice, theory, research, training*. Toronto: University of Toronto Press.

Canada, Dominion of. (1884). *Statutes of Canada, 47 Victoria: Volumes I–II*. Ottawa: Drow Chamberlin, Law Printers to the Queen's Most Excellent Majesty.

———. (1927). *Revised statutes of Canada, 1927: Volume II*. Ottawa: Frederick Albert Acland, Law Printer to the King's Most Excellent Majesty.

Canadian Association for Social Work Education (CASWE). (2008, May). *Standards for accreditation*. Ottawa. Retrieved Apr. 14, 2009 from http://www.caswe-acfts.ca/en/Board_of_Accreditation_33.html.

———. (2009). *Board of accreditation*. Retrieved Apr. 9, 2009 from http://www.caswe-acfts.ca/en/Board_of_Accreditation_33.html.

Canadian Association of Social Workers (CASW). (1994). The social work profession and Aboriginal peoples: CASW presentation to the Royal Commission on Aboriginal Peoples. *The Social Worker 62*(4): 158.

———. (2005a). *Code of ethics*. Ottawa: CASW. Retrieved Jan. 2009 from http://www.casw-acts.ca/practice/codeofethics_e_000.pdf.

———. (2005b). *Guidelines for ethical practice*. Ottawa: CASW. Retrieved Jan. 2009 from http://www.casw-acts.ca/practice/guidelines_e.pdf.

———. (2005c). *Social work practice in child welfare*. Retrieved Apr. 2, 2009 from http://www.casw-acts.ca/practice/publicmessage_e.pdf.

———. (2009). *CASW provincial/territorial member organizations*. Retrieved Apr. 2009 from http://www.casw-acts.ca/canada/prov_e.html.

Canadian Council on Social Development (CCSD) and Native Women's Association of Canada (NWAC). (1991). *Voices of Aboriginal women: Aboriginal women speak out about violence*. Ottawa: CCSD.

Canda, E. R. (1983). General implications of shamanism for clinical social work. *International Social Work 26*(4), 14–22.

Carniol, B. (1995). *Case critical: Challenging social services in Canada*, 3rd ed. Toronto: Between the Lines Press.

———. (2005). *Case critical: Social services and social justice in Canada*, 5th ed. Toronto: Between the Lines Press.

Carter, S. (1990). *Lost harvests: Prairie Indian reserve farmers and government policy.* Montreal: McGill–Queen's University Press.

CBC News. (2007, September 13). *Canada votes "no" as native rights declaration passes.* CBC.ca. Retrieved Apr. 9, 2009 from http://www.cbc.ca/canada/story/2007/09/13/canada-indigenous.html.

Chambers, C. (1963). *Seedtime of reform: American social service and social action 1918–1933.* Minneapolis: University of Minnesota Press.

———. (1986, March). Women in the creation of the profession of social work. *Social Services Review*, 1–33.

Chandler, R. (1986). *The profession of social work*. In J. Turner and F. Turner (eds.), *Canadian Social Welfare*, 2nd ed., pp. 331–44. Don Mills, ON: Collier Macmillan.

Child Welfare League of Canada (CWLC). (2007). *The welfare of canadian children: It's our business.* Retrieved Nov. 3, 2008, from http://www.cwlc.ca/files/file/policy/Welfare%20of%20Canadian%20Children%202007.pdf.

Clarkson, L., Morrissette, V., and Regallet, G. (1992). *Our responsibility to the seventh generation: Indigenous peoples and sustainable development.* Winnipeg: International Institute for Sustainable Development.

Code, L. (1993). Feminist theory. In S. Burt, L. Code, and L. Dorney (eds.), *Changing patterns: Women in Canada*, pp. 19–57. Toronto: McClelland and Stewart.

Collier, K. (1993). *Social work with rural peoples*. Vancouver: New Star Books.

Compton, B., and Galaway, B. (1999) *Social work processes,* 6th ed. Pacific Grove, CA: Brooks/Cole.

Compton, B., Galaway, B., and Cournoyer, B. (2005). *Social work processes,* 7th ed. Belmont, CA: Brooks Cole – Thomson Learning.

Correctional Services Canada. (2002). *Race profile population trends.* Retrieved Jan. 13, 2004 from http://www.elizabethfry.ca/eweek07/pdf/aborig.pdf

Couture, J. E. (1996). The role of Native Elders: Emergent issues. In D. A. Long and O. P. Dickason (eds.), *Vision of the heart: Canadian Aboriginal issues.* Toronto: Harcourt Brace.

Cowger, C. (1997). Assessing client strengths: Assessment for client empowerment. In D. Saleebey, *The strengths perspective in social work practice,* pp. 59–76. White Plains, NY: Longman.

Cowger, D., and Snively, C. (2002). Assessing client strengths: Individual, family and community empowerment. In D. Saleebey, *The strengths perspective in social work practice,* pp. 106–23. Boston: Allyn and Bacon.

Cox, R. (1998). The consequences of welfare reform: How conceptions of social rights are changing. *Journal of Social Policy 27*(1): 1–16.

Crooks, V., Lubben, J., Petitti, D., Little, D., and Chiu, V. (2008). Social network, cognitive function and dementia incidence among elderly women. *American Journal of Public Health, 98*(7): 1221–27.

CTV.ca. (2007, March 28). *Campaign finds ways to prevent hospital errors.* CTV.ca. Retrieved Apr. 9, 2009 from http://www.ctv.ca/servlet/ArticleNews/story/CTVNews/20070328/safer_heatlhcare_070328/20070328/.

———. (2007, September 13). *Canada votes against UN Aboriginal declaration.* CTV.ca. Retrieved Apr. 9, 2009 from http://www.ctv.ca/servlet/ArticleNews/story/CTVNews/20070913/aboriginal_rights_070913/20070913?hub=Canada.

Culleton, B. (1992). *In search of April Raintree.* Winnipeg: Peguis.

Daly, C. (1995). An historical perspective on women's role in social work in Canada. In P. Taylor and C. Daly (eds.), *Gender dilemmas in social work: Issues affecting women in the profession.* Toronto: Canadian Scholars' Press.

Davis, A. (1991). A structural approach to social work. In J. Lishman (ed.), *Handbook of theory for practice teachers in social work.* London: Jessica Kingsley.

Davis, L. (1986). Role theory. In F. Turner (ed.), *Social work treatment: Interlocking theoretical approaches,* 3rd ed., pp. 541–63. New York: Free Press.

Day, S. (2007). *Defending the rights of mothers.* National Association of Women and the Law Conference, Mothering in Law: Defending Women's Rights in 2007, Friday May 11 (Ottawa). Retrieved Aug. 6, 2008 from http://www.nawl.ca/ns/en/Actions/conference2007.html.

Dei, G. J. S. (1996). *Anti-racism education: Theory and practice.* Halifax: Fernwood.

Dei, G. J. S., and Calliste, A. (eds.). (2000). *Power, knowledge and anti-racism education: A critical reader.* Halifax: Fernwood Publishing.

DeJong, P., and Berg, I. (2007). *Interviewing for solutions*, 3rd ed. Pacific Grove, CA: Brooks/Cole.

Deloria, V. Jr., and Wildcat, D. R. (2001). *Power and place: Indian education in America*. Golden, CO: American Indian Graduate Center and Fulcrum Resources.

Dewees, M. (2006). *Contemporary social work practice*. New York: McGraw-Hill.

Dickason, O. (2006). *A concise history of Canada's First Nations*, 4th ed. Toronto: Oxford University Press.

Dion Buffalo, Y. R. (1990). Seeds of thought, arrows of change: Native storytelling as metaphor. In T. A. Laidlaw, C. Malmo, and Associates, eds., *Healing voices: Feminist approaches to therapy with women*, pp. 118–42. San Francisco: Jossey-Bass.

Dominelli, L. (1997). *Sociology for social work*. London: Macmillan.

———. (2002). *Feminist social work theory and practice*. Houndmills, UK: Palgrave.

———. (2006). *Women and community action*. Bristol, UK: Policy Press.

Dominelli, L., and McLeod, E. (eds.). (1989). *Feminist social work*. London: Macmillan Education.

Driedger, D. (1993). Women with disabilities: Naming oppression. *Resources for Feminist Research/Documentation sur Recherche Feministe 20*(1–2): 5–9.

Driedger, L. (1996). *Multi-ethnic Canada: Identities and inequalities*. Toronto: Oxford University Press.

———. (2003). *Race and ethnicity: Finding identities and equalities*. Toronto: Oxford University Press.

———. (2008). Multiculturalism: Bridging ethnicity, culture, religion and race. *Forum on Public Policy Online*, Spring 2008 edition. Retrieved April 8, 2009 from http://forumonpublicpolicy.com/archivespring08/driedger.pdf

DuBois, B., and Miley, K. (1992). *Social work: An empowering profession*. Boston: Allyn and Bacon.

Dunsenberry, V. (1962). *Montana Cree: A study in religious persistence*. Stockholm: Almquist and Wicksell.

Duran, E., and Duran, B. (1995). *Native American postcolonial psychology*. Albany, NY: State University of New York Press.

Eichler, M. (1997). Feminist methodology. *Current Sociology 45*(2): 9–36.

Elliott, G., Levin, R., Lafrance, J., and Herbert, M. (2005). Culturally competent social work practice in health: A focus on urban Aboriginal populations. In T. Heinonen and A. Metteri (eds.), *Social work in health and mental health: Issues, developments, and actions*, pp. 170–89. Toronto: Canadian Scholars' Press.

Ellison Williams, E., and Ellison, F. (1996). Culturally informed social work practice with American Indian clients: Guidelines for non-Indian social workers. *Social Work* *41*(2): 14–151.

Epstein, R. (1993, Summer/Fall). Breaking with tradition. *Healthsharing*: 18–22.

Erikson, E. (1950). *Childhood and society.* New York: Norton.

Ermine, W. (1995). Aboriginal epistemology. In M. Battiste and J. Barman (eds.), *First Nations education in Canada: The circle unfolds*, pp. 101–12. Vancouver: University of British Columbia Press.

Falk, J. H. T. (1928). Social work in Canada. In International Conference of Social Work, *1st Conference report*, pp. 223–47. Paris: International Conference of Social Work.

Ferguson, E. (1998). The child care debate: Fading hopes and shifting sands. In C. Baines, P. Evans, and S. Neysmith (eds.), *Women's caring*, pp. 191–217. Toronto: Oxford University Press.

Fisher, R., and Karger, H. (1997). *Social work and community in a private world.* New York: Longman.

Fleras, A., and Elliott, J. L. (1999). *Unequal relations: An introduction to race, ethnic, and Aboriginal dynamics in Canada.* Scarborough, ON: Prentice Hall/Allyn and Bacon.

————. (2006). *Unequal relations: An introduction to race, ethnic, and Aboriginal dynamics in Canada.* Toronto: Prentice Hall.

Fonow, M., and Cook, J. (1991). *Beyond methodology: Feminist scholarship as lived research.* Bloomington, IN: Indiana University Press.

Fook, J. (1993). *Radical casework: A theory of practice.* St. Leonard's, Australia: Allen & Unwin.

Forte, J. (2007). *Human behavior and the social environment: Models, metaphors and maps for applying theoretical perspectives to perspectives.* Belmont, CA: Thomson/Brooks-Cole.

Fraser, N. (1989). Struggle over needs: Outline of a socialist–feminist critical theory of late-capitalist political culture. In N. Fraser (ed.), *Unruly practices: Power, discourse and gender in contemporary social theory*, pp. 161–87. Minneapolis: University of Minnesota Press.

Freedman, J., and Combs, G. (1996). *Narrative therapy: The social construction of preferred realities.* New York: W. W. Norton & Company.

Freire, P. (1970). *Pedagogy of the oppressed.* New York: Herder and Herder.

Frumkin, M., and Lloyd, G. (1995). Social work education. In *Encyclopaedia of Social Work*, 19th ed., vol. 3, pp. 2238–46. Washington, DC: NASW Press.

Fusco, L. (1999). The techniques of intervention. In F. Turner (ed.), *Social work practice: A Canadian perspective*, pp. 48–57. Scarborough, ON: Prentice Hall/Allyn and Bacon Canada.

Galper, J. (1975). *The politics of the social services.* Englewood Cliffs, NJ: Prentice-Hall.

Garrett, M. T. (2003). Counseling Native Americans. In N. A. Vace, S. B. DeVaney, J. M. Brendel (eds.), *Counseling multicultural and diverse populations: Strategies for practitioners,* 4th ed., pp. 27–54. New York: Brunner Routledge.

Garrett, M. T., and Myers, J. E. (1996). The rule of opposites: A paradigm for counseling Native Americans. *Journal of Multicultural Counseling and Development 24*(2): 82–88.

George, U., and Ramkissoon, S. (1998). Race, gender, and class: Interlocking oppressions in the lives of South Asian women in Canada. *Affilia 13*(1): 102–19.

Gerhart, U. C. (1990). *Caring for the chronic mentally ill.* Itasca, IL: F. E. Peacock.

Germain, C. (1979). *Social work practice: People and environments.* New York: Columbia University Press.

———. (1984). *Social work practice in health care: An ecological perspective.* New York: The Free Press.

———. (1991). *Human behavior in the social environment: An ecological view.* New York: Columbia University Press.

Germain, C., and Gitterman, A. (1980). *The life model of social work practice.* New York: Columbia University Press.

———. (1995). Ecological perspective. In *Encyclopaedia of Social Work,* 19th ed., vol. 2, pp. 816–24. Washington, DC: NASW Press.

Gitterman, A. (1996). Ecological perspective: Response of professor Jerry Wakefield. *Social Service Review 70*(3): 472–75.

Gitterman, A. and Germain, C. (2008). *The life model of social work practice: Advances in theory and practice.* 3rd ed. New York: Columbia University Press.

Golan, N. (1986). Crises theory. In F. Turner (ed.), *Social work treatment: Interlocking theoretical approaches,* 3rd ed., pp. 296–340. New York: Free Press.

Goldstein, E. (1984). *Ego psychology and social work practice.* New York: Free Press.

———. (1986). Ego psychology. In F. Turner (ed.), *Social work treatment: Interlocking theoretical approaches,* 3rd ed., pp. 514–40. New York: Free Press.

———. (2002). The literary and moral foundations of the strengths perspective. In D. Saleebey, *The strengths perspective in social work practice,* pp. 23–46. Boston: Allyn and Bacon.

Goldstein, H., Hillbert, H., and Hillbert, J. (1984). *Creative change: A cognitive-humanistic approach to social work practice.* London: Tavistock.

Golightley, M. (2006). *Social work and mental health,* 2nd ed. Exeter, UK: Learning Matters.

Good Tracks, J. G. (1989). Native American noninterference. In D. R. Burgest, (ed.), *Social work practice with minorities,* 2nd ed., pp. 273–81. Metuchen, NJ: Scarecrow Press.

Gordon, W. (1962). A critique of the working definition. *Social Work 7*(4): 3–13.

———. (1969). Basic constructs for an integrative and generative conception of social work. In G. Hearn (ed.), *The general systems approach: Contributions toward a holistic conception of social work*, pp. 5–12. New York: Council on Social Work Education.

Government of Manitoba. (2003). *Manitoba Freedom of Information and Protection of Privacy Act (FIPPA).* Retrieved Dec. 29, 2008 from http://www.gov.mb.ca/chc/fippa/index.html.

Government of Ontario. (2007, October 30). *Child protection standards and tools.* Ministry of Children and Youth Services. Retrieved Nov. 15, 2008 from http://www.gov.on.ca/children/english/resources/child/STEL02_179886.html.

Graham, J., Swift, K., and Delaney, R. (2000). *Canadian social policy: An introduction.* Scarborough, ON: Prentice Hall/Allyn and Bacon Canada.

Graham, T. C. (2002). Using reason for living to connect to American Indian healing traditions. *Journal of Sociology and Social Welfare, XXIX*(1), 55–75.

Grant, K., Amaratunga, C., and Armstrong, P. (2004). *Caring for/caring about: Women, home care and unpaid caregiving.* Toronto, ON: Broadview Press.

Green, J. (1995). *Cultural awareness in the human services: A multi-ethnic approach.* Needham Heights, MA: Allyn and Bacon.

Grinnell, R. (1993). *Social work research and evaluation*, 4th ed. Itasca, IL: F. E. Peacock.

Gross, L. W. (2003). Cultural sovereignty and Native American hermeneutics in the interpretation of the sacred stories of the Anishinaabe. *Wicazo Sa Review, 18*(3), 127–34.

Guo, S., and Andersson, P. (2006). *Non/recognition of foreign credentials for immigrant professionals in Canada and Sweden: A comparative study.* 2005–2006 PCERII Working Paper Series, No. WP04-05. Prairie Centre of Excellence on Immigration and Integration, Edmonton, AB.

Guttiérez, L. (1991). Empowering women of color: A feminist model. In M. Bricker-Jenkins, N. Hooyman, and N. Gottlieb (eds.), *Feminist social work practice in clinical settings*, pp. 199–214. Newbury Park, CA: Sage.

Halli, S., and Driedger, L. (eds.). (1999). *Immigrant Canada: Demographic, economic and social challenges.* Toronto: University of Toronto Press.

Hallowell, A. (1992). *The Ojibwa of Berens River, Manitoba: Ethnography into history.* Edited with preface and afterword by J. Brown. Fort Worth, TX: Harcourt Brace Jovanovich College.

Hampton, M., Hampton, E., Kinunwa, G., and Kinunwa, L. (1995). Alaska recovery and spirit camps: First Nations community development. *Community Development Journal 30*(3): 257–64.

Hangan, C. (2006). Introduction of an intensive case management style of delivery for a new mental health service. *International Journal of Mental Health Nursing 15*(3): 157–62.

Hanmer, J., and Statham, D. (1988). *Women and social work: Towards a woman-centred practice*. London: Macmillan Educational.

———. (1999). *Women and social work: Towards a woman-centred practice,* 2nd ed. Houndmills, UK: British Association of Social Workers/Macmillan Press.

Hare-Mustin, R. (1978). A feminist approach to family therapy. *Family Process 17*: 181–94.

Hart, M. (1992). The Nelson House medicine lodge: Two cultures combined. In M. Tobin and C. Walmsley (eds.), *Northern perspectives: Practice and education in social work,* pp. 61–66. Winnipeg: Manitoba Association of Social Workers and University of Manitoba Faculty of Social Work.

Hart, M. A. (2008). Critical reflections on an Aboriginal Approach to Helping. In M. Gray, J. Coates, and M. Yellow Bird (eds.), *Indigenous social work around the world: Towards culturally relevant education and Practice,* pp. 129–40. Burlington, VT: Ashgate Press.

Harvard Mental Health Letter (2006). Assertive community treatment. 23(5): 4–5.

Healey, S. (1994). Diversity with a difference: On being old and lesbian. *Journal of Gay & Lesbian Social Services 1*(1): 109–17.

Hearn, G., (1958). *Theory building in social work*. Toronto: University of Toronto Press.

Hepworth, D., Rooney, R., and Larsen, J. (1997). *Direct social work practice: Theory and skills,* 5th ed. Pacific Grove, CA: Brooks/Cole.

———. (2002). *Direct social work practice: Theory and skills,* 6th ed. Pacific Grove, CA: Brooks/Cole.

Herberg, D. (1993). *Frameworks for cultural and racial diversity: Teaching and learning for practitioners.* Toronto: Canadian Scholars' Press.

Herrick, J., and Stuart, P. (eds.). (2005). *Encyclopedia of social welfare history in North America.* Sage Publications.

Herring, R. D. (1996). Synergetic counseling and Native American Indian students. *Journal of Counseling and Development 74*(6): 542–47.

Hick, S. (1998). *Canada's unique social history.* Retrieved Nov. 3, 2008 from http://www.socialpolicy.ca/cush/index.htm.

———. (2004). *Social welfare in Canada: Understanding income security.* Toronto: Thompson Educational Publishing.

———. (2006). *Social work in Canada: An introduction,* 2nd ed. Toronto: Thompson Education Publishing.

Holmes, G. (1997). The strengths perspective and the politics of clienthood. In D. Saleebey (ed.), *The strengths perspective in social work practice,* 2nd ed., pp. 151–64. White Plains, NY: Longman.

Homan, M. (1999). *Promoting community change: Making it happen in the real world.* Pacific Grove, CA: Brooks/Cole Publishing.

Hooyman, N. (1991). Supporting practice in large-scale bureaucracies. In M. Bricker-Jenkins, N. Hooyman, and N. Gottlieb (eds.), *Feminist social work practice in clinical settings,* pp. 251–70. Newbury Park, CA: Sage.

Hubble, M., Duncan, B., and Miller, S. (1999). *The heart and soul of change: What works in therapy.* Arlington, VA: American Psychological Association.

Hughes, B., and Mtezuka, M. (1992). Social work and older women: Where have the older women gone? In M. Langan and L. Day (eds.), *Women, oppression and social work,* pp. 220–41. London: Routledge.

Hughes, M. (2007). Older lesbians and gays accessing health and aged-care services. *Australian Social Work, 60*(2): 197–209.

Humphreys, C. (2007). A health inequalities perspective on violence against women. *Health and Social Care in the Community, 15*(2): 120–27.

Ife, J. (2002). *Community development: Community-based alternatives in an age of globalisation.* Frenchs Forest, NSW, AU: Pearson Education Australia.

Indian and Northern Affairs Canada. (2002, December). *Social development—Health and social indicators.* Retrieved Jan. 13, 2004 from http://www.ainc-inac.gc.ca/gs/soci_e.html.

International Federation of Social Workers (IFSW). (2000). *Definition of social work.* Retrieved Nov. 28, 2008 from http://www.ifsw.org/p38000208.html.

———. (2004). *Ethics in social work, statement of principles.* Retrieved Nov. 28, 2008 from http://www.ifsw.org/f38000032.html.

Inuit Tapiriit Kanatami. (2008). *About ITK: Facts.* Retrieved Aug. 6, 2008 from http://www.itk.ca/media/backgrounder-itk.php.

Irving, A., Parsons, H., and Bellamy, D. (1995). *Neighbors: Three social settlements in downtown Toronto.* Toronto: Canadian Scholars' Press.

Irwin, L. (1994). Dreams, theory, and culture: The Plains vision quest paradigm. *American Indian Quarterly 18*(2): 229–45.

Ivanoff, A., Blythe, B., and Tripodi, T. (1994). *Involuntary clients in social work practice: A research-based approach.* New York: Aldine deGruyter.

Jaco, R. (2002). Individual treatment. In F. J. Turner (ed.), *Social work practice: A Canadian perspective,* pp. 255–69. Toronto: Pearson Education Canada.

James, C. (1995). *Seeing ourselves: Exploring race, ethnicity and culture.* Toronto: Thompson Educational.

———. (2003). *Seeing ourselves: Exploring race, ethnicity and culture.* Toronto: Thompson Educational.

James, C., and Shadd, A. (eds.). (2001). *Talking about identity: Encounters in race, ethnicity and language*. Toronto: Between the Lines Publishing.

Janzen, H. L., Skakum, S., and Lightning, W. (1994). Professional services in a Cree Native community. *Canadian Journal of School Psychology 10*(1): 88–102.

Jennissen, T., and Lundy, C. (2008). Keeping sight of social justice: 80 years of building CASW. Retrieved Nov. 2008 from http://www.casw-acts.ca/aboutcasw/building_e.pdf.

Johnson, D. W., and Johnson, F. (2003). *Joining together: Group theory and group skills*. Boston: Allyn and Bacon.

Johnson, L., McClelland, R., and Austin, C. (2000). *Social work practice: A generalist approach*, Canadian ed. Scarborough, ON: Prentice Hall/Allyn and Bacon Canada.

Johnston, B. (1990). *Ojibway heritage*. Lincoln, NE: University of Nebraska Press.

Johnston, P. (1983). *Native children and the child welfare system*. Toronto: Canadian Council on Social Development in association with James Lorimer and Co.

Kanel, K. (2007). *A guide to crisis intervention,* 3rd ed. Belmont, CA: Thomson Brooks/Cole.

Katz, R., and St. Denis, V. (1991). Teachers as healers. *Journal of Indigenous Studies 2*(2): 23–36.

Kidneigh, J. (1965). History of American social work. In *Encyclopaedia of social work*, 15th ed., pp. 3–18. New York: NASW.

Kiresuk, T., Smith, A., and Cardillo, J. (1994). *Goal attainment scaling: Application, theory and measurement*. Hillsdale, NJ: L. Earlbaum Associates.

Kirst-Ashman, K., and Hull, G. (2009). *Understanding generalist practice,* 5th ed. Belmont, CA: Brooks/Cole.

Kitsuse, J. (1962). Societal reaction to deviant behaviour. *Social Problems 9*(3): 247–56.

Konopka, G. (1983). *Social group work: A helping process*, 3rd ed. Englewood Cliffs, NJ: Prentice-Hall.

LaDue, R. A. (1994). Coyote returns: Twenty sweats does not an Indian expert make. *Women and Therapy 15*(1): 93–111.

Laird, J. (1995). Family-centred practice: Feminist, constructionist, and cultural perspectives. In N. Van Den Bergh (ed.), *Feminist practice in the 21st century*, pp. 20–40. Washington, DC: NASW Press.

Langan, M., and Lee, P. (1989). Whatever happened to radical social work? In M. Langan and P. Lee (eds.), *Radical social work today*, pp. 1–18. London: Unwin Hyman.

Lawrence, M. (1992). Women's psychology and feminist social work practice. In M. Langan and L. Day (eds.), *Women, oppression and social work*, pp. 32–47. London: Routledge.

Leighninger, L. (1987). *Social work search for identity*. New York: Greenwood Press.

Lemert, E. (1951). *Social pathology*. New York: McGraw-Hill.

Leonard, P. (1997). *Post modern welfare: Reconstructing an emancipatory project.* London: Sage.

Leslie, J., and Maguire, R. (1978). *The historical development of the Indian Act,* 2nd ed. Ottawa: Treaties and Historical Research Centre, Indian and Northern Affairs Canada.

Levine, H. (1989). Feminist counseling: Approach or technique? In J. Turner and L. Emery (eds.), *Perspectives on women in the 1980s,* pp. 74–98. Winnipeg: University of Manitoba Press.

Li, P. (1999). *Race and ethnic relations in Canada.* Don Mills, ON: Oxford University Press.

———. (2003a). *Deconstructing Canada's discourse of immigrant integration,* PCERII Working Series, No. WP04-03, Prairie Metropolis Centre, Edmonton, AB.

———. (2003b). *Destination Canada: Immigration debates and issues.* Don Mills, ON: Oxford University Press.

Lieby, J. (1978). *A history of social welfare and social work in the United States.* New York: Columbia University Press.

Locke, B., Garrison, R., and Winship, J. (1998). *Generalist social work practice: Context, story and partnerships.* Pacific Grove, CA: Brooks/Cole.

Loewenberg, F., Dolgoff, R., and Harrington, D. (2000). *Ethical decisions for social work practice.* Itasca, ILL: F.E. Peacock Publishers.

Longclaws, L. (1994). Social work and the medicine wheel framework. In B. Compton and B. Galaway (eds.), *Social work processes,* 5th ed., pp. 24–33. Pacific Grove, CA: Brooks/Cole.

Lundy, C. (2004). *Social work and social justice: A structural approach to practice.* Peterborough, ON: Broadview Press.

MacInnis, G. (1953). *J. S. Woodsworth: A man to remember.* Toronto: Macmillan.

Malloch, L. (1989). Indian medicine, Indian health: Study between red and white medicine. *Canadian Women Studies 10*(2/3): 105–12.

Mann, H. (1968). *Notes for a history: School of Social Work, University of Manitoba.* Winnipeg: University of Manitoba.

Marr, W. L. (2008). Industrialization. In J. Marsh, et al. (eds.), *The Canadian Encyclopedia.* Retrieved Nov. 3, 2008 from http://www.thecanadianencyclopedia.com/index.cfm?PgNm= TCE&Params=A1ARTA0003992.

Maslow, A. (1970). *Motivation and personality,* 2nd ed. New York: Harper and Row.

Masten, A. (1994). Resilience in individual development: Successful adaptation despite risk and adversity. In M. Wang and E. Gordon (eds.), *Educational resilience in inner city America: Challenges and prospects.* Hillsdale, NJ: Erlbaum.

Mawhiney, A. M. (1995). The First Nations in Canada. In J. C. Turner and F. J. Turner (eds.), *Canadian social welfare,* 3rd ed., pp. 213–30. Scarborough, ON: Allyn and Bacon.

McCormick, R. (1995). The facilitation of healing for the First Nations people of British Columbia. *Canadian Journal of Native Education 21*(2): 251–322.

McHardy, M., and O'Sullivan, E. (2004). *First Nations Community Well-Being in Canada: The Community Well-Being Index (CWB), 2001*. Ottawa: Strategic Research and Analysis Directorate, Indian and Northern Affairs Canada. Retrieved Aug. 6, 2008 from http://www.ainc-inac.gc.ca/pr/ra/cwb/index_e.html.

McIntosh, P. (1989, July/August). White privilege: Unpacking the invisible knapsack. *Peace and Freedom*, 10–12.

McKenzie, B., and Morrissette, V. (2003). Social work practice with Canadians of Aboriginal background: Guidelines of respectful social work. *Envision: The Manitoba Journal of Child Welfare 2*(1): 1–39.

McMahon, M. (1994). *Advanced generalist practice with an international perspective*. Englewood Cliffs, NJ: Prentice-Hall.

Mesbur, E. (2002). Social group work practice: The Canadian Experience. In F. J. Turner (ed.), *Social work practice: A Canadian perspective,* pp. 282–300. Toronto: Pearson Education Canada.

Meyer, C. (1983). *Clinical social work in an eco-systems perspective*. New York: Columbia University Press.

———. (1988). The eco-systems perspective. In R. Dorfman (ed.), *Paradigms of clinical social work*, pp. 275–94. New York: Brunner/Mazel.

Migliardi, P., Blum, E., and Heinonen, T. (2004). Immigrant and refugee women's action against violence: A prevention strategy. In C. Ateah and J. Mirwaldt (eds.), *Within our reach: Preventing abuse across the lifespan,* pp. 76–89. Halifax: Fernwood Publishing.

Miley, K. (2002). Unacknowledged resources of aging: Empowerment for older adults. In M. O'Melia and K. Miley, (eds.), *Pathways to power: Readings in contextual social work practice,* 2nd ed. Boston: Pearson/Allyn and Bacon.

Miller, J. R. (2000). *Skyscrapers hide the heavens,* 3rd ed. Toronto: University of Toronto Press.

Milloy, J. (1999). *A national crime: The Canadian government and the residential school system, 1879 to 1986.* Winnipeg, MB: University of Manitoba Press.

Ministry of Children and Youth Services – Ontario. (2007a). *Child protection standards in Ontario.* Ottawa, ON: Queen's Printer.

———. (2007b). *Child protection standards in Ontario,* Standard 10. Ottawa, ON: Queen's Printer. Retrieved Apr. 2, 2009 at http://www.gov.on.ca/children/graphics/stel02_179887.pdf, pp. 71–76.

Monture-Angus, P. (1995). *Thunder in my soul: A Mohawk woman speaks.* Halifax, NS: Fernwood.

Moreau, M. (1979). A structural approach to social work practice. *Canadian Journal of Social Work Education 5*(1): 78–94.

Moreau, M., and Frosst, S. (1993). *Empowerment II: Snapshots of the structural approach in action.* Ottawa: Carleton University Press.

Moreau, M., with Leonard, L. (1989). *Empowerment through a structural approach to social work: A report from practice.* Montreal: École de service social.

Morrisseau, C. (1998). *Into the daylight: A wholistic approach to healing.* Toronto: University of Toronto Press.

Morrissette, V., McKenzie, B., and Morrissette, L. (1993). Towards an Aboriginal model of social work practice. *Canadian Social Work Review 10*(10): 91–108.

Morrissey, M. (1997). The uses of culture. *Journal of Intercultural Studies 18*(2): 93–107.

Mullaly, R. (1997). *Structural social work: Ideology, theory, practice,* 2nd ed. Toronto: Oxford University Press.

———. (2002). *Challenging oppression: A critical social work approach.* Don Mills, ON: Oxford University Press.

———. (2007). *The new structural social work,* 3rd ed. Toronto, ON: Oxford University Press.

Nabigon, H. (2006). T*he hollow tree: Fighting addictions with traditional Native healing.* Kingston, ON: McGill-Queen's University Press.

Nabigon, H., and Mawhiney, A. (1996). Aboriginal theory: A Cree medicine wheel guide for healing First Nations. In F. J. Turner (ed.), *Social work treatment: Interlocking theoretical approaches,* 4th ed., pp. 18–38. Toronto: The Free Press.

Naples, N., with Clark, E. (1996). Feminist participatory research and empowerment: Going public as survivors of childhood sexual abuse. In H. Gottfried (ed.), *Feminism and social change: Building theory and practice,* pp. 160–83. Chicago: University of Illinois Press.

National Association of Women and Law. (2007, September 20). *Harper government working to silence women.* Retrieved Nov. 18, 2008 from http://www.nawl.ca/ns/en/Actions/20070920Press.html.

National Union Research. (2000). Workfare: A low-wage strategy for the Canadian economy. Retrieved Dec. 5, 2008 from http://www.nupge.ca/publications/workfare%20complete.pdf.

Nelson, C. H., Kelley, M. L., and McPherson, D. H. (1985). Rediscovering support in social work practice: Lessons from Indian Indigenous human service workers. *Canadian Social Work Review 2*: 231–48.

Nes, J., and Iadicola, P. (1989). Toward a definition of feminist social work: A comparison of liberal, radical, and socialist models. *Social Work 34*(1): 12–21.

Neysmith, S. (ed.). (2000). *Restructuring caring labour: Discourse, state practice and everyday life.* Don Mills, ON: Oxford University Press.

Neysmith, S., Bezanson, K., and O'Connell, A. (2005). *Telling tales: Living the effects of public policy.* Black Point, NS: Fernwood Press.

Ng, R. (1993). Racism, sexism, and immigrant women. In S. Burt, L. Code, and L. Dorney (eds.), *Changing patterns: Women in Canada*, pp. 279–307. Toronto: McClelland and Stewart.

Nixon, K. (2009). *The construction of intimate partner woman abuse in Alberta's child protection policy and the impact on abused mothers and their children.* Unpublished doctoral dissertation, University of Calgary, Calgary, Alberta, Canada.

Nye, A. (1988). *Feminist theory and the philosophies of man.* New York: Routledge.

O'Connor, P. J. (1986). *The story of St. Christopher's House 1912–1984.* Toronto: Toronto Association of Neighbourhood Services.

O'Meara, S. (1996). Epilogue. In S. O'Meara and D. A. West (eds.), *From our eyes*, pp. 123–41. Toronto: Garamond Press.

Odjig White, L. (1996). Medicine wheel teaching in Native language education. In S. O'Meara and D. A. West (eds.), *From our eyes*, pp. 107–22. Toronto: Garamond Press.

Ontario Association of Children's Aid Societies. (2008). *History of child welfare.* Retrieved Nov. 3, 2008 from http://www.oacas.org/childwelfare/history.htm.

Ontario Human Rights Commission. (2009). Race policy dialogue papers. Retrieved Nov. 23, 2008 from http://www.ohrc.on.ca/en/issues/racism/racepolicydialogue.

Osennontion and Skonaganleh:rá. (1989). Our world. *Canadian Woman Studies 10*(2/3): 7–19.

Parker, J., and Bradley, G. (2007). *Social work practice: Assessment, planning, intervention and review*, 2nd ed. Exeter, UK: Learning Matters.

Parrott, L. (2002). *Social work and social care.* London: Routledge.

Payne, M. (2005). *Modern social work theory*, 3rd ed. Chicago: Lyceum Books Inc.

Payne, M., Adams, R., and Dominelli, L. (2002). On being critical in social work. In M. Payne, R. Adams, and L. Dominelli (eds.), *Critical practice in social work,* pp. 1–12. Houndmills, UK: Palgrave.

Peat, F. D. (1994). *Lighting the seventh fire: The spiritual ways, healing, and science of the Native American.* Toronto: Canadian Manda Group.

Perlman, H. (1957). *Social casework: A problem solving process.* Chicago: University of Chicago Press.

Popple, K. (2002). Community work. In R. Adams, L. Dominelli, and M. Payne (eds.), *Critical practice in social work,* pp. 149–58. Houndmills, UK: Palgrave.

Pumphrey, R., and Pumphrey, M. (1961). *The heritage of American social work.* New York: Columbia University Press.

Radford, L., and Hester, M. (2006). *Mothering through domestic violence.* London: Jessica Kingsley Publishers.

Ramsey, R. (1984). Snapshots of practice in the twentieth century. *The Social Worker* *52*(1): 11–15.

Razack, S. H. (2000). Gendered racial violence and specialized justice. The murder of Pamela George. *Canadian Journal of Law and Society 15*(2): 91–130.

Reamer, F. (2006). *Social work values and ethics*. New York: Columbia Press.

Regnier, R. (1994). The sacred circle: A process pedagogy of healing. *Interchange 25*(2): 129–44.

Reinharz, S., and Chase, S. (2003). Interviewing women. In Holstein, J. and Gubrium, J. (eds.), *Inside interviewing*. Thousand Oaks, CA: Sage.

Richmond, M. (1917). *Social diagnosis*. New York: Russell Sage Foundation.

Ridgely, E. (2002). Family treatment. In F. Turner, (ed.), *Social work practice: A Canadian perspective*, pp. 270–82. Toronto: Pearson Education Canada.

Ristock, J., and Pennell, J. (1996). *Community research as empowerment: Feminist links, postmodern interruptions*. Toronto: Oxford University Press.

Robison, W., and Reeser, L. C. (2000). *Ethical decision making in social work*. Boston: Allyn and Bacon.

Rodway, M. (1986). Systems theory. In F. Turner (ed.), *Social work treatment: Interlocking theoretical approaches*, 3rd ed., pp. 514–40. New York: Free Press.

Roe, D., Dekel, R., Harel, G., and Fennig, S. (2006). Clients' reasons for terminating psychotherapy: A quantitative and qualitative inquiry. *Psychology and Psychotherapy: Theory, research and practice 79*(4): 529–38.

Rooney, R. (1992). *Strategies for work with involuntary clients*. New York: Columbia University Press.

Ross, R. (1992). *Dancing with a ghost: Exploring Indian reality*. Markham, ON: Octopus Books.

———. (1996). *Returning to the teachings: Exploring aboriginal justice*. Toronto: Penguin Books.

Rothman, J. (1994). *Practice with highly vulnerable clients: Case management and community-based services*. Englewood Cliffs, NJ: Prentice-Hall.

———. (1996). The interweaving of community intervention approaches. *Journal of Community Practice 3*(3/4): 69–99.

Russell, M. N. (1989). Feminist social work skills. *Canadian Social Work Review 6*(1): 69–81.

Saleebey, D. (1992). *The strengths perspective in social work practice*. White Plains, NY: Longman.

———. (1997a). Community development and individual resilience. In D. Saleebey (ed.), *The strengths perspective in social work practice*, 2nd ed., pp. 199–216. White Plains, NY: Longman.

———. (1997b). Introduction: Power in the people. In D. Saleebey (ed.), *The strengths perspective in social work practice*, 2nd ed., pp. 3–20. White Plains, NY: Longman.

———. (1997c). *The strengths perspective in social work practice*, 2nd ed. White Plains, NY: Longman.

———. (2002). *The strengths perspective in social work practice,* 3rd ed. Boston: Allyn and Bacon.

———. (2006a). Introduction: Power to the people. In D. Saleebey (ed.), *The strengths perspective in social work practice,* 4th ed., pp. 1–24. Boston: Pearson Education Inc.

———. (2006b). *The strengths perspective in social work practice*, 4th ed. Boston: Pearson/Allyn and Bacon.

Sapers, H. (2006). *Annual report of the Office of the Corrections Investigator, 2006–2007.* Ottawa: Minister of Public Works and Government Services.

Saulnier, C. (1996). *Feminist theories and social work: Approaches and applications.* New York: The Haworth Press.

Schact, S., and Ewing, D. (1997). The many paths of feminism: Can men travel any of them? *Journal of Gender Studies* 6(2): 159–76.

Schur, E. (1971). *Labeling deviant behavior.* New York: Harper and Row.

Sheafor, B., and Horejsi, C. (2008). *Techniques and guidelines for social work practice*, 8th ed. Boston, MA: Pearson/Allyn and Bacon.

Shera, W. (2002). Empowering mental health consumers: Assessing the efficacy of a partnership model of case management. In M. O'Melia and K. Miley (eds.), *Pathways to power: Readings in contextual social work practice,* pp. 214–30. Boston: Pearson/Allyn and Bacon.

Shulman, L. (1999). *The skills of helping: Individuals, families, groups and communities*, 4th ed. Itasca, IL: Peacock.

———. (2006). *The skills of helping: Individuals, families, groups, and community,* 5th ed. Belmont, CA: Thomson/Brooks/Cole.

Sibbald, B. (2002). Off-reserve Aboriginal people face daunting health problems: StatsCan. *Canadian Medical Association Journal* 167(8): 912.

Simmons, J. (1994). Community-based care: The new health social work paradigm. *Social Work in Health Care* 20(1): 35–46.

Smith, D. (1990). *The conceptual practices of power: A feminist sociology of knowledge.* Toronto: University of Toronto Press.

Spearman, L. (2005). A developmental approach to social work practice in mental health: Building on strengths. In T. Heinonen and A. Metteri (eds.), *Social work in health and mental health: Emerging developments and international perspectives*, pp. 45–64. Toronto: Canadian Scholars' Press.

Specht, H., and Specht, R. (1986). Social work assessment: Route to clienthood (part I). *Social Casework* 67: 525–32.

Stanley, L., and Wise, S. (1993). *Breaking out again: Feminist ontology and epistemology.* London: Routledge.

Statistics Canada. (2001). *Aboriginal peoples in Canada.* Ottawa: Statistics Canada.

———. (2003). *Aboriginal peoples survey 2001: Initial findings—Well-being of the non-reserve Aboriginal population.* Ottawa: Statistics Canada.

———. (2008a). Ethnicity. Retrieved Apr. 8, 2009 from http://www.statcan.gc.ca/concepts/definitions/ethnicity-ethnicite2-eng.htm.

———. (2008b). Race (ethnicity). Retrieved Apr. 8, 2009 from http://www.statcan.gc.ca/concepts/definitions/ethnicity-ethnicite-eng.htm.

Stiegelbauer, S. M. (1996). What is an Elder? What do Elders do? First Nations Elders as teachers in culture-based urban organizations. *The Canadian Journal of Native Studies 16*(1): 37–66.

Strickberger, M. (1990). *Evolution.* Boston: Jones and Bartlett.

Suchar, C. (1978). *Social deviance: Perspectives and prospects.* New York: Holt, Rinehart, and Winston.

Sullivan, N., Mesbur, E. S., Lang, N., Goodman, D., and Mitchell, L. (eds.). (2003). *Social work with groups: Social justice through personal, community and societal change.* Binghamton, NY: The Haworth Press.

Sullivan, P. (1994). A long and winding road: The process of recovery from mental illness. *Innovations and Research 3*(3): 20.

Sullivan, W., and Rapp, C. (2002). Environment context, opportunity, and the process of recovery: The role of strengths-based practice and policy. In D. Saleebey (ed.), *The strengths perspective in social work practice*, pp. 247–66. Boston: Allyn and Bacon.

Symington, A. (2004). Intersectionality: A tool for gender and economic justice. *Women's Rights and Economic Change, 9,* 1–8.

Taylor, J. (1997). Niches and practice: Extending the ecological perspective. In D. Saleebey (ed.), *The strengths perspective in social work practice*, 2nd ed., pp. 217–28. White Plains, NY: Longman.

Thompson, N. (1993). *Anti-discriminatory practice.* London: BASW/Macmillan.

Titley, B. (1986). *A narrow vision: Duncan Campbell Scott and the administration of Indian Affairs in Canada.* Vancouver: University of British Columbia Press.

Trecartin, W., Tasker, R., and Martin, K. (1991). *Moses Coady.* National Film Board of Canada. (Videotape).

Tripodi, T. (1994). *A primer on single-subject design for clinical social workers.* Washington, DC: NASW.

Turner, C., and Turner, F. (eds.). (2009). *Canadian Social welfare,* 6th ed. Toronto: Pearson.

Turner, F. (1999a). The theoretical base of practice. In F. Turner (ed.), *Social work practice: A Canadian perspective*, pp. 23–33. Scarborough, ON: Prentice-Hall/Allyn and Bacon Canada.

———. (1999b). Theories of practice with vulnerable populations. In D. E. Biegel and A. Blum (eds.), *Innovations in practice and service delivery across the lifespan,* pp. 13–31. New York: Oxford University Press.

———. (2002). The theoretical bases of practice. In F. Turner (ed.), *Social work practice: A Canadian perspective,* pp. 46–56. Toronto: Pearson Education Canada.

Tutty, L. (2002). The setting of objectives and contracting. In F. Turner, ed., *Social work practice: A Canadian perspective,* pp. 165–79. Toronto: Pearson Education Canada.

United Nations (2007, September). *United Nations Declaration on the Rights of Indigenous Peoples.* Retrieved Aug. 5, 2008 from http://www.un.org/esa/socdev/unpfii/documents/DRIPS_en.pdf.

Valentich, M. (1986). Feminism and social work practice. In F. Turner (ed.), *Social work treatment: Interlocking theoretical approaches*, pp. 564–89. New York: Free Press/Macmillan.

Valverade, M. (1991). *The age of light, soap, and water: Moral reform in English Canada, 1885–1925.* Toronto: McClelland and Stewart.

Van Den Bergh, N., and Cooper, N. (eds.). (1986). *Feminist visions for social work.* Silver Springs, MD: NASW.

Wakefield, J. (1996a). Does social work need the eco-systems perspective? Part 1: Is the perspective clinically useful? *Social Service Review 70*(1): 1–32.

———. (1996b). Does social work need the eco-systems perspective? Part 2: Does the ecosystems perspective save social work from incoherence? *Social Service Review 70*(2): 183–213.

———. (1996c). Does social work need the eco-systems perspective? Reply to Alex Gitterman. *Social Service Review 70*(3): 476–81.

Waldram, J. B. (1997). *The way of the pipe: Aboriginal spirituality and symbolic healing in Canadian prisons.* Peterborough, ON: Broadview Press.

Walton, R. (1975). *Women in social work.* London: Routledge & Kegan Paul.

Waring, M. (1996). *Three masquerades: Essays on equality, work and human rights.* Toronto: University of Toronto Press.

Weaver, H. N. (2001). Indigenous identity: What is it, and who *really* has it? *American Indian Quarterly, 25*(2), 240–55.

Weaver, J. (1997). Native American studies, Native American literature, and communitism. *Ayaangwaamizin, 1*(2), 23–33.

Weick, A., Kreider, J., and Chamberlain, R. (2006). Solving problems from a strengths perspective. In D. Saleebey (ed.), *The strengths perspective in social work practice*, 4th ed., pp. 116–27. Boston: Pearson Education Inc.

Wendell, S. (1993). Toward a feminist theory of disability. In D. Shogan (ed.), *A reader in feminist ethics*, pp. 223–47. Toronto: Canadian Scholars' Press.

Wharf, B. (ed.). (1990). *Social work and social change in Canada.* Toronto: McClelland and Stewart.

Wharf, B., and McKenzie, B. (2004). *Connecting policy to practice in the human services.* Toronto: Oxford University Press.

White, R. (1963). *Ego and reality in psychoanalytic theory.* New York: International Universities Press.

Wicks, R., and Parsons, R. (1984). *Counseling strategies and intervention techniques for the human services.* New York: Longman.

Williams, A. and Crooks, V. (2008). Introduction: Space, place and geographies of women's caring work. *Gender, Place & Culture, 15*(3): 243–47.

Williams, F. (1989). *Social policy: A critical introduction.* Cambridge, UK: Polity Press.

———. (1992). Women with learning difficulties are women too. In M. Langan and L. Day (eds.), *Women, oppression and social work*, pp. 149–68. London: Routledge.

Wills, G. (1995). *A marriage of convenience: Business and social work in Toronto 1918–1957.* Toronto: University of Toronto Press.

Yelaja, S. (1985). *An introduction to social work practice in Canada.* Scarborough, ON: Prentice-Hall Canada.

Yoder, J., and Kahn, A. (1992). Toward a feminist understanding of women and power. *Psychology of Women Quarterly 16*: 381–88.

Young, D., Ingram, G., and Swartz, L. (1989). *Cry of the eagle: Encounters with a Cree healer.* Toronto: University of Toronto Press.

Young, I. M. (1990). *Justice and the politics of difference.* Princeton, NJ: Princeton University Press.

Yuval-Davis, N. (2006). Intersectionality and feminist politics. *European Journal of Women's Studies, 13*(3): 193–209.

Zastrow, C. (1995). *The practice of social work*, 5th ed. Pacific Grove, CA: Brooks/Cole.

Zieba, R. A. (1990). Healing and healers among the northern Cree. Unpublished master's thesis, Natural Resources Institute, University of Manitoba, Winnipeg, Manitoba.

Ziegler, O. (1934). *Woodsworth, social pioneer.* Toronto: Ontario Publishing.

Index

A

ABC mode, in crisis intervention, 182
Aboriginal approach, 247–274
    antiracist practice, 132
    application of, 266–271
    assessment, 199–200
    background, 254
    comparative summary, 326–333
    conventional social work and, 253, 271–272
    core of, 254–255
    ecosystems framework and, 272–273
    helping, 263–266, 272
    historical context, 248–249, 261
    key concepts, 255–259
    overview, 199
    perceptions of functioning, 261–263
    perceptions of persons, 260–261
    present context, 250–252
    problem-solving approach vs., 271–272, 321
    values, 259
Aboriginal peoples
    apprehension of children, 77, 252
    client–social worker relationship, 114
    culture, 249
    defined, 274n1
    diversity of, 254, 267–268
    feminist approach, 286
    health of, 250–252
    history of, 248–249, 261
    labelling, 119
    oppression, 248–252, 261
    present context, 250–252
    values of, 39–40
    See also Aboriginal approach
Acceptance, 105–106
Acculturation, 128
Act for the Prevention of Cruelty to and Better Protection of Children, 75
Act for the Protection and Reformation of Neglected Children, 75
Adams, R., 304
Addams, Jane, 19, 69
Advocacy, 57–59, 310
Affirmation, 291
Affirmative action, 33n, 134
Agency. *See* Individual agency; Social agencies
Aging, women and, 287–288

Aitken, L., 264
Alcoholics Anonymous, 239
Alienation, 236
All Peoples Mission, 20
Alternative social services, 306
Amnesty International Canada, 250
Anthony, W., 231
Anti-oppressive practice, 3, 10, 138–139, 190–192, 298–300
Antiracist practice, 132–133
Antle, B., 41
Apollo, A., 101
Apprehension of the child, 89–92, 252–253. *See also* Child rescuing
Approach, concept of, 171
Arbitration, 65
Assessment, 202–224
    Aboriginal approach, 199–200
    anti-oppressive practice, 191
    application of, 212–223
    case example, 213–223
    client role, 208–209, 241–242
    cognitive theory, 179
    community development, 188
    crisis theory, 182–183
    cultural factors, 192–193
    determinants of, 204–212, 223, 224n1
    ecosystems framework, 193–194
    ego psychology, 180
    eligibility assessment, 213
    family relationships and processes, 184
    feminist approach, 200–201
    focused, 204
    groups, 186
    inductive vs. deductive, 204–205, 224
    involuntary clients, 115–116, 120
    knowledge base, 324
    labelling theory, 196–197
    multidimensional, 204, 223, 324
    problem solving process, 148–151, 213
    purpose of, 204
    risk in, 209–211
    role theory, 195
    social worker role, 206–208
    strengths-based practice, 198, 213
    structural approach, 189
    subjective and objective aspects, 116
    workplace role in, 211–213

Authority
  in client–social worker relationship, 111–112
  as source of knowledge, 170
Autonomy, 108–109

B

Bachelor of Social Work (BSW) programs,
    25–26
Bailey, R., 299, 305
Baines, D., 277
Baker, Simon, 262
Balance, 256–257
Bandura, Albert, 178
Barnett, Samuel and Henrietta, 19
Barnlund, D., 128
Becvar, D., 184
Becvar, R., 184
Behavioural and learning theory, 178
Bellamy, D., 19–20
Belonging, 236–239, 242–243
Best interest principle
  child protection, 78
  consumer-driven approach vs., 165
  involuntary clients, 121, 164–165
  strengths approach vs., 234–235
Bill 210, 77, 78
Biology, 173–174, 238
Bishop, Ann, 191, 299
Blaming the victim, 303
Boldt, M., 264
Boston Center for Psychiatric Rehabilitation,
    231
Boundaries, 149
Brake, M., 299, 305
Brant, C., 260
Bricker-Jenkins, Mary, 279, 289
Brill, N., 162
British North America Act, 75
Brown, H. C., 287–288
Bruce, Lucille, 286
Bunch, Charlotte, 278
Burns, D., 178
Business contracts, 152
Butler, A., 132

C

Caillou, S., 259
Calliste, A., 132
Camilleri, P., 27n3
Campbell, Carolyn, 298
Canada Assistance Plan (CAP), 76

Canadian Association for Social Work Education
    (CASWE), 7–8, 26
Canadian Association of Schools of Social Work
    (CASSW), 26
Canadian Association of Social Workers
    (CASW), 24, 34–37, 45, 211, 253
  See also Code of Ethics (CASW)
Canadian Charter of Rights and Freedoms, 77, 251
Canadian Mental Health Association, 231
Canadian social work. *See* History of Canadian
    social work
Capacity for change, 106–108
Capitalism, 283–285
Care and concern, 103–104
Carleton University, 302
Carniol, B., 27n3, 306
Case advocacy. *See* Advocacy
Case examples
  Aboriginal approach, 268–269
  assessment, 213–223
  child protection services, 79–93
  client–social worker relationship, 100,
      103–109, 111–114, 118, 120–122
  feminist approach, 292–293
  introduction to social work, 2–6
  oppression, 135–138
  problem solving, 147, 151–155, 158–159,
      163–164
  social work roles, 50–53, 55–60, 62, 64–68, 70
  strengths-based practice, 228–229, 234–237,
      239–240, 243
  structural approach, 307–309, 311–317
  theoretical diversity, 179, 181, 183–190,
      192–200
Case management, 3, 53–56
Casework, 8, 15–16
Caseworkers, 16
CASW. *See* Canadian Association of Social
    Workers (CASW)
CASWE. *See* Canadian Association for Social
    Work Education (CASWE)
Ceremonies, 265
Chalmers, Thomas, 16
Chambers, C., 27n3
Change, nature of, 262–263
Charity movement, 15–17
Charity Organization Society (COS), 16–17
Chief and Council system, 249
Child abuse
  category of, 76–77
  reporting, 81–82, 110

response to, 82–93

Child protection services, 73–95
  case example, 79–93
  challenges of, 83
  dual purpose of, 92
  generalist practice, 94
  overview, 74–78
  provincial responsibility for, 78
  role separation, 80
  social work practice in, 78
  specialist practice, 94
  teams, 83

Child removal. *See* Apprehension of the child

Children's Aid Societies, 75, 76

Children's Protection Act, 75

Child rescuing, 77. *See also* Apprehension
  of the child

Child sexual abuse, 77

Child welfare, 74

Child Welfare Transformation Agenda, 77

Class advocacy, 58

Class oppression, 191, 299

Clients
  assessment of, factors in, 208–209, 241–242
  defining, 98
  involuntary, 98–100, 112, 114–123
  risk to self or others, 210–211
  voluntary, 98
  See also Client–social worker relationship

Client–social worker relationship, 97–124
  Aboriginal approach, 114
  acceptance, 105–106
  capacity for change, 106–108
  care and concern, 103–104
  commitment, 112–113
  components, 102–114
  confidentiality, 109–111
  consumer-driven approach, 233–235
  context and structure, 113–114
  cultural and other factors, 114, 139–142
  defining, 100–102
  empathy and honesty, 104–105
  endings, 122, 160–162
  feminist approach, 102, 114
  helping vs. social control, 98–99
  power, authority, and control, 111–112, 154,
    164
  problem solving, 146
  reciprocity, 235–236
  self-determination and autonomy, 108–109
  significance of, 101, 323

strengths-based practice, 233–236
  structural approach, 114
  values conflicts, 40–41

Clinical evaluation, 68

Clinical practice, 56

Coach, social work role of, 62–64

Coady, Moses, 15, 69

Coalitions, 310

Code of Ethics (CASW), 34–37, 41, 44, 45, 98,
    103, 109, 112, 133, 187, 304

Codes of ethics, 34–37, 41

Cognitive distortion, 178

Cognitive restructuring, 178

Cognitive theory, 178–179

Collective action, 303, 305–306, 310

Collier, K., 253

Colonization, 248, 252–253, 261

Commitment, in client–social worker
    relationship, 112–113

Communication, in client–social worker rela-
    tionship, 102

Communitism, 255

Community development, 8
  assessment, 188
  outreach and, 66
  principles, 187–189
  settlement houses as source of, 15, 19
  social work role of, 69
  top-down vs. bottom-up, 187

Community organization, 8, 15, 19

Community practice, 68–70

Compton, B., 111, 320

Concern. *See* Care and concern

Confidentiality, 35, 109–111, 110

Conflict negotiation. *See* Mediation and conflict
    negotiation

Conflict perspective, 298, 301–302

Consciousness, 261–262

Consciousness-raising, 290–291, 315

Conservative ideology, 30–31

Construction of reality, 106

Consumer-driven approach, 3, 165, 233–235

Contracts
  business contracts, 152
  establishing, 153
  involuntary clients, 121–122
  no harm contracts, 152
  power and, 154
  practice contracts, 152
  problem solving, 152–154
  written contracts, 153

Control, in client–social worker relationship, 111–112

Cooper, Lynn, 278, 279

Co-operative Commonwealth Federation (CCF), 20

Cooperative movement, 69

Coping, 175

Correctional Services of Canada, 251

Council on Social Work Education (CSWE), 25–26

Counsellors, 3, 56–57

Cournoyer, B., 111, 320

Cowger, D., 149

Crisis theory and intervention, 160, 181–183

Cross, Terry, 255

Cross-cultural practice, 142, 324

Culleton, Beatrice, *In Search of Raintree*, 130, 282

Cultural competence, 140–142, 324

Culturally competent strengths approach, 3, 241–243

Culture
 Aboriginal peoples, 249
 acceptance and, 105
 assessment, 192–193
 belonging/membership, 242–243
 client–social worker relationship, 114, 139–142
 concept of, 127–128
 cultural competence, 3, 140–142, 241–243, 324
 identity and, 126–127
 individual vs. collective emphasis in, 108
 as source of knowledge, 169
 strengths-based practice, 241–243
 support, 242
 values and, 39–41
 See also Ethnoculture

Cyclical nature of life, 261

D

Day, S., 279

Decision making
 ethics, 43–44
 involuntary clients, 120–121, 164–165

Deductive assessment, 204–205, 224

Defence mechanisms, 180

Deficit perspective, 226

Dei, G. J. S., 132

Determinants of assessment, 204–212, 223, 224n1

Deviance, 117

Diagnosis, 149–151. *See also* Assessment; Social diagnosis

Differential Response, 77

Dion Buffalo, Y. R., 258, 261

Direct practice, 56, 303–304

Disabilities, women with, 286–287

DisAbled Women's Network (DAWN), 287

Discharge planning, 48

Discrimination, 33n, 133–134, 299. *See also* Oppression; Racism

Diversity of theory, 168–169, 176, 204, 223

Domestic violence, 82–93, 282

Dominelli, L., 283, 304

Driedger, Diane, 287

Duncan, B., 102

Duran, B., 261

Duran, E., 261

E

Ecology, 173–174

Ecosystems framework, 3, 172–176
 Aboriginal approach and, 272–273
 assessment, 193–194
 background, 172–173
 essential principles, 175–176
 origins, 24–25
 overview, 173–175
 strengths approach and, 198, 238
 structural approach and, 306–307
 value of, 8
 See also Person-in-the-environment

Educational programs
 accreditation of, 25–26
 graduate-level, 25–26
 history of, 21–26, 76
 undergraduate-level, 25–26

Education equity, 134

Educator, social work role of, 62–64, 310

Ego psychology, 179–181

Elders, 264–265

Eligibility assessment, 213

Elliott, T., 132

Emic approach, 131–132

Empathy, 104–105

Empowerment, 58, 200, 232–233. *See also* Enabling

Enabling, 59–61, 239, 310. *See also* Empowerment

Endings, 160–162
 referral, 160–161
 termination, 122, 161
 unplanned, 161–162

Entropy, 173

Equilibrium, 173
Erikson, Erik, *Childhood and Society*, 180
Ermine, W., 262
Ethical dilemmas, 42–45
Ethical Principles Screen, 43–44
Ethics, 41–45
    decision making, 43–44
    defined, 41
    dilemmas, 42–45
Ethnic competence, 140–142
Ethnicity
    concept of, 128–129
    ethnic competence, 140–142
    identity and, 126–127
    See also Ethnoculture
Ethnoculture
    concept of, 126–127
    emic approach, 131–132
    ethnocultural competence, 140–142
    etic approach, 130–131
    See also Culture; Ethnicity
Etic approach, 130–131
Evaluation
    everyday practice, 157–159
    informal, 156, 159
    involuntary clients, 160
    problem solving, 156–160
    process, 157
    qualitative, 156
    quantitative, 156
    short-term contacts, 159–160
    social work role of, 68
Evaluation time-outs, 158–159
Evangelia, Toronto, 19
Experience, 169
Expertise, and power, 154, 164

F
Fabian socialism. *See* Socialism
Facilitating. *See* Enabling
Falk, J. H. T., 17, 21, 23, 27n3
Family life cycle, 184
Family norms, 184
Family relationships and processes, 183–185
Feedback loops, 144, 173
Feedback mechanism, 145
Feminist approach, 275–296
    Aboriginal peoples, 286
    application of, 288–295
    assessment, 200–201

background and context, 278–280
    central concepts, 200, 202
    client–social worker relationship, 102, 114
    comparative summary, 326–333
    diversity of clients, 285–288, 295
    liberal orientation, 281
    men and, 294
    orientations in, 281–285
    overview, 200–201, 276–277
    power, 293–294
    problem solving and, 321–322
    radical orientation, 282–285
    research, 280–281
    socialist orientation, 283–285
Fields of practice, 8, 48
First Nations peoples. *See* Aboriginal peoples
Focused assessment, 204
Fook, Janis, *Radical Casework*, 298
Forte, J., 168, 176
Framework, concept of, 7, 171
Framing, 302
Frankel, Sid, 224n1
Fraser, Nancy, 302
Freud, Sigmund, 30
Freudian theory, 24, 168, 180
Friendly visitors, 16

G
Galaway, B., 111, 320
Garrison, R., 101
Gender
    Aboriginal relationships, 260–261
    power and, 282
    stereotypes, 291–292
    See also Women
Generalist social work, 7–10, 25–26
    child protection services, 94
    roles in, 49–71
    specialized agencies and, 211–212
Genocide, 261
Germain, C., 24–25, 174
Gitterman, Alex, 24–25, 174, 175
Goal attainment, 157
Goal attainment scaling, 157, 166n
Goal setting, 151–152, 158, 266
Good life. *See* Mino-pimátisiwin
Goodness of fit, 175
Gordon, W., 32
Gordon, William, 172
Graham, Thomas Crowfoot, 255

Green, J., 140
Group work, 8
  settlement houses as source of, 15, 19
  theories, 186
  types of groups, 185–186
Group workers, 60–62
Growth
  in Aboriginal approach, 258, 261
  personal, 227–228
Guidelines for Ethical Practice (CASW), 36–37,
  164, 210

H
Habitat, 174
Hanmer, J., 279
Harmony, 258
Healing, 258–259, 265, 271
Hearn, Gordon, 172
Helping
  Aboriginal approach, 263–266, 272
  charity movement and, 15–16
  client–social worker relationship, 98–99
  healing vs., 271–272
  ideology of, 30
Herberg, Dorothy, 128
Hick, Steve, 31
Hierarchy of needs, 43, 46n2
History of Canadian social work, 14–27
  charity movement, 15–17
  development of the profession, 23–25
  educational programs, 21–26
  Industrial Revolution, 14–15
  settlement house movement, 17–20
  social gospel movement, 20
  women's role, 27n3
Homeostasis, 173
Honesty, 104–105
Horejsi, C., 103
Hubble, M., 102
Hull House, Chicago, 19
Human dignity, 33, 34
Human nature, 260
Human rights, 33
Human services, 30
Humour, 264

I
Identity, 126–127
Ideological lens, 32, 74
Ideology
  conservative, 30–31

foundations of social work, 30–32
  liberal, 31
  socialist, 31
  social welfare policy, 30–31
  social work practice, 31–32
IFSW. *See* International Federation of Social
  Workers (IFSW)
Immigrants
  case example, 136–137
  discrimination, 134
  group and community helping, 138
  social work practice, 135
Inclusiveness, 36
Indian Act, 249
Individual agency, 108
Individualism, among Aboriginal peoples,
  255
Individual orientation, in social work, 162–163,
  168, 172. *See also* Micro practice
Inductive assessment, 204–205, 224
Industrial revolution, 14–15
Institutional racism, 130
Institutions. *See* Social institutions
Interface, 172, 272
International Federation of Social Workers
  (IFSW), 6, 32–34, 36–37, 44, 45
Intersectionality, 276
Intervention, 154–156, 209–210, 232
Inuit peoples. *See* Aboriginal peoples
Involuntary clients, 114–123
  assessment, 115–116, 120
  case example, 100
  decision making, 120–121, 164–165
  defined, 98
  evaluation, 160
  labelling, 116–119
  negotiation and contracting, 121–122
  power relationships, 98
  prior experiences of, 116
  reaching out, 119–120
  social control, 98–99, 112, 164–165
  social support, 122–123
  termination, 122
  types, 99, 115
Involuntary contacts, 160
Irving, A., 19–20

J
James, C., 128
Johnson, D. W., 61
Johnson, F., 61

K

Kanel, K., 181–182, 211
Kelso, Henry, 75
Kierkegaard, Søren, 262
Knowledge
    Aboriginal approach, 265
    acquisition, 169
    sources, 169–170
    types, 106
Knowledge base, 169–170, 204, 223, 324

L

Labelling, 106, 116–119, 162–163, 210
Labelling theory, 24, 117, 196–197.
    See also Role theory
Labour, 278, 283
Lawrence, M., 277
Least restrictive approach, 78
Leonard, P., 191
Lesbian women, 287–288
Levine, Helen, 279
Liberal feminism, 281, 284
Liberal ideology, 31
Licensing, 48
Life, cycle of, 261
Life experience, 169
Life model of social work, 174
Locke, B., 101
London School of Economics, 24
Long, J. A., 264
Longclaws, L., 260
Lundy, Colleen, 188, 301

M

Mackenzie King, William Lyon, 20
Macro practice, 8
    advocacy, 58–59
    community development, 187–189
    community practice, 68–70
    educating/teaching/coaching, 62–64
    enabling, 59–60
    evaluation, 68
    mediation, 64–65
    outreach, 66–67
    social brokers, 67
    social work roles, 49–50
    structural approach, 189–190
    on theoretical continuum, 177–178
    See also Structural approach
Mandated involuntary clients, 99
Mandated organizations, 99

Mann, H., 21
Maslow, Abraham, 43, 46n2, 291
Master of Social Work (MSW) programs,
    25–26
McGill University, 24, 76
McHardy, M., 252
McIntosh, P., 135
McKenzie, B., 302
Mediation and conflict negotiation, 8, 64–65
Medical model, 16–17, 145, 150–151,
    227, 231, 320
Medicine wheel, 254, 255–257, 261
Membership, 236–239, 242–243
Men, feminist social work and, 294
Mental health, recovery in, 231
Methods, 8, 23
Métis peoples. *See* Aboriginal peoples
Meyer, C., 24
Mezzo practice, 8
    advocacy, 58–59
    case management, 53–55
    counselling, 56
    educating/teaching/coaching, 62–64
    enabling, 59–60
    evaluation, 68
    family relationships and processes,
        183–185
    group work, 185–187
    mediation, 64–65
    outreach, 66–67
    social brokers, 67
    social work roles, 49–50
    on theoretical continuum, 177–178
Micro practice, 8
    advocacy, 58–59
    case management, 53–55
    cognitive theory, 178–179
    counselling, 56
    crisis theory and intervention, 181–183
    educating/teaching/coaching, 62–64
    ego psychology, 179–181
    enabling, 59–60
    evaluation, 68
    mediation, 64–65
    outreach, 66–67
    social brokers, 67
    social work roles, 49–50
    on theoretical continuum, 177–178
    See also Individual orientation, in social work
Miller, S., 102
Mining Act, 250

Mino-pimátisiwin (the good life), 199, 259–263, 266, 271
Modelling, 63
Morality, charity movement and, 16
Moreau, Maurice, 298
  Empowerment through a Structural Approach to Social Work, 302
Morrissey, M., 127
Motivation, 263
Mullaly, R., 37, 133, 135, 139, 191, 253, 298–300, 304, 306, 310
Multiculturalism, 133
Multidimensional assessment, 204, 223, 324
Multiple theoretical languages, 168, 204
Multi-theory practice, 176

N
Narrative, 157
National Association of Social Workers (NASW), 24
National Institute for Mental Health, 54
Negative discrimination, 33
Negotiation, involuntary clients, 121–122
Neo-Freudian theory, 24, 168, 180
New Democratic Party (NDP), 20
Niches, 237–239
  concept of, 174
  enabling, 239
  personal niche, 237
  social niche, 238
Nixon, K., 78
No harm contracts, 152
Noninterference, 40
Nye, A., 282

O
Observation, as source of knowledge, 170
Open systems, 173, 174
Oppression
  Aboriginal peoples, 248–253, 261
  capitalism, 283
  challenging, 300
  effects of, 291, 299
  impact of, 10
  multiple forms of, 135–138, 288, 299
  racism, 129–130
  social work contribution to, 252–253
  types, 190
  women, 276, 282–283
  See also Anti-oppressive practice;
    Discrimination

Order perspective, 301
Organizational policy, 110
O'Sullivan, E., 252
Outcomes, 157
Outreach, 66–67. *See also* Reaching out

P
Paradigm, 37
Parents' rights, 78
Parsons, H., 19–20
Patriarchy, 282
Payne, M., 176, 178, 304
Peat, F. D., 265–266
Perlman, Helen, 101, 102, 145, 320
  Social Casework, 24, 149
Personal growth, 227–228
"Personal is political," 261, 279, 283, 290
Personality theories, 179
Personal niche, 237. *See also* Niches
Person-in-the-environment
  development of, 24, 168, 172
  ecological basis of, 173–174
  goodness of fit, 174, 175
  See also Ecosystems framework
Perspective, concept of, 171
Philanthropy, 14
Positive discrimination, 33n
Power
  Aboriginal concept of, 263
  client–social worker relationship, 111–112, 154
  contracts and, 154
  dynamic nature of, 293–294, 317
  expertise as form of, 154, 164
  feminist approach, 293–294
  gender and, 282
Practice. *See* Social work practice
Practice contracts, 152
Prevention, 154
Primary deviance, 117
Primary groups, 185
Primary prevention, 154
Privacy. *See* Confidentiality
Private practice, 152
Problem definition, 146–148
Problem solving, 143–166
  Aboriginal approach vs., 271–272, 321
  assessment, 148–151, 213
  client–social worker relationship, 146
  comparative summary, 326–333
  contracts, 152–154

defining the problem, 146–148
endings, 160–162
evaluation, 156–160
extending, 320–322
feminist approach, 321–322
goal setting, 151–152, 158
implications, 162–165
individual orientation, 162–163
intervention, 154–156
power and, 154, 164
process, general, 144
process, social work practice, 145–162
restorative vs. promotional approach, 163–164
in social work, 6
strengths-based practice and, 226–230, 321
structural approach vs., 305–306, 321–322
Process evaluation, 157
Pro-feminist men, 294
Profession, social work
history of, 23–25
social science disciplines vs., 171–172
values of, 35–36
Professional lens, 3, 206–208, 223
Professional role, 48
Promotional approach, 163
Provinces
child welfare responsibilities, 78
social work regulation responsibilities, 36
Psychoanalysis, 184
Psychodynamic theories, 179
Psychology, 24
Public, as client, 115
Public education, 63

Q

Qualitative evaluation, 156
Quality of life, 227–228
Quantitative designs, 157
Quantitative evaluation, 156
Quebec, 27n1

R

Race, 129
Racism
Aboriginal peoples, 251
antiracist practice, 132–133
concept of, 129–130
institutional, 130
See also Discrimination
Radical feminism, 282–283
Radical social work, 298–299, 301, 317

Rapp, C., 231
Reaching out, 119–120. *See also* Outreach
Reciprocity, 235–236, 241
Recovery in mental health, 231
Reeser, L. C., 44
Reference groups, 185
Reference points, 157–158
Referral, 160–161
Reflexivity, 140, 191, 304
Refugees, 135
Relational worldview, 255
Relationships, in Aboriginal approach, 257–258, 260–261, 263–264
Religion
charity movement, 15–17
social gospel movement, 20
as source of knowledge, 169
See also Spirituality
Research, feminist, 280–281
Research methods, 68
Resilience, 239–240
Resources, availability of, 37–38
Respect, 259
Respectful individualism, 255
Restorative approach, 163, 229
Richmond, Mary, 320
Social Diagnosis, 16, 144, 145
Ridgely, E., 184
Rights
human rights, 33
indigenous peoples, 250–251
parents, 78
women, 281
Risk
assessment of, 183, 209–211
intervention as, 209–210
Robison, W., 44
Role ambiguity, 195
Role conflict, 195
Role modelling, 264
Role-playing, 63–64
Roles. *See* Professional role; Social work roles
Role theory, 24, 194–196. *See also* Labelling theory
Ross, R., 40, 263
Rural women, 286
Russell, N. M., 290, 291

S

Safety planning, 84, 86–87
Saleebey, D., 106, 289

Scott, Duncan Campbell, 249
Secondary deviance, 117
Secondary prevention, 154
Self-determination, 37–39, 108–109
Self-help, 239
Settlement houses, 14–15, 17–20
  cultural practices, 126
  early workers, 18
  reformers, 18–19
  service providers, 19–20
Sharing, 259
Sheafor, B., 103
Shulman, Laurence, 104, 303
Silence, 265
Single-subject designs, 157
Snively, C., 149
Social action, 310
Social activism, 69–70
Social agencies
  assessment role of, 211–213
  origins of, 16
  structure provided by, 7, 113
  types, 211
  values conflicts, 40–41
Social brokers, 67
Social change, 7, 303–304, 309, 314–315.
  See also Social transformation
Social control
  child protection and, 78, 92, 94
  client–social worker relationship, 98–99,
    112, 164–165
  defined, 98–99
Social diagnosis, 16–17, 145
Social gospel movement, 20
Social institutions, 14. *See also* Structural
  approach
Socialism, 24, 31
Socialist feminism, 283–285
Social justice, 6, 33–34
Social labelling. *See* Labelling
Social location, 132
Social movements, 300
Social niche, 238
Social policy
  context for social work, 7
  ideological bases of, 30–31
  settlement houses and, 18
  social change and, 7
  social work practice in relation to, 79–93
Social safety net, 19, 31
Social sciences, 171–172

Social support, 122–123
Social transformation, 299. *See also* Social change
Social welfare
  ideological bases of, 30–31
  social activism for, 70
  See also Welfare state
Social Welfare League, 21
Social work
  defined, 6, 17
  dual purpose of, 324
  fields of practice, 8
  generalist, 7–10, 25–26
  history of Canadian, 14–27
  ideological foundations, 30–32
  methods, 8, 23
  oppressive practices of, 252–253
  range of approaches and knowledge, 323–325
  social sciences in relation to, 171–172
  specialist, 7–9
  system size, 8
  values, 32–45
  women and, 27n3, 277–278
  See also Social work practice; Social workers
Social Work Code of Ethics (CASW), 34, 41,
  98, 133
Social workers
  assessment role, 206–208
  positions, 8
  See also Client–social worker relationship;
    Social work roles
Social work practice
  in child protection, 78
  comparative summary of approaches, 325–334
  context and foundations, 322–323
  ideology and, 31–32
  social policy in relation to, 79–93
Social work roles, 47–71
  advocate, 57–59, 310
  case manager, 53–56
  community developer, 69
  counselling, 56–57
  educator/teacher/coach, 62–64, 310
  enablers/facilitators, 59–60, 310
  evaluator, 68
  field of practice and, 48
  generalist, 49–71
  group worker, 60–62
  macro systems, 49–50
  mediator, 64–65
  mezzo systems, 49–50
  micro systems, 49–50

multiple, 50
outreach worker, 66–67
social activist, 69–70
social broker, 67
types, 48–49
Solution-focused therapy, 8, 231–232
Speaking from the heart, 265–266
Specialist social work, 7–9, 94
Spirituality, 249, 254–255, 262, 265, 272
Standards of Accreditation (CASWE), 7–8
Statham, D., 279
Statuses, 194
Steady state, 173
Stereotyping, 106, 291–292. *See also* Labelling
Stopard, N., 132
Storytelling, 264
Strengths-based practice, 225–245
    assessment, 198, 213
    basis of, 226
    belonging/membership, 236–239, 242–243
    client–social worker relationship, 233–236
    comparative summary, 326–333
    culturally sensitive practice and, 241–243
    developmental focus of, 227
    ecosystems framework and, 198, 238
    elements, 232–243
    empowerment, 232–233
    goals, 227
    overview, 197
    principles, 230
    problem solving and, 226–230, 321
    recovery in mental health, 231
    resilience, 239–240
    solution-focused therapy, 231–232
Strengths perspective, 106–107, 226
Stress, 175
Structural approach, 297–318
    anti-oppressive practice, 299–300
    application of, 304–311
    assessment, 189
    background, 300–301
    capacity for change and, 107
    client–social worker relationship, 114
    comparative summary, 326–333
    direct practice and, 303–304
    discrimination, 133–134
    ecosystems framework and, 306–307
    example of, 311–318
    foundations of, 298–304
    goals, 301
    institutional racism, 130

overview, 189
problem-solving approach vs., 305–306, 321–322
radical social work and, 298–299
role of, 302–303
settlement house movement as early form of, 15
social worker roles, 309–310
See also Macro practice
Subcultures, 127
Suicide, 210–211
Sullivan, W., 231
Support
    cultural, 242
    social, 122–123
Support groups, 185
Systems theory, 168, 173–174, 183–184

T
Task groups, 185
Taylor, J., 238
Teacher, social work role of, 62–64
Temporary guardianship, 90
Termination, 122, 161. *See also* Endings
Testing, as source of knowledge, 170
Theoretical diversity, 168–169, 176, 204, 223
Theoretical framework, 16
Theoretical repertoire, 205
Theory
    Aboriginal approach, 199–200
    anti-oppressive practice, 190–192
    assessment and, 204–205
    cognitive theory, 178–179
    community development, 187–189
    crisis theory, 181–183
    culture and, 192–193
    diversity of, 168–169, 176, 204, 223
    ecosystems framework, 172–176, 193–194
    ego psychology, 179–181
    family relationships and processes, 183–185
    feminist approach, 200–202
    group work, 185–187
    labelling theory, 196–197
    meanings of, 171
    micro to macro continuum, 177–178
    role theory, 194–196
    in social work, 170–171
    strengths-based practice, 197–199
    structural approach, 189–190
    unified, 168
Thompson, N., 132
Time, Aboriginal concept of, 260

Toronto, 19
Toynbee Hall, London, 18, 19, 24
Tradition, 169
Transaction, 172, 272
Transformative action, 291
Treatment groups, 185
Turner, Francis, 168, 171, 176
Turtle Island, 254, 267, 274n2

U

Unconsciousness, 261–262
United Nations Declaration on the Rights of
    Indigenous Peoples, 250–251
University of Manitoba, 21, 76
University of Toronto, 21, 24, 25, 76
Unwilling clients, 99

V

Valentich, Mary, 279, 294
Validation, 200, 289
Values, 32–45
    Aboriginal approach, 259
    application of, 37–41
    concept of, 32
    conflicts of, 40–41
    core, 32–37
    culture and, 39–41
    ethics and, 41–45
Van Den Bergh, Nan, 278, 279

Voluntary clients, 98
Volunteers, 76

W

Wakefield, Jerome, 175
Walton, R., 27n3
Welfare state, 24. *See also* Social welfare
Wendell, S., 286
Wharf, B., 302
White, R., 180
Wholeness, 255–256
Whole person development, 291–292
Wilfrid Laurier University, 25
Williams, Fiona, 31
Winnipeg, 21
Winship, J., 101
Wisdom, 169
Women
    caregiving responsibilities of, 278
    oppression, 276, 282–283
    rights of, 281
    settlement house workers, 18
    in social work, 27n3, 277–278
    See also Feminist approach
Woodsworth, J. S., 20–21, 26, 69
Workplace, assessment role of, 211–213

Y

Young, Iris Marion, 298